The Kingship of Jesus in the Gospel of John

The Kingship of Jesus in the Gospel of John

Sehyun Kim

FOREWORD BY
Peter G. Bolt

◆PICKWICK *Publications* · Eugene, Oregon

THE KINGSHIP OF JESUS IN THE GOSPEL OF JOHN

Copyright © 2018 Sehyun Kim. All rights reserved. Except for brief quotations in critical publications or reviews, no part of this book may be reproduced in any manner without prior written permission from the publisher. Write: Permissions, Wipf and Stock Publishers, 199 W. 8th Ave., Suite 3, Eugene, OR 97401.

Pickwick Publications
An Imprint of Wipf and Stock Publishers
199 W. 8th Ave., Suite 3
Eugene, OR 97401

www.wipfandstock.com

PAPERBACK ISBN: 978-1-5326-1722-5
HARDCOVER ISBN: 978-1-4982-4177-9
EBOOK ISBN: 978-1-4982-4176-2

Cataloguing-in-Publication data:

Names: Kim, Sehyun. | Bolt, Peter G., foreword

Title: The Kingship of Jesus in the Gospel of John / Sehyun Kim.

Description: Eugene, OR: Pickwick Publications, 2018 | Includes bibliographical references.

Identifiers: ISBN 978-1-5326-1722-5 (paperback) | ISBN 978-1-4982-4177-9 (hardcover) | ISBN 978-1-4982-4176-2 (ebook)

Subjects: LCSH: Bible. John—Criticism, interpretation, etc. | Bible. John—Theology. | Jesus Christ—Royal office.

Classification: LCC BS2615.52 K5 2018 (print) | LCC BS2615.52 (ebook)

All Scripture quotations, unless otherwise indicated, are taken from the Holy Bible, New International Version®, NIV®. Copyright ©1973, 1978, 1984, 2011 by Biblica, Inc.™ Used by permission of Zondervan. All rights reserved worldwide. www.zondervan.com The "NIV" and "New International Version" are trademarks registered in the United States Patent and Trademark Office by Biblica, Inc.™

Manufactured in the U.S.A.   08/20/18

To Grace Dal-Nae Park, Esther Song-Ha Kim,
and Deborah Sun-Hah Kim

Contents

Foreword by Peter G. Bolt | ix
Acknowledgments | xi
Abbreviations | xiii

1. Introduction | 1
   Research Questions   1
   Preliminary Remarks   3
   A Review of Literature   8
   Outline of the Research   14

Part I: The Kingship of Jesus in the Gospel of John

2. Background and Methodology | 19
   The Multiple Purposes of the Gospel of John   20
   Backgrounds of the Gospel of John and Kingship   30
   Methods and Theories   39
   Summary of the Chapter   60

3. Kingship and Johannine Christological Titles | 62
   Two Important Factors for the Understanding of Johannine Christological Titles   62
   Messiah/Christ and Kingship   67
   Son of God and Kingship   87
   Son of Man and Kingship   95

Prophet and Kingship   104
Savior of the World and Kingship   112
Lord and "My Lord and My God," and Kingship   117
The Kingship Motif in the Johannine Christology   124

4. The Kingship of Jesus in the Use of the Title Βασιλεύς and the Term Βασιλεία | 129
   A Survey of the Meanings of King/Kingdom   130
   King/Kingdom in the Gospel of John   137
   Summary of the Chapter   158

Part II: A Postcolonial Reading of the Kingship of Jesus in the Gospel of John

5. Identity Matters of the Groups in the Gospel of John | 161
   A Perspective of a Korean Reader on Conflict and Identity Matters   162
   Identification of the Groups in the Gospel of John   168
   Summary of the Chapter   207

6. Reading John as a Postcolonial Text: Jesus and His Function as King | 208
   Identification of the Johannine Jesus   209
   The Function of the Johannine Jesus   235
   Summary of the Chapter   238

7. Conclusion | 240

   Bibliography | 245

Foreword

As a multipurpose document to a multicultural audience, Dr. Kim argues that the Gospel of John uses multiple titles to give maximal emphasis upon the kingship of Jesus as a better alternative to the rulers of this world. Functioning as resistance literature, John urges belief in Jesus as the key to overcoming the pain, violence, and divisions of a post-colonial world. Granting Dr. Kim's argument, the Gospel of John seems to be exactly what our present world needs to hear.

—Peter G. Bolt (Sydney College of Divinity)

Acknowledgments

First of all, I confess that the love of God my Father, the grace of my Lord Jesus, and the indwelling of the Holy Spirit have sustained me in wonderful ways so that I have been able to complete this book for His kingdom.

I especially give many thanks to my supervisor, Professor Loveday Alexander at the University of Sheffield, who encouraged and supported me in the completion of my thesis. Her abundant knowledge and academic experience were essential during this long and painful, but joyful process. Her patience and kind guidance encouraged me to continue my research without giving up in spite of my shortcomings academically and in English. Her illuminating supervision has influenced, widened, and deepened me more than I can express. I enjoyed writing my thesis because she gave information and suggestions with a warm heart and careful concern. To her I give my gratitude and respect.

I want to express my appreciation to the entire Department of Biblical Studies at the University of Sheffield, especially Dr. Jorrun Økland, who supervised me during my first two years and challenged me to explore (post) modern methodology, and advised the use of a postcolonial methodology. In addition, I appreciate all the scholars, whose academic works I consulted in writing my thesis.

I am truly thankful to many others who helped me shape my thesis and polish my language. In particular, I appreciate Anne Cocker, who corrected my English, and suggested many alternative expressions, which made my argument clearer. Without her, I could not have completed my study. There are also many others, to whom I owe a debt of love, in particular, my dear friends Tae-Il Kang, Sun-Jung, and Tim Bateman.

I specially give my thanks to Professor Jim Harris, who encouraged me in publishing my PhD thesis, to Professor Peter Bolt, who wrote the preface of this book, and to Professor Diane Speed and Professor Honam Kim who opened the door for me to explore my academic journey in Sydney College of Divinity Korean School of Theology.

Finally, I must reserve my deepest thanks for my family, my lovely wife Dal-Nae who has always been with me, and my beautiful daughters Song-Ha and Sun-Hah who have always been precious and my pleasure. Because of them, I have always been happy, taken courage, and kept going in my academic journey in Sheffield as well as in Sydney, where I would have been lonely without them. In addition, our parents, brothers and sisters, who are my great supporters, deserve thanks. Our parents have prayed unceasingly for my family, and have provided all our needs. With their prayers, support, and encouragement, I was able to finish my work.

Abbreviations

1 Apol.	*Apologia i (First Apology)*
AB	Anchor Bible
ABD	*Anchor Bible Dictionary.* Edited by D. N. Freedman. 6 vols. New York, 1992
ABR	*Australian Biblical Review*
ANRW	*Aufstieg und Niedergang der römischen Welt: Geschichte und Kultur Roms im Spiegel der neueren Forschung.* Edited by H. Temporini and W. Haase. Berlin, 1972–
AThRSup	Anglican Theological Review Supplementary Series
BA	*Biblical Archeologist*
BAGD	Bauer, W., W. F. Arndt, F. W. Gingrich, and F. W. Danker. *Greek-English Lexicon of the New Testament and Other Early Christian Literature*, 2d ed. Chicago, 1979.
BBR	*Bulletin for Biblical Research*
BDAG	Danker, F. W., W. Bauer, W. F. Arndt, and F. W. Gingrich. *Greek-English Lexicon of the New Testament and Other Early Christian Literature.* 3d ed. Chicago, 1999
BDB	Brown, F., S. R. Driver, And C. A. Briggs. *A Hebrew and English Lexicon of the Old Testament.* Oxford, 1907
BETL	Bibliotheca ephemeridum theologicarum lovaniensium
Bib	*Biblica*
Bijdr	*Bijdragen, tijdschrift voor filosofie en theologie*
BJRL	*Bulletin of the John Rylands University Library of Manchester*
BNTC	Black's New Testament Commentaries

BSac	*Bibliotheca Sacra*
BTB	*Biblical Theology Bulletin*
CBQ	*Catholic Biblical Quarterly*
CC	*Continental Commentary*
CIA	*Corpus Inscriptionum Atticarum* 1873—97.
CIL	*Corpus inscriptionum latinarum*
Corp. Herm.	*Corpus Hermeticum*
CP	*Classical Philosophy*
De Medic.	*De Medicina*
Dial.	*Dialogus cum Tryphone* (*Dialogue with Trypho*)
DJG	*Dictionary of Jesus and the Gospels*. Edited by J. B. Green and S. McKnight. Downers Grove, 1992
DLNT	*Dictionary of the Later New Testament and Its Developments*. Edited by R. P. Martin and P. H. Davids. Downers Grove, 1997
DNTB	*Dictionary of New Testament Background*. Edited by Craig A. Evans and Stanley E. Porter. Downers Grove, 2000.
DPL	*Dictionary of Paul and His Letters*. Edited by G. F. Hawthorne and R. P. Martin. Downers Grove, 1993
EDNT	*Exegetical Dictionary of the New Testament*. Edited by H. Balz, G. Schneider. ET. Grand Rapids, 1990–1993
Haer.	*Adversus haereses* (*Against Heresies*)
Hist.	*Historiae*
Hist. eccl.	*Historia ecclesiastica* (*Ecclesiastical History*)
HTR	*Harvard Theological Review*
IBS	*Irish Biblical Studies*
IC	*Interpretation Commentary*
IG	*Inscriptiones graecae*. Editio minor. Berlin, 1924—
IGRR	*Inscriptiones Graecae ad res Romanas Pertinentes*. Edited by R. Cagnat et al.
ILS	*Inscriptiones Latinae Selectae*. Edited by H. Dessau.
Int	*Interpretation*
IvE	*Die Inschriften von Ephesos*
JBL	*Journal of Biblical Literature*

JSNTSup	Journal for the Study of the New Testament Supplement Series
JSOTSup	Journal for the Study of the Old Testament Supplement Series
LCL	Loeb Classical Library
LSJ	Liddell, H. G., R. Scott, H. S. Jones, *A Greek-English Lexicon*. 9th ed. With revised supplement. Oxford, 1996
NCBC	The New Century Bible Commentaries
NBD3	*New Bible Dictionary*. Edited by J. D. Douglas, N. Hillyer, and D. R. W. Wood. 3d ed. Downers Grove, 1996
NICNT	The New International Commentary on the New Testament
NIDNTT	*New International Dictionary of New Testament Theology*. Edited by C. Brown. 4 vols. Grand Rapids, 1975—1985
NovT	*Novum Testamentum*
NovTSup	Supplements to Novum Testamentum
NTS	*New Testament Studies*
OGSI	*Orientis graeci inscriptiones selectae*. Edited by W. Dittenberger. 2 vols. Leipzig, 1903—1905.
OPetr	Ostraca in Prof. W.M. Flinders Petrie's Collection at University College, London
Philops.	*Philopseudes (The Lover of Lies)*
PLond	Greek Papyri in the British Museum, Catalogue with Texts
PMich	Michigan Papyri
PNTC	The Pillar New Testament Commentaries
POslo	Papyri Osloenses
POxy	The Oxyrhynchus Papyri
PRyl	Catalogue of the Greek and Latin Papyri in the John Rylands Library
PSI	Papiri greci e latini
PTeb	The Tebtunis Papyri
SB	*Sammelbuch Griechischer Urkunden aus Ägypten*. Edited by F. Preisigke and et al. Vols. 1-, 1915—
SC	Sources chrétiennes. Paris, 1943—
SE	*Studia evangelica I, II, III* (= TU 73[1959], 87 [1964], 88 [1964], etc.)
SBLDS	Society of Biblical Literature Dissertation Series

SBLSymS	Society of Biblical Literature Symposium Series
SEG	*Supplementum Epigraphicum Graecum*
SHR	Studies in the History of Religions (supplements to *Numen*)
SIG	*Sylloge Inscriptionum Graecarum*. Editied by W. Dittenberger 4 vols. 3d ed. Leipzig, 1915—1924
SJT	*Scottish Journal of Theology*
SJLA	Studies in Judaism in Late Antiquity
SNTSMS	Society for New Testament Studies Monograph Series
TDNT	*Theological Dictionary of the New Testament*. Edited by G. Kittel and G. Friedrich. Translated by G. W. Bromiley. 10 vols. Grand Rapids, 1964—1976
TDOT	*Theological Dictionary of the Old Testament*. Edited by G. J. Botterweck and H. Ringgren. Translated by J. T. Willis, G. W. Bromiley, and D. E. Green. 8 vols. Grand Rapids, 1974—
VCSup	Vigiliae Christianae Supplement
Vesp.	*Vespasianus*
WUNT	Wissenschaftliche Untersuchungen zum Neuen Testament
ZNW	*Zeitschrift für die neutestamentliche Wissenschaft*

Ancient Jewish Sources

b.	*Babylonian Talmud*
Ber.	*Berakot*
Sanh.	*Sanhedrin*
b. Sanh.	*Babylonian Sanhedrin*
Qoh. R.	*Midrash Koheleth Rabbah*
Mekh. Ex.	Midrash *Mekhilta* (Oldest Rabbinic Commentary on Exodus)
Pirqe Scheq.	*Pirqe Schequalim*
1*Pesiq.*	*1 Pesiqtha*
Tanch.	*Tanchuma (Midrash)*
Tg. 1 Chr.	*Targum of 1 Chronicles*

Josephus

J. W.	Jewish War
Ant.	Jewish Antiquities
B. J.	Bellum Judaicum
Vita	Vita

Philo

Aet.	De aeternitate mundi (On the Eternity of the World)
Arg.	De argrigultura (On Agriculture)
Cher.	De cherubim (On the Cherubim)
Congr.	De congressu eruditionis gratia (On the Confusion of Tongues)
Decal.	De decalogu (On the Decalogue)
Det.	Quod deterius potiori insidari soleat (That the Worse Attacks the Better)
Gig.	De gigantibus (On Giants)
Jos.	De Iosepho (On the Life of Joseph)
Leg.	Legum allegoriae I, II, III (Allegorical Interpretation 1, 2, 3)
Legat.	Legatio ad Gaium (On the Embassy to Gaius)
Mos.	De vita Mosis I, II (On the Life of Moses 1, 2)
Migr.	De migratione Abrahami (On the Migration of Abraham)
Mut.	De mutatione nominum
Opif.	De opificio mundi (On the Creation of the world)
Post.	De posteritate Caini (On the Posterity of Cain)
Plant.	De plantatione (On Planting)
QG	Quaestiones et solutiones in Genesin I, II, III, IV (Questions and Answers on Genesis 1, 2, 3, 4)
Sacr.	De sacrificiis Abelis et Caini (On the Sacrifices of Cain and Abel)
Somn.	De somniis I, II (On Dreams 1, 2)
Spec.	De specialibus legibus I. II. III. IV (On the Special Laws 1, 2, 3, 4)
Virt.	De virtutibus (On the Virtues)

1. Introduction

Research Questions

THE GOSPEL OF JOHN uses many ambiguous and complex concepts and motifs. Among them is the kingship motif as applied to Jesus. This Gospel also has intricately interconnected theological perspectives, such as its Christology. The Johannine Jesus might be designated as the king who came to liberate his people from the darkness, and to lead them into his new world. Particularly relevant for an exploration of the kingship motif are the Johannine christological titles, which were employed to show Jesus as king, i.e., the Messiah/Christ, the Son of God, the Son of Man, the Prophet, the Savior of the World, the Lord (My Lord and My God), the King of Israel/the Jews, etc.

In addition, the author of this Gospel (John) employs both christological terms and many literary devices to deepen the kingship of Jesus. A study of those terms and concepts in the Johannine Gospel, therefore, may well open a new horizon offering new perspectives on the Gospel. In particular, the terms and concepts employed to describe Jesus as king were used in contrast with the similar ones of the marginal groups and those of the center as well. Their meanings are significant, but indirect, suggestive, and implicational, so that there may be many interpretations concerning them. However, the kingship of Jesus could be easily recognized by its first century readers who had diverse origins, because the terms and concepts used to connote his kingship were historically developed and deep-rooted in their worldviews, and were adapted in the Fourth Gospel.

In the first part of this book, I will explore the kingship of the Johannine Jesus, which might be familiar to readers from diverse origins, to discuss whether the kingship motif might be a key to the interpretation of the Gospel. It is meaningful to do so, because the kingship has not been researched as the key to the interpretation of the Johannine Gospel. In part two, I will attempt a postcolonial reading of the Gospel of John in terms of kingship.

In order to do this, I will employ postcolonial theory as a major research methodology. However, I admit that it would not be useful to adopt postcolonial theory in interpreting the Gospel of John without an evaluation or criticism of its limits as a theory. To begin with, this theory needs to be modified adequately in order to attempt a new reading of the Fourth Gospel which sees the kingship of Jesus as not only a contemporary issue in the first century CE, but also as a current issue today. Finally, I will use this theory expecting to obtain good insights from it concerning three major areas of research: 1. the portrait of Jesus in the Gospel of John; 2. the identification of various groups and their relation and function in the Roman Empire; 3. the message of the Johannine Jesus to the (post)colonial world.

More specifically, concerning the portrait of the Johannine Jesus, I have these research questions: Does the Gospel of John describe Jesus as king? What kind of king was Jesus from the perspective of a variety of readers of the first century CE?

Concerning the second area of my research, the identification of various groups and their relation and function, we need to ask the following questions: Was the Roman Empire regarded as the center of the world? What was her particular relationship with other marginal groups? How are the Jews, particularly the Jewish leaders, described in the Gospel of John? What were their relationships with the Roman Empire and with Jesus? Can we deduce the essential characteristics of the Johannine community through reading the Gospel of John? Were they a marginal group? What were the purposes of the Gospel of John toward its readership?

Regarding the message of the Johannine Jesus to the postcolonial world, we should answer these questions: Why should we research the kingship of Jesus in the Gospel of John in the postcolonial era? What is the meaning of the kingship of Jesus in this world? What do the Johannine terms—love, forgiveness, freedom, service, and peace—mean in the postcolonial world? Can the message of the fourth Gospel provide an alternative vision of reconciliation and peace for society rather than the violence and conflict common in today's world?

Before beginning to research these questions, it is first necessary to make some preliminary remarks concerning my research on the kingship motif with reference to the Johannine Jesus.

1. INTRODUCTION

Preliminary Remarks

The Gospel of John is estimated to have been written in the late first century CE.[1] This view has been widely accepted,[2] although there are still debates over the date.[3] Particularly, it is probable that the Gospel of John was written in the mid-nineties, during the reign of Domitian.[4] Following Martyn's argument, it is widely accepted that the Johannine community had been in conflict with the Jews from the middle of the first century CE and as a result were estranged from the Jerusalem Temple and the synagogues (John 9:22; 12:42; 16:2).[5] This supports the view that the Fourth Gospel was written to consolidate the Johannine community in order to overcome its conflict with the Synagogue.[6] However, this is not the only serious problem, which con-

---

1. The date of the Gospel of John is important because "the dating . . . brings us to the question of the political ideology of the text" (Alexander, "Relevance," 123).

2. Kümmel, *Introduction*, 246; Smalley, *John*, 82–84; Cassidy, *John's Gospel*, 3; Brown, *Introduction*, 206–15; Keener, *Gospel of John*, 140–42; Lincoln, *Gospel*, 18.

3. Robinson, Cribbs, and Wallace propose an earlier date (in the late 50s or in the 60s) for the composition of the Gospel of John (Robinson, *Redating*, 254–311; Robinson, *Priority*, 67–93; Cribbs, "Reassessment," 38–55; Wallace, "John 5,2," 237–56). However, this view is not supported by many scholars (see Blomberg, *Historical Reliability*, 42–44). For example, the expulsion from the synagogue is not likely to have occurred much earlier than the eighties (Lincoln, *Gospel*, 18). Carson suggests tentatively a date in the early eighties (Carson, *The Gospel*, 82–86). However, supposing John knew the Synoptic Gospels, its date suggests an earliest date of 85 CE (Keener, *Gospel of John*, 140). In addition, because of the discovery of Papyrus Egerton 2 (P_{52}, the two sides of a fragmentary leaf from a codex of the Gospel of John, written probably between 100 and 150, being the oldest known copy of any book of the New Testament) dates in the second century seem now to have lost their foundation (see Metzger, "Recently Published Greek Papyri," 25–44, esp. 40; Keener, *Gospel of John*, 141–42; Carson, *Gospel*, 24, 82; Lincoln, *Gospel*, 17–18).

4. Domitianic persecution and the motif of ruler cult are important elements to date the Gospel of John to the reign of Domitian.

5. About the expulsion from the Synagogue, see Martyn, *History and Theology*; Brown, *Gospel*, xxxiv–xl, xcviii–cii; Brown, *Introduction*, 58–89; Meeks, *Prophet-King*; Meeks, "Man from Heaven," 44–72; Lincoln, *Gospel*, 82–89; Kysar, "Community and Gospel," 355–66; Smith, "Presentation of Jesus," 367–78; Painter, "Farewell Discourses," 525–43.

6. Many scholars follow Martyn's view on the Johannine community (an attempt to reconstruct the historical context of the readers to whom the Gospel was first addressed). In this book, I also employ the term "the Johannine community" to develop my argument, because, in the textual level, we can reconstruct the Johannine community, which has a variety of backgrounds in the multicultural world, in conflict with other groups (on the reconstruction of the Johannine community as the ideal reader in the textual level, see chapter 5 of this book). However, it is impossible for us "to produce a portrait of the historical reader that is so complete that it guarantees the meaning of the text, and even as we gain some clarity about the first-century

fronted the Johannine community. A more dangerous situation arose from Rome.[7] The Roman Empire was persecuting Christians for several reasons. One of them seems to be related to Emperor-worship.[8] The Roman Emperors were worshipped as supra human beings or gods.[9] It is also probable

---

context we are still confronted with questions about how the text can speak to its twentieth-century readers in a compelling way" (Koester, "Spectrum," 6). Accordingly, as Koester concludes, "The final form of the Gospel envisions a heterogeneous readership," in other words, "the final form of the Gospel was shaped for a spectrum of readers" (Koester, "Spectrum," 9, 19; see also Culpepper, *Anatomy*, 221, 225; Lincoln, *Gospel*, 88). I define, therefore, the Johannine community as the ideal reader, which had various origins and was in conflict with others in the text. In other words, in the presupposition that John bore in mind a variety of readers with a wide spectrum of origins, I contend that the Gospel of John was written to the Johannine community as the ideal/implied readers, which were marginal in the Empire (on the relationship between the implied readers and the Johannine community, see Segovia, "Journey(s)," 23–54, esp. 47–49; Sim, "Gospels," 3–27).

Apart from the Johannine community theory, Bauchkam contends the circular reading of the Gospel (see Bauckham, "For Whom," 9–48). Just as Robinson's criticism on Martyn's view as "highly imaginative" (Robinson, *Redating*, 272–75), while denying the reality of the Johannine community, Bauckham argues that the Gospel was written for wide circulation among its first century readers ("a very general Christian audience"). Barton also argues the impossibility of the reconstruction of the Johannine Community (Barton, "Christian Community," 279–301). In terms of the written place of the Gospel, Cribbs also says that "different scholars can find sufficient evidence so as to argue that such diverse centers as Alexandria, Ephesus, Antioch, or Jerusalem were the locale in which this gospel originated, suggests to us that John was a 'circular gospel' written from an influential center of Christianity during a period of crisis in the life of the early church" (Cribbs, "Reassessment," 55). In addition, Cassidy focuses on the final form of the Gospel, which was copied and circulated within the early Christian Community in the Roman Empire (See Cassidy, *John's Gospel*, 1–5). However, it is hard to deny "Christian churches were . . . the primary intended readers of the Gospels. It is within the realms of possibility that any given Evangelist envisaged a broader readership, but these readers would have been very close to his own community in both geographical and theological terms" (Sim, "Gospels," 27).

7. It is important to recognize that the Johannine community, i.e., the readers, lived under the Roman ruling power, which was harsh to the margins (see Rensberger, *Johannine Faith*, 15–36; Carter, *John*, 170–71). About the exercise of Roman power on the margins through a hierarchical social structure and economic, military, social, ideological, rhetorical, and judicial means, see Cassidy, *John's Gospel*, 6–26; Cassidy, *Christians and Roman Rule*, 37–50; Carter, *Matthew and Empire*, 9–53; Lincoln, *Gospel*, 88–89; Lincoln, *Truth on Trial*, 265–307.

8. About the view of the imperial cult and Christian persecutions, see Price, *Rituals and Power*; Frend, *Martyrdom and Persecution*; Charlesworth, "Some Observations," 26–42. Three emperors, Gaius, Nero, and Domitian, had been especially attracted to these practices (Cassidy, *Christians and Roman Rule*, 13).

9. It came from Augustus and his successors who were acclaimed as supra human (Cassidy, *Christians and Roman Rule*, 12). On the practice of emperor worship as a legitimate ancient religion and political phenomenon, see Price, *Rituals and Power*;

that the Johannine community needed to consolidate itself with strong faith in order to prevent apostasy[10] and to confront and overcome persecution.[11] It was Domitian (81–96 CE) who claimed the title "lord and god"[12] and was responsible for a major persecution of Christians due to his profound hostility toward any form of religious unorthodoxy,[13] particularly, as the

Price, "Rituals and Power," 47–71; Fantin, "Lord of the Entire World," 70–134. Price says that "the imperial cult, along with politics and diplomacy, constructed the reality of the Roman empire" (Price, *Rituals and Power*, 248), while indicating most scholars' "overemphasis" on the political dimension of the imperial cult, and providing detailed analyses of the rituals, sacrifices, and images of the cult in Asia Minor.

10. Smallwood says about the Jewish tax as a categorizing criterion of self-confessed Jews and proselytes: "The record of attempts made during Domitian's reign to conceal one's circumcision by the surgical operation of epispasm or by other means (Celsus, *De Medic.* vii. 25, suggesting that the operation was well known at the time of publication [before *c.* 90; the work is mentioned by Quintilian xii, 11, 24]) will concern apostates, who it is reasonable to suppose wanted to escape the tax as well as to pass as gentiles socially" (Smallwood, *Jews*, 376). This description shows one fragmentary example of the complex responses of the margins toward the center. It is likely that whether to survive, to keep one's position, or to conceal one's national identity for property, in the first century, there were various, complex relations among the groups under Roman rule. In addition, the remark below shows clearly a variety of Jewish attitudes to the Romans: "The Herodian rulers and their party were naturally pro-Roman. The High priests also generally favored cooperation, as did the Sadducees. The Essenes withdrew to the desert, while the Zealots worked for armed rebellion. The Pharisees saw as their first loyalty absolute adherence to the Mosaic Law and traditions. They refused to take an oath of loyalty to Herod (Josephus *Ant.* 17.42); some actively resisted Roman rule, but others were more acquiescent. The common people must have simply scraped a living in a society where there was great inequality between rich and poor and much scope for oppression" (Edwards, "Rome," 713). It might be no exception for first-century Christians. In giving a thought of this complex historical background, it is quite probable that the Gospel of John was written to the first century readers in the Imperial world.

11. About the account of Roman persecution in the Gospel of John, see John 16:2 (a warning of persecution), more strikingly the passion narrative (death on the cross as a way of Roman execution), and 21:18–19 (Peter's martyrdom).

12. *Dominus et deus noster* (Suetonius *Domitian* 13.2); *domini deique nostri* (Martial, *Epigram* 5.8.1; 8.2.6); *deus praesens* (Cuss, *Imperial Cult*, 139). Domitian appears to have persuaded himself that he was "*Deus et dominus*," and ordered his courtiers and poets to greet him as such (Suetonius, *Domitian*, 4.4, 13.2; Dio Cassius, 68.7). In particular, "[i]t was under Domitian that the practices of taking an oath by the Emperor's genius, of offering libation and incense before his statue, and addressing him as *Dominus* grew up" (Frend, *Martyrdom and Persecution*, 213). On Domitian having recognition as divine, see Martial, *Epigram* 8.21; Statius, *Silvae* 1.1 (cf. Jones, "Christianity," 1033).

13. On abuses of imperial religion and Domitianic persecution, see Frend, *Martyrdom and Persecution*, 210–17, esp. 212–13; Sordi, *Christians*, 43–53; Fox, *Pagans and Christians*, 433; Wright, *New Testament*, 355–56; Jones, "Christianity," 1033–35; Moore and McCormick, "Domitian (Part i)," 74–101; Moore and McCormick, "Domitian (Part ii)," 121–45.

traditional provenance of the Gospel of John was in Ephesus.[14] The imperial

---

Roloff upholds the systematic promotion of imperial cults throughout the empire during the reign of Domitian (Roloff, *Revelation of John*, 9–10). Boring argues that there was an increase in imperial cults under Domitian, which came from above as well as from the populace that led to this development (Boring, *Revelation*, 21). However, this view is disputable between scholars in the discipline of New Testament studies (not usually working with the archaeological artifacts) and those in Roman studies (not usually analyzing early Christian literature) because of their different research area (see Friesen, *Imperial Cults*, 3; Smallwood, *Jews*, 372–74, 376–85). Scholars in Roman studies argue that Nero and Domitian were no more offensive than others were. Particularly, Fantin says that the negative portrayal of Domitian seems to be exaggerated, and that there is little evidence for a major persecution under Domitian (Fantin, "Lord of the Entire World," 123, 185; see also Smallwood, "Domitian's Attitude," 1–2, 7–9; Collins, *Crisis and Catharsis*, 69–73; Thompson, *Book of Revelation*, 104–7; Friesen, *Imperial Cults*, 147–51). Collins says that the evidence for the persecution of Christians as Christians under Domitian is rather slight in non-Christian texts. Smallwood also argues that the early Christian tradition about Domitian as the second persecutor is by its probable apologetic function doubtful.

In spite of their exaggeration about Domitian, it is reasonable that Domitianic persecution was laid to Domitian's charge. On this, Frend argues with evidence from different sources that "when one discounts the senatorial prejudices of Tacitus and Suetonius, the Emperor stands out as a shrewd but jealous-minded ruler, a strong upholder of public right and the state religion, whose prejudices and fears for his own safety increased with age" (Frend, *Martyrdom and Persecution*, 213–14). In addition, according to Eusebius (*Hist. eccl.* 3.33.2), there were partial attacks in various provinces, although there was no open persecution. Because relations between the Jews and the majority of educated Romans went from bad to worse, the Christians regarded as Jews were not an exception (Smallwood, *Jews*, 381). In a letter written to the Corinthians by Clement of Rome (ca. 96) (*I Clement* 1:1, The sudden and successive misfortunes and accidents; 59:4ff, Rescue those of our number in distress . . . release our captives), Domitianic persecution is alluded to (see Jones, "Christianity," 1033–34). Although he had not persecuted indiscriminately as Nero did, Domitian singled out individual Christians. Domitianic persecution was "a succession of short, sharp, assaults—a series of sudden and repeated misfortunes" as Clement wrote (see Barnard, "Clement of Rome," 251–60). In addition, the Jewish tax ("*didrachmon* tax") increased due to financial stringency might have become a heavy burden in psychological, religious, and economic terms as well (Domitian enforced stringent measures for its collection), and when in natural disasters the Christians were treated harshly by the Romans, they felt that they were under persecution. Moreover, under Domitian for the first time people in public documents began to swear by the genius of the living emperor. This shows that the time of Domitian rule was difficult for the Christians. Collins says, "The practice of the ruler cult by those who wished to flatter Domitian seems to have been the occasion for John to call for intensified exclusiveness over against the surrounding Greco-Roman culture" (Collins, *Crisis and Catharsis*, 77). It cannot be denied, therefore, that under Domitian, who was called a living god on earth (see Moore and McCormick, "Domitian (Part i)," 74–101), and for whose divine worship temples were already being built during his lifetime, that many Christians suffered martyrdom, and that anti-language, symbolism, and apocalyptic mood were intensified.

14. Eusebius, *Hist. eccl.* 3.1.1; Irenaeus, *Haer.* 3.1.2. There is no other location, except Ephesus, which the church Fathers supported as the provenance of the Gospel of

cult in Domitian's time was a strong challenge to the Christians in Ephesus, who were the first possible readers of the Gospel of John. The fact that a gigantic marble statue of Domitian in the new imperial temple in Ephesus, the center of the imperial cult in Asia Minor, was dedicated to Rome and "the divine Julius,"[15] implies the existence of religious conflict for the Christians in Ephesus. It is probable, therefore, that the Fourth Gospel was, at least, written to consolidate faith in the era of persecution for the Johannine community or the Christians, who experienced both estrangement from the Synagogue and harsh persecution from Roman rule.[16] If it is probable that the Gospel of John was written against these religious-political backgrounds in an era of conflict and persecution, it is quite likely that John adapted several terms, which originally indicated the Roman emperors and applied them to Jesus, as the real king to be followed throughout life.[17]

It is meaningful to say that just as the author and the audience or readers of this Gospel, regardless of whether they were Jewish or non-Jewish, lived in a world which was a melting-pot of cultures, the Gopsel is a multicultural melting-pot. That is, the Gospel of John was written in the context of an Empire, which had a multicultural, multilingual, multireligious, and multiethnic character.[18] Therefore, we can recognize these multicultural features, which are absorbed into the Fourth Gospel. John belonged to a society "that constituted part of the ancient world, and in spite of the uniqueness of their message, still had much in common with their contemporaries."[19] It is natural that he used them in the composition of the Gospel for his readers. Thus, Hellenized readers would be able to understand this Gospel when

---

John (see Carson, *Gospel*, 86–7). Harris sets out as evidence a higher rate of literacy than other Greek cities of the Roman Empire on the basis of observation of the massive production of catalogued inscriptions by the Ephesians (*Ancient Literacy*, 274). In addition, van Tilborg illustrates "how John's text . . . could have been read in first century Ephesus" (Tilborg, *Reading*, 3). On other possible provenances, Alexandria, Antioch, or Jerusalem, see Barrett, *Gospel*, 128–31; Brown, *Gospel*, ciii–civ; Cribbs, "Reassessment," 38–55; Johnson, "Early Christianity," 1–17; Carter, *John and Empire*; Tilborg, *Reading*.

15. Jones, "Christianity," 1034; Caird, *Commentary on the Revelation*, 29; Koester, *History, Culture, and Religion*, 1:316.

16. On the purpose(s) of the composition of the Gospel of John, see chapter 2 of this book.

17. About various forms of the title used for Roman rulers, see Deissmann, *Light*; Koester, "Savior," 667.

18. See Carter, *John*, 188–93.

19. Edwards, "Hellenism," 316–17. Because John lived in an era of persecution, he was "very aware of the Roman world and of the challenge that Jesus presents to it. It is part of the complex, multicultural world in which they lived and to which they attempt to address the good news" (Carter, *John*, 193).

they met the familiar terms during their reading.[20] In short, the author used these terms to show Jesus' identity so that the readers could easily recognize it by linking christological titles with imperial ones.[21]

In addition, several titles employed to designate the identity of Jesus as king are also closely linked to the Jewish traditions, particularly the Hebrew Bible.[22] That is, among the Johannine christological titles, the Messiah, the Prophet, the Lamb of God, and the Son of Man (cf. the Son of God, the Son) are much rooted in the Jewish traditions. However, because the Gospel of John was written for Greek speaking readers including Jews and non-Jewish people, these titles were mixed into one another to reveal the identity of Jesus. The Johannine christological titles, therefore, have their own unique meanings in the Gospel, which reveal the identity of Jesus as king.

A Review of Literature

The topic of this book, the kingship as attributed to Jesus in the Gospel of John, is an attempt to read the Gospel from a postcolonial perspective. The Johannine Gospel has traditionally been approached from the perspective of Jewish traditions. Recently, new materials and perspectives, which reveal its close relation to the Graeco-Roman context, have stimulated Johannine

---

20. Terms and concepts, e.g., *logos*, life, light, truth, rebirth, descending and ascending savior, dying and rising deity, mystic knowledge of God, sacramental communion, new life, and immortality through partaking of the flesh and blood of a deity in the Gospel of John, were familiar to the readers in the Hellenistic world. See Gunther, "Alexandrian Gospel," 583–84; Carter, *John*, 190; Barrett, *Gospel*, 101; Dodd, *Interpretation*, 8–9. In addition, on similarities between Philo and the Gospel of John (the concepts of *Logos*, a heavenly man, and the symbols of light, water, and shepherd), see Dodd, *Interpretation*, 54–73; Gunther, "Alexandrian Gospel," 584–88.

21. Cassidy emphasizes this point in terms of John. He argues, "[I]n depicting Jesus' identity and mission within his Gospel, the evangelist John was concerned to present elements and themes that were especially significant for Christian readers facing Roman imperial claims and for any who faced Roman persecution." He also argues that John "*consciously chose* to include and even to emphasize particular elements and themes" to depict the identity and mission of the Johannine Jesus (Cassidy, *John's Gospel*, 1, 28). In addition, Carter, in his attempt at an anti-imperial reading in the Gospel of Matthew, emphasizes a similar concept about "that of historical context of the Gospel (to use conventional language)," namely, "the audience's knowledge or experience that the Gospel text assumes," or "authorial audience." He sees "this authorial audience playing an active part in interpreting the text" (See Carter, *Matthew and Empire*, 3–6).

22. On the use of the Hebrew Bible (*Graphe*) in the Gospel of John, see Beutler, "Use of 'Scripture,'" 147–62; Freed, *Old Testament Quotations*; Hanson, *Prophetic Gospel*; Brown, *Introduction*, 132–38. On the relationship with other backgrounds, see chapter 2 of this book.

scholars to see the Gospel in the Graeco-Roman context.[23] Particularly, a gap, which research on the relation of the Johannine christological titles to those of Jewish traditions could not fill,[24] seems to be more or less filled through the products of the new materials and perspectives. These two tendencies and academic research, however, have been paying little attention to the kingship motif of Jesus in John's Gospel as one of the major themes of it.

The twentieth century saw a rapid development in the study not only of the Graeco-Roman world but also of the Hebrew Bible and Jewish traditions when investigating the texts of the New Testament. These studies have had a remarkable influence on the study of the Fourth Gospel. New perspectives have been developed and new approaches of interpretation have been suggested. Hence, no one can deny that research into the background of the New Testament is necessary when examining the kingship motif in the John's Gospel.

Early in the twentieth century, a German scholar, Adolf Deissmann, in his book entitled *Light from the Ancient East*, shows how closely the world of the New Testament is connected to the Graeco-Roman world. In his book, Deissmann translates and interprets inscriptional evidence, which describes Roman emperors. Several concepts and titles ascribed to Roman emperors had developed as the result of Emperor-worship. This development was one of the major backgrounds of the formation of the Christianity. He emphasizes that the titles used for Roman emperors were adapted by Christians to magnify Jesus. He compares the titles of Roman emperors with those of Jesus to show similarity between them.[25] He has opened a way of research on the King-Christology of the New Testament by presenting the similarity of titles between Roman emperors and Jesus. His broad research underlines the importance of the Graeco-Roman world for the study of the New Testament. In particular, his viewpoint throws light on the necessity of the study of Johannine Christology in association with the Imperial titles, because several titles attributed to Roman emperors are used to identify the Johannine Jesus.

A half century later, in 1967, Wayne A. Meeks published a book entitled *The Prophet-King*. In this book, Meeks puts his emphasis on the possible

23. Cassidy, *John's Gospel*, 1–2.

24. Mainly, the Gospel of John presents Jesus as king using the prevailing Roman titles such as "Lord," "Savior of the world," and "Lord and God," while Jewish titles such as "Son of Man," "King of Israel (the Jews)," "Messiah," definitely are used to identify Jesus as king. In addition, the expression, "friend of Caesar" in John 19:12, shows that the Gospel is related to the Roman key terms that appeal the kingship of the Johannine Jesus.

25. Deissmann, *Light*, 346.

links between Mosaic traditions and Johannine Christology. He explores the kingship of "the Prophet" both in the Hebrew Bible and in Jewish traditions. He demonstrates Jesus as the Prophet, indicative of the King who was promised to come as the Prophet like Moses in the Hebrew Bible. Ten years later, in 1977, M. de Jonge in his book entitled *Jesus: Stranger from Heaven and Son of God* also argues for a relationship between Jewish Messianism and Jesus as the Prophet and king in the Gospel of John. According to Meeks and de Jonge, the kingship of Jesus in the Gospel of John is also in close relation to Jewish traditions.

In 1990, Craig R. Koester[26] focuses on the title, "the Savior of the World," which is confessed by the Samaritans in John 4:42, a term that was never used in Samaritan traditions. Rather, it used to be applied to Roman emperors only by the Romans. Koester argues that John used this term on purpose to reveal Jesus as the king through the lips of the Samaritans. He compares the scenes of triumphal entries into the towns of Roman emperors with those of the Samaritans' reception of the Johannine Jesus. He suggests these two are very similar to each other.

In 1992, Richard J. Cassidy published a book entitled *John's Gospel in New Perspective*. In this book, he researches three significant Imperial titles, which are employed to designate Jesus in the Gospel of John: "Savior of the World," "Lord," and "Lord and God." He demonstrates how these three Imperial titles were employed in the process of the deification of Roman emperors. He comments that the intention to strengthen the position of emperors seems to lead to the deification of Roman emperors. He mentions, "so many political factors were intertwined with so many religious factors that it is extremely difficult to delineate the boundary between these two dimensions."[27] Cassidy indicates that the political and religious factors of Rome might well be a strong background for the Gospel of John.

M. É. Boismard in his book entitled *Moses or Jesus* suggests a new interpretation of the usage of "Son of Joseph," which may relate to the Messianism of Samaritan traditions. According to Boismard, one of the backgrounds to John's Gospel is the Samaritan tradition, in which two Messiahs are prophesied: "Son of David," and "Son of Joseph." "Joseph" in Samaritan tradition is the son of Jacob in Genesis, who was a savior of the Israelites.

Many scholars currently conduct studies on the Graeco-Roman background of the New Testament.[28] They suggest that studies on Rome, Roman

---

26. Koester, "Savior," 665–80.

27. Cassidy, *John's Gospel*, 11.

28. See Brent, *Imperial Cult*; Koester, *History, Culture, and Religion*, 366–73; Carter, *Matthew and Empire*; Carter, *Roman Empire*; Novak, *Christianity*; Cassidy, *Christians and Roman Rule*; Aune, "Roman Emperors," 233–35; Edwards, "Hellenism," 312–17;

emperors and the Imperial cult could be quite closely related to the New Testament studies. In particular, Frederick W. Danker's research[29] on the benefactor, because the word, "benefactor," was used as a title of Roman emperors and deities at that time. Danker uses data derived especially from Graeco-Roman inscriptions in which the benefactor-pattern is reasonably certain, to determine whether particular sections of the New Testament that suggest adoption of the Graeco-Roman benefactor model do in fact connote such to a reasonable degree of certainty. He examines particularly the ideas of ἀρετή (excellence), ἀνηρ ἀγαθός (good man), and καλοκἀγαθός. He proposes that the ideas are common in concept and meaning, and are synonymous alternative expressions of benefactor. The concept of benefactor seemed to be applied to the kingship of the Johannine Jesus.[30]

Some scholars[31] convey the knowledge of the Jewish and Hellenistic background by conducting their research on the shepherd-king motif in the Gospel of John. The book entitled *The Shepherd Discourse of John 10 and its Context*[32] edited by Beutler and Fortna is an important one to consider when studying the shepherd-king motif.

In addition, recently, some scholars have pursued a fuller understanding of Jesus in his religious, social, political, and economic context. David R. Kaylor attempts to delineate the political elements of Jesus' ministry and teaching in his book entitled *Jesus the Prophet*. He intends to interpret the political dimensions of Jesus, not to reconstruct a political Jesus. An attempt to explore Jesus in a political context, which is closely connected with the religious one, in the Gospel of John has its usefulness, although the Gospel explains much more beyond the political dimension of Jesus. It is necessary, therefore, to have some understanding of the religious-political context to explore what the Fourth Gospel wants to reveal about Jesus.

David Rensberger, in his book *Johannine Faith and Liberating Community*, argues the possibility of such in relation to Christology and politics by the rediscovery of its social and historical settings. He intends to show "that in the late first century CE, when Jewish and Christian theology and politics could seldom be totally separated, the author of the Gospel had a distinctive conception of what those connotations were."[33] He, finally, argues that

---

Edwards, "Rome," 710–15; Reasoner, "Emperor," 321–26.

29. Danker, *Benefactor*; Danker, "Benefactor," 58–60.

30. On the relationship between the kingship motif of the Johannine Jesus and the good man in the Gospel of John, see Kim, "Jesus as 'Good Man.'"

31. Manning, *Echoes of a Prophet*; Johnson, "Shepherd, Sheep," 751–54; Keener, "Shepherd, Flock," 1090–03.

32. Beutler and Fortna, *Shepherd Discourse of John 10*.

33. Rensberger, *Johannine Faith*, 90.

the Johannine Gospel seems to support a theology of liberation because of its overruling Christology. Accordingly, he remarks that this Gospel is "the product of an oppressed community."[34]

Jerome H. Neyrey in his book *An Ideology of Revolt* focuses on the cultural system or perception of the cosmos reflected in the christological statements of the Gospel of John. He focuses also on the conflict and competition with other colonized Jewish groups and within the Johannine community itself.

In 2002, the book entitled *John and Postcolonialism*[35] was published to examine the making and distribution of power on earthly spaces by tracing the journeys within the Johannine narrative. In this collection of essays, some authors show how the Gospel of John approves of certain travellers invading foreign spaces and how these foreign peoples can reread the Gospel to support decolonization.[36] Some authors seek to identify the exclusive boundaries, while others seek to open up closed boundaries so that all travellers can descend from heaven to earth. Still others trace the journeys and places occupied by women in the Johannine story and in colonial settings. Some authors highlight how colonial history has changed the reading practices of certain communities, while others read this Gospel in order to understand the complex power relations that characterize readers as the colonizers, the collaborators, and the colonized.

Particularly, Musa W. Dube, in her article entitled "Reading for Decolonization,"[37] attempts to highlight some of the main imperial ideological constructions of the Johannine narrative. Her hypothesis on reading the Johannine texts for decolonization seems to be subjected to the hypothesis on "the Bible as imperializing texts." She seems to admit a premise of postcolonial perspective on Imperialism: Imperialism pursues power, mostly violence and military power, to dominate foreign spaces. In addition, Dube, in her article "Savior of the World but not of This World,"[38] points out where her reading of the Gospel of John differs, i.e., in refusing to ignore the Roman imperial setting in the Gospel, refusing to abstract the biblical texts from modern and contemporary international structures, and refusing to read the biblical text in isolation from other works of literature. Dube's aim is to highlight colonizing strategies and their similarity to the Gospel of

---

34. Rensberger, *Johannine Faith*, 110.

35. Dube and Stanley, *John and Postcolonialism*.

36. This book shows "how the Johannine text was used to justify the invasion of others' land, and how the same text can be read for decolonization and emancipation" (Sugirtharajah, "Postcolonial Biblical Interpretation," 71).

37. Dube, "Reading for Decolonization," 51–75.

38. Dube, "Savior of the World," 118–35.

John. She argues, "the exalted space of Jesus as a savior of the world, who is not of this world, is shown to be a colonizing ideology that claims power over all other places and peoples of the earth—one which is not so different from other constructions in secular literature."[39] However, we need to ask if the Bible, in particular the Gospel of John, is, in fact, an imperializing text. The Johannine Jesus does not justify a colonizing ideology because he rejects the logic of power that contains violence. Rather, the Johannine Gospel describes Jesus as a decolonizer who attempts to liberate the world from the darkness with love, forgiveness, freedom, service, and peace.

Richard A. Horsley highlights in his book, *Jesus and Empire*, that it is important to recognize the relationship of the Gospels and the Roman Empire in order to research the identity of Jesus. That is, he highlights the political aspect in the study of Jesus. His remark has much in common with an academic trend of Johannine study, which emphasizes the relation of this Gospel and the Roman Empire. Horsley points out the similarity between Jesus' movement of the kingdom of God and the postcolonial agenda, "recent and current anti-colonial (or anti-imperial) movements in which the withdrawal (or defeat) of the colonizing power is the counterpart and condition of the colonized people's restoration to independence and self-determination."[40] Meaningfully, the judgmental aspect of the Kingdom of God and the eschatological teaching of Jesus indicate emancipation from the foreign power, the Roman Empire. His view is particularly linked with the Johannine new world where the Johannine Jesus reigns as the king. That is, the functions of the Kingdom of God, as Horsley points out, are those of the Johannine Jesus. The Fourth Gospel also implies emancipation of the people from the darkness. This emancipation from the darkness is linked to a constructive alternative, the Johannine new world where all people can live in love, forgiveness, freedom, service, and peace.

Most recently, Warren Carter surveys the central issues of the Gospel of John in his book, *John: Storyteller, Interpreter, Evangelist*. He introduces a consideration of the Gospel's negotiation of the Roman imperial world. He notes that Jesus' ministry reveals God's life-giving purposes for all people, including those marginalized by the hierarchical imperial social structure.[41] He also notes that in the inclusion of such people in John's community, John thus interprets traditions about Jesus in relation to

---

39. Dube, "Savior of the World," 132.

40. Horsley, *Jesus and Empire*, 14.

41. The low-status poor, lacking power, honor, and resources, such as the man who has been sick for thirty-eight years (5:1–9) and the man born blind (9:1–8), a child (4:46–54), a woman and a Samaritan (ch. 4), low-status Galileans (ch. 6), and those who habitually ignore the law (7:49).

Rome's world. He argues that the Johannine new world as God's life-giving and just purpose is shown to be contrary to and resistant to the Roman Empire. Namely, the Roman Empire is revealed to be under judgment in the Gospel of John. In addition, he notes that the Fourth Gospel reveals to the community of Jesus believers, that is, the Johannine new world, that it participates in and anticipates a vastly different reality, namely, the life of God which is given through faith in Jesus. He highlights also that "this alternative community . . . reflected in, and shaped by, the gospel's anti-language, is commissioned to continue to do the works Jesus did (14:12–17), to reveal God's life-giving purposes even though it will be a tough and resisted work (15:18–25)."[42] Furthermore, Carter explains that the Johannine meaning of life is "countercultural in that it is marked by love and service, not domination as in Roman imperial society, and material and physical, since it participates in God's life-giving and just purposes of salvation."[43] Finally, Carter concludes that in John's Gospel various christological titles, which are related to kingship, are used throughout the Gospel to emphasize the identity and tasks of Jesus as God's agent.

Outline of the Research

This book consists of two major parts: the first part is about the identity of the Johannine Jesus (from chapter 2 to 4), and the second part the function of the Johannine Jesus (from chapter 5 to 6).

First, in chapter 2, I will discuss the textual features of the Johannine Gospel in relation to its purposes and recipients. Then, I will describe the two pillars of the background of the kingship of Jesus in the Gospel of John: Jewish traditions and Graeco-Roman traditions. Thirdly, I will discuss the importance of the combination of the two traditions to understand the kingship motif of Jesus in John's Gospel. Finally, I will discuss the method of this book: postcolonialism.

From chapter 3 onwards, I will investigate christological titles, which present the kingship motif of Jesus and their distinctive usage in the Gospel of John. In chapter 3, I will point out important factors for understanding the Johannine christological titles: the Johannine christological titles as hybridized products of hybridized society, and their distinctive usage in mixture. Then, I will discuss the Johannine christological titles in terms of kingship, particularly, the Messiah, the Son of God, the Son of Man, the Prophet, the Savior of the World, and the Lord/ My Lord and My God.

42. Carter, *John*, 172.
43. Carter, *John*, 53.

In chapter 4, I will research the title, "the king of Israel/the Jews" which explicitly reveals the kingship of Jesus in the Fourth Gospel. To begin with, I will survey the meanings of "king" (βασιλεύς) in comparing with both Graeco-Roman and Jewish understandings of this particular office. Then, I will examine that title in the particular context of the Johannine Gospel.

In the second part of the book, I will research the function of the Johannine Jesus from a postcolonial perspective. To do so, in chapter 5, I will deal with "identity matters," that is, the identities of the groups in the Gospel of John: the Roman Empire as the center, the Jews not the ordinary Jews but the Jews of Jerusalem as the collaborators, and the Johannine Group as the margins but also as a group to overcome the center. Then, I will deal with the subtle relationship between the center and the margins under the Roman Empire, and with the matter of collaborators with the Empire. In addition, I will research a complex and delicate conflict between the center and the margins.

Finally, in chapter 6, I will define the identity of the Johannine Jesus. I will discuss Jesus as space to identify him as a universal king, and his functions as a decolonizer, and his vision toward his new world where people live in harmony with love, service, peace, freedom, and forgiveness.

PART I

The Kingship of Jesus in the Gospel of John

2. Background and Methodology

IN THE PRECEDING CHAPTER, I argued that the Johannine community was in conflict with the synagogue as well as with Roman imperial power. Accordingly, it is quite probable that the Gospel of John was written for the consolidation of the community in faith, although it does not seem that this is the only purpose of its composition, as I will argue further in this chapter. Then, I raised a significant question: why are so many christological titles employed in the Johannine Gospel? In my argument, I contend that John adapted a variety of the titles that were used to indicate the Jewish kingly Messiah and the Roman emperors in order to portray Jesus as the real king worthy of the audience's lifelong allegiance in their complex and multicultural world.

In the present chapter, first, while regarding the Fourth Gospel as a product of a multicultural and hybridized society which accommodated multicultural features, I will argue that the Gospel was written for multiple purposes: it was written for multicultural readers in order to present Jesus as king; to make the readers believe in him whom they could follow for eternity; and to challenge them to live in the world according to the ruling ideology of the Johannine new world to overcome conflict and oppression. In order to do this, I need to begin by dealing with the purposes of the composition of this Gospel and to scrutinize the kingship motifs therin, because they are closely related to the identity of the Johannine Jesus.

In order to discuss this matter, in the first section of this chapter, I will present three major views of the purpose of the Gospel of John, including an investigation of the Johannine community as multicultural readers. In the second section, I will survey the kingship motif against the Jewish background and the Graeco-Roman to corroborate my research. In the last section, I will deal with postcolonialism as a major methodology of this book.

The Multiple Purposes of the Gospel of John

The Gospel of John may quite well have more than one purpose as well as a variety of intended recipients.[1] The purposes of the Gospel have been described in various ways, and three major purposes, namely missionary, polemic, and parenetic,[2] can be distinguished.

A Missionary Document for Various Groups and Individuals

The first suggested purpose of the Gospel of John is that it has a missionary aim. In it, we can find evidence of concerns about world mission: for example, references to the sending and coming motif;[3] the emergence of the Greeks who seek Jesus (12:20); the Samaritans identifying Jesus as the Savior of the World (4:42); Jesus' mention of other sheep which are not of this fold (10:16); most of all, God's love for the world (3:16–17).[4] In John 20:21, moreover, the sending motif could be applied to followers of Jesus, which then is a challenge to the Johannine readers. On this, Okure argues, "Thus the terminology of sending/coming not only focuses attention on the Father and Jesus, it emphasizes the intimate and exclusive relationship which exists between them in this missionary enterprise."[5] Segovia also argues that the Gospel of John, particularly the last two chapters,

> [pursue] the proper and correct role of the disciples in the world, especially with regard to their assigned mission in and to the

---

1. For more than one purpose and one potential audience, see Tanzer, "Salvation Is for the Jews," 285–300, esp. 285–86.

2. Brown gives a clear definition of the terms, polemic, apologetic, and missionary: "The most virulent tract of one group of Christians against others usually wants to show how their position is wrong (apologetic), how they horrendously distort Jesus' message (polemic), and how they can be brought to the truth represented by the writer of the tract (missionary)" (Brown, *Introduction*, 152).

3. In this Gospel, God the Father is presented as the one who sent Jesus the Son (5:23, 36, 37; 6:44, 57; 8:18; 12:49; 20:21), and Jesus as the one sent (3:34; 5:38; 6:29; 17:3), and as the one who has come into the world (5:43; 12:46; 16:28; 18:37; cf. 7:28; 8:42; see also 1:9, 11; cf. 1:5, 10; 1:15, 27, 30; 3:31; 3:2; 11:27; 7:27, 31, 41, 42; 6:14; 12:13, 15; 4:25–26). Particularly, although the term "mission" is not used in the Gospel, this motif using different terms, various forms of πέμπειν (5:37; 6:44; 7:28; 8:16, 26, 29; 12:49; 5:23; 7:33; 12:44, 45; 13:20; 15:21; 16:5; 5:24; 4:34; 5:30; 6:38, 39; 7:16; 9:4; 14:23) and ἀποστέλλειν (5:36; 20:21; 11:42; 17:3, 8, 18, 21, 23, 25; 3:17, 34; 5:38; 6:29, 57; 7:29; 8:42; 10:36), is insistently repeated in the text.

4. See Sheppard, "Gospel of John," 2; Okure, *Johannine Approach*, 1–3.

5. Okure, *Johannine Approach*, 3.

world . . . the section makes it very clear that the disciples must carry out their assigned role in and to the world and that they must do so under the guidance and direction of Jesus himself.[6]

We can read, therefore, in this Gospel that "the foundation of the fellowship of the Johannine community in the divine commission to continue the witness of the Johannine Jesus kept it oriented toward the world."[7] In this sense, mission seems to be the primary task of the Johannine community.[8]

From this position, some scholars regard the Gospel as a missionary document for Diaspora Jews or Christian Jews.[9] However, the Johannine Gospel cannot be categorized in such a narrow way. There seem to be various inner-groups in the Johannine Community, suggesting a multicultural readership.[10] The Johannine community might well consist of those groups whose origins were not simply defined by ethnicity or location.[11] To define the Johannine community, therefore, various aspects of its origin must be considered: a variety of classes, ethnicities, and genders and of religious, cultural, political and economic backgrounds, because the descriptions in the Gospel show the complex aspects of relationships or conflicts between the Johannine community and others. For example, many groups and individuals, with which Jesus meets in the Gospel, show a variety of relationships: Individual Jews (Jesus' disciples and followers; particularly, women (e.g., Mary and Martha, a Samaritan woman, etc), the sick (e.g., the invalid

6. Segovia, "Final Farewell of Jesus," 178–79.

7. Nissen, "Community and Ethics," 194–95.

8. Perkins, *Love Commands*, 106.

9. On the Gospel of John as a missionary document for Diaspora Jews, see Smith, *Jesus in the Gospel*; van Unnik, "Purpose of the Fourth Gospel," 410; Robinson, "Destination and Purpose," 117–31; Nicol, *Semeia*, 146; Moule, *Birth*, 136–37; Carson, "Purpose," 639–51.

10. For example, Philip and Nicodemus are Greek names, while Simon and Nathanael are Jewish names in the Gospel of John. This employment of the Jewish and Greek names implies that this Gospel "seems best . . . to posit a mixed audience for the immediate group addressed, bearing in mind the undeniably cosmic dimensions and setting of the Gospel" (Okure, *Johannine Approach*, 280–81).

11. See Esler, *Community and Gospel*, 220. Esler sees that religious and socioeconomic positions are important to understand the identification of the community. He argues that the Gospel of Luke was written for legitimating Christianity to his audience, especially perhaps to the Roman readers among them. Esler's argument gives a good application to understand the Johannine community as the audience or the readers of the Gospel in the multicultural societies of the Roman Empire. On this, Okure argues, "the Christians of the first century were not provincial in their outlook, movements or mentality, we have no reason to surmise that either the works or the problems addressed were restricted to the geographical area from which they originated" (Okure, *Johannine Approach*, 280–81).

for 38 years; the man born blind, etc), and high-ranking individuals (Nicodemus, the royal official, and Joseph of Arimathaea, etc) and Jewish groups (e.g., the Jews of Jerusalem, the disciples of John the Baptist, and the crowds, etc), and non-Jewish people (e.g., a Samaritan woman and the Samaritans,[12] Greeks, Roman governor and soldiers), and so on.

The characters and groups, which seem to reflect the reality of the Johannine community,[13] show complicated and complex inter-relationships in the Gospel. From these relationships we may infer that it is highly possible that, within this multiple and hybridized society, the Gospel of John was written for the Johannine community which consisted of readers who were from multicultural environments.[14] Accordingly, as a missionary document, this Gospel had not only the Jews in view.[15] Its target readership must be wider. It is safe to say that the Gospel was written for a community that consisted of Greek-speaking readers including Jewish and non-Jewish people, and that, to them, the christological titles were mixed into one another to reveal the identity of the Johannine Jesus more clearly.

Polemic/Apologetic Purpose of the Gospel

The second suggested purpose of the Johannine Gospel is as a polemic.[16] As I mentioned in the previous chapter, the Gospel was written to justify the Johannine community in the setting of contention with the synagogue, and to strengthen the faith of readers who were suffering persecution and martyrdom under Roman rule. This implicit conflict, for example, is revealed by

---

12. On the relationship between Samaritan tradition and the Gospel, see chapter 3 of this book. Freed argues that John 4 was written to win Samaritan converts (Freed, "Did John Write His Gospel?," 241–56). Meeks also contends that the secondary aim of the Gospel is to win Samaritan converts (Meeks, *Prophet-King*, 313–19; Meeks, "Galilee and Judea," 159–69, esp. 169; Meeks, "'Am I a Jew?,'" 163–86, esp. 178).

13. On the relationship between ideology and reality, see the section "Methods and Theories" of this chapter.

14. On this, Wind concludes, "It is therefore not improbable that the purpose of John's Gospel is as broad as its universalistic character seems to suggest: 'that you may believe', that is the faith that saves and defeats the world (John iii 16 and I John v 5)" (Wind, "Destination and Purpose," 69).

15. On the openness to Gentiles or Gentile Christians in the Gospel, see Dodd, *Interpretation*, 9; Hengel, *Johannine Question*, 123; Brown, *Community*, 55–58; Culpepper, *Johannine School*, 287–88; Wind, "Destination and Purpose," 26–69. For example, insertions of Greek terms to clarify Aramaic phrases (1:41, 42; 4:25) show that the author considered Greek-speaking readers (Brown, *Community*, 57; Kysar, *John*, 44).

16. Polemic purposes against several groups, for example, Gnosticism, Docetists, the followers of John the Baptist, and so on, have been suggested by scholars. For good surveys on it, see Morris, *Gospel*, 30–34; Lindars, *Gospel*, 58–63.

the comments of the high priest in John 11:49–53, and in the passion narrative where the complicated conflict is revealed sharply: the conflict between the Jewish leaders and Jesus, between Pilate and Jesus, and between Pilate and the Jewish leaders.[17]

Accordingly, if there is a polemic in the Gospel, it is not simply against the Jews. The Gospel of John might attempt to dialogue with a variety of groups, even though the major group was the Jews. Thus, the purpose of the composition of the Gospel can be categorized as apologetic.[18] It is quite probable that John was partly "writing for a pagan audience with a philosophical and cultural interest in Eastern religion."[19] Fiorenza says,

> Jews as well as Christians appealed to the Greco-Roman world and used the means and methods of Hellenistic religious propaganda.... The appropriation of such missionary propagandistic forms was necessary if Judaism as well as Christianity were to succeed in the face of competition from other religions, especially those of Oriental origin, as well as competition from the philosophical movements of the time.[20]

In this respect, Johannine Christianity was not exceptional. Cassidy also argues that John was conscious of Roman realities and provided support for Christians under Roman rule.[21] It may be safe to say, therefore, that the Fourth Gospel has some apologetic characteristics. In short, the polemic (toward other Christians) and/or apologetic (toward unbelievers) purpose has its own basis in the Gospel. It is probable that the Gospel of John was written for the promotion and defense of Johannine Christianity.

---

17. See Rensberger, *Johannine Faith*, 87–134; Carter, *John and Empire*.

18. On the apologetic purpose of the Gospel of John, the defense of the faith of the Johannine community before unbelievers and/or other Christian groups, see McGrath, *John's Apologetic Christology*, esp. 232; Fortna, *Gospel of Signs*, 224, 229–31; Nicol, *Semeia*, 145; Meeks, "Divine Agent," 43–67, esp. 44; Geisler, "Johannine Apologetics," 333–43; Brown, *Introduction*, 151–83; Alexander, "Acts of the Apostles," 15–44.

19. Alexander, "Acts of the Apostles," 17–18.

20. Fiorenza, "Miracles, Mission and Apologetics," 2. Droge also gives a good explanation: "Apologetic in the New Testament comprises a study of the 'act of persuasion' employed by the early Christians. Such persuasion evolved in a context of Jewish and Hellenistic thought and laid a foundation from the second century apologists.... Much of early Christian literature, including the New Testament, was written to promote and defend the Christian movement. The early Christians attempted to appeal to the inhabitants and used methods of Hellenistic religious propaganda. The appropriation of such apologetic-propagandistic forms was essential if Christianity was to succeed in the face of competition from other religions" (Droge, "Apologetics," 302–7, esp. 302).

21. See Cassidy, *John's Gospel*.

Consolidation of the Johannine Community

The last suggested purpose of the Gospel, which is widely accepted, is parenetic, namely, the need to strengthen the faith of the Johannine community. This last one is related to the historical situation with which the Johannine community was faced. Although the historical situation of the Johannine Jesus in the text was related to Judaism in Palestine, that of the Johannine community was related to a multicultural society if we accept that the Gospel was written in Asia Minor, particularly in Ephesus. In other words, it is likely that the author and the readers of the Gospel belonged to the colonial environment regardless of whether it was composed in Palestine or in Asia Minor.[22] Accordingly, it is acceptable that the text describes a complex and hybridized society. It is reasonable to infer from this that the readership of the text has experience of such a society whether in Palestine or in Asia Minor.

Supposing the Gospel to have a closed metaphorical system (sectarian), Meeks argues that individuals or groups outside of the Johannine community could not understand it.[23] However, the Gospel of John seems not to have been unreadable and not understandable to the outsiders of the Johannine community.[24] Beutler argues that the Gospel was written to deepen the faith of the Christians, as well as to encourage them to confess this faith openly in the face of conflict and trials and even death.[25] In addition, McKnight's comment on the Bible is helpful for my argument: "The Bible is read in the context of continuing communities of faith, and even readers who do not share the faith of those communities are influenced by that fact."[26] In McKnight's explanation, the Gospel was not only read by the Johannine community (the first recipients of the Gospel). Rather, it is probable that

---

22. The implicit expression of the persecution (9:22; 12:42; 16:2; cf. Domitian's claim being "Lord and God" in John 20:28; Jesus' death on the cross as a Roman execution; Peter's martyrdom in 21:18–19) might show that the Johannine community had been struggling not only with the Synagogue but also with the Roman power (see chapter 3 of this book).

23. Meeks, "Man from Heaven," 44–72; Meeks, "Am I a Jew?," 163–86; see also Fuglseth, *Johannine Sectarianism*; Segovia, "Love and Hatred," 258–72; Culpepper, *Johannine School*, 287; Brown, *Gospel*, lxx–lxxv; Kysar, *Fourth Evangelist*, 149–65; Wind, "Destination and Purpose," 31–32.

24. See chapter 6 of this book.

25. See Beutler, "Faith and Confession," 19–32. The Fourth Gospel shows various examples of figures who confess Jesus as their object of faith: Nicodemus, the Samaritan woman, the man born blind, Peter, the beloved disciple, Thomas and the disciples, Mary Magdalene, and Joseph of Arimathea and the Crypto-Christians.

26. McKnight, "Reader-Response," 239.

the Gospel would be spread to readers inside and outside the Johannine community in order to be read at the same time (at least, partly because of the missionary and apologetic purpose of the Gospel).[27] Accordingly, even readers who were not in the same community could read the Gospel. Consequently, it is highly probable that the insiders of the Johannine community and even the outsiders of various backgrounds could understand what we being said about the identity of Jesus because of the variety of the Johannine christological titles and terms, which had been adapted from those of both the Jewish and the Graeco-Roman world.[28]

In short, the important point is that the Johannine metaphorical system is not only for the closed Johannine community[29] (the Gospel as a closed sectarian document), but for the Johannine community which opened toward the world (the Gospel as an open document).[30] Although it has a symbolic language of resistance against the center, the Gospel would be mainly given to the margins in the first century CE who longed for liberty from oppression.[31] Lincoln comments exactly on this:

> To all those who found their confession about the identity of Jesus in dispute and who suffered the consequences, this Gospel's interpretation of his mission was meant to provide reassurance about the confession and about its being the means of experiencing the life and well-being of the age to come in the midst of present conflict and trials.[32]

Seeing the Johannine community in the larger environment, therefore, namely the Johannine community in the Roman world, opens a possibility of re-reading the Fourth Gospel with multiple purposes.

---

27. See also Burridge, "About People," 113–45, esp. 144. On a fairly wide and rapid dissemination and circulation of the texts in the first century, see Thompson, "Holy Internet," 49–70; Alexander, "Ancient Book," 71–105; Bauckham, "John for Readers," 147–71; Barton, "Can We Identify?" 173–94.

28. Nissen, "Community and Ethics," 197.

29. On the rejection of the sectarian nature of the community, see Cullmann, *Johannine Circle*; Brown, *Community*.

30. On this, see chapter 5 of this book.

31. See Rensberger, *Johannine Faith*. Rensberger argues that John is a kind of liberation theologian. However, it does not mean that the Gospel of John is written only for the poor. It was also written for the rich, for example, the positive roles of Joseph and Nicodemus in the burial of Jesus (van Bruggen, *Jesus*). On this matter, see also chapter 6 of this book.

32. Lincoln, *Gospel*, 88.

Purposes of the Gospel of John: A Synthetic Approach

Until now, we have discussed the possible purposes of the Gospel of John, missionary, polemic/apologetic, and parenetic. These three major possibilities must have their claim based upon proper grounds. In this sub-section, it is necessary to remark that the purpose of the Gospel is not categorized in an exclusive way. It is fairly acceptable that the Gospel "was intended to serve the needs of the community."[33] In terms of the needs of the community, it is quite probable that the Gospel was destined to meet a variety of apologetic, polemic, and parenetic needs in a multicultural and colonial society.[34] I contend, therefore, that as a postcolonial text, the Johannine Gospel includes all these possible purposes in it, because it was written for first century readers who were in the colonial era in the process of the hybridization of culture. For that reason, it is appropriate to discuss a synthetic approach to the purpose of the composition of the Fourth Gospel.

As a synthetic approach, some scholars argue, "the purpose of the Gospel of John is to evangelize Jews, to evangelize Hellenists, to strengthen the church, to catechize new converts, to provide materials for the evangelization of Jesus and so forth."[35] On this matter, Okure's question about the possibility of the interrelationship of the motives of the purpose(s) of the Gospel of John is appropriate.

> The question raised, then, is whether these efforts to meet the various needs of the community can be considered as missionary work. In other words, do the apologetic, polemic and parenetic motifs serve a missionary purpose? Or does outreach to pagans constitute the exclusive meaning of missionary work?[36]

Fiorenza gives a sharp answer to the question: "apologetics and missionary propaganda functioned like two sides of the same coin."[37] While saying that "in whole or in part the Gospel was written with an apologetic,

---

33. Okure, *Johannine Approach*, 11–12.

34. Segovia proposes the five possible functions of the plot of the Gospel of John, which shows comprehensively the synthetic purpose of the Gospel (a very strong didactic function; a very strong polemical function; a very prominent admonitory function; a clear consolatory function; a very important exhortatory function). See Segovia, "Journey(s)," 47–49.

35. Carson, *Gospel*, 89; See also Beasley-Murray, *John*, lxxxviii–xc; Barrett, *Gospel*, 26; de Jonge, *Jesus*, 1–3.

36. Okure, *Johannine Approach*, 14.

37. Fiorenza, "Miracles, Mission and Apologetics," 3; see also Alexander, "Acts of the Apostles," 15–44, esp. 17–18, 39–40.

2. BACKGROUND AND METHODOLOGY 27

polemic, or missionary motif in regard to one or all of those groups,"[38] Brown also argues that these goals are not mutually exclusive.[39] Although Brown's view on the purpose of the Gospel (that it was written to intensify people's faith and make it more profound) is different from Okure's (the Gospel was written for mission), their views on the interrelation of these motives for the writing of the Gospel meet in a common place. Furthermore, Segovia sees the Johannine community as the ideal/implied readers of the Gospel of John, which

> is initiated, confirmed, or reinforced as children of God . . . who believe in Jesus and carry out his commands . . . should see itself as deeply estranged from and at odds with the world . . . are specifically warned thereby that an acceptance of the ways and values of God in the world implies and entails severe opposition from the world [as well as] a very privileged position indeed while in the world, ultimate victory over the world, and an abiding union with God in the world above . . . should expect nothing but hatred and oppression in and from the world [as well as] shall receive glory not only in the world of human beings but also in the world of God . . . are also urged thereby to carry on with their own mission in the world, regardless of dangers or consequences, in obedience to the plan of God and following the example of Jesus.[40]

Segovia's view clearly shows that the Gospel of John is coincident with the multiple needs of the community.

In addition, these possible purposes have their own basis on a textual variant of John 20:31. At the textual level, this synthetic approach is closely related to a textual variant of John 20:31. Two possible translations of this verse from the Greek text could be proposed in relation to the tense of the main verb *"you may believe"* (πιστεύ[σ]ητε) because of different manuscript readings.[41]

---

38. Brown, *Introduction*, 151–52.

39. Meeks also says that "the history of the Johannine mission and apologetics must have been far more complex" (Meeks, "Divine Agent," 60).

40. Segovia, "Journey(s)," 47–49.

41. The witnesses for the first reading (πιστευητε; present subjunctive: "you may continue to believe") given in NA27 include P66vid ℵ* B Θ 0250. 892s. *l* 221 1; and for the second reading (πιστεύσητε; aorist subjunctive: "you may begin or to come to believe"), ℵ2 A C D L W ψ 0100 F1.13 33, etc. (see Bruce, *Gospel*, 395; Metzger, *Textual Commentary*, 256; de Jonge, *Jesus*, 1–7; Okure, *Johannine Approach*, 9; Beutler, "Faith and Confession," 19–20).

Firstly, this verb can be parsed as the aorist tense[42] of the subjunctive mood. In this case, the subject of the verb (second person plural) "you," as the recipients of the Gospel stands for non-believers whether or not they were real historical figures. That is, the author of the Gospel wrote it for non-believers in order to make them believe in Jesus as the Christ and the Son of God through their reading of this Gospel; as a result of their belief in Jesus, they might have life in his name which they did not have before believing. In this case, the purpose of the composition of the Gospel might be missionary.

Secondly, the verb can be parsed as the present tense[43] of the subjunctive mood. In this case, the subject could be interpreted as the believers who have not seen Jesus in the flesh. In this case, the purpose of the composition of the Gospel was to be for subsequent generations of believers who have not actually seen Jesus (*you may continue to believe*).[44] In other words, John wrote it for believers in order to strengthen their faith that Jesus is the Christ and the Son of God; in order to emphasize the fact that they already have life in his name, because they had already believed in Jesus so that they need to have no doubt of the facts of their faith in any circumstances. In this case, the purpose of the composition of the Gospel might be closely linked to the consolidation of the Johannine community in Christ.

According to Metzger,[45] both readings have the support of early witnesses. The problem cannot be resolved on the basis of textual evidences alone but on the general suggestion of the Gospel.[46] Because of the possibility of the motives (missionary, polemic/apologetic, parenetic) for the writing of the Gospel, these two possible variant readings of John 20:31 could give the possibility of the multifaceted purpose of the composition

---

42. In Greek, the aorist form always expresses the perfect aspect of the verb, which describes the action as a complete event, without commenting on whether or not it is a process. Therefore, in ἵνα-clauses (purpose), aorist subjunctive means the action as a complete event in the future. It is, therefore, that πιστεύσητε can be translated as "you, who have not believed yet, may begin to believe."

43. In Greek, the present form always expresses the imperfect aspect, which describes the action as a process. Therefore, in ἵνα-clauses (purpose), present subjunctive means the action as a process from the past. It is, therefore, that πιστεύητε can be translated as "you, who have believed, may continuously believe."

44. Bryne, "Faith of the Beloved Disciples" 93. De Jonge also comments that the subjunctive sentence in the Johannine literature "reflects catechetical instruction within the Johannine communities rather than missionary practice" (de Jonge, *Jesus*, 2). See also Brown, *Gospel*, 1056; Schnackenburg, *Gospel*, 3:337–38; Fee, "On the Text," 193–206.

45. Metzger, *Textual Commentary*, 256.

46. Kysar, *Fourth Evangelist*, 147–65; Kysar, *John*, 18–26.

of the Gospel: the purpose of mission (missionary propaganda/apologetic), and the purpose of strengthening the faith of the Johannine Christians. On this, Carson says, "it can easily be shown that John elsewhere in his Gospel can use *either* tense to refer to *both* coming to faith and continuing in the faith."[47] On the one hand, John might write the Gospel to believers in order to consolidate their faith in the time of persecution and conflict, and in order to challenge them to evangelize the world, which was negative toward Jesus and his followers. On the other hand, to the non-believers, at least, it could be presented as an evangelistic document, which challenges them to have faith in the Johannine Jesus. Consequently, I argue that the Gospel functions as a multipurpose document.

If these two variant readings could be acceptable, in addition, how did those readers in the first century, "you" in John 20:31, understand Jesus? Lincoln sees that "you" of 20:31 "can be seen as embracing a wide variety of implied readers" in terms of different levels of understanding and knowledge of the Jesus story, of Hebrew or Aramaic terms, of Jewish customs, and of Scriptures and Synoptics.[48] Lincoln's comment exactly explains the reason why among many other titles and concepts employed to designate Jesus in the Gospel, John emphasizes Jesus as the Christ and the Son of God at the end of the Gospel to present clearly the purpose of its composition. In other words, the Johannine kingship motif is central to John's purpose of introducing Jesus as king to first-century readers in a multicultural society.

Therefore, all the questions about the purpose of the Gospel can be explained in relation to the kingship of Jesus, because Jesus is described in terms, which indicate his kingship in the Gospel. Furthermore, the Johannine Jesus has already predicted in the Gospel that his followers will find themselves in situations where they will be treated harshly by the world (John 9:22; 12:42; 16:2). By adapting many christological titles and using them distinctively in the text, the Gospel on the one hand is simply giving maximum emphasis to the portrait of Jesus as king and its impact on its readers to encourage their faith. On the other hand, through representing Jesus as king and his kingly function, the Gospel challenges the readers to evangelize the world.

Therefore, the purposes of the Gospel could be summarised thus: The Johannine Gospel was written with multi-purposes for multi-recipients. It was written for the insiders of the community which consisted of people of

47. Carson, *Gospel*, 662.

48. Lincoln, *Gospel*, 88. Culpepper also argues, "a distinctive group of readers . . . is in view, but it is not necessarily a homogeneous group," through surveying all the data of five areas (persons, places, languages, Judaism, and events) to which the narrator refers (see Culpepper, *Anatomy*, 211–23).

many different backgrounds, in order to consolidate their faith in Jesus as king and to challenge them to live out that faith for the new world; simultaneously it was written for the outsiders of a multicultural society in order to lead them to believe in Jesus as king.

Backgrounds of the Gospel of John and Kingship

In the previous section, I discussed the different purposes of the composition of the Gospel for the multicultural readers in the Johannine community in order to explain the necessity of the identity of Jesus as king, because the kingship of Jesus gives answers to their various needs. In this section, I will survey the kingship of the Johannine Jesus in terms of multicultural backgrounds: Jewish and Graeco-Roman.

Two Pillars of the Background of the Gospel of John and the Kingship Motif

My argument is that the kingship of Jesus functions as one of the crucial characteristics of Johannine Christology, reflecting its multicultural features. In order to argue this, first, I have to say that specific terms, which conveyed royal concepts originating from the various cultures, are employed in the Gospel to designate the identity of Jesus as king. MacRae argues that many of the most striking elements of Johannine symbolism and literary technique are simply not paralleled in Jewish literature but in other more unmistakably Hellenistic types, both Jewish and non-Jewish.[49] Smith also contends that although the origin of Johannine Christianity is to be understood as processes centering on Judaism and Jewish Christianity, the motifs in the Johannine literature go beyond Judaism and reflect a later stage in the development of the Johannine community.[50] McGrath also concludes that "the paradox of Johannine Christology is an aspect of John's development of traditions he inherited, utilizing motifs current in his day and age."[51] Horbury further argues that there was a strong relationship between Christianity and Judaism, emphasizing the significance of messianic hope within the Scripture and Jewish traditions in the Second Temple period.[52] In addition, he argues that there was a close resemblance to contemporary Gentile cults

---

49. MacRae, "Fourth Gospel," 14–15.
50. Smith, "Johannine Christianity," 222–48, esp. 47.
51. McGrath, *John's Apologetic Christology*, 234.
52. See Horbury, *Jewish Messianism*.

of heroes, sovereigns, and divinities so that the cult of Christ was essentially a "Gentilized manifestation of Christianity."[53]

It is not easy, therefore, to define the meaning of the christological terms employed in the Gospel to depict the Johannine Jesus without prior understanding of the terms in relation to the Jewish and the Graeco-Roman,[54] or other cultural backgrounds.[55] The meanings of the terms have been originated, developed, and changed in various different contexts through the hybridization of various cultures.[56] It is important to know, however, that even though the terms in the different contexts could convey different nuances of meanings, there must be common meanings, which penetrate the terms in general.[57]

For example, the term "the Christ" is closely related to the kingship of Jesus in the Gospel, although it could be understood as having different meanings in different contexts.[58] To begin with, the meaning of "the Christ," namely "the Messiah" in Hebrew, might be defined slightly differently in Jewish society from that of other societies. In Jewish society after the Exile the political features of the term had been emphasized more and more. Under

---

53. Horbury, *Jewish Messianism*, 3.

54. For surveys of backgrounds of the Gospel of John, see Lindars, *Gospel*, 35–42; Barrett, *Gospel*, 27–41. Lindars argues that "the author derives his thought from the Jewish and Christian tradition; but it is altogether probable that he writes for Greeks, and duly takes their way of thinking into account" (Lindars, *Gospel*, 35). Some scholars see both possibilities of the perception of Jewish and Gentile influence on the Gospel (Casey, *From Jewish Prophet*, 11–14; Barclay, *Jews in the Mediterranean Diaspora*, 402–13; McGrath, *John's Apologetic Christology*, 6–27).

55. About the relationship between the Gospel of John and the Samaritan traditions, see chapter 6 of this book.

56. For example, the influence of the Hellenistic culture on Judaism was extensive (see Engberg-Pedersen, "Introduction," 1–16), but resistance of the Jewish people resulted in different situations in various regions and periods (Lindars, *Gospel*, 49; see also Barrett, *Gospel*, 27). Hengel argues that because of a smooth penetration of Hellenistic influences into Judaism for centuries, there was respect on both sides between Jew and Greek. However, he argues that a furious defensive reaction occurred when the Greeks tried to go too fast, make Hellenization obligatory and outlaw the Law (see Hengel, *Judaism and Hellenism*).

57. MacRae contends that because he and his readers were in the multicultural environment of Roman Hellenism, John "may have tried deliberately to incorporate a diversity of backgrounds into the one gospel message, precisely to emphasize the universality of Jesus, creating his own gospel 'style,' and heaping up Christological titles" (MacRae, "Fourth Gospel," 15, 17, 19). In my view, John exquisitely employed many Christological titles to reveal the universal kingship of Jesus. The titles were not "heaped up," but arranged elaborately in the text by the author's highly intended literary strategy. I will discuss this in chapter 3 of this book.

58. De Jonge, "Jewish Expectation," 246–70; Fitzmyer, *One Who Is to Come*.

the oppression of foreign powers, the Jews had anticipated a Messiah as the descendant of King David, who would emancipate them from oppressive foreign powers.[59] The concept of the Messiah had emphasized the kingly messiah of the Jews as a savior in Jewish society. In the Gospel of John, however, the term "the Christ" is not only an indicator of the Jewish messianic king, but also when the term is applied to Jesus it is used to describe Jesus as the universal king who could unite all the differences of the colonial world into one harmonious whole.[60] The Johannine Jesus, therefore, rejects his earthly kingship but affirms his higher kingship in front of Pilate (18:33–38), and also that people such as John the Baptist (chapter 1), Andrew and Philip (1:41), the Samaritan woman (4:29), the crowds (chapter 7), and Martha (11:27) who meet Jesus and confess him as the Christ are not only the Jews in this Gospel. The more important thing is that they are mainly people on the margins of society who cannot go into the center of the colonial environment. It is important, therefore, to understand the kingship of the Johannine Jesus in a multicultural and hybridized society, rather than simply according to ethnic or religious backgrounds. In the Graeco-Roman world, on the other hand, the concept of the Christ had no special religious significance prior to the influence of ancient Jewish and Christian usage.[61] To understand the proper meaning of the Christ in the Gospel of John, therefore, knowledge about the Jewish term "the Messiah" is needed.

In the Graeco-Roman background, however, "the Savior of the World" was used to designate kings and generals, including Roman emperors, who were victors in ancient wars.[62] The term "the Savior of the World" (4:42), which is employed to confess the identity of the Johannine Jesus from the lips of the Samaritans,[63] is closely linked to the term "the Messiah" in the context (4:29, 42). If this is accepted, therefore, those terms which point to the identity of the Johannine Jesus as king could be understood in relation to kingship.

59. Strauss, *Davidic Messiah*, 35–57. See also Caragounis, "Kingdom of God/Kingdom of Heaven," 418.

60. That is the reason why John describes Jesus fleeing the crowd's attempt to make him king by force (6:15), while in other passage he affirms Jesus as the king (12:13; in the passion narrative). Moreover, the use of the phrase, "Jesus the Nazarene, the king of the Jews," (19:19–20) on the cross written in Hebrew, Greek, and Latin indicates, ironically, his universal kingship.

61. Hurtado, "Christ," 106.

62. See chapter 3 of this book; Dodd, *Interpretation*, 238–39; Schneider and Brown, "σωτήρ," 217; Koester, "Savior of the World," 667.

63. Dodd comments that "the evangelist may even have been conscious of a certain dramatic propriety in putting it in the mouth of Samaritans, who in this gospel represent in some sort the Gentile world over against the Jews" (Dodd, *Interpretation*, 239).

In short, my argument is that the author presents Jesus as the universal king using terms the meaning of which a variety of readers from various backgrounds could understand when they read the Gospel of John. Therefore, to justify my argument, we need to survey two backgrounds of this Gospel: the Jewish and the Graeco-Roman.

The Kingship Motif and the Jewish Background

Among a variety of terms in the Johannine Gospel, which imply the kingship of Jesus, many of them might come from the Hebrew Bible and other Jewish sources.[64] Particularly, Davidic royalty (cf. John 7:42) and the Jewish messianic expectation form a major area of research into the background of the kingship motif in Jewish literature.[65] In Jewish literature, kingship is closely related to God and his representatives who ruled ancient Jewish society. Furthermore, this term was also used for the redeemer king.[66] Although for nearly 500 years after the fall of Jerusalem there was no king, the Jews expected the emancipation of Israel from foreign power and looked to a leader to come, the Messiah, to be their king in the restoration of the nation. Predictions of the coming king, which includes that of a religious and political leader, are referred to in the Hebrew Bible and Davidic royal terms are employed in passages referring to Israel's restoration.[67] Consequently, the anticipated king would be the political and religious head of the people, as well as a representative of God in order to emancipate them.

---

64. See Fitzmyer, *One Who Is to Come*, 82–133; Horbury, *Jewish Messianism*; Day, *King and Messiah*; Collins, *Scepter and the Star*, 20–48; Neusner, Green, and Frerichs, *Judaisms*.

65. In the New Testament, Messiah bears this title "king" in close dependence on the Hebrew Bible and Jewish usage. For example, John 12:34 (the Messiah remains forever) is reminiscent of Ezek 37:25 (David my servant shall be their prince forever) and Ps 89:37 (David's offspring shall endure forever). The remaining of the Messiah in John 12:34 is understood in terms of kingship. On the background of the Davidic Messiah, see Strauss, *Davidic Messiah*, 35–75; Fitzmyer, *One Who Is to Come*, 8–81; Schmidt, "βασιλεύς, βασιλεία," 576).

66. Strauss, *Davidic Messiah*, 35. Von Rad describes the complex of religious and political ideas linked with the empirical king as forming the soil for Messianic belief and that the true point of connection or starting-point of the Messianic belief was the person of David and especially the Davidic covenant (2 Sam 7) (see von Rad, "βασιλεύς," 566–68).

67. It is "with the collapse of the Davidic monarchy and the Babylonian exile" that "expectation for the restoration of the monarchy became a common feature—though not universal—within the more general hope for Israel's renewal" (Strauss, *Davidic Messiah*, 38). On the very diversity of the development of the hope for their restoration before the Exile, see Barton, "Messiah in Old Testament Theology," 365–79.

Some examples in the Hebrew Bible, particularly prophetic passages, are relevant to the discussion in my book.[68]

Firstly, in Isaiah 9:1–7 the king as the powerful and mighty ruler will establish his kingdom and will sit and reign on the throne of David over his kingdom forever.[69] He is "a great light" who will come to the people who walk in darkness (Isa 9:1–2). He will deliver them from the oppression of their oppressor and will end war by destroying the instruments of war (Isa 9:3–4). The Johannine Jesus can be matched to this Davidic kingly figure. As "the light of the world," Jesus comes to the world in darkness to rescue the people in darkness by non-violent means.[70] The Johannine Jesus shows how to be free from oppression (8:32), promises peace which the world cannot give (14:27; 16:33; 20:19, 21),[71] and will sit on the throne by glorification through the cross. Moreover, a Davidic Messianic figure in Isaiah 11:1–10 (a shoot from the stem of Jesse[72] and a branch from his roots in Isa 11:1, the root of Jesse to whom the Jews and the Gentiles will resort in Isa 11:10) stands for the representative of an enormous social transformation.[73] The utopian description in Isaiah 11:1–10 represents a reformed community and a true kingdom of God on earth which is reminiscent of the new world of the Johannine Jesus: the new world in which the center and the margins can live in harmony. Like the king of this utopian nation (the shoot, the branch or the root) who will unite both Jews and Gentiles, the Johannine

---

68. See Williamson, "Messianic Texts," 238–70; Mason, "Messiah," 37–38.

69. Williamson emphasizes the nature of king as agent through whom God will work, which is reminiscent of the Johannine Jesus as God's agent (see Williamson, "Messianic Texts," 254–58).

70. See Prologue of the Gospel of John; John 8:12–59; 18:1–11, 35–37.

71. In the Qumran literature, as in rabbinic tradition, the branch, son of David, appears as a man of peace after the battle has been won (Johnson, "Davidic-Royal Motif," 148).

72. This image as a favorite metaphor for the coming Davidic king was used by the exilic and post-exilic prophets (Strauss, *Davidic Messiah*, 38).

73. Klappert, "King, Kingdom," 374. "The branch" in the Qumran literature as well as in the Hebrew Bible appears as the Messianic figure (see Collins, *Scepter and the Star*, 49–73; Fitzmyer, *One Who Is to Come*, 103–4; Johnson, "Davidic-Royal Motif," 146–48). In 4QBt3 (4Q504), for example, God has chosen the tribe of Judah and made a covenant with David who was to be shepherd and prince of the people (see Johnson, "Davidic-Royal Motif," 146); the Messiah of Righteousness is called the Branch of David (see Vermès, *Complete Dead Sea Scrolls*, 494; Allegro, "Further Messianic References," 174–87). Particularly, in 4QSefM (4Q285) 7:1–6, which quotes Isa 10:34—11:1, the titles "scion of David" and "Prince of the congregation" indicates the same person, and "identifies 'the shoot from the stump of Jesse,' indirectly giving that passage of Isaiah a messianic connotation, which it did not have in preexilic times" (Fitzmyer, *One Who Is to Come*, 104).

Jesus comes to his world (1:10) to assemble his flock from among the Jews as well as from amongst other sheep (10:16), and will receive them into heavenly dwelling places (14:2–3).

Secondly, Haggai and Zechariah also describe the king as a religious and political leader.[74] Haggai is concerned with the building of the temple by Zerubbabel who is a Davidic prince and the natural leader of the nation. Zerubbabel is made the signet of God (Hag 2:23) and foreign powers would be defeated. Similarly, in Zechariah a man called "the Branch" will build the temple of God and he will be a ruler (6:12–13; cf. 3:8[75]). The role of the Branch, Zerubbabel, is that of the king. In addition, the king, mounted on a donkey will come to Israel (Zech 9:9), speak peace to the Gentiles and rule the whole world (9:10). The coming king is also related to rescue from oppression and to bringing war to an end (9:8, 10). We can link the Johannine Jesus with the king in Zechariah 9:9–10. Jesus enters into Jerusalem riding on a donkey (John 12:12–19). The multitude welcomes him shouting "Hosanna! Blessed is he who comes in the name of the Lord! Blessed [even] the King of Israel." The multitude regards and welcomes Jesus as the King of Israel. Those prophets who hoped for the restoration of the nation and saw the Branch as a decolonizing king have meaning in terms of the national emancipation. The concept of the king in the post-exilic period of Jewish society is linked to that of the political and religious leader as the decolonizer.[76]

Thirdly, in Micah 5:1–15 a ruler (מָשַׁל) of Israel (LXX: ἄρχοντα ἐν τῷ Ἰσραηλ) would come not only from Bethlehem Ephrathah but from the beginning (LXX: ἀπ᾽ ἀρχῆς) and even the days of eternity as well. He was a shepherd who will feed his flock, and bring peace to Israel. The ruler of Israel in Micah 5:1 is also related to the Johannine Jesus.[77] In the Gospel of John, the origin of Jesus is "the beginning," like the ruler of Israel in Micah 5:1, although his origin from Bethlehem is not revealed (cf. 7:41–42). Rather, his Galilean origin is employed in the controversy over his messiahship. His pre-existence in the Gospel might be linked to this verse.

74. See Mason, "Messiah," 340–49; Toy, "King," 157–60.

75. The concept of a fig tree (Zech 3:10) is linked to John 1:48. In that context, being called under a fig tree marked the arrival of the "Branch" (Zech 3:8), who was understood to be the Davidic Messiah foretold in the Law (Gen 49:10) and the Prophets (Jer 23:6; 33:16; Zech 3:8; 6:12–13) (Koester, *Symbolism*, 40).

76. In the book of Jeremiah, the concept of king stresses the political qualities of the king. That is, the function of the king in the book of Jeremiah is that of political ruler. The coming king as a branch of David in Jer 33:15–16 will rule on "the earth" with justice and righteousness, and Israel will be saved and safe under him. The king in Jeremiah also functions as a decolonizer.

77. Von Rad, "βασιλεύς," 567, 569.

The ruler of Israel as a shepherd who will feed his flock foreshadows the Johannine Jesus in the good shepherd discourse in John 10:1–11, and the multitude's attempt to force him to be their king after he fed them in John 6:1–15. Moreover, the prophecy that the ruler of Israel would bring peace to Israel is also suggestive of the message of Jesus about peace (14:17; 16:33) before his crucifixion and after his resurrection (20:19–23). Consequently, just as Lambert comments that the biblical concept of messianism has two main features (the Messiah as a descendent of King David and as an ideal king),[78] it is also fair to say that some of the christological titles of the Johannine Jesus have these two features.

The Kingship Motif and the Graeco-Roman Background

The kingship of the Johannine Jesus is more deeply revealed when Johannine christological terms and titles are investigated in comparison with terms and titles in the Graeco-Roman world. Research into the relationship between the Gospel of John and the Graeco-Roman world[79] reveals terms and titles which were popularly known in Graeco-Roman culture, and might be employed to reveal the identity of Jesus as king in the Fourth Gospel. For example, some specific terms, i.e., the Savior of the World, my Lord and my God, which are employed to confess Jesus as their king by the believers or the crowds might be used to reveal the kingship of Jesus.[80] In this section, I will cite some references, which could elucidate the Graeco-Roman background of the kingship of the Johannine Jesus.

Firstly, it is interesting that the term, ἐυεργέτης (benefactor) was a favourite and striking title for the Hellenistic kings and Roman Emperors, whose funcion was linked with that of Jesus in the Johannine narratives (supplying new wine, feeding thousands, 10:1–18, and the passion narrative). The nature and task of the king is revealed clearly in the fact that he is a benefactor to the whole world.[81] Danker demonstrates the Graeco-Roman documents, which attest "the consistency of thematic interest and formulaic patterns in language relating to the benefactor figure."[82] Particularly,

---

78. Lambert, "Kingship in Ancient Mesopotamia," 69.

79. To consult recent research, see Cassidy, *John's Gospel*; Koester, "Savior," 665–80; Carter, *John*.

80. About "Savior" or "Savior of the World," see chapter 3 of this book; about "My Lord and My God" see also chapter 3 of this book.

81. See Danker, *Benefactor*, 36–42, 202–36; Danker, "Benefactor," 58–60; Kleinknecht, "βασιλεύς," 565; Neyrey, "God, Benefactor and Patron," 465–92, esp. 471–76.

82. Danker, *Benefactor*, 29.

inscriptions and documents to give honor to kings in terms of benefactor are likely to relate to the kingship of the Johannine Jesus. We can propose that the Gospel of John characterizes Jesus as the "benefactor" par excellence in terms of kingship.

Secondly, the Hellenistic idea of divine kingship originated with Alexander the Great,[83] and was revived in the cult of the Roman emperor. In the time of Augustus (63 BCE–14 CE), the concept of the incarnation of divinity in the emperor took over this idea.[84] The Johannine proclamation of Jesus as the incarnate form of God could be the cause of a crucial ideological confrontation with the Roman authorities and be the cause of the persecution of Christians in the period of the Early Church (Prologue; 10:30; 14:8–16:33).[85]

Thirdly, the stories of Vespasian's miracles,[86] the healing of a blind man and of a man with a withered hand, are reminiscent of the miraculous healings of the Johannine Jesus. In particular, the healing of a blind man by Vespasian is directly paralleled with the healing of the man born blind by Jesus in John 9:1–12. The healing of the blind man with his saliva is similar to that of the man born blind in John 9:6.

In addition, according to Eusebius, both Vespasian and Domitian ordered the hunting down of all who claimed to be a descendent of David.[87] It is also possible that Domitian insisted on the title *dominus et deus* ("lord and god"), which is reminiscent of the confession of Thomas about Jesus, "my Lord and my God!" (John 20:28).[88] If it is accepted that the Gospel of John was written during the period of persecution, the readers could read

---

83. To be exact, the divine kingship is rooted in the kingship of the Pharaoh in ancient Egypt and the kings in the Ancient Near East. For example, the Pharaoh was regarded as both a god and as the son of a god, the incarnation of god; in the Sumerian period in Mesopotamia, the king was deified and regarded as representative of the god (see Day, "Canaanite Inheritance," 81–82; see also Rajak et al., *Jewish Perspectives*).

84. See chapter 1 of this book; Klappert, "King, Kingdom," 372–73.

85. The Christian proclamation of the New Testament "Jesus is the Lord!" might be a crucial anti-language against Rome. On Christ's challenge to the living Caesar, the polemical purpose of the term, Christ, see Fantin, "Lord of the Entire World," 174–240. Fantin argues that "given the relational nature of κύριος and the exclusive nature of *supreme lord*, using the title for Christ with explicit features such as unique modifiers, creedal formulas, and praise hymns would be viewed by the original readers as challenging the default *supreme lord*" (Fantin, "Lord of the Entire World," 240).

86. Johnson, "Davidic-Royal Motif," 136–37; Tacitus, *Hist.* 4.81, 5.13; Dio Cassius, *Hist.* 65.8.1, 66.1.4; Josephus, *Jewish War* 3.399–404, 6.310–315; Suetonius, *Vesp.* 4.5. In Suetonius, *Vesp.* 7, the second man was lame.

87. Eusebius, *Hist. eccl.* 3.12; cf, Eusebius *Hist. eccl.* 3.20, 1–6; Johnson, "Davidic-Royal Motif," 150.

88. Ferguson, *Backgrounds*, 38; Barrett, *New Testament Background*, 20.

Johannine stories of miracles as a kind of resistance document against Imperialism. In addition, the Samaritans' coming to welcome Jesus into their village (John 4:40), and the triumphal entry of Jesus into Jerusalem and the rapturous welcome of the crowd (John 12:12–14) are reminiscent of the triumphal returns of the generals or the kings into the towns of the Graeco-Roman world.[89] In short, as I have briefly pointed out concerning the relationship between the Graeco-Roman background and the Gospel of John, the kingship of the Johannine Jesus can be clarified more when giving due consideration to this Gospel in the wider context of the Graeco-Roman world.

The Necessity of the Combination of the Two

Nobody denies that the two main pillars of the background of the Gospel of John are the Jewish and the Graeco-Roman worlds. Consequently, reading the Fourth Gospel with knowledge of these two backgrounds throws a new light on interpretation.[90] In order to combine the knowledge from research into these backgrounds, I attempt to discover the common meanings of the terms employed to designate the kingship of the Johannine Jesus.

A reading of this Gospel in the context of Jewish culture could provide an understanding of the text as a microscopic view of Jewish society. The historical subtle and complex relationships of various groups in Jewish society may be seen, namely the conflict between the Jews and the Christians, particularly that of the Jews and the Johannine community, the estrangement between them, and the necessity of a description of the identity of Jesus and their faith, and so on. However, this kind of reading without consideration of the Roman Empire restricts the view of the macroscopic perspectives to be found in the Gospel. In other words, when we consider

---

89. Josephus presents imperial connotations as examples of welcoming visiting rulers/emperors: Tiberius (*J. W.* 398); Vespasian (*J. W.* 741); Titus (*J. W.* 425; 752–3) (Koester, "Savior," 665–80; Catchpole, "'Triumphal' Entry," 319–34). In addition, in Israelite kingship ritual, we can find the ultimate precedents. Particularly, in 1 Kgs 1:32–40 (cf. Zech 9:9) a ceremonial entry with acclamation is described when the king-designate precedes a celebrating crowd. The king rides the royal animal and the crowd play on pipes and rejoice with great joy. This image seems to be "a more or less fixed pattern of triumphal entry" (Catchpole, "'Triumphal' Entry," 319).

90. For good examples of this attempt, see Rajak et al., *Jewish Perspectives*; Moore, *Empire and Apocalypse*. Moore's comment shows well the necessity of these backgrounds for the clarification of the Johannine Jesus' kingship: "And whereas the principal topic of Jesus' dialogues with 'the Jews' was his relationship to the God of Israel, the principal topic of his dialogue with the Roman prefect will be his relationship to that other, more proximate, god, the Roman Emperor" (Moore, *Empire and Apocalypse*, 55).

the macro world relations into the reading of the Fourht Gospel, we could conclude that there were more subtle and complex relationships existing in the Johannine world. In the colonial situation, conflicts between the center and the margins, conflicts among marginal groups and the conflicts caused by the collaborators in the marginal society can be discovered in the Gospel. When we admit that the Johannine world was under colonial power, the identity of the Johannine Jesus can be newly identified in postcolonialism. Therefore, our reading does not imply a totally different manner of reading of the Gospel in relation to the Jewish background or in relation to the Graeco-Roman world. Because the Johannine group/readers and Jewish society were already in the Graeco-Roman world and because the Gospel was a product of the colonial world, we should read this Gospel with the combination of the main two backgrounds of a hybridized society.

Therefore, understanding the postcolonial perspective and its application in the reading of the Gospel is very useful. It is helpful in identifying individuals or groups from the perspective of colonial and postcolonial relations. In particular, the identity and function of the Johannine Jesus can be newly interpreted. The Johannine community, the Jews and the Jewish leaders can also be reinterpreted.

It also helps us to see the subtle relationships among the groups. In the light of power struggles, we can see the suffering and hope of the marginal groups and their pursuit of the ideal destiny by overcoming their oppressors. A reading of the Johnnine Gospel from a postcolonial perspective can throw new light on its interpretation. When we read the Gospel as a postcolonial text, in the conflicts between Jesus and the Jewish leaders, between the Johannine community and the Jews, between the Jewish leaders and Pilate who was the representative of the Roman Empire, and so on, Jesus is regarded as the solution to these conflicts. In this book, I shall offer a reading of the Gospel of John from a postcolonial perspective, particularly identifying the kingship in its portrait of Jesus.

Methods and Theories

In order to read the Gospel of John from a postcolonial perspective and to identify the Johannine Jesus as the universal king, I will now deal with methods and theories of this book with priority given to postcolonialism.[91]

---

91. For an introductory reading on postcolonialism from non-biblical critics, see Césairé, *Discourse on Colonialism*; Sartre, "Preface", 7–26; Moore-Gilbert, *Postcolonial Theory*; Childs and Williams, *Introduction*; Gandhi, *Postcolonial Theory*; Loomba, *Colonialism*; Ashcroft, Griffiths, and Tiffin, *Postcolonial Studies*; Ashcroft, Griffiths, and

To begin with, it is necessary to define the word "postcolonial." The adjective, postcolonial, is defined as the frame of mind "that problematizes the imperial/colonial phenomenon as a whole, and in so doing, attains a sense of conscientization which pursues independence from imperialism."[92] Therefore, a postcolonial focus encompasses not only the discourses of imposition and domination but also the anti-discourses of opposition and resistance.[93] In addition, Samuel defines postcolonial literature and discourse, referring to it as:

> the literature and discourse that springs from a colonized population during or after the colonial experience, that critically scrutinizes and engages the colonial contacts and perceptions of power. Generally, it is a complex, ambivalent and incongruous discourse that accommodates and disrupts the colonialist perceptions and perspectives of domination.[94]

In terms of definitions, it is plausible to say that there is postcoloniality in the Gospel of John. The Fourth Gospel as a product of the Roman colonial world clearly presents a way of resistance and decolonization to its first century readers, who were mostly colonized and marginalized by the center, using the imperial language as well as that of the fringes. In this way, the Johannine Gospel is a kind of postcolonial text.

In this section, I will explore postcolonial theory as long as it is relevant to my book. First, I will deal with the relationship between ideological criticism and postcolonialism; with the relationship between postcolonial agenda in comparison with colonial imperialism; with the relationship between postcolonialism and literary criticism; and lastly, with the major concepts in a postcolonial approach: hybridentity and diaspora.

Tiffin, *Empire Writes Back*; Young, *Postcolonialism*.

For important readings on postcolonialism from non-biblical critics, see Memmi, *Colonizer and the Colonized*; Fanon, *Wretched of the Earth*; Said, *Orientalism*; Bhabha, *Location of Culture*; Spivak, *Critique of Postcolonial Reason*. Said, Bhabha, and Spivak are regarded as the major figures in postcolonial criticism (for a critical survey of them, see Moore-Gilbert, *Postcolonial Theory*, 34–151).

On critical approaches of postcolonialism in biblical studies, see Donaldson and Sugirtharajah, *Postcolonialism*; Sugirtharajah, *Asian Biblical Hermeneutics*; Sugirtharajah, *Postcolonial Bible*; Sugirtharajah, *Bible and the Third World*, 244–75; Sugirtharajah, "Postcolonial Biblical Interpretation," 64–84; Fiorenza, *Jesus and the Politics*; Segovia, *Interpreting Beyond Borders*; Segovia, *Decolonizing Biblical Studies*; Samuel, "Postcolonial Reading"; Dube and Staley, *John and Postcolonialism*; Moore, *Empire and Apocalypse*.

92. Segovia, "Interpreting," 12.

93. See Segovia, "Interpreting," 13–14.

94. Samuel, "Postcolonial Reading," 3.

2. BACKGROUND AND METHODOLOGY 41

Ideological Criticism as a Basis for Postcolonialism

Postcolonialism has plural theoretical roots from Marxism, the pioneer of modern critical theory, to Post-structuralism in terms of critical theories. Particularly, "poststructuralist concepts of the political nature of the language of race, gender, and class have had profound effects on postcolonial writers preoccupied with subject-identity and oppositional discourses."[95] In addition, it is likely that in the broader category of critical theories, postcolonialism could belong to both a kind of reader-response and ideological criticism. Hence, through the diffusion of these roots, a plurality of application in postcolonial studies is possible. In this sub-section, for my argument I will explore the relationship between ideological criticism and postcolonial studies.

On the one hand, ideology reflects reality, on the other hand, there is no ideology, which corresponds to reality as it is.[96] Moreover, reality affects ideology. Since this is so, ideology, particularly at the textual level, needs to be interpreted in order to comprehend reality in history.[97]

In the Gospel of John, there seems to be ideology, in particular Christology (whether or not it is regarded as a political issue), which reflects not only the real Johannine world but also that which could be employed to reveal the ideal world which the Johannine Jesus/John/the Johannine community might pursue. Hence, ideology in the Gospel needs to be interpreted at the textual level to discover the reality of the Johannine world with which the Johannine community was confronted. The Johannine reality also needs to be reconstructed to seek for the influential elements in the formation and

---

95. See Samuel, "Postcolonial Reading," 12–17, esp. 14.

96. On the relationship between reality and ideology in detail, see Althusser, "Ideology," 294–304; Eagleton, *Literary Theory*, 169–89; Younger, *Ancient Conquest Account*, 47–51. Younger argues that "ideology embraces both normative and allegedly factual elements; and these elements are not necessarily distorted" (Younger, *Ancient Conquest Account*, 48). Hoskins also argues, "Yet distortion is by no means inherent to every definition of the term. It can be defined in a neutral way that does not necessitate distortion" (Hoskins, *Jesus as the Fulfillment*, 8). However, Culpepper argues, "the influence of the perspective, the culture, and the social location of the interpreter is being recognized. No text, no interpretation, is ever completely unbiased or neutral. Some interests are advocated, privileged, or defended, while others are denied or subjugated" (Culpepper, "Gospel of John," 118). Therefore, "there is no basic or neutral literary language uncolored by perception and response" (McKnight, "Reader-Response," 231).

97. If reality could be reconstructed through reading the text or historical research, ideology in the text could be revealed more clearly, because reality influences to key points of the formation and development of ideology. Conversely, if ideology could be read more clearly in the text level, reality could be inferred more exclusively as well through reading the text.

development of ideology in this Gospel.[98] In the case of the Fourth Gospel, for example, the author might put his ideology into the composition of the Gospel, reflecting the real world to which he and his community belonged, in order to describe the ideal world where Jesus as the king reigns using terms, concepts and literary devices which had developed through the mixture of the cultures of the center and the margins.[99]

As a result, no interpretation of ideology in the text can be done in a vacuum. The important thing in the interpretation of Johannine ideology and reconstruction of the Johannine world, therefore, is to discover the relationship of the Johannine community and the conditions of the world in which the community is represented.

The difference and gap between the reality of the Johannine world and the ideological Johannine world occurs and exists because ideology reflects reality and reality has an effect on ideology. Consequently, it might be true that a greater or lesser gap (description with different angles, hyperbole, maximization or minimization) of representation of the real world would occur in the author's representation of ideology in the text. Furthermore, more twist and gap of representation of the real world would occur in the readers' interpretation of the ideology. In spite of the series of twists and gaps, however, through interpretation of ideology in a particular text we can reconstruct a hypothetical world, which reflects the real world, as described in the text and can discover the factors that influenced the formation of the ideology, though an interpretation is dependent on the interpreter's circumstances. We cannot help but being interpreted by our circumstances when seeking to interpret the ideology of the Gospel.[100] Therefore, an analysis of the interpreter is necessary in order to interpret the ideology of this Gospel from a postcolonial perspective.[101]

---

98. Just as the real world to which the author belongs could have an effect on the placement of ideology through creative written works of the text by the author, those of the readers as well could have an effect on the interpretation of ideology, and on the reconstruction of the real world through interpretation of ideology by the readers.

99. All the readers through all the generations might have interpreted ideologies in the Gospel of John to justify their own ideologies reflecting their real worlds, i.e., reading the Gospel in their own ideological contexts. For example, in the period of modern colonialism, the Gospel has been read as an advocate of colonialism. Ideological readings of the text produce very different interpretations.

100. Segovia, "Journey(s)," 23–54.

101. On an analysis of myself as an interpreter, see chapter 5 of this book.

Postcolonialism vs. Colonial Imperialism[102]

First, to read the Gospel of John from a postcolonial perspective, it is important to know that one of the main topics of postcolonial reading in biblical studies is a discourse on "identity matter." In terms of identity, differences and similarities between the colonizer and the colonized have been recognized as one of the most important factors. That is, postcolonial theory has been employed to clarify various identities and the complex relations between them in colonial society. For example, Bhabha[103] scrutinizes the matters of similarity and mixtures between the colonizer and the colonized, while Said[104] describes differences and opposition between them in his colonial discourses.[105] Likewise, the Fourth Gospel implies that the identities of the individuals and the groups in the Gospel perform their various and complex mutual relations with difference and similarity.[106] In addition, the relationship between the center and the margins as encompassing both social and cultural reality from a number of different angles shows a range of disciplines within postcolonial studies.[107] Among postcolonial themes, perspectives on the relations between the center and the margin and hybridized identities in the colonial society will be employed in my book. In short, clarifying their identities in a colonial society can be a key to postcolonial interpretation of the Gospel of John, particularly regarding the identity of the Johannine Jesus as decolonizer,[108] knowing that difference and similarity

---

102. According to Samuel, "imperialism" refers to "the authority/power of a state over another territory" and "colonialism involves consolidation of such power either by creating military and civilian settlements in such a territory or by exploiting its people and resources or by lording over its indigenous inhabitants" (Samuel, "Postcolonial Reading," 3). He uses these terms interchangeably.

103. See Bhabha, "Of Mimicry and Man," 33; Bhabha, *Location of Culture*.

104. Said, *Orientalism*; Said, *Culture and Imperialism*.

105. Childs and Williams, *Introduction*, 122.

106. On the hybridization of ideas, images, languages, and political and cultural practices between the center and the margins, see Alexander, *Images of Empire*; Hengel, *Judaism and Hellenism*; Barclay, *Jews in the Mediterranean Diaspora*; Horsley, *Paul and Empire*.

107. See Segovia, "Interpreting Beyond Borders," 11. On the disciplinary range of postcolonial studies (the study of imperialism and colonialism; the complicated relationship between the center and margins; the study of imposition and domination as well as of opposition and resistance; the study of the different phrases or periods within imperialism and colonialism [pre, post, neo]), see also, Segovia, "Interpreting Beyond Borders," 13–14. On the four models of postcolonial reading practiced in biblical studies, see Samuel, "Postcolonial Reading," 23–44.

108. See chapters 5 and 6 of this book. On the recognition of the significance of postcolonial theory in the study of Roman imperialism, see Webster and Cooper, eds.,

between the colonizer and the colonized is a major contact point between postcolonialism and the Fourth Gospel.

Secondly, one of the topics of postcolonial reading in biblical studies is a discourse of resistance and emancipation. Segovia says,

> The proposed postcolonial optic in biblical studies is obviously a discourse of resistance and emancipation. It takes as its reading lens the geo-political relationship between center and periphery, the imperial and the colonial, not only at the level of the text but also at the level of interpretation, of readings and readers of the text. It does so, moreover, with decolonization and liberation in mind, as it proceeds to highlight the periphery over the center and the colonial over the imperial.[109]

Sugirtharajah also says,

> [Postcolonialism] is an active confrontation with the dominant system of thought, its lopsidedness and inadequacies, and underlines its unsuitability for us. Hence, it is a process of cultural and discursive emancipation from all dominant structures whether they be political, linguistic or ideological.[110]

In the Gospel of John, we can discover a discourse of resistance and liberation. By the employment of a variety of christological titles from the center as well as from the margins, the Gospel presents the identity of Jesus as king. It challenges its readers in the colonial world to believe and follow him as the real king who liberates the margins of the colonized world and eventually, from the darkness.

Thirdly, when "postcolonial studies engage in examining the complex web of desire and distantiation between the colonists and the colonized,"[111] three major concepts, such as ambivalence, mimicry, and hybridentity, become "touchstones for debates over colonial discourse, anti-colonial resistance, and post-colonial identity."[112]

1) Ambivalence is used to describe a continual interchange between both opposites, namely the center/the colonizer and the margins/the colonized. Therefore, it suggests both compliance and resistance in a colonial

---

Roman Imperialism; Mattingly, *Dialogues*; Goodman, *Roman World*, 100–56; Horsley, *Jesus and Empire*.

109. Segovia, *Decolonizing Bible*, 140; see also Sugirtharajah, *Asian Biblical Hermeneutic*, ix–x.

110. Sugirtharajah, "Postcolonial Exploration," 93.

111. Samuel, "Postcolonial Reading," 48.

112. Childs and Williams, *Introduction*, 123–24.

subject. In postcolonialism, it refers to a simultaneous attraction and repulsion, which marks the complex relationship between them.[113] In this respect, collaboration and resistance in a colonial society become unavoidable. In addition, postcolonial ambivalence gives the margins room for collaboration with the central power and/or resistance against the center. As a result, "ambivalence decenters authority from its position of power" to that of the margins.[114] For example, the Johannine readers as the margins could see a resistant tendency in the Gospel against this earthly Imperialism, but a collaborating tendency toward the heavenly kingdom (the Johannine new world), when they met its ambivalent usage of the Johannine christological titles, which could imply various definitions in different contexts.

2) Postcolonial mimicry is also used to describe the ambivalent relationship between the colonizer and the colonized. The phrase, "a difference that is almost the same, but not quite,"[115] conveys the force of mimicry quite well. Mimicry requires simultaneous similarity and dissimilarity. It relies on resemblance, on the colonized becoming like the colonizer, but always remaining different. In addition, mimicry is related to the fear of loss. Van Bruggen remarks,

> After the exile the Jews were not the only inhabitants of Palestine. They lived among all kinds of non-Jews, and this made it necessary for them to preserve a clear identity if they were to avoid being absorbed into the other cultures in Palestine. This potential loss of Jewish identity had been a real threat on several occasions.[116]

In postcolonialism, however, the fear of loss that had been a real threat to the colonized on the one hand, works as a kind of resistance against the colonial power on the other. "Mimicry, as a repetition that is 'almost but not quite' the same as an original, queries not only the definition but the self-identity of the 'original.'"[117] Therefore, mimicry also produces a disturbing effect on colonial rule.[118]

> Mimicry is another ambivalent (re)assertion of similarity and difference and it therefore poses a challenge to the normalized

---

113. See Ashcroft, Griffiths, and Tiffin, *Postcolonial Studies*, 12; Samuel, "Postcolonial Reading," 50–51.

114. Samuel, "Postcolonial Reading," 51; see also chapter 6 of this book; Thiong'o, *Moving the Center*.

115. Bhabha, *Location*, 86.

116. van Bruggen, *Jesus*, 36.

117. Childs and Williams, *Introduction*, 132.

118. Childs and Williams, *Introduction*, 130.

> knowledge of colonized and colonizer; not least by making one an imitation of the other while preserving differences of, for example, liberty, status, and rights. . . . The imitation must always remain distinguishable from the original and so poses two troubling questions. On the one hand, it asks what constitutes the "original" and preserves its difference from any "imitation." . . . On the other hand, it asks what "deformation" of this original is visible in the imitation, which is never exactly a copy and therefore something more or less than the "original."[119]

In this respect, we can see that John uses mimicry in the Gospel, particularly, in the christological titles in terms of kingship. We can regard the employment and adaptation of them for kingly identification of Jesus as mimicry in terms of resistance. The Gospel of John adapts many christological titles originating in and used by a variety of cultures to introduce Jesus as king, but more fully describes Jesus as a universal and ideal king than those described as king in various other contexts. For example, Jesus as Messiah in the Gospel is a more fully idealized Messiah (Christ)/king than is found in Jewish culture (1:49; 7:31; 11:27). Jesus is *truly* the Savior of the World (4:42) rather than the Roman emperors. Jesus is *of a truth* the Prophet like Moses (Deut 18:15)[120] who is to come into the world (7:14). Jesus is a more fully personalized, dramatized Lord and God (*My Lord and My God*) than any other one, and so on.

To attempt a new reading of the Gospel of John from a postcolonial perspective, therefore, I will employ three major postcolonial subjects in my book: 1) identity issues of the characters, using differences and similarities between the colonizer and the colonized (mimicry as a colonial process as well as a kind of resistance);[121] 2) a discourse of resistance and emancipation; 3) the ambivalent relationship between the center and the margin in hybridentity.

Literary Criticism and Postcolonial Theory

In this sub-section, in order to discover some bases of postcoloniality in this Gospel, I will deal with the relationship between literary criticism and postcolonial theory, and as an example, I will discuss the matter of the genre of the Gospels.

---

119. Childs and Williams, *Introduction*, 131.
120. However, Jesus is greater than Moses in the Fourth Gospel is (see John 6:32).
121. See chapter 3 of this book. In this section, I will deal with 2) and 3).

First, it is necessary to indicate that both inside and outside biblical scholarship there is a growing variety of conflicting views on the subject of the value of the Bible, the difference between biblical texts, and between biblical texts and other literary texts. Without any clear consensus of definitions of terms, of critical/philosophical understandings of disciplines, and of methods of interpretations of biblical texts, various interpretations of the biblical texts flood the world.[122]

We can say that literary theory provides not only a means of dealing with differences of critical opinion, but also provides the basis for constructing a more rational, adequate and self-aware discipline of literary studies. Jefferson and Robey say that "[l]iterary theory is not something that has developed in a vacuum, but has arisen for the most part in response to the problems encountered by readers, critics, and scholars in their practical contact with texts."[123] Questions raised by the readers might be answered in a number of different ways and the established ways of answering them should not be taken for granted. These ways of answering might cover a range of possibilities only; all elements in them can be open to challenge, and in practice most theories seem to concentrate on some more than others do, or even exclusively to others.

Since the 1970s, trends of biblical interpretation have rapidly changed and developed, the main focus of it passing onto the reader especially onto the modern reader.[124] This new trend has a tendency to ignore the ancient background of the texts because of its tendency to make a distinction between the intention of the original author and the meaning of the text.[125] However, in order to interpret the biblical texts better, I believe, we need to

---

122. On the variety of the biblical methodology, see Haynes and McKenzie, *To Each Its Own Meaning*; Black and Dockery, *Interpreting the New Testament*. On attempts at a dialogue between the historical approach and the literary approach, see Barton, "Historical Criticism," 3–15; de Boer, "Narrative Criticism," 35–48; Motyer, "Method" 27–44.

123. Robey and Jefferson, *Modern Literary Theory*, 13.

124. Segovia, "Journey(s)," 23–54; Segovia, "Biblical Criticism," 49–65. For example, Segovia remarks that there has been the development of biblical criticism as a process of "liberation" and "decolonization," one with reference to a fundamental transformation "in theoretical orientation and reading strategy" as well as "in the ranks of the discipline" (Segovia, "Biblical Criticism," 51–52).

125. The meaning of the text and the author's intention are not automatically and completely the same. About "intentional fallacy," the presupposition that one can find the meaning of the text exclusively through the intention of its author, see Barthes, "Death," 167–72. About the "surplus meaning" of the text, that is, meaning that written texts acquire beyond the meaning intended by the author, see Ricoeur, *Interpretation Theory*.

consult the products of the various scholarly works including not only those of traditional critics, but also those of post-modern critics.

In this sense, postcolonialism has significant advantages for the interpretation of the biblical texts as well as serious shortcomings. Some scholars are alarmed that one of the effects of imperialism as a major force is to reflect and reproduce dominant cultural assumptions about the margins, which not only fail to represent the diversity in the lives of the marginal groups but also promote unrealistic expectations about normal marginal behavior.[126] Hence, postcolonialism has provided a useful corrective to the imperial perspectives of the interpretation of the biblical texts and has promoted a new perspective, which reads the biblical texts with the eyes of the margins. To borrow Alcoff's phraseology, John as a voice of the margins in the first century offers the Johannine community at the margins the new world of Jesus as "a positive alternative and a vision of a better future."[127] The new world of the Johannine Jesus can motivate the readers to sacrifice their time and energy toward its realization in the colonized world.

However, postcolonial theory has a tendency which has denied the uniqueness of the biblical texts when compared with other texts (generalization of the Bible),[128] and has a methodological limitation because it is problematic that it applies a post-modern critical theory to interpret biblical texts. In addition, another problem is a tendency to regard the biblical texts as unhistorical (neglect of the historicity of the Bible), although it is not the only problematic assumption in postcolonial theory.

Secondly, while emphasizing the postcoloniality of the Gospel of John, I take the view that the New Testament Gospels are uniquely special literature,[129] so that even though the Gospel is a hybridized product of the colonial, imperial world, and there is similarity to the ancient Graeco-Roman texts, particularly ancient Greek biography, yet the Gospel has a uniqueness of its own.[130] Many scholars regard the Gospel as a modified form of ancient

126. These major forces, however, "including social discourses and social practices, are apparently not overdetermined, resulting as they do from such a complex and unpredictable network of overlapping and crisscrossing elements that no unilinear directionality is perceivable and in fact no final or efficient cause exists" (Alcoff, "Cultural Feminism," 416).

127. Alcoff, "Cultural Feminism," 419.

128. On the limitations of the method of reader-response criticism, which have analogies to those of postcolonial criticism, see McKnight, "Reader-Response," 247–48.

129. On the variety of view of the genre of the Gospels, see Aune, "Gospels," 205–06; Aune, *New Testament*, 17–115; Carter, *John*, 3–16.; Burridge, *What Are the Gospels?*, 26–54; Attridge, "Genre Bending," 3–21 (Attridge focuses on diverse genres within the gospel but pays little attention to the gospel genre itself); Blomberg, "Diversity," 272–95.

130. Aune, "Gospels," 204–6; Carter, *John*, 9–10; Blomberg, "Diversity," 275. There

Greek biography, while others do not. While criticizing modern categories of genre, which "are misleading and even inimical to actual understanding" of the biblical texts, Osborne also points out that the characteristics of the ancient genres are a key to interpreting biblical texts.[131]

Hence, in order to interpret the Johannine Gospel better, we need to define the genre of the Gospels. I define the Gospels as a unique genre, which though similar to types of ancient literature which quickened, and grew in the first century owing to cultural mixture, yet it displays unique characteristics of its own.[132] In other words, just as the Gospels display a mixing of genres[133] (narrative, parables, proverbs, poetry, biography, teaching, and apocalyptic) and still function overall as Gospels ("like and yet not like"),[134] the Gospel of John functions as unique literature and as a postcolonial text.[135] While introducing the flexibility and various literary types of Hellenistic biography which continued to change and develop, Aune contends,

> It is methodologically incorrect to try to link the Gospels rigidly only with that specific type of ancient biography.... The canonical Gospels then constitute a subtype of Hellenistic biography, one that exhibits *the syncretistic insertion of a Judaeo-Christian message in a Hellenistic envelope*.[136]

Aune concludes that the Gospels are on a par with the other forms of early Christian literature, which "reflect the complexities of the syncretistic world within which they arose."[137] I can endorse this description, but

---

might be utterly no new creation from nothing in the material world. Therefore, the Gospel of John contains many features of the Jewish and the Graeco-Roman world. However, the New Testament, particularly the Fourth Gospel, came from the multicultural society, although the Gospels show formal parallels to other historical and biographical writings, materially they remain unique. For example, almost half of this Gospel (chapters 12–21) deals with the passion and resurrection of Jesus.

131. Osborne, *Hermeneutical Spiral*, 149.

132. See Aune, *New Testament*, 46–76.

133. Attridge, "Genre Bending," 3–21.

134. Longman argues, "While it is true that the individuality of many compositions must be maintained, the similarities between the form and content of text must not be denied. That there are similarities between texts which can serve as a rationale for studying them as a group is especially true for ancient literature where literary innovations were not valued highly as they are today" (Longman, "Fictional Akkadian Royal Autobiography," 3–4 [re-quoted from Osborne, *Hermeneutical Spiral*, 150]).

135. Kümmel argues that the Gospels are a new creation in terms of a literary form (Kümmel, *Introduction*, 37; see also Hurtado, "Gospel," 276–82).

136. Aune, "Biography," 81 (Italics are mine).

137. Aune, "Gospels," 204–5.

would prefer to substitute "colonial" for "syncretistic." What we see in the evangelist's adaptation of ancient biographical genres is a classic example of postcolonial "mimicry," producing something that is "like and yet not like" other ancient genres.

A simple list of the possible genres of the Gospels suggested by modern scholars shows the potential for postcolonial mimicry in the Gospel of John. There is a variety of possible categories of scholarly views on the definition of the genre of the Gospels: 1) not a unique genre; 2) a unique literary type (*kerygma*, replacement for the Torah; an unliterary form of folk literature); 3) Hellenistic romance or popular fiction; 4) OT biographical narratives; 5) Jewish novel; 6) Greek comedy or tragedy; 7) Hellenistic biography (*Bios*); 8) a pool of genres and narrative devices; 9) an ancient revelatory biography.[138] It is justifiable to say that scholars have been able to find partly the generic features of various ancient genres in the Gospel, but there is no exact fit with ancient genres and no consensus among scholars. This suggests that we should regard the Gospel as a hybridized text. The Gospel contains hybridized features of a variety of cultures in the Roman colonial world (e.g., the employment of variety of christological titles). The Fourth Gospel is a kind of postcolonial literature, not only as a mixture of a variety of culture and literature including mixing genres, and as a hybridized product of the multicultural society, but also as a unique writing about the life and death of Jesus. That is, there is no other text that describes the life of Jesus in more detail than the Gospels. It is important to acknowledge the uniqueness and rarity of the gospels concerning the life of Jesus.[139] In this respect, therefore, I contend that in terms not only of genre but also of content, the Johannine Gospel is a product of hybridentity in a multicultural society.

In summary, the concept of hybridentity as a key concept of a postcolonial theory may be employed not only to denote the complication of the presence and absence of the colonial areas (Jewish society), but also to feature the discourse of power and resistance, of rejection and acceptance, with and against the dominance of the Imperial Roman culture.

---

138. Blomberg, "Diversity," 273–77.

139. There are some different emphases and slightly different descriptions of the life of Jesus among the Gospels, because they were written for their own purposes for their own readers, and in their specific historical backgrounds. However, it is also probable that the authors of the Gospels used their contemporary literary devices, terms, genres, and so on in their compositions, but as a postcolonial text, the Gospel of John in particular was produced as a hybridized one, namely, a sort of the Christian literature, which was generated from the first century, in multicultural society. In addition, Blomberg comments, "more differences than similarities appear between the Gospels, and these various genres so that none of these identifications is widely held today" (Blomberg, "Diversity," 274).

2. BACKGROUND AND METHODOLOGY 51

Hybridization and Identity

One of the visions of postcolonialism is the pursuit of one world, in which all people have an equal right to benefits, material as well as cultural.[140] To accomplish this postcolonial vision, to begin with, it is necessary to recognize individual, ethnic, and especially national identities, because self-identity is the starting point of the accomplishment of postcolonial visions.[141] Generally speaking, postcolonialism draws and pays attention to problems of identity in relation to broader national histories and futures,[142] because of this postcolonial vision.[143] Therefore, it is said that we never reach one ideal world without any objective confrontation with colonial histories as well as postcolonial realities in the society.[144] To reach one world by overcoming colonial histories, problems of identity should be pointed out.

In this respect, identity problems arising in the (post) colonial society must be complicated, because there exist delicate, complex, and not easily explained matters between the colonizer and the colonized.[145] There must exist simultaneously "differences and opposition" and "similarity and mutual transactions" between the colonizer and the colonized. Attempts to identify individuals, groups, or a whole society in the (post) colonial environment often result in discovering in them different identities, which the colonized would never expect as their identities.

HYBRIDENTITY (= HYBRID IDENTITY)

Hybridentity is a useful term which is employed to explain the intricate relationship between the colonizer and the colonized and ambivalent conditions in colonial societies. Most postcolonial writing, which has concerned itself with cultural exchange as a mutual process in the colonial and postcolonial societies, emphasizes the strength of the hybridized nature of postcolonial culture.

---

140. Young, *Postcolonialism*, 2; see also Gandhi, *Postcolonial Theory*, 122–40.

141. As Fanon writes, "[The consciousness of self] is not the closing door to communication. Philosophic thought teaches us, on the contrary, that it is its guarantee. National consciousness, which is not nationalism, is the only thing that will give us an international dimension" (Fanon, *Wretched*, 199).

142. Selden, Widdowson, and Brooker, *Reader's Guide*, 226.

143. So, Ghandi says that "[p]ostcoloniality, we might say, is just another name for the globalisation of cultures and histories" (Gandhi, *Postcolonial Theory*, 126).

144. See Gandhi, *Postcolonial Theory*, 7.

145. Bhabha, *Location*, 1–2.

> [Most postcolonial writing] lays emphasis on the survival even under the most potent oppression of the distinctive aspects of the culture of the oppressed, and shows how these become an integral part of the new formations which arise from the clash of cultures characteristic of imperialism. Finally, it emphasizes how hybridentity and the power it releases may well be seen to be the characteristic feature and contribution of the post-colonial, allowing a means of evading the replication of the binary categories of the past and developing new anti-monolithic models of cultural exchange and growth.[146]

Because the mutual transactions and influences generate hybridentity in both societies, the notion of in-between-ness or ambivalence in the concept of hybridentity gives some space for achievement of the postcolonial vision: globalization, one ideal world, or international welfare.

Some postcolonial critics' works, however, tried/trended to "downplay the bitter tension and the clash between colonizer and colonized and therefore misrepresent the dynamics of anti-colonial struggle."[147] Although hybridentity, because of cultural transactions, occurred mutually in (post) colonial societies, it does not mean an equal-value-transaction among the cultures. Accordingly, when one group among culturally discrete groups has dominated the others and when this cultural domination of one group is linked with political and economic profits, it has produced huge suffering in those colonial societies; its side effects have been felt unceasingly in those colonial and postcolonial societies.

In addition, when the culture in the colonial society is manipulated by the dominant culture that influences or causes mutations in every area of the society, it breeds ambivalent and uncertain conditions, blurred cultural boundaries both inside and out, as well as an otherness within the society.[148] Ultimately, the society experiences an alteration, a different society from that of its master but similar to its master's. In the process of colonization, therefore, a problem of colonial identity arises between the colonizer and the colonized.

In many cases, the conflict and competition is generated radically and intensely in colonial resistance against the dominant culture. In these cases, the colonized society is in the negative but offensive mood, in suspense and in agitation. The hearts of the colonized are filled with emotions of oppression, exploitation, restriction, the absence of liberty, subordination, and so

---

146. Ashcroft, Griffiths, and Tiffin, *Postcolonial Studies Reader*, 183.
147. Loomba, *Colonialism*, 181.
148. Young, *Postcolonialism*, 23.

on. Painful experiences beyond description and negative images have been inscribed on the hearts of the colonized, no matter how tremendous the profits of colonization are. The more radical and intensive the feelings of oppression and bitterness, and the longer period of oppression they experience, the more negative emotions remain in the hearts of the colonized.

The opposite direction of influence, however, occurs spontaneously in the dominant culture.[149] While the dominant culture has experience of modification of itself in some way by the influence of the colonial culture, a similar ambivalence and uncertainty, blurring of cultural boundaries and otherness are generated in that society. In many cases, this kind of transformation results in positive formations in the end, while supplementing the weakness of the dominant culture, strengthening their establishments, and increasing the wealth and benefits of the dominant society.

Diaspora

The term "diaspora," with "hybridentity," is effective when examining the mutual contagion and subtle intimacies between the colonizer and the colonized because of their remarkable analytic versatility and theoretical adaptability.[150] Theoretically speaking, the concept of diaspora could be employed to elaborate "the notion of in-between-ness conjured up by the term hybridity."[151]

Many of the colonized had to leave their original places for several reasons. In these difficult exilic situations, panic beyond imagination grew in the hearts of the diaspora. Their destinies were to be slaves or wanderers in foreign places. During their survival in foreign places, having lost their possessions the diaspora experienced on the one hand a loss of their original identities, although they attempted to keep them. On the other hand, they could not help accepting foreign influences, which caused a modification of their identities. The diasporic peoples, therefore, underwent modifications of their identities, with (no) relation to the ways in which they attempted to survive. In this kind of diasporic situation, their identities became more and more hybridized. Crucially, in this situation, the diaspora were sometimes not welcomed by either the colonizer or the colonized, like the Samaritans in Jewish society. Eventually, most of them could not return to their homeland after the emancipation of their home country from foreign power.

---

149. The prime example of it is the spread of Christianity in the Roman Empire. As a result, Christianity became the national religion in 313 CE

150. Gandhi, *Postcolonial Theory*, 130.

151. Gandhi, *Postcolonial Theory*, 131.

We can find a typical example of hybridentity and diaspora in the diasporic Hellenized Jews in the first century. One of the groups of readers of the Gospel of John might have been the diasporic Jews. In their hybridized identities, their reading of the Gospel might quite well have been different from that of the Palestine Jews. Supposing that John bore in mind not only the diasporic Jews, but also other readers whose origins were also very varied,[152] it would have been acceptable for the author to adapt and employ many christological titles in order to identify Jesus as a universal king without any misunderstanding. John, with literal logic, seems to use various christological titles together, in a series, and simultaneously, in order to persuade the readers from a wide spectrum of origins.[153]

Postcolonial Reading of the Gospel of John

In early Christianity, the huge influence of the empire upon multiple cultures had permeated into marginal groups.[154] Jewish society, which is the background of the story of the Johannine Jesus as well as the Johannine community, was no exception. From the time of the Babylonian exile, Jewish society had been a kind of hybrid society in various ways. For example, in Babylonia the diasporic Jews on the one hand made themselves comfortable and, apparently, accepted the rule of the Chaldeans and afterward of the Persians, with some degree of contentment. On the other hand, there had also been resistance movements against the foreign powers.[155] For example, the relationship between Tyre and Sidon and Galilee could be an appropriate case of hybrid processing.[156] In addition, more particularly, the significance of the Roman occupation of the cultivatable arc of territory in the Near East and its relation to the surrounding marginal areas underlines the possibility of the hybridizing of the culture.[157] Consequently, there is no doubt that Jewish society had been a kind of hybridized society for a long time through a series of resistance movements and

---

152. The readers in Asia Minor, particularly in Ephesus, the traditional location for Gospel.

153. See chapter 3 of this book.

154. Van Bruggen remarks, "This dilemma is rather unproductive, however, because no clear dividing line can be drawn between Jewish and Greek culture due to the fact that there was a great deal of mutual influencing of cultures during the Hellenistic period" (van Bruggen, *Jesus*, 172).

155. Toy, "King," 157. See also Horsley, *Bandits, Prophets, and Messiahs*; Horsley, *Jesus and Empire*, 35–54.

156. Schmiz, "Sidon," 17–18; Edwards, "Tyre," 686–92.

157. Millar, *Roman Near East*, 16–23, 506–22.

accommodation to foreign influence. In short, the society was already in the process of diaspora and hybridentity and had been for a long time, even though some groups within Jewish society had tried to protect themselves from foreign influences.[158]

In the time of the Johannine community, various groups were coexisting in society. Early Christianity, in particular, was a typical group marked by hybridentity and diaspora. For example, the description of the formation of the early Church in the book of Acts shows this feature of hybridentity and diaspora. The Johannine community would not be an exception. In this process, what was the direction of the pursuit of early Christianity, particularly that of the Johannine community? In the process of hybridentity and diaspora, their direction was neither a return to Judaism, nor submission to the Roman Empire, but the pursuit of a new world, in which Jesus reigns as the universal king. They had to pursue the new world where the various groups or individuals could live in harmony regardless of their origins. This vision of the Johannine community and that of postcolonialism reach each other at this point. In addition, the Johannine Gospel pursues not only the new world in which the various groups live together in unity and harmony, but also seeks to open larger and more extensive solidarities in the name of Jesus, the universal king. The globalization of postcolonialism reaches to the new universal world in the Fourth Gospel also at this point.

Postcolonialism and the Gospel of John

No texts were ever written in a cultural vacuum.[159] That means texts should be read with an understanding of the backgrounds: when/ where/ how/ why/ by whom texts were written. However, because of the difficulty or impossibility of knowing the exact backgrounds of the text and the authorial purpose of its composition, because of the admitted value of the reader-oriented reading of the text, it is possible and valuable to read the ancient text with current reading perspectives.

1) Hybridentity: Some researchers of the possible historical situations of the Johannine Community have spoken of the conflicts between the Jews and the Johannine community and/or within the Johannine community.[160]

---

158. See Fiensy, *Social History*; Hengel, *Judaism and Hellenism*.

159. We can admit that "a reading of the past in terms of the present, 'contemporization,' or 'actualization,' is an inevitable aspect of any translation" (Rajak, "Introduction," 3).

160. On a new exegetical framework derived from social-scientific ideas relating to intergroup conflict and its reduction, see Esler, "Jesus and the Reduction," 185–205.

However, the Johannine community had a relation to not only the Jews in Palestine and the diaspora, but also to Samaritan and non-Jewish groups.[161] In the Fourth Gospel, in fact, these various elements, which indicate the relationship of John and many other communities, seem to co-exist.[162] Then, why is it that many scholars have found common places in which John and other religious groups could stand together? One of the reasons is John's concern for the universal kingdom in which Jesus reigns as king. To describe the Johannine Jesus as the universal king whom every group could understand when they read or heard this Gospel, John borrowed, modified and used a number of terms from both Jewish and non-Jewish cultures, which included a kingship motif.

2) Mimicry: Jewish society in the first century was not only suffering under colonial power, but also pursuing it. After the failure of their attempts for independence through a long military resistance to the Roman power, it is most probable that Jewish society had gradually admitted the reality of the Roman Empire and had been in the process of hybridentity under Roman influence. Being under the foreign power for a long time, Jewish society had not been able to maintain its purity in every aspect. In particular, the process of hybridentity proceeded rapidly after the collapse of the temple of Jerusalem, which had always been an important symbol of Jewish identity.

For example, in the process of the hybridization of the Jewish society in the first century CE, a new leading group, namely the Pharisees, grasped political power after the collapse of the Jerusalem temple. They adjusted to Roman power and obtained ruling power in Jewish society. That is the reason why the Pharisees are the major opponents of Jesus in the Gospel of John.[163] They worked hand in hand with the religious leaders, namely the high priests, and as members of the Sanhedrin, they yielded immense power in society. Possibly, there was friendly collaboration with the Roman authorities in order to grasp political power or maintain their position in peace under *Pax Romana*. Childs and Williams briefly describe this aspect:

> One aspect of the contemporary imperialist dispensation is its hegemonic—rather than directly coercive—power, its ability to persuade the post-colonial world to adopt its priorities, imitate its styles, above all, perhaps, accept its inevitability.[164]

---

161. See chapter 3 of this book.

162. See chapter 5 of this book.

163. Lindars, *Gospel*, 37; Bruce, *New Testament History*, 81; Ferguson, *Backgrounds*, 515.

164. Childs and Williams, *Introduction*, 48.

When we read the Gospel from this perspective, the subtle relationships among the groups of Jewish society and complexity of their power relations can be seen. The political situation of Jewish society described in the Gospel seems to indicate that the Jewish leaders ruled Jewish society with hegemonic power rather than with military suppressing power. The Jewish leaders had already accepted the Roman power as an inevitable reality (John 11:47-57). They adopted Roman priorities to maintain their power, and imitated its styles to eliminate their opponents, Jesus and his followers (18:3). The hegemonic power of the Jewish leaders functioned like an imperialist dispensation. They persuaded Jewish society to adopt the imperial priorities, which enabled them to keep their ruling positions, which included the authority to cast the Jews out of the synagogues (9:22). It is probable that the Gospel of John describes these politico-religious situations, which caused tremendous conflicts between them, to demonstrate the necessity of a solution, which could reduce or remove the conflicts. Therefore, the Johannine community might need to resist this compromising power in order to consolidate themselves and to accomplish their mission to overcome the conflicts.

3) Ambivalence: The world to which the Johannine community belonged was a hybridized one. Therefore, the Johannine literary strategy, which the author could adapt to resist the reality of the circumstances of their society, should be an effective one for the hybridized society. One effective strategy is an adaptation of multicultural elements, which are common in pluralistic societies. The adaptation of a variety of Johannine christological titles in the Gospel is a particular illustration of this. This Gospel adapted them to reflect the multicultural diversity of the Roman world, particularly in order to present Jesus as the king. The Fourth Gospel functions as a resistant literature in the hybridized society under imperial power.

> While one of the best forms of resistance to this is the process of creolization itself, which combines diverse cultural elements, rather than holding up one culture as the model to be emulated by others.... Its cross-cultural transmission and fertilization represent the positive dynamic, processual becoming of Diversity, rather than the incorporative fixity of the being of Sameness.[165]

A literary strategy of resistance that combines various cultural elements into one category is mainly employed in the Gospel. In particular, in the part of the revelation of the identity of Jesus, a variety of cultural elements which indicate the kingship of Jesus exist as a complex combination, particularly the combination of Jewish and Graeco-Roman elements. It is therefore possible

165. Childs and Williams, *Introduction*, 48.

to describe the Gospel as a text of (post)colonialism,[166] which utilizes hybridized cultures for its literary purpose. However, unlike the most obvious form of resistance in the colonial debates, namely violent resistance, the message of the Gospel rejects it. Rather, the Johannine Jesus throws himself into the colonial context to stop the violent and suppressive world, and to lead it into a new world where forgiveness, love, service, freedom and peace function as ruling apparatuses.

> Since [the colonialists] do not want to give up power, "decolonization is always a violent phenomenon." . . . In addition, violence has an effect on the colonized people both in general and as individuals. For the former, it overturns the divide and rule techniques of colonialism, and brings together regions, religious and ethnic groups in a united opposition. For the latter, violence is both cleansing and restorative; it purges feelings of inferiority and impotence, and restores self-respect.[167]

The Gospel of John presents a method of decolonization, but it never accepts that violence is the way to achieve it. While the Jewish leaders attempt to bring together regions and religious and ethnic groups in a united opposition so as to maintain their ruling position, the Johannine Jesus attempts neither. He does not attempt to overturn the colonial power, rather, he allows himself to be killed by its violence in order to deliver others from the violent techniques of colonialism. Moreover, the Johannine Jesus breaks down the walls between the oppositional groups to bring them into a new world where all will live in harmony without competition, struggle, and oppression. He never intends to bring together regions and religious ethnic groups in a united opposition; rather he teaches how to live a liberating life of forgiveness, service, freedom, peace and love. The Johannine Jesus combines the center and the margin into one by his life and message. In this sense, Jesus is the Universal King.

As Fanon says "Decolonization is the veritable creation of new men,"[168] the Gospel of John presents a way to "the veritable creation of new men" through the life and teaching of Jesus.

> Colonialism imposed its control of the social production of wealth through military conquest and subsequent political dictatorship. However, its most important area of domination was the mental universe of the colonized, the control, through

---

166. Dube, "Reading for Decolonization," 51–75.
167. Childs and Williams, *Introduction*, 54.
168. Fanon, *Wretched*, 28.

culture, of how people perceived themselves and their relation to the world.[169]

If we read the Gospel of John as a literature of resistance against colonialism, we find that the Jewish leaders in the Gospel attempted to control society in order to keep their political and religious positions through collaboration with the imperial power. They sought to prevent Jesus' resistance movement against colonialism in darkness. Their ambitions for power drove them to believe that the multitude, which followed Jesus, was stupid (John 7:49), and that they were the only elite group which could get rid of that kind of stupidity. Eventually, their political ambitions reached their climax when they sought to eliminate their opponent, Jesus.

The Jewish leaders in this Gospel were afraid that the world was breaking away from their political control as well as from their religious and spiritual domination because they saw the world following Jesus' movement (John 12:19). Individuals from not only Jewish groups but also from many other groups follow Jesus. From this perspective, we may read of the Johannine Jesus as the decolonizer.[170]

Similarities and Differences (Mimicry): The "Collaborators"

It is not easy to determine the identity of the Jewish leaders in the Gospel of John because they are regarded as both victims of institutionalized oppression and are also allied with it.[171] In Jewish society, the Jewish leaders had a mixed identity as the colonized and the colonizer. The term, "collaborator" is particularly appropriate to them. They had the discrete and pure identity neither of the colonizer nor of the colonized. Jewish society at the end of the first century CE was neither a pure nation nor did it maintain a society of a pure single race. It was colonized and had lost its identity as a single independent nation. They had to try to discover an answer to the problem of how to live with the present new empire, Rome. They were seeking a satisfactory alternative. In these circumstances, the Roman Empire emphasized her benefits to the colonized. Some of the Jews accepted the new ethics of the Empire and tried to enjoy gradually its benefits. For their own sakes, they collaborated with the Empire in the colonial society. They gained high positions and became rulers for the colonizer. As a result, they

169. Thiong'o, *Decolonialising the Mind*, 16.
170. See chapter 6 of this book.
171. See chapter 5 of this book. They were victims of suppression by the Roman Empire as well as taking up a position of other new suppressors of Jewish society for the Roman Empire at the end of the first century CE.

were both the colonized under the power of the Empire, and the colonizer as rulers of the colonial society.

While dominant power colonizes in the name of civilization, colonization results in de-civilization, brutal oppression and the degradation of the colonizer. Moreover, it reveals the buried instincts of the colonizer of covetousness, violence, race hatred and moral relativism.[172] In the process of hybridentity, "internal" colonists can absorb these negative features. In the Gospel of John, these negative features of colonization can be found in the character of the Jewish leaders. They justify the use of violence to maintain their positions. Their covetousness drives them into de-civilization. They seek to kill Jesus without any hesitation and to justify their actions; they use their own judicial process as well as that of the Romans. Moreover, they put pressure on the Roman governor, Pilate, to sentence Jesus to death. They ask for the crucifixion of Jesus instead of releasing him. An example of their moral relativism is that they want to keep the Passover and the Sabbath according to the Law (19:31), but they are willing to commit the murder of an innocent man.[173] The Jewish leaders in the Gospel act like the Romans who cruelly destroy their enemies by eliminating their opponent, Jesus. Their character is typical of collaborators who cooperate with the colonial power but who suppress the colonized in the colonial society.

Summary of the Chapter

In this chapter, I first discussed the textual features of the Gospel of John in relation to its purposes and its readership. I pointed out that as a postcolonial text the Fourth Gospel was written in a multicultural and hybridized society, and that it is highly possible that the purpose of the composition of this Gospel was for a variety of readers who were from multi cultural environments. Then, I described the two pillars of the background of the kingship of Jesus in the Johannine Gospel: Jewish traditions and Graeco-Roman traditions. Through a survey of the two major backgrounds to the Gospel, I clarified that the kingship of the Johannine Jesus is included in the use of various christological terms. The meanings of these titles could be understood by a variety of readers from varied backgrounds could understand in common when they read the Gospel. I also pointed out the importance of the combination of the two traditions in order to understand the kingship motif

---

172. Césaire argues that "colonization works to decivilise the colonizer, to brutalise him in the true sense of the word, to degrade him, to awaken him to buried instincts, to covetousness, violence, race hatred, and moral relativism" (A. Césaire, *Discourse*, 13).

173. See Orchard, *Courting Betrayal*.

of Jesus in this Gospel. In the spiral of the mixture of the meaning of the christological titles from the two backgrounds, I demonstrated a common meaning of the terms, namely the kingship of Jesus. In particular, I have argued that the Gospel as a hybridized product of this multicultural society accommodates various multicultural aspects. This Gospel was written for multicultural readers in order to present the Johannine Jesus as king, to lead them to believe in him as the true king whom they would follow for eternity and to challenge them to live according to the ruling ideology of the Johannine new world. Therefore, the Johannine Gospel encourages its readers and seeks to consolidate their faith in Jesus, and challenges them to live/spread out the Johannine ideology of the new world in/to the world.

Secondly, I researched the methodology of this book, postcolonialism. Because the Johannine world was under colonial power, the identity of the Johannine Jesus as decolonizer could be newly identified in colonialism. Therefore, a very different manner of reading of the Gospel in relation to the Jewish background or in relation to the Graeco-Roman world is not necessary. I also argued that the Johannine Jesus is regarded as the solution to the conflicts among the various groups, when we read the Gospel as a postcolonial text. In order to attempt a postcolonial reading of the Gospel, particularly to identify the kingship motif in the Johannine Jesus, I surveyed 1) differences and similarities between the center and the margins (mimicry), 2) the subtle relationship between the center and the margins (ambivalence), 3) hybridentity and diaspora in postcolonialism, as major theoretical tools of postcolonialism. While I defined the Gospel as a discourse of resistance and emancipation, I pointed out the complex and subtle relationship between the center and the margins in the Gospel.

Finally, I argued that hybridentity and diaspora are in a sense unavoidable in a colonial society. Thus, it is necessary to admit that a postcolonial society is a hybridized and diasporic society. The postcolonial hope, therefore, is to make a new utopian society through mutual transactions of the center and the margin, thus overcoming institutionalized violence and suffering. The Johannine new world pursued in the Gospel is like this: entry into the new hybrid society, which overcomes institutionalized violence and sufferings means entering the new world of peace, forgiveness, service, freedom, and love. The postcolonial hope is linked to the Johannine Utopia where Jesus as the universal king reigns for all the people regardless of whether their origins were the center or the margin.

3. Kingship and the Johannine Christological Titles

THE VARIETY OF THE christological titles used in the Gospel of John is an eminent indicator of the hybridity of the multiculture of the first century. The various backgrounds of these titles show that their separate use can generate various different responses by different groups of readers. However, in the Fourth Gospel, because these titles are brought together, they work with and against each other to reveal the identity of Jesus as king to first century readers. In order to argue this point, in this chapter I will, first of all, point out two important factors for the understanding of the Johannine christological titles: the relationship of their various backgrounds, and the use of the titles to create a unique and distinctive identity of Jesus. Secondly, I will explore the Johannine christological titles, which are used to designate Jesus as king, through demonstration of their distinctive use in this Gospel.

Two Important Factors for the Understanding of Johannine Christological Titles

Christological Titles as Hybridized Products of a Hybridized Society

As I argued in the previous chapter, the Gospel of John was written in a hybridized society for hybridized readers.[1] This specific but multifaceted condition of the hybridized societies of the first century is one of the major points for consideration in the interpretation of the kingship of the Johannine Jesus.[2] Accordingly, this opens up the possibility that the trajectory of

---

1. On the Gospel of John as a product of a hybridized society, see chapter 2 of this book.

2. Johannine Christology is developed not only in contrast with Jewish thinking but also with other Christological views (see de Jonge, "Jewish Expectations," 246–70). De Jonge remarks, "It uses Jewish terms commonly employed in early Christian statements about Jesus (as Christ, Son of God and Son of Man), but explains and develops

the unique life of the Johannine Jesus could be exposed more clearly in the light of various backgrounds of the titles.[3] In particular, the Gospel designates Jesus using hybridized products engendered mainly from the combination of the Jewish and the Graeco-Roman backgrounds.[4] That is, the Gospel of John in describing Jesus living and working in Jewish society is the reason for the importance of the knowledge of the Jewish background.[5] For the same reason, the fact that Jewish society in first century Palestine had been under foreign influences, particularly Roman rule, is the reason for the importance of knowledge of the Graeco-Roman background.[6] Moreover, it is quite clear that the Roman Empire did not simply rule the Jews politically, but resulted in other cultural, religious and economic influences merging into Jewish society so that Jewish society was not pure and monolithic, but a complex and hybridized one. For that reason, John never freed himself from the concept of the christological titles, which were linked to that of the Graeco-Roman. Rather, it is likely that the author used them to designate Jesus for hybridized readers. Therefore, John as well as his readers living together in a hybridized society could have a common context for understanding the various christological titles which were employed to designate the Johannine Jesus. In short, it is necessary to know these backgrounds in order to understand better the kingship of Jesus in the Gospel of John.[7]

---

them in a process of elaboration and radicalization" (de Jonge, "Christology," 214–15).

3. Koester remarks, "The actions appropriate and redefine associations that readers would bring to the text from the literary context, the Old Testament and Jewish traditions, and the wider Greco-Roman cultural context" (Koester, *Symbolism*, 81).

4. Lincoln says, "In terms of its broad intellectual and cultural setting, the Fourth Gospel sits squarely within the religious thought-world of the Judaism of the late first century CE. This was a Judaism . . . that had interacted in a variety of ways with the social codes of its Mediterranean world and with the political, economic, and cultural aspects of its dominant Graeco-Roman environment" (Lincoln, *Gospel*, 82).

5. Keener remarks that the Gospel of John adapted distinctively Christological terms, which were used more broadly in other streams of early Judaism and Jewish Christianity (see Keener, *Gospel of John*, 280–330). For comprehensive surveys of the history and religion of the Jewish people before and during the New Testament era, see Schürer, *History of the Jewish people*; Moore, *Judaism in the First Centuries*; Smallwood, *Jews Under Roman Rule*; Sanders, *Judaism*.

6. Cassidy argues, "John's indication of Jesus' exalted status also functions to affirm Jesus' sovereignty in the face of competing claims of sovereignty made by various Roman officials" (Cassidy, *John's Gospel*, 29). See also chapter 2 of this book.

7. It seems to be agreed by most scholars that the Gospel is an exemplary mixture of Jewish and Graeco-Roman elements.

Distinctive Usage of the Christological Titles in the Gospel of John

In the first place, it is necessary to point out that there are various sequences of confessions or designations of Jesus in the Gospel of John, which are arranged in the Gospel by special authorial intention. For example, "Logos" (1:1–18), "Lamb of God" (1:29, 36), "Messiah" (1:41), "the Son of God, and the King of Israel" (1:49) where the "Son of God" is intended to be understood in kingly messianic terms alongside that of the Roman emperors, "a" or "the prophet" (4:19 – the prophet awaited by the Samaritans?), "the Savior of the World" (4:42), "the Holy One of God" (6:69), "the prophet" (7:40 – like Moses?), "the Son of Man" (9:35), "the King of the Jews" (19:19), and "my Lord and my God" (20:28).

These progressions of thought concerning the identity of Jesus might well show that the author wrote the Gospel with due consideration given to the varied backgrounds of his readers. Van Bruggen emphasizes that "no matter how new the message of Christ was, it was tuned to his listeners' wavelength."[8] Then, in terms of authorial intention, we can question if John did use these terms to describe Jesus in consideration of the readers' wavelength. If the answer is yes, we must ask whether the author employed them to describe Jesus in such a way so as to lead the Johannine readers beyond their wavelength in order to discover a new aspect of his character.

Accordingly, the author's unique way of narrative description, particularly with regard to the christological titles, creates the unique Johannine Jesus. In other words, John might know that the Johannine readers could, at first, understand the christological titles in relation to the meanings they already knew.[9] However, he might also use them in his own way to uniquely depict the Johannine Jesus. Thus, in the Gospel, the concepts of the christological terms were adapted and arranged to portray Jesus as a unique character. In short, the author places them elaborately into the narratives so that when they read the Gospel repeatedly and deeply, his readers could find a new understanding of Jesus, that is, Jesus as king.

In the second place, a peculiar thing in the employment of various christological titles is that those terms seem to be used synonymously with one another in terms of the kingship motif in the Gospel and so create

---

8. Van Bruggen, *Jesus*, 13. Van Bruggen's emphasis on the listeners' wavelength in association with the meanings of terms can be also applied to the readers' wavelength in association with the meanings of the Christological terms of the Gospel.

9. Pryor remarks, "Johannine Christianity does not live in an isolated part of the globe, cut off from other Christian traditions, for it shares a common vocabulary" (Pryor, *John*, 144).

a distinctive image of the Johannine Jesus as king. It seems that the author must intentionally have considered the employment of these various terms to reveal a new identity of Jesus as king and to lead his readers to reach this conclusion as well.

The contemporaries of John could identify the Johannine Jesus in terms of conventional categories and popular understanding. However, the use of the titles in the Gospel goes beyond everyday language and conventional meaning[10] by their usage in a Johannine manner.[11] Petersen argues on this point,

> We cannot help but acknowledge that his usage stands in fundamental contrast to everyday usage. John and his people speak and think in ways that are in contrast with the speech and thought of others in their social environment. . . . We cannot appreciate John's special use of language without acknowledging its social function as an affirmation of difference over against the sameness of the world around him and his people, a world that has also rejected what they affirm. Indeed, we will find that the fact of social rejection is the motivating force behind the affirmation of a difference that has been imposed upon John and his people. In terms of the narrator's use of language . . . difference is represented both by his creation of synonyms out of words that in everyday language are not synonyms and by his relentless use of contrastive expressions. . . . Synonymy raises the fundamental conceptual problem of the *reference* of his special use of language. . . . Any better understanding we might obtain will come not from reference but from *difference*.[12]

Because of the unique Johannine use of language and, in particular, the employment of the christological titles for the identification of Jesus which have different origins and meanings, they could be rendered synonymously in the context when the author used them to refer to the identity of Jesus as king. In this sense, "John *creates* synonyms"[13] in the

---

10. On anti-language, anti-society, see Malina and Rohrbaugh, *Social-Science Commentary*; Halliday, "Anti-languages," 570–84; Halliday, *Language*; Petersen, *Gospel of John*.

11. The Gospel of John seeks the implementation of new values in place of old ones (Malina and Rohrbaugh, *Social-Science Commentary*, 6). John is "consciously used for strategic purposes, defensively to maintain a particular social reality or offensively for resistance and protest" (see Halliday, *Language*, 178–79).

12. Petersen, *Gospel of John*, 21.

13. Petersen, *Gospel of John*, 10. Petersen also argues that "'Rabbi/teacher' and 'lord' (meaning 'master') are synonymous when people use them to refer to Jesus as their superior or leader, or simply out of difference. Similarly, 'Messiah/Christ,' 'king' (of Israel/the

Johannine semantic field. In addition, although the Johannine Jesus was characterized by the common and general meanings of the terms in the first century, the unique Johannine use of various christological titles and their sequence in the narratives created a different, distinctive and unique identity of Jesus: Jesus as king.[14]

In summary, it is probable that, in terms of authorial intention, this synonymous but distinctive use of the Johannine christological titles was employed to express the Johannine unique way of understanding who Jesus was.[15] It also reflects that the author wrote the Gospel in due consideration of its intended readership consisting of inner groups from various origins within the Johannine community.[16] It is quite likely that the christological titles have synonymy among them in the narratives in terms of the indication of a distinctive characteristic of the Johannine Jesus as king. As a result, it is necessary to research the meanings of the christological titles in the Johannine Gospel giving due consideration to this tendency of mixture and synonymy.

In the following sections of this chapter, as a result of research into the various backgrounds of the Johannine christological titles, I will discuss a number of the titles which contain implicit or explicit references to the kingship motif to verify that the kingship of Jesus is one of the major themes of this Gospel. In order to do this, I will first discuss two titles, Messiah (the Christ) and the Son of God, both of which are directly employed to reveal the identity of Jesus as the purpose of the composition of the Gospel of John (20:21–22). Then, I will discuss another important title, the Son of Man, and other christological titles, such as Prophet, Lord, my Lord and my God, and Savior of the World. Finally, after dealing with various Johannine christological titles, I will demonstrate the kingship motif, which is found throughout the Gospel.

Jews), 'Son of God,' 'Holy one of God,' and 'Savior of the world' are everyday synonyms when used to refer to Jesus' royal role in the world" (Petersen, *Gospel of John*, 57).

14. It also explains that this literary device might be created to reflect "the situation of the evangelist and his intended readers at the time of writing" (Culpepper, *Anatomy*, 67–68). Dodd argues that John "develops his teaching in part, by way of opposition to such ideas" because of the effect of the controversy with his contemporary Jews. For example, the title, the Messiah as the Son of David, is not employed in the Gospel of John, even though it is a most common Jewish messianic title (Dodd, *Interpretation*, 228).

15. This implies that the Gospel of John, as a product of a hybridized society, was written for hybridized readers, facing various conflicts with synagogues and with Roman rule as well. See chapter 1 of this book.

16. See chapter 6 of this book.

Messiah/Christ and Kingship

Messiah in Pre-Christian Texts

It is true that the knowledge of the term, the Messiah, in pre-Christian texts should give a better understanding of the identity of the Johannine Jesus as king. It is important to know just what Messianism in the first century CE meant in Jewish society. The main traditional Jewish view of the Messiah was of a kingly Messiah, Messiah the son of David.[17] Accordingly, the Davidic royalty and the Jewish messianic expectations[18] are one of the major areas of research into the background of the kingship motif in Jewish literature.[19] I will deal with some representative texts in this section.

---

17. Vermes, *Jesus the Jew*, 130; Fitzmyer, *One Who Is to Come*, 182.

18. The expectation of the royal Davidic Messiah is one of the various different concepts of the Messiah to come. On the issues of the origins of Jewish Messianism and its influence on early Christianity, see Horbury, *Jewish Messianism*; Fitzmyer, *One Who Is to Come*; Keener, *Gospel of John*, 283–89; Charlesworth, *Messiah*; Collins, *Scepter and the Star*; Strauss, *Davidic Messiah*, 35–57; Day, *King and Messiah*; Neusner, Green, and Frerichs, *Judaisms and Their Messiah*; Nickelsburg, *Ancient Judaism*, 98–117. On other messianic pretenders contemporary with Jesus, see Horsley, "Popular Messianic Movements," 471–95; Horsley, *Bandits, Prophets, and Messiahs*.

19. Horbury (*Jewish Messianism*, esp. 1–4) argues for the diversity of Second Temple messianism and the close relationship between Judaism and early Christianity, emphasizing themes of kingship and national liberation as congruent with messianism. He argues that the continuity is in homage to the messiah as attested in the LXX and in the targums and rabbinic texts. Horbury further argues that "recognition of Christ as messianic king, beginning in the ministry of Jesus and intensified in the earliest Christian community, shaped address to Christ according the tradition of homage . . . and led to the acclamations and titles preserved in the New Testament." In addition, he argues, "Early Christianity also offers signs of continuity with the developed messianic expectation of ancient Judaism. . . . These developments of an inherited messianism were encouraged by its parallel continuation in the Jewish community of ruler-cult under both Greek and Roman Rule." "In the case of the Christ-cult, messianism in particular formed the link been Judaism and the apparently gentilic acclamation of *Kyrios Iesous Christos*."

Fitzmyer also surveys the roots of messianic hopes in the Hebrew Bible and its developments in later extrabiblical Jewish writings. However, Fitzmyer argues the Christian Messiah is different from the Jewish Messiah in terms of his mission, namely, deliverance in a spiritual sense rather than in a political and economic sense, and his coming for all human beings, not for a chosen people (see Fitzmyer, *One Who Is to Come*, esp. 182–83).

Collins examines the crucial links and similarities between Jewish and Christian models of the messiah (a Shoot from the Stump of Jesse, the Messiahs of Aaron and Israel; Teacher, Priest and Prophet; the Messiah as the Son of God; the Danielic Son of Man). Collins explains the birth of messianic thought and its impact for Jews and Christians alike in ancient—as well as modern—times (Collins, *Scepter and the Star*).

Strauss investigates one theme within Lukan Christological "proclamation from

Messiah in the Hebrew Bible

In the Hebrew Bible, all the occurrences of the term,[20] which refer to the contemporary king of Israel, seem to underscore the very close relationship between God and the king[21] (Note. In the Gospel of John, Jesus as the Son was sent by God the Father into the world to be king, among other roles). Two major Messianic passages in the Hebrew Bible (2 Sam 7:11–17; Psalm 2) are not exceptional in this respect. I will discuss briefly these two passages, which contribute to the presentation of the kingship of the Johannine Jesus.[22]

2 SAM 7:11–17

2 Sam 7:11–17 is one probable basis for the kingship of the Johannine Jesus.[23] It is the expectation of a royal Messiah as a descendant of David, where the permanence of the Davidic throne and the father-son relationship are emphasized. The Davidic king would be a son of God, and his kingdom

---

prophecy and pattern" motif, that of the coming king from the line of David. To determine the background to this theme, Strauss examines the Davidic promised tradition in its first century context of meaning. While the diverse writings of first century Judaism exhibit a range of eschatological expectations, he explores evidence of widespread hope for a coming Davidic deliverer, described as a new "David," a "seed" or "shoot" from David. Strauss also proposes "a plausible synthesis" to explain "the unity and diversity of Luke's Old Testament Christology." He sees that "Luke links the Jesus event particularly to the Isaianic portrait of eschatological salvation, where the messianic deliverer is at the same time prophet, servant and king." In this way, according to Strauss, Luke "is able to show that Jesus is the Christ promised in Scripture and that through his life, death, resurrection, and exaltation he has fulfilled the promise made to the fathers" (see Strauss, *Davidic Messiah*, esp. 35–75, 325, 343).

Nickelsburg discusses the variety of Jewish messianic notions. For some Jews the Messiah would be an exalted heavenly figure. For others he would be an earthly ruler. In still other sources there is no reference to a Messiah. Such a complicated picture of messianic notions calls into question earlier Christian presuppositions about Jewish "unbelief." Claims made about a Messiah, and about Jesus as Messiah, "would not have been universally taken for granted even among pious, eschatologically oriented Jews" (see Nickelsburg, *Ancient Judaism*, 116).

20. The anointed of God: 1 Sam 24:7, 11; 26:9, 11, 16, 23; 2 Sam 1:14, 16; 19:22; Lam 4:20. The anointed of the God of Jacob: 2 Sam 23:1. His, my, your anointed one: 1 Sam 2:10, 35; 12:3, 5; 16:6; 2 Sam 22:51; Isa 45:1; Hab 3:13; Ps 2:2; 18:51; 20:7; 28:8; 84:10; 89:39, 52; 132:10, 17; 2 Chr 6:42.

21. Roberts, "Old Testament's Contribution," 39.

22. For other relevant texts from the Hebrew Bible, see chapter 2 of this book.

23. See Strauss, *Davidic Messiah*, 35–74; Collins, *Scepter and the Star*, 23; Pomykala, *Davidic Dynasty Tradition*, 13.

would be forever. The kingship of the Johannine Jesus as the Messiah and the Son of God is linked with this prophecy, although his identity as the Davidic descendant is weak in the Gospel of John.[24] Instead, a common view of the Christ by his contemporaries is shown in John 7:42. The multitudes know that the Christ would come from the offspring of David and from Bethlehem, the town of David.[25] In the context of this passage, the Christ as the Davidic descendant comprises one aspect of the identification of Jesus. In John 10:22-42, furthermore, there is the controversy between Jesus and the Jews in the context of the healing of the man born blind (10:19-21) and of the parable of the Good Shepherd (10:1-18).[26] The Messiahship and kingship of Jesus is a crucial theme in this narrative. When the Jews ask if Jesus is the Christ (10:22), Jesus answers by affirming that he is the Son of the Father, his mission from God, and more strikingly that he and the Father are one (10:30). This shows the close relationship between the Christ and the Son of God in the Gospel of John. In addition, Jesus repeatedly answers that he is the Son of God (10:36) and that the Father is in him and he in the Father (10:38; cf. 1:18). The intimate relationship between the Father and the Son, which is reminiscent of the prophecy in 2 Sam 7:11-17, implicitly shows the kingship of Jesus throughout the Gospel. It is, therefore, clear that the Davidic king as the Messiah and the Son of God contributes to the presentation of the kingship of the Johannine Jesus.

Psalm 2

Psalm 2 is another root for the kingship of the Johannine Jesus, where the king is the Lord's anointed (Messiah) as well as the son of God and will be the universal king and the judge of the world. In the Gospel, Jesus is the king

---

24. The origin of the Johannine Jesus is "in the beginning" in the Gospel. His filial relationship with God, however, is more emphasized than that with his earthly father, Joseph in the Gospel (in 1:34, Jesus is described as the son of Joseph, which might imply Davidic royal descent). Particularly, the Father-Son relationship is emphasized in the Gospel, and the title "the Son" without any modifiers ("of God" or "of Man") is one of the crucial Johannine Christological titles (1:14; 1:18; 3:16-17; 3:35-36; 5:19-23, 26; 6:40; 8:35-36; 14:13; 17:1). The Gospel of John presents the kingship of the Johannine Jesus as the Son [of the Father], or the Son of God/Man, which are used together, or interchangeably with one another, in the narratives.

25. The Gospel reports that some of the multitudes deny Jesus' Messiahship because of Jesus' Galilean origin (7:41). However, it is their misunderstanding of Jesus' origin. The Gospel emphasizes his pre-existence (1:1-18) and his coming from above (3:12-21—the Son of Man and the Son or the Son of God are represented together to designate Jesus), not his Galilean origin.

26. Shepherd motif is linked to the ideal king in the ancient Near East.

and the judge as the Son (of God). In John 1:18 and 3:16, Jesus is the only unique begotten Son, which is reminiscent of Psalm 2:7. In John 3:16–22, the mission of the Son is not judgment of the world but the salvation of it (3:17). However, judgment is unavoidable because of the world's unbelief in the Son of God (3:18). In chapter 5, the kingship of Jesus revealed in his divine sonship is depicted through the mixture of the titles, the Son, the Son of Man, and the Son of God. Jesus as the Son (of God/of Man) is portrayed as the life-giver and also the judge in this passage (5:20–30). The authority and power of God is given to Jesus and Jesus will execute this power over the world when the hour is come (5:25–27). The divine sonship of the king in Psalm 2:7 is a basis for the kingship of Jesus in the Gospel of John.

Messiah in Extra-Biblical Texts

I will discuss three significant sources for the Messianic expectation of Israel and the expected Redeemer figure in this sub-section.[27] They are *Psalms of Solomon* 17–18, *1 Enoch* 37–71, and *4 Ezra*.

PSALMS OF SOLOMON 17–18

In the Inter-testamental period, the first significant source concerning the Messianic hope, which underlies the kingship of the Johannine Jesus, is the *Psalms of Solomon* (an anti-Hasmonean and anti-Roman collection from the first century BCE[28]). The *Psalms of Solomon* 17 and 18 are prayers for the coming of the promised redeemer from the house of David, depicting the Messiah as an earthly king who will remove the Romans without force.[29] Particularly, the *Psalms of Solomon* 17 expresses the notion that the king over Israel will be David and that his kingdom will be a permanent one (17:4). The king of the future, i.e., the son of David (17:21)[30] will shatter unrighteous rulers and judge the world (17:22 17:31; cf. Jesus

---

27. See van Bruggen, *Jesus*, 132–39.

28. Charlesworth, *Old Testament Pseudepigrapha*, 2:640–41. See also Atkinson, "On the Herodian Origin," 435–60.

29. Especially, see 17:23–36 and 18:6, 8; cf. Isa 11. The Messiah was expected to be a king descended from King David, victor over the Gentiles, and Savior and restorer of Israel; he is not merely a warrior king but a new establisher of God's justice as "the final ruler portrayed by Isaiah 11 and Jewish Messianic thought in General" (See Vermes, *Jesus the Jew*, 131).

30. The title, the Son of David, is the most common title for the Messiah in the rabbinic literature (See Strauss, *Davidic Messiah*, 41).

as the judge). He will be mighty due to the anointing of the Holy Spirit (17:37; cf. John 1:29-34 – the Spirit descending and remaining on Jesus as the Son of God; Acts 4:25). He will be "one anointed by God" (17:36 – χριστὸς κυρίου as the future Davidic savior; cf. Jesus as χριστὸς κυρίου in Luke 2:11). The king will gather together both Jews and Gentiles and will reign over them (17:26, 30-31; cf. John 10:16 – Jesus has two flocks of sheep and will bring them into one flock with one shepherd), and will faithfully and righteously shepherd the flock of the Lord (17:40-41; cf. Jesus as the good shepherd in John 10). He will purge Jerusalem from the nations that are intent on her destruction (17:22) in order to make her holy (17:30). This prophecy of the purge of Jerusalem is reminiscent of the purge of the Temple in Jerusalem (John 2:13-22). The Messianic hope in the *Psalms of Solomon* 17 is another explicit source for understanding contemporary Jewish ideas of Messiah in terms of kingship.

1 Enoch and 4 Ezra

Among the Jewish Apocalyptic literature, *1 Enoch* and *4 Ezra* describe a messianic figure with allusions to the Davidic line, which could be linked to the kingship of the Johannine Jesus.[31]

1. *1 Enoch* 37—71

In *1 Enoch* ("Similitudes"; second and first century BCE[32]), the Messiah is a heavenly figure who executes judgment on the day of judgment especially against oppressive kings and exploitative landowners. In *1 Enoch* 37—71, 48:10, and 52:4 are instances of the name "His Anointed," which alludes to Psalm 2 (cf. Ps 2:2 – *the LORD and his anointed*). This refers to the same figure who is also called "the Elect One"[33] (49:3; 62:1-2; cf. Isa 11:2). Especially, this "Elect One" will restore and judge the righteous (61:5, 8). More frequently the same figure is called "the Son of Man"[34] (esp. ch. 46 – the revelation of the Son of Man) who will judge the world. This Messianic figure as the king and judge in *1 Enoch* is reminiscent of Jesus in John 5:19-30. God

---

31. Strauss, *Davidic Messiah*, 45.

32. Charlesworth, *The Old Testament Pseudepigrapha*, 1:6-7.

33. According to Collins, this title is routinely referred to as "the king messiah" in the *Targumim* and *Midrashim* (Collins, *Scepter and the Star*, 65).

34. It is based on the Danielic Son of Man. For further echoes of the Danielic Son of Man, see ch. 47; the vision of the heavenly throne room, cf. Dan 7:9-10; ch. 52; the vision of the great image made of metal mountains, cf. Dan 2:31-48 (see Nickelsburg, "Salvation," 58-64).

as the Father gives all judgment to Jesus as the Son [of God and of Man] (5:22, 26–27). The Son will judge justly (5:30 – My judgment is just; ἡ κρίσις ἡ ἐμὴ δικαία ἐστίν) because he is the Son of Man (5:27), and the dead will rise either to life or to judgment when they hear the voice of the Son of God (5:25; cf. John 10:27; 18:37).[35]

2. *4 Ezra*

In *4 Ezra* (a Jewish document from the first century CE), the Danielic and royal-Davidic Messianic figure is alluded to. Especially, the Messiah as the seed of David in *4 Ezra* 12:31–34 will come to judge the world at the end of the days. These verses are linked with Davidic Messianic expectations "which emphasize the role of the king as Warrior, Savior and Judge (esp. Isa 11; Ps 2)."[36] In the Gospel of John, this Messianic judgment, which recalls the *Psalms of Solomon* 17 and draws its image from Isaiah 11 and Psalm 2, is reminiscent of the Johannine Jesus' role as the judge. In addition, *4 Ezra* 7:28–29 expresses the revealing and the death of "my Son the Messiah."[37] Similarly, we can find the combined concept of "the Son and the Messiah" in the Gospel of John: Jesus is the Messiah and the Son of God in his divine Sonship. Furthermore, in *4 Ezra* 13, a Messianic man who will rise from the sea on the clouds is reminiscent of the Danielic Son of Man (Dan 7: One like a son of Man coming with the clouds) as well as the Davidic Messiah.[38] This Messiah as the Man rising from the sea with the clouds of heaven (13:2–3) will speak, and his voice out of his mouth will be heard by all (13:4; cf. John 5:25–30 – the dead will hear the voice of the Son of God). *4 Ezra* 13 expresses there will be war against the Man (13:5–7), and the Man will gain victory by peaceful means (13:8–11). Finally, he will gather another peaceable multitude (13:12–13; cf. John 10:16 – another flock which will hear Jesus voice and become his flock). The Man as a Man ascending from the heart of the sea is also expressed as "my Son" (13:32). Here also, *4 Ezra* 13 presents a background of kingship relevant to the Johannine Jesus. Jesus as the Man (John 19:5) brought before Pilate by the Jewish leaders (John 18:29–19:37) gains the victory by non-military means (the Cross and the Resurrection; cf. John 16:33 – "I have overcome the world").

---

35. That there is a mixed use of the titles is important evidence of the interchangeability.

36. Strauss, *Davidic Messiah*, 48.

37. In *2 Baruch* 30:1, the Messiah's return to heaven is described. This is reminiscent of the Jesus' death as glorification.

38. Collins, *Scepter and the Star*, 65.

The Qumran Texts

It is in the formative period of Christian origins that the diversity of messianic expectation exists.[39] The Qumran texts (i.e., 1QSa 2:11-17[40]; 4Q174 3:11-12) also feature two major eschatological figures, a Davidic Messiah (the anointed king of Israel) and a high priest (the anointed high priest).[41] Among some thirty Qumran texts[42] describing Messianic figures, about half of them[43] refer to the traditional royal Messiah.[44] For example, 1QSa 2:11-12 "When God will have be[got]ten the anointed one among them [the Mess]iah of Israel" (cf. Ps 2:2, 7) is echoed in the description of the

---

39. Keener, *Gospel of John*, 286-89. Collins distinguishes four Messianic figures: king, priest, prophet, and heavenly king or Son of Man (see also Collins, *Scepter and the Star*). The variations in the use of the words in Qumran fragments prove that the term, the anointed, was not yet reserved for one figure alone (see van Bruggen, *Jesus*, 137).

40. Vermes, *Complete Dead Sea Scrolls*, 161.

41. Messianic expectations centered on two Messiahs in Qumran seem to reflect the political changes. It is likely that the domination of Palestine by Rome resulted in an increase in royal-Davidic expectation in the sect's later years (c. 4 BCE to CE 68) according to Various Cave 4 documents, while priestly messianic expectations were dominant during its classical period (from c. 110 BCE onward) (Strauss, *Davidic Messiah*, 43-44).

42. Texts of the royal Messiah – CD 12:23-13:1; 14:19 (= 4Q266 frg. 18, 3:12); 19:10-11; 20:1; 1QS 9:11; 1QSa 2:11-12, 14-15, 20-21; 4Q252 frg.1 v. 3-4; 4Q381 frg.15 7; 4Q382 frg.16 2; 4Q458 frg. 2, 2:6; 4Q521 frg.2 ii. 1; 4Q521 frg.7 5. Texts of Messianic figures who are not said to be "anointed" – CD 7:19-20 (=4Q266 frg.3 4:9); 1QSb 5:20; 1QM 3:16, 5:1; 4Q496 frg.10 3-4; 4Q161 frgs.2-6 2:17; 4Q285 frg.4 2; 4Q285 frg.4 6; 4Q285 frg.6 2; 4Q276 frag.1 3:1; Jubilees 31:18; Sibylline Oracles 3:469. Texts of a Branch of David – 4Q161 frags. 7-10 3:22; 4Q174 frags. 1-3 1:11; 4Q252 frag.1 5:3-4; 4Q285 frag.5 3-4. Text of the Scepter as the expected Messiah – 1QSb 5:27-28; 4Q161 frags.2-6 2:17. Texts of Son of God – 4Q246 1:9; 2:1; 4Q369 frag.1 2:6.

43. CD 12:23-13:1 (the coming of the Messiah of Aaron); CD 14:19 (the coming of the Messiah of Aaron and Israel who will pardon their iniquity); CD 19:10-11 (the coming of the anointed of Aaron and Israel); CD 20:1 (the anointed of Aaron of Israel appears); 1QS 9:11 (until there shall come the Prophet and the Messiahs of Aaron and Israel); 1QSa 2:11-12 (When God will have be[got]ten the anointed one among them, [the Mess]iah of Israel); 1QSa 2:14-15 (the Messiah one of Israel); 1QSa 2:20-21 (the Messiah of Israel shall extend his hand over the bread, [and] all the congregation of the Community [shall utter a] blessing, [each man in the order] of his dignity); 4Q252 frag.1 v. 3-5 (For the ruler's staff (xlix, 10) is the Covenant of kingship, [and the clans] of Israel are the divisions, until the Messiah of Righteousness comes, the Branch of David. For to him and his seed is granted the Covenant of kingship over his people for everlasting generations which he is keep); 4Q381 frag.15 7 (As for me, Thine anointed one, I have understood); 4Q382 frag.16 2 ([an]ointed one of Isra[e]l); 4Q458 frag.2 2:6 (one anointed with the oil of the kingdom); 4Q521 frag. 2 ii.1 ([the hea]ven and the earth will listen to His Messiah); 4Q521 frag.7 5 ([when] he Life-giver will raise the dead of His people).

44. See Evans, "Messianism," 701-2; Strauss, *Davidic Messiah*, 43.

Johannine Jesus as the only begotten Son (1:18; 3:16, 18). Secondly, 1QSa 2:20–21 "the Messiah of Israel shall extend his hand over the bread, [and] all the congregation of the Community [shall utter a] blessing, [each man in the order] of his dignity" has resonances with the feeding of thousands in John and the multitude's attempt to make Jesus king by force (6:15). This they did because they perceived Jesus to be "the Prophet who is to come into the world" (6:14), and this could be linked to a Messianic figure in 1QS 9:11 (until there shall come the Prophet and the Messiahs of Aaron and Israel), where the various Messianic figures speak. It could also be linked to the various Messianic expectations mentioned by (the Messiah and the Prophet). Thirdly, 4Q521 frag.7 5 ([when] the Life-giver will raise the dead of His people) can be linked to the Johannine Jesus as the life-giver (John 5:20–30). Finally, 4Q502 4:5 describes the Messianic figure as the shepherd, which could belong to the background of the Johannine kingship of the good shepherd in John 10.

To summarize, it is evident that a variety of Messianic titles and concepts in the kingly Messiah texts of the Hebrew Bible as well as Jewish extra-biblical texts form the background to the kingship of the Johannine Jesus, and that this kingship is closely linked to these various Jewish Messianic expectations. Hence, the Johannine Jesus can be better understood in the light of these Jewish Messianic backgrounds. However, it seems that the Johannine Jesus also stands apart from thses Jewish Messianic figures. In order to see this more clearly, it is necessary to scrutinize the Johannine texts.

Messiah/Christ in the Gospel of John

It is generally accepted that "there were many Jews in Jesus' day who put their hope for national recovery in the person of the coming Messiah, the new king of the end times."[45] We can also find that the contemporaries of Jesus and, later, the Johannine community, both Jews (John 1:20, 25; 3:28) and Samaritans (John 4:25), had various eager expectations that the Messiah would come.[46] Inquiries by the crowds and the Jews of Jerusalem concerning the identity of both John the Baptist and Jesus using several titles such as

---

45. Van Bruggen, *Jesus*, 15. "It is striking that the various rebel readers are not called *Messiah*. This confirms that God's anointed is a figure belonging to God's future—not a political but an eschatological future" (Van Bruggen, *Jesus*, 40–41; see also Horsley, *Bandits, Prophets, and Messiahs*, 88–134).

46. Painter remarks that "even when we make allowance for the diversity of messianic expectations in second temple Judaism, the identification of Christ as the Messiah is the starting point of John's Christology" (Painter, "Point of John's Christology," 250).

the Prophet, Elijah, the Christ, illustrate this. Hence, these kingly messianic claims are important to identify Jesus in the Gospel of John.

It is this distinctive Johannine way of describing Jesus that is linked to the traditional Jewish heritage.[47] However, it also seems that the Gospel is ambivalent as to which kind of messiah is described. Dahl argues, "to the contemporary Jews, the Messiah is a political king (6:15; 11:48; 19:12)."[48] However, Schürer argues, "the messianic hope was a remarkable mixture of political and religious ideals."[49] That is, "the political freedom of the nation which they longed for was viewed as the goal of God's way." Carter also points out that "in the Roman world there was no separation between the religious and political spheres. Religion was not a private matter for individuals. Religion was a civic and public practice, visible to and observed by others."[50] Rowland argues,

> Early Christian writings present us with a classic example of a radical movement engaging in that process of accommodation with the wider world leading to the channelling of the charismatic vision in a way which would guarantee preservation. The hope for the transformation of the world was kept alive, though Christians were increasingly accepting of many of the institutions of society while they enjoyed, and looked forward to, the messianic kingdom. The early Christians did not reject Jewish political messianism, therefore, by replacing it with a doctrine of a spiritual Messiah, at least immediately.[51]

In this view, it is fair to say that the Johannine Christ is much more than the "Messiah" in the Jewish or Samaritan sense of this term.[52] Particularly, this claim is found in the series of titles in the Gospel of John. For example, they are employed in the narrative where the Jewish leaders asked about the identity of John the Baptist, and in the various titles which are used by the disciples to identify Jesus in chapter 1; in the dialogue with a Samaritan woman in chapter 4; in the debate with the Pharisees in chapter 7; on the occasion of the

---

47. Dodd, *Interpretation*, 228.
48. Dahl, "Johannine Church," 127.
49. Schürer, *History of the Jewish People*, 527; see also, Cassidy, *John's Gospel*, 11.
50. Carter, *Matthew and the Margins*, 20.
51. Rowland, "Christ," 494.
52. John alone in the New Testament brings the title in its original form, the Messiah (1:41; 4:25). It shows that the background to the concept of the title, Messiah, is obviously and intensely Jewish (see Ashton, *Understanding the Fourth Gospel*, 240). However, "this term is used in the Jewish (Samaritan) sense of the word or with a Christian meaning presupposing or correcting Jewish usage" (de Jonge, "Use of the Word *Kristos*," 71).

expulsion from the synagogue of the man born blind in chapter 9; in the confessions of Peter (6:69) and Martha (11:27); and in the summary statement of the purpose of the composition of the Gospel (20:31).

So, then, what kind of kingship of the Johannine Jesus is presented in the Gospel in terms of the Messiah? The Johannine Gospel surely presents the messiahship of Jesus in conjunction with the kingship so that when the people called Jesus the Messiah/Christ, it is mainly used in the context of the revealing of his kingship.[53] The kingship of the Johannine Jesus, however, goes beyond this sphere, as he is a king in quite another sense (17:16; 18:33-37).[54] The Johannine Jesus does not belong to this world, as his kingdom is not of this world. He is a transcendent being, but he came to earth. He came to save the world as the expected Messiah, but in an unexpected way, namely through the cross. Smalley remarks on an important aspect of the concept of the Messiah in relation to the kingship of the Johannine Jesus,

> John is also aware . . . of the kingly and triumphal implications of the figure of Messiah—whether these were by association political, or religious, or both. However, once more John's Christology . . . is taken further. To this end John interprets the messiahship of Jesus by linking it to the notions of "derivation" and (in a developed sense) "kingship."[55]

The Gospel of John through all its chapters reports that Jesus is the Christ/the Messiah in a unique way (John 1:36; 1:41; 4:29, 42; 6:68–69; 7:26, 31, 41, 48–49; 11:27; 12:30–31; 20:31). It is necessary, henceforth to scrutinize the meaning in the Johannine narratives where the title is employed.

John 1:19–34

In John 1:19–34, the possible answers to the question of the true identity of John the Baptist are "the Christ," "Elijah" or "the Prophet." These three possible answers can be related to the various Jewish expectations of

---

53. Kalyor argues, "God's kingdom is larger than Israel since God is king of all the earth. So also the messiah to come is destined to rule not only Israel but the whole world" (Kaylor, *Jesus*, 82). This logic is found in the Gospel of John, particularly in explaining the purpose of the crucifixion of Jesus (John 11:51–52: prophesied that Jesus was about to die for the people, and not for the people only, but also in order to gather together the children of God scattered abroad into one).

54. Dodd says, "The kingship of the Messiah is the sovereignty of the Truth which He reveals and embodies" (Dodd, *Interpretation*, 229).

55. Smalley, *John*, 218.

the Messianic King.[56] In particular, a clear correlation exists between the Christ and the Prophet in John 1:19–34 and the various messianic kingly titles in John 7:10–44.

In addition, the title, "the Lamb of God,"[57] in John 1:29 and 36 (ὁ ἀμνὸς τοῦ θεοῦ), which is announced by John the Baptist, may contain similar implications about the identity and function of Jesus as a triumphal Messiah, namely as a king. Dodd argues that "the Lamb of God" here, in its first intention, is a messianic title virtually equivalent to "King of Israel."[58] Jesus "will take away sin as king and he will enact God's rule and represent God's purpose."[59] Moreover, Petersen remarks that "three expressions, 'only son,' 'Son of God,' and 'Lamb of God,' all refer to Jesus, and . . . they are being used synonymously."[60]

In this context, the christological titles testified to by the lips of John the Baptist, i.e., "the Lamb of God" (1:29, 36), "a Man" (1:30), and "the Son of God" (1:34), indicate the Johannine Jesus. In particular, this term, ἀνήρ (a man), is only used to describe Jesus on one other occasion in John's Gospel—John 4:18.[61] This Man (ἀνήρ), as testified to by John the Baptist as one who existed before him and ranked higher than himself, is the one upon whom the Spirit descended from heaven and remained on. This man who

---

56. Van Bruggen, *Jesus*, 117–18. It is striking that in the Gospel of John, Jesus is identified with the Prophet by people in the crowd (6:14; 7:40–44). But Jesus is never identified with Elijah in the Gospel of John, while other titles, the Prophet, and the Christ were messianic designations in connection with Jesus (see Robinson, "Elijah, John and Jesus," 270).

57. On the background of this term, see Dodd, *Interpretation*, 230–40. The origin of the term, ἀμνός, is problematic. In Jewish literature, the concept of the lamb might be related to that of sacrificial animals, e.g., the Paschal Lamb and the Passover as a type of the death of Christ (Exod 12:5, 46; Num 9:12; cf. Ps 34:20; and John 12:46), that of the lamb of the sin-offering (1 Kgs 25:25; cf. John 10:15; 11:50–52; 17:19; 1 John 2:2), that of the suffering Servant in Isa 53:7 (cf. John 19:9), or the young ram, i.e., the Messiah as King of Israel grounded in apocalyptic symbolism (*1 Enoch* 89; cf. John 1:41, 52). Dodd argues that "the 'Lamb' is the Messiah, and primarily the militant and conquering Messiah; but in the Christian writing, which has in view the historical crucified Messiah, the bellwether of God's flock is fused with the lamb of sacrifice" (see Dodd, *Interpretation*, 232).

58. Dodd, *Interpretation*, 236–38. It is significant that this title, the king of Israel, is accepted as a legitimate title of Christ in the Gospel of John (1:49; 12:13), while it is used only in mockery in Matthew and Mark.

59. Carter, *John*, 58.

60. Petersen, *Gospel of John*, 26.

61. In *1 Enoch* 89: 30, 35–36, a sheep as a leader of the people of God became *a man* and gathered the other flock into one, built a house for the Lord of the sheep, and placed the sheep in it. This is reminiscent of the function of the Johannine Jesus as the good shepherd (see John 10:16; 11:52; 14:2–3).

will baptize in the Holy Spirit (οὗτος ἐστιν ὁ βαπτίζων ἐν πνεύματι ἁγίῳ), is the Lamb of God and the Son of God as well. It is likely that this term is linked to the kingship of Jesus in the Passion Narrative, because it is reminiscent of Pilates reference to Jesus as "this Man" (τοῦ ἀνθρώπου τούτου) in John 18:29 and 19:5 (ὁ ἄνθρωπος). Jesus is accused by the Jewish leaders of being an evildoer in John 18:30 (οὗτος κακὸν ποιῶν). Later they clamour for Pilate to pronounce a sentence of death because Jesus made himself out to be the Son of God (19:7). In the following narrative, Jesus is described as the opponent of Caesar by the lips of the Jewish leaders in 19:12 (Before this Pilate had made efforts to release him, but the Jews cried out, saying, "If you let *this Man* go, you are no friend of Caesar. Anyone who claims to be a king opposes Caesar"; ἐὰν τοῦτον ἀπολύσῃς, οὐκ εἶ φίλος τοῦ Καίσαρος· πᾶς ὁ βασιλέα ἑαυτὸν ποιῶν ἀντιλέγει τῷ Καίσαρι)."

Furthermore, the title "the Lamb of God" is used to identify Jesus as king alongside that of Messiah (1:41; cf. 1:45), the Son of God and the King of Israel (1:49), and the Son of Man (1:51). In addition, the concept of the Lamb of God who takes away the sin of the world could be linked to the concept of the expiatory sacrifice as in the ironic words of Caiaphas (11:50–52), and is explained in 1 John 2:2 (cf. 1 John 3:5).

In the New Testament there are two other uses of the term "lamb (ἀμνός)," in namely Acts 8:32 and in 1 Peter 1:19 as well as John 1:29, 36.[62] This term in Acts 8:32 is used to explain that the Messianic prophecy in Isaiah 53:7[63] is fulfilled in Christ. In addition, in the Revelation of John, a different word for lamb, ἀρνίον,[64] is used to identify the Messiah (5:5 – the Lion of the tribe of Judah, the Root of David; 5:6 – the Lamb). In the Revelation of John, the Lamb is sacrificed (5: 6, 12 – the Lamb that was slain; 7:14 – in the blood of the Lamb) for the redemption of man (5:9 – for you [Lamb] was slain, and you purchased for God with your blood [men] from every tribe, tongue, people, and nation). Furthermore, the Lamb is the leader or shepherd (7:17 – for the Lamb in the center of the throne will rule them, and shall lead them to springs of living waters; cf. Jesus as the Good shepherd in John 10 and as the living water in John 4:13 and 7:37–38). The Lamb stands on Mount Sion (14:1; cf. *4 Ezra* 13 and *1 Enoch* 89:32, 33 – the Messiah who stands on the Mount and wins the war; he makes war against the enemies of God and overcomes them; 17:14 – . . .the Lamb will conquer them, because

---

62. On the Christian view of Messiah as the Savior of his people from their sin, see Acts 5:31; 8:26; Matt 1:21.

63. The Lamb in 1 Pet 1:19 is linked not only to the paschal lamb (Exod 12:46; Num 9:12) but also to that of Isa 53:7 in the LXX.

64. In the Jewish apocalypses, ἀμνός, as well as ἀρήν, κριός and πρόβατον, is used of the bellwether of the flock (Dodd, *Interpretation*, 236).

He is Lord of lords and King of kings. . . .). It is likely, therefore, that the concept of the Lamb in the New Testament is closely linked to the sacrificial work of the Messianic king.

The removal of sin by the Messiah is also expressed in Jewish literature. For example, in the *Psalms of Solomon* 17:29, the Messiah Son of David will remove unrighteousness. In *the Testament of Levi* 18:9, the priestly Messiah will terminate sin; in the *Apocalypse of Baruch* 73:1–4, the Messiah will eliminate all evil. In addition, in *1 Enoch* 89:41–50, which is reminiscent of the story of David, particularly 89:45–46 shows that David is represented as a lamb (ἀρήν) which becomes a ram, a ruler and leader of the sheep (εἰς κριὸν εἰς ἄρχοντα καὶ εἰς ἡγούμενον τῶν προβάτων).[65] In addition, the death of the Messiah in *4 Ezra* 7:28–29 "my son the Messiah . . . my son the Messiah shall die" might be linked to the titles "the Messiah" and "the Lamb of God," as the king who will die for the sin of world.

John 1:35–51

In John 1:35–51, the author reports that some disciples of Jesus confess their beliefs in Jesus as the Messiah[66]: by Andrew, as "the one Moses wrote about in the Law, and about whom the Prophets also wrote—Jesus of Nazareth, the Son of Joseph" by Philip, and as "the Son of God, the King of Israel" by Nathanael. This employment of a series of confessions in the narrative is meant to give more than a survey of messianic titles and designations. It is used to emphasize that they find their true meaning and fulfillment in Jesus. In short, it is likely that various titles employed to designate the identity of Jesus in this narrative seem to be linked with a major common concept, kingship, although it cannot explain all the complexity of the Christology in the Fourth Gospel.

This episode consists of three witnesses to the identity of Jesus, the two disciples of John the Baptist and Nathanael. First, after meeting Jesus together, the two disciples of John the Baptist separately acknowledge Jesus using different terminology. However, their confessions of Jesus both point to his true

---

65. In *1 Enoch* 89, the people of God are represented symbolically as a flock, and its leaders as sheep or rams (cf. *the Testaments of the Twelve Patriarchs, Joseph* 19:8, which was mainly written between BCE 250–100; see also Charlesworth, *Old Testament Pseudepigrapha*, 1:777–78; the figure, the Lamb, symbolizes the coming Messiah; see on the argument on *the Testaments of the Twelve Patriarchs* as an early Christian document, de Jonge, *Jewish Eschatology*, 148–51, 160–63).

66. The title, Christ and Messiah, is used slight differently in the Gospel of John. This title, Christ and Messiah, is used together by people who come to believe in him (1:41) or want to know his identity as more than the Jewish Messiah (4:25, 29).

identity: the Messiah. In this sense, these terms are used to depict the unique Johannine Jesus even though it would be admitted that they have more or less different meanings in the extra Johannine texts. Their confessions are closely linked together in the narrative. Jesus is referred to as Rabbi by the two disciples (John 1:35),[67] but identified as the Messiah in their testimonies. Moreover, the identity of Jesus is revealed at the climax of Nathanael's confession that he is the Son of God and the King of Israel. In this sense, the title, the Christ/Messiah, is also used more clearly to identify the Johannine Jesus as king with "the Son of God, and the king of Israel" (1:50).[68]

Secondly, Andrew witnesses to his brother Simon that "we have found the Messiah" and brings Simon to Jesus. Although there is no record of any confession by Simon himself, the account given shows that Simon agrees with Andrew's declaration in that he receives from Jesus a new name. This means Simon becomes a disciple of Jesus. Later, in John 6:68–69, Simon Peter confesses Jesus as the Holy one of God.[69] His confession of Jesus is the same of that of Andrew, although he does not use the term "the Messiah."

---

67. Nathanael also refers to Jesus as Rabbi (1:49). Bultmann argues that this term, Rabbi, brings out the paradox that the Son of God appears as a Jewish Rabbi (Bultmann, *Gospel*, 1971), 100). On ironic aspects of the notion of Jesus as a Rabbi, see Duke, *Irony*, 71–73.

68. Ashton, *Understanding*, 260–62; Koester, "Messianic Exegesis," 23–34; Koester, *Symbolism*, 40. The title "King of Israel" is related to expectations concerning the coming of a royal messiah, and the title "Son of God" is also messianic. The Hebrew Bible (2 Sam 7:14; Ps 2:2, 6–7) says that the heir to David's throne will be a "son" to God. Schnackenburg has emphasized that the entire passage 1:19–51 is purposely centered on the question of the fulfillment of Jewish messianic expectations in Jesus (see Schnackenburg, *Gospel*, 1:507–14).

69. This title is especially used to refer to God in the Hebrew Bible and in early Judaism; however, it could function as an acceptable title for one of God's servants conjoined with "of God" (see Keener, *Gospel of John*, 697). In some manuscripts ("the Christ" in Tert; "the Christ and the Holy of God" in P66 samss ac2 bo; the Christ and the Son of God in C3 Θ Ψ0250 f1.13 33 R lat sy bomss), this expression is linked to that of 1:49 (the Son of God and the King of Israel), 11:27 (the Christ and the Son of God); cf. 20:31; cf. Matt 16:16 (You are the Christ and the son of the living God); Mark 8:29 (You are the Christ); Mark 1:24; Luke 4:34; Acts 2:14 (the Holy and Righteous one); Acts 2:27 (Thy Holy one, quotation from Ps 16:10). In addition, in John 10:36, this term is linked to the Johannine Jesus who has been sanctified by the Father and sent into the world, and in 17:19, who brings his mission to its God-ordained culmination in consecrating himself as a sacrifice for the world. Moreover, Lindars argues that as the first person "your [God's] holy one" in Ps 16:10 refers directly to "one individual, presumably David," and that in this sense, this term is related to Jesus as the Davidic Messiah (Lindars, *New Testament Apologetic*, 40–42; Lindars, *Gospel*, 276). It is quite probable that Ps 16:10 provides strong evidence of the Holy one of God in terms of the Davidic Messiah. Therefore, it is safe to say that in the Gospel of John, the title "the Holy one of God" is used as a further description of Jesus as the Davidic Messiah.

3. KINGSHIP AND THE JOHANNINE CHRISTOLOGICAL TITLES   81

Finally, this story goes further and more specifically in the words of Philip, who witnesses to Nathanael "we have found the one Moses wrote about in the Law, and about whom the Prophets also wrote—Jesus the Son of Joseph from Nazareth." His confession matches that of Andrew, "we have found the Messiah." The meaning of the Messiah is clarified by the response of Nathanael, who replies, "Nazareth! Can *anything good* come from there?" Nathanael is skeptical about Nazareth as the place from which the Messiah would come. However, his biased thinking is corrected when he meets Jesus. He confesses Jesus as "the Son of God and the King of Israel." In this incident, the identity of Jesus is revealed as the Messiah synonymous with the Son of God and the King of Israel. Thus, Nathanael's confession reveals important messianic implications: "Jesus is the embodiment of the new and true messianic community, and its leader."[70] In this narrative, therefore, a series of christological titles contributes significantly to the depiction of Jesus as king.

John 4

In John 4:25, the Samaritan expectation of the coming of the Messiah is clearly stated. Although the portrait of Jesus is again revealed as the Christ (4:29), his identity is more fully revealed as king, when they confess him as the Savior of the World (4:42).

The Samaritan woman herself expects the coming Messiah to be the one who will tell them all things (4:25).[71] Jesus reveals himself to be the

---

70. Smalley, *John*, 218.

71. It is important to remark that "the expectation of the Prophet like Moses occupied a very important place in Samaritanism, because the Samaritan Pentateuch adds Deut 5:28–29; 18:18–22; and 5:30–31 immediately after Exod 20:21, that is, after the Decalogue" (de Jonge, *Jesus*, 105). This remark shows that messianic belief in Samaritan traditions is closely linked to that of the Prophet like Moses to come, rather than to that of the Davidic messiah. Particularly, the Samaritan messiah is the "Taheb," the "restorer," "the Returning one," a prophet like Moses (on this, see Keener, *Gospel of John*, 619–20; Cullmann, *Christology*, 19; Bruce, *New Testament History*, 37–38; Brown, *Gospel*, 172–73; Purvis, "Fourth Gospel, "161–98; Meeks, *Prophet-King*, 216–57). Barrett argues that the Samaritans, who made messianic use of Deut 18:15, 18, "appear to have thought of Taheb as a teacher but also a political leader" (Barrett, *Gospel*, 239), while MacDonald says that the Samaritans did not expect the Taheb to be a king (MacDoland, *Theology of the Samaritans*, 362). As Samkutty argues that the author of Luke-Acts intends his readers to see the legitimacy of the Samaritan community as part of God's people, an apologetic purpose which he very strongly signals throughout the Samaritan stories (see Samkutty, "Samaritan Mission"), if the Johannine readers "could be expected to catch the allusion, the greater-than-Moses imagery in John 4 would reinforce the picture of Jesus as the Taheb" (Keener, *Gospel of John*, 620; see also

Messiah/Christ to the Samaritan woman (John 4:26).[72] She then reports to the Samaritans that she has met a man who told her all the things that she has ever done (4:29) and asks, "Could this be the Christ?" – the one they were waiting for. At last, the meaning of the Messiah/Christ is clarified in the confessions of the Samaritans at the end of the account, when they confess Jesus as *"indeed* the Savior of the world" (John 4:42), whose title was employed to praise the Roman Emperors.[73] They came to Jesus like those who welcome a king or a victorious general who returns in triumphal procession. This image is more strongly revealed in the episode of Jesus' entry into Jerusalem in chapter 12.[74]

The use of the christological titles in chapter 4 shows that "the interconnections between the particular and the universal aspects of the identity of Jesus are integral to the Johannine Christology."[75] The Samaritan story in chapter 4 relates Jesus to Samaritan tradition and Graeco-Roman conventions as well as Jewish religious tradition. The use of the terms Messiah and Christ in chapter 4, therefore, shows that Jesus fulfills the hopes of these traditions.[76] In addition, the author uses both traditions and Graeco-Roman conventions to describe the distinctive Johannine Jesus as king by using diverse christological titles in the same context. Using christological titles in chapter 4, therefore, is evidence that this Gospel is the product of hybridity

---

Burge, *Anointed Community*, 195). Moreover, Koester argues that "the narrative subsumes Samaritan expectations under the Jewish expression Messiah, since Samaritans did not use the term Messiah or await the coming of someone like David, who was a Jewish king, but expected a prophet like Moses to appear" (Koester, *Symbolism*, 43). In this narrative, therefore, the Johannine Jesus is the one whom the Jews expected as the promised prince of the house of David and at the same time the one whom the Samaritans expected as the prophet like Moses (Bruce, *Gospel*, 111). The Johannine Jesus in this narrative is identified more deeply than the Samaritan messiah, Taheb. The Johannine Jesus is represented as the universal king in this narrative (4:26, 42) who "breaks the socio-religious and ethnico-geographical boundaries of his day and prepares the ground for and anticipates a mission to the Samaritans" (Samkutty, "Samaritan Mission," 268).

72. Jesus accepts here the title Messiah as a self-designation: "I am He, the one who is speaking to you" (Ἐγώ εἰμι, ὁ λαλῶν σοι; cf. LXX of Isa 52:6). The similar expression of "I am He" in John 18:6, 8 reveals the dramatic moment of his authority: "He said to them 'I am He (Ἐγώ εἰμι).' And they drew back and fell to the ground." In addition, in John 9:35–38, Jesus revealed himself as the Son of Man (εἶπων αὐτῷ ὁ Ἰησοῦς, καὶ ἑώρακας αὐτὸν καὶ ὁ λαλῶν μετὰ σοῦ ἐκεινός ἐστιν) to the man born blind and he worshipped (προσεκύνησεν) Jesus.

73. Dodd, *Interpretation*, 239.

74. Here different titles are employed (John 12:13, 15).

75. Koester, *Symbolism*, 42.

76. See Josephus, *Ant.* 18.85–88; de Jonge, *Jesus*, 102–6.

3. KINGSHIP AND THE JOHANNINE CHRISTOLOGICAL TITLES 83

of the multiculture of the first century and that Jesus' hybridentity is also produced by using various titles.

John 7–10

The title "the Christ" in John chapters 7 to 10 is employed in the debates among the crowds about the identity of Jesus, while "the Messiah" is used to reveal Jesus' identity in chapters 1 to 4. This point might show the author's consideration for non-Jewish readers when it is considered that on the one hand he reveals the Christ as the translation of the term, the Messiah (1:41). On the other hand, the term "the Christ" could be more appropriate in showing the various messianic kingly expectations to the various readers in a multicultural, hybridized society, and could be regarded as the broader concept of the kingship of the Johannine Jesus.

1. In John 7:10–52, various views as to the identity of Jesus are expressed by the crowds as they debate among themselves, i.e., a good man vs. a deceiver; the Prophet or the Christ. In the following debate by the crowds, some confess Jesus as the Christ, while others claim that he is the Prophet (7:40). In this episode, the origin of the Christ is the cause of the argument (7:25–27, 42). This title, the Christ, again is linked to the kingship of Jesus. The Christ was known to be the offspring of David and to come from Bethlehem, the town of David. The connection of the Christ and David shows again that the meaning of the Christ is closely related with kingship.

2. In John chapter 9, the parents of the man born blind are afraid of the Jews (the Jewish leaders, mostly the Pharisees in the narrative) because they had already agreed that if anyone should confess Jesus to be Christ, he should be put out of the Synagogue (9:22). They avoid replying to the Pharisees as to how it was that their son could now see. This story implies indirectly that his parents believe in Jesus as the Christ but they would not confess publicly because of their fear of being excommunicated. This episode comes to a climax in Jesus' self-affirmation as the Son of Man and being worshipped by the man born blind (9:35–8). It is striking that in the episode that shows Jesus receiving worship as the son of Man, he is also in reality accepting it as the king because God is the king of the Jews.

3. In John 10:22–40, the Jews ask directly whether or not Jesus is the Christ. In reply, Jesus reveals his identity more specifically: "I and the Father are one" (10:30); "the Father is in me, and I in the Father" (10:38). The Gospel of John reveals the identity of Jesus more clearly as the chapters proceed. The meaning of the Christ in this episode links more strikingly

with the kingship of Jesus. Jesus emphasizes his authority as the king using oneness with God.

John 11:27–37

The confession of Martha, "You are the Christ, the Son of God, who was to come into the world (σύ εἶ ὁ χριστὸς ὁ υἱὸς τοῦ θεοῦ ὁ εἰς τὸν κόσμον ἐρχόμενος)," (11:27) is given immediately after she is told of the raising of her brother by Jesus. Here, the title "the Christ" is given along with "the Son of God" which is similarly expressed in the same formula in John 20:31 (Jesus is the Christ and the Son of God; Ἰησοῦς ἐστιν ὁ χριστὸς ὁ υἱὸς τοῦ θεοῦ) and 6:14 (this man is indeed the Prophet *who comes into the world*; οὗτός ἐστιν ἀληθῶς ὁ προφήτης ὁ ἐρχόμενος εἰς τὸν κόσμον). The meaning of Martha's confession is clarified effectively when Lazarus is raised from death. In this event, Jesus as the Christ and the Son of God shows his authority as the one who rules over death. His power is the same as that of God (cf. 5:19–31; 10:30). The death of Lazarus is for the glory of God as well as for the Son of God (11:4).

This episode is followed by the conspiracy to kill Jesus by the members of the Sanhedrin, Mary's anointing of Jesus, and his entry into Jerusalem.[77] The members of the Sanhedrin conspire to kill Jesus otherwise, the Romans will come and take away both their place and their nation (11:48). Here political and nationalistic perspectives are revealed. They are afraid of Jesus' becoming king but he is anointed as king by Mary (12:18 – the death of Christ is the way to enthrone the king) and enters Jerusalem as the triumphal king. The entry of Jesus into Jerusalem is reminiscent of the enthronement (coronation) of a king in ancient times.

The title "the king of Israel"[78] which appears in the narrative of the triumphal entry of Jesus into Jerusalem highlights his kingship. Strikingly,

---

77. Freed, "Entry into Jerusalem," 332.

78. In the narrative, the great multitude hailed Jesus as the Messiah (He who comes in the name of the LORD) and the King of Israel (12:13). It is meaningful to compare the parallel passages of the Synoptics: In Matthew, Jesus was called the Son of David and the Messiah (21:9). Particularly, Matthew adds that Jesus is referred to as the Prophet by the multitudes in 21:11; In Mark, Jesus was called the Davidic Messiah (11:9); the King as the Messiah in Luke 19:38. The designation "the King of Israel (of the Jews)" refers to He who comes in the name of the LORD, namely, the Davidic kingly Messiah. This term, therefore, is used for "the Messiah, the Son of God" (John 1:49; 12:13; cf. Mark 15:31–32; Luke 19:38). Furthermore, in a number of the extra Johannine texts in the New Testament, the title "Son of God" is employed together with "Son of David" or "Messiah" (Mark 12:35–37; 14:61–62; Rom 1:3–4) (de Jonge, *God's Final Envoy*, 106), and these occurrences of Son of God should be seen in the context of the use of the

the promised figure of the Johannine Messiah is a king, so the recognition of Jesus as the Messiah goes hand in hand with honoring him as king (John 12:13).[79] The Jewish people believe that the signs point to the coming of the Messiah.[80] The multitudes bear witness that what Jesus had done was this sign (12:18).

Although he knows that the Jewish leaders are seeking to seize him (10:39), and to stone him (11:8), Jesus comes across the Jordan again in order to raise Lazarus. The readers must feel the heightening crisis as Jesus performs this miraculous sign demonstrating his power over life and death. Ironically, although Jesus has power to raise a man from death, he himself is seized and killed. This leads the readers to believe that Jesus is not killed because he has no power against the authorities, but rather that his death was a voluntary act to save the world. The raising of Lazarus resulted in divided responses: on the one hand, many people come to believe in Jesus (11:45; 12:11), on the other hand, the Jewish leaders hold a council and decide to kill him (11:47–57). Outwardly, the popularity of Jesus is increasing more and more, but inwardly the shadow of death is growing stronger (11:47–57; 12:11; 12:19).

It is in this situation that Jesus enters Jerusalem to a massively enthusiastic reception by the multitudes who are calling him "the King of Israel," like the procession of a victorious king returned from war, or like the coronation of a king. By contrast, the Pharisees are fearful of his increasing popularity (12:19). Ultimately, Jesus is arrested and killed in Jerusalem but his purpose is to save the world as king.[81] In the trial of Jesus before Pilate, the kingship of the Johannine Jesus is indeed intensified in connection with the origin of Jesus as king.[82] It is evident that the main purpose of putting the accounts in

---

term to denote the Davidic king in the Hebrew Bible (2 Sam 7:11–14; Ps 2:7; 89:3–4; 1 Chr 17:13; 22:10; 28:6; cf. 4QFlor 1:10–14, quoting from 2 Sam 7:11–14 in connection with the "Branch of David," and the much discussed apocalypse 4Q246). The title, the Christ, is, therefore, that of king.

79. In the Gospel of Matthew, the title Son of David often occurs in conjunction with him as the Lord (Matt 9:27–28; 15:22; 20:30–31). In the Jewish traditions, we can find that these two terms are linked (2 Sam 7:10–16, 25–29; Ps 132:11–18—his throne would last forever; Isa 7:14; 9:1–7; 11:1–10; 32:1–8; Mic 5:2–5—a future righteous ruler, a shoot from the stump of the tree that had been cut down; this servant of the LORD will be a most marvellous king; Jer 23:5–8; Ezek 34:23–31—the coming son of David; Mic 5:1—the one is who was born king of the Jews).

80. Dodd, *Interpretation*, 89–90.

81. Smalley, *John*, 219. Smalley remarks that "at one level, then, the kingship of Jesus could be understood and accepted in worldly terms, but at another level the kingship of Jesus was 'not from the world' (18:36; 6:15)."

82. De Jonge, *Jewish Eschatology*, 80.

this particular sequence is to emphasize the kingship of Jesus and to show the increasing crisis of his approaching death. In particular, in comparison with similar passages in the Synoptic Gospels,[83] the title "the King of Israel" is exclusively used in John in order to emphasize his kingship.[84]

To summarise, it is necessary to raise a question again, what did the readers understand by the term "the Messiah/Christ" when they encountered it in the Gospel of John? The Jews familiar with the Hebrew Bible could appreciate it as the figure who was sent by God for special missions.[85] The meaning of the Messiah might be developed in the series of mixtures of Jewish messianic expectations. They hoped that the Messiah would give them solutions to their contemporary problems that arose out of their being a colonized society. In the Gospel of John, Jesus is described frequently as the one who was sent by God (1:41, 45; 7:41–42; 12:34).[86] As a result, Jesus is the Messiah (the anointed one), the long-promised savior, sent by God. If we consider that from ancient times, the king was the religious and political head of the nation, Jewish expectations of the Messiah were a complex of religious and political ideals. Furthermore, considering the fact that Jewish society had long been colonized under various empires, it is likely that the Jews expected that the Messianic king would come, emancipate them, and restore their nation as prophesized in the Hebrew Bible. It is, therefore, quite possible that the contemporaries of the Johannine community regarded the Messiah as the king. Van Bruggen remarks, "the frequent occurrences of the title 'the Christ' in the Gospels are, as far as content is concerned, in keeping with Judaism's scripturally based expectations about a coming divine savior (anointed by God)."[87] Therefore, the introduction and the confession of Jesus as the Messiah with other christological titles in the Gospel of John are closely linked to the revelation of Jesus as the king who is sent by God as the fulfillment of his promises.

83. Cf. "Your king" in Matt 21:5 and the Son of David in 21:9; "he" and the coming kingdom of our father David in Mark 11:9–10; "the King" in Luke 19:38.

84. This term is used in the confession of Nathanael, "You are the Son of God, and the King of Israel" in John 1:49. Furthermore, in the narrative of the crucifixion the title "the King of the Jews" is employed in relation with his kingship.

85. For example, Matthew shows an expectation of the Messianic king among the Jews. In Matt 2:4, Herod asks, "where the Christ was to be born." In this context, however, his question is just a reiteration of the question put by the wise men about "one who has been born king of the Jews." The wise men clearly point to the ruler promised by the prophets. "This is why Herod asks the teachers of the law where 'the *anointed* [king]' is to be born. Here 'the anointed' is an independent (substantival) adjective, used to indicate what sort of king is being referred to" (see van Bruggen, *Jesus*, 138).

86. Koester, *Symbolism*, 42.

87. Van Bruggen, *Jesus*, 138.

Son of God and Kingship

The title "the Messiah" is an exclusively Jewish concept and linked to the fulfillment of prophecy in the Hebrew Bible. However, the other title used in John 20:31, "the Son of God," even if accepted as linked to the Jewish background,[88] is very different in concept from that of the Messiah, when it is read in comparison with Roman imperial titles.[89] The purpose of the study of the title "the Son of God" is to show that, in terms of hybridentity, it was very closely consistent with the background of both Jewish traditions and Roman imperial titles in indicating the kingship of the Johannine Jesus.

The Jewish Background of the Son of God

First, it is necessary to survey briefly the Jewish background of the term. Smalley emphasizes the Jewish background, although he admits there is also a Greek background[90] to the title.[91] He remarks,

> In the Old Testament Israel was chosen by Yahweh to be his "son," and Israel's kings were "sons" of God in the sense of being the representatives of Yahweh's people. Similarly, in Hellenistic Judaism the expression "son of God" could be used of a righteous man who was loyal to God's law.[92]

"The Son of God" is used in both the Hebrew Bible and Jewish literature to identify the people of Israel (Exod 4:22; Deut 32:5-6, 18-19; Jer 31:20; Hos 11:1), the king (2 Sam 7:14; Ps 2:7; 89:26-7), angels (Job 38:7), and the righteous person who lives faithful to the covenant guidelines (*Sir.* 4:10; *Wis.* 2:18; 5:5; *Jub.* 1:24-5; *Ps. Sol.* 17:26-7, cf. 13:8, 18:4). Although the title "the Son of God" could then be used to refer to various figures in the

---

88. On the motif of the Messiah as the Son of God in the Jewish, and especially Qumran, tradition, see Collins, *Scepter and the Star*, 154-72; on the Qumran text about the Son of God, see Collins, "Son of God," 65-82.

89. On the background of the title, see Levin, "Jesus," 418-21; Vermes, *Jesus*, 194-99.

90. On research of the term in Hellenistic background, see Hengel, *Son of God*; Nicol, *Semeia*. In Hellenistic thought, extraordinary men such as sages, statesmen, prophets, and wonder workers were seen as partly divine, as *theioi andres* (Nicol, *Semeia*, 48).

91. Ashton's remark, "Son of God may be the most important—it is certainly the most misunderstood—of all titles," shows that the meaning of the title has been widely debated (see Ashton, *Understanding*, 260).

92. Smalley, *John*, 216. Hengel also points out that the Aramaic text "makes one thing clear, that the title 'Son of God' was not completely alien to Palestinian Judaism" (Hengel, *Son of God*, 45).

Hebrew Bible,[93] it is its usage as the royal messianic son of God (2 Sam 7:14; Ps 2:7)[94] which corresponds in particular with New Testament usage (Mark 13:32; 14:61; 15:39; Matt 11:27; 16:16; Luke 1:31-2, 35, etc). In addition, *1 Enoch* 105:2 (the description of the Messiah as my son) and *4 Ezra* 7:28-29; 13:32, 37, 52; 14:9 are important relevant passages containing the term. In the Qumran writings, the expected royal Messiah could be also linked with the concept of the Son of God (1QSa 2:11-12; 4Q174 1:10-12,[95] where the begetting of the Messiah as the public appointment of Israel's royal savior[96] is closely linked to Jesus as the only begotten son (1:14; 18; 3:16-18). As kings were regarded as the representative of God in the Hebrew Bible (Ps 2:2, 6-7 – the son of God who is anointed to be king of Zion; Ps 45:2-8 – a king anointed by God who is also addressed as God; Isa 7:14 – Immanuel = Mighty God – Isa 11:2; Isa 32:1-8),[97] the Johannine Jesus is the representative "of God's empire who is commissioned to enact these concerns in the present and to accomplish their full enactment in the final yet-future completion of God's purposes."[98] In the Gospel of John, furthermore, this correspondence is more decisive. Particularly, the Johannine way in which Jesus is called "the Son" or "the Son of God" is unique. For example, the distinct use of the terms υἱός and τέκνον in the Gospel of John shows the unique origin and divine sonship of Jesus.[99] In the Gospel, the term υἱός is used exclusively to designate the identity of Jesus in terms of his filial relationship with God the Father, while the other term, τέκνα (1:12; 8:39; 11:52), indicates those who are the children of God through believing in Jesus. The Gospel designates Jesus not only as the Son of God, but also as the Father's Son in terms of the Father-Son relationship. This is in the same way, as a person would be introduced as somebody's son and grandson in the ancient era.[100] According to this introduction formula,

---

93. For example, the children of God; a good Jew; a charismatic holy Jew; the king of Israel; in particular, to the royal Messiah; and an angelic or heavenly being.

94. Vermes, *Jesus and the World of Judaism*, 72; Vermes, *Jesus the Jew*, 194–99.

95. "*The Lord declares to you that he will build you a House* (2 Sam Vii, 11c). *I will raise up your seed after you* (2 Sam Vii, 12). *I will establish the throne of his kingdom [for ever]* (2 Sam Vii, 13). *[I will be] his father and he shall be my son* (2 Sam Vii, 14). He is the Branch of David who shall arise with the Interpreter of the Law [to rule] in Zion [at the end] of time. As it is written, *I will raise up the tent of David that is fallen* (Amos ix, 11). That is to say, the fallen *tent of David* is he who shall arise to save Israel" (Vermes, *Complete Dead Sea Scrolls*, 526).

96. Vermes, *Jesus the Jew*, 198–99.

97. See Smalley, *John*, 216.

98. Carter, *Matthew and the Margins*, 68–69.

99. See Carter, *John*, 60.

100. See Price, *Rituals and Power*, 8–9. A symbolic statement avoids the difficulties

Jesus' origin is from God, who is understood as the true king of Israel and he is the Father's Son. Therefore, the title "the Son of God" has implications of kingship within it.

The Son of God in Roman Imperial Titles and in the Gospel of John

Secondly, research on the title "the Son of God" in relation to the titles of the Roman emperors gives an enhanced meaning to the kingship of the Johannine Jesus.[101] To begin with, it is necessary to indicate that it is likely that the contemporaries of Jesus and the Johannine community understood their messianic king to possess the title, the Son of God, as well as the Roman emperors. The title "Son of God" was connected with the Emperor Augustus as well as being used to refer to other emperors.[102] It is helpful to survey the term "son of god" in the titulature of Roman emperors from Augustus to Domitian to understand the kingship of the Johannine Jesus in relation to this title.

Augustus[103] was called "Emperor Caesar son of god Augustus"[104] while he was still alive ([Α]ὐτοκράτωρ Καῖσαρ Θεοῦ υἱὸς Σεβαστὸς), "god Caesar son of god, Augustus, savior of freedom" (θεοῦ Καίσ[α]|ρος θεοῦ υἱοῦ

---

inherent in either/both literal or/and metaphorical approach. "It does permit us to accept that people mean what they say but it does not entail the crude 'literalist' consequences. People can mean what they say without their statements being fully determinate" (Price, *Rituals and Power*, 9). For example, as a symbolic statement, "Jesus is the Son of God" could be meant literally (Jesus really is [believed in] the Son of God) or metaphorically (Jesus is [only believed] *like* the Son of God). However, the Johannine usage creates a new way, which avoids the weakness of these approaches, being not falsifiable by a literal approach.

101. See Cassidy, *John's Gospel*, 10–16; Carter, *Matthew and Empire*, 1–49; Kim, "Anarthrous," 221–41; Mowery, "Son of God," 100–110; Cook, Adcock, and Charlesworth, *Cambridge Ancient History*; Ehrenberg and Jones, *Documents*; Sherk, *Roman Documents*; Millar and Segal, *Caesar Augustus*; Smallwood, *Documents Illustrating*; McCrum and Woodhead, *Select Documents*; Charlesworth, *Documents Illustrating*. In the Graeco-Roman world, the same term also identifies miracle workers, teachers, kings, and emperors (see Martitz, "υἱός," 336–40; Vermes, *Jesus the Jew*, 200).

102. Deissmann, *Light*, 350.

103. "Augustus was honored as a god in the East during his reign, and some Greek texts hail him as both θεός and θεοῦ υἱός (See *IGRR* I 853; *SIG* III 778; *SEG* XXXIX 752). He was formally designated a *divus* in Rome after his death. His successor and adopted son Tiberius could therefore call himself 'son of god Sebastos'" (Mowery, "Son of God," 102) (*Σεβαστός = Augustus).

104. Sherk, *Roman Documents*, n. 61; Ehrenberg and Jones, *Documents*, n. 99.

Σεβαστοῦ Σωτῆρος Ἐλευθερίου),[105] "the mastery of Caesar son of god" (ἡ καίσαρος κράτησις θεοῦ υἱοῦ),[106] "Caesar son of god, Emperor" (καῖσαρ θεοῦ υἱὸς Αὐτοκράτωρ),[107] "Emperor Caesar son of god, Zeus the liberator, Augustus" (Καίσαρος αὐτοκράτωρ θεοῦ υἱὸς Ζεὺς ἐλευθέριος),[108] and "Emperor Caesar Augustus, savior and benefactor" (Αὐτοκράτωρ Καῖσαρ Σεβαστὸς σωτὴρ καὶ εὐεργέτης).[109] Kim remarks, "it was not mere flattery when people called Augustus savior, lord, god, benefactor, etc. To the minds of ordinary people he was every bit what they called and praised."[110]

Tiberius was hailed as son of the divine Augustus: "of the Emperor Tiberius Augustus, son of Augustus" (Τοῦ αὐτοκράτορος Τιβερίου Σεβαστοῦ υἱοῦ Σεβαστοῦ),[111] "[Tiberius Caesar] child of Augustus" ([Τιβερίῳ Καίσαρος] Σεβάστῳ παίδα),[112] "[Tiberius Caesar, god, Au]gustus, so[n of A]ugustus, chief priest" ([Τιβέριος Καῖσαρ θεοῦ Σεβ]αστοῦ υἱὸ[ς Σ]εβαστὸς ἀρχιερεὺς),[113] "Emperor Tiberius Caesar Augustus, son of god" (Τιβέριος καῖσαρ Σεβαστὸς θεοῦ υἱὸς αὐτοκράτωρ),[114] "Emperor Tiberius Caesar, new Augustus, son of Zeus the liberator" (Τιβέριος Καῖσαρ νέος Σεβαστὸς αὐτοκράτωρ θεοῦ Διὸς ἐλευθερίου),[115] and called a god[116] as well as a "god and son of god Sebastos (Augustus)"[117] (Τιβερίωι Καίσαρι Σεβαστῶι θεῶι θεοῦ Σεβαστοῦ υἱῶι| αὐτοκράτορι ἀρχιερεῖ μεγίστωι δημαρχικῆς ἐξουσίας).[118]

Gaius Caligula was identified as "grandson of Tiberius Caesar" and "descendent of god Sebastos" (θεοῦ Σεβαστοῦ ἔγγονος; [Αὐτοκ]ράτωρ Σεβαστὸς Καῖσαρ, θεοῦ Σεβαστοῦ ἔ[γγ]ονος, Τιβερίου Καί[σα|ρος υἱ]

---

105. *SEG* XI 922–3; Ehrenberg and Jones, *Documents*, n. 102; Deissmann, *Light*, 350.

106. PRyl 601; PSI 1150.

107. PTeb 382.

108. POslo 26; *SB* 8824.

109. *SB* 8897.

110. Kim, "Anarthrous," 237.

111. *IGRR* IV. 206; Ehrenberg and Jones, *Documents*, no. 93.

112. *IG* XII. 2, 540; Ehrenberg and Jones, *Documents*, no. 94.

113. *SEG* XI. 922–3; Ehrenberg and Jones, *Documents*, no. 102.

114. *SB* 8317.

115. POxy 240.

116. *SEG* XXXVI 1092, *IGRR* III 715; IV 144; Burnett, Amandry, and Repolles, *Roman Provincial Coinage*, 1:2344–46.

117. See also *IGRR* I 659; III 933 (cf. *IGRR* III 721).

118. *OGIS* 583; Ehrenberg and Johnes, *Documents*, no. 134.

3. KINGSHIP AND THE JOHANNINE CHRISTOLOGICAL TITLES 91

ωνός).[119] Claudius was honored as god in the East during his lifetime,[120] i.e., "Claudius god" (θεὸς Κλαύδιος),[121] "Caesar god" (θεὸς Καῖσαρ)[122], and he was affirmed a *divus* in Rome after his death.[123]

During the reign of Nero, the emphasis on the divine sonship of the emperor reappeared. Nero was called "the lord" (Νέρων ὁ κύριος),[124] "Lord of the whole world' (ὁ τοῦ παντὸς κόσμου κύριος Νέρων),[125] "Nero Claudius Caesar . . . the savior and benefactor of the inhabited world" (Νέρων Κλαύδιος Καῖσαρ . . . ὁ σωτὴρ καὶ εὐεργέτης τῆς οἰκουμένης),[126] "Nero Caesar the lord" (Νέρων Καῖσαρ ὁ κύριος),[127] "The good god of the inhabited world, the beginning of all good things" ('Αγαθὸς Δάιμων τῆς οἰκουμένης ἀρχὴ ὤν τε πάντων ἀγαθῶν),[128] "descendant of god Sebastos" (θεοῦ Σεπαστοῦ ἀπέγονος/ἔγγονος),[129] and "son of the god Claudius" (θεοῦ Κλαυδίου υἱός).[130]

Vespasian was consecrated as *divus* in Rome after his death ["Vespasian god" (θεὸς Οὐεσπασιανός)].[131] As a result, his sons Titus and Domitian could each claim to be "son of god Vespasian." He was also acclaimed as lord ["Vespasian the lord" (Οὐεσπασιανὸς ὁ κύριος)].[132] Titus in turn was deified and designated as a *divus* after his death. He could be simultaneously hailed as both "god" and "son of god Vespasian" ["son of god Vespasian"[133] (θεοῦ

---

119. *ILS* 8792; *IG* VII, 2711; Smallwood, *Documents*, no. 361. See also, *IGRR* IV 1094 – "new god" (νέωι θεῶι); *CIA* III 444a – "son of Ares" (Ἄρηος υἱόν); *CIA* III 444 – "son of Augustus, a new Ares" (Σεβαστοῦ υἱὸν νέον Ἄρη).

120. *POxy* 2555; *SEG* XXXVII 1221 (Smallwood, *Documents*, no. 135: Τιβέριον Κλαύδιον Καίσαρα Γερμανικὸν αυτο|κράτορα θεὸν Σεβαστὸν).

121. *PSI* 1235; *POxy* 713; *PMich* 244 – "Augustus god" (θεὸς Σεβαστός). About Lord, see *SB* 4331 – "Tiberius Claudius lord" (Τιβέριος Κλαύδιος κύριος); *OPetr* 209 – "The lord" (ὁ κύριος).

122. *POxy* 808; *POxy* 1021.

123. "By the grace of the god Claudius" in *IGRR* I 126 (See Mowery, "Son of God," 102–3).

124. *PLond* 1215; *POxy* 246; *GOA* 1038.

125. *SIG* 814.

126. *OGIS* 668.

127. *OPetr* 288; *POxy* 246.

128. *POxy* 1021.

129. *SEG* IX 352; Charlesworth, *Documents*, Part II, no. 4b.

130. *ILS* 8793; *IGRR* IV 1124; *SIG* 810; Smallwood, *Documents*, no 412(b).

131. *POxy* 257; *POxy* 1112. See also *GOA* 439.

132. *POxy* 1439; *SB* 1927.

133. See also *IGRR* IV 1599 and *IGRR* III 724 – θεοῦ υἱός; cf. *IGRR* IV 846.

Οὐεσπασιανοῦ υἱός),[134] "god" and "son of god Vespasian" (θεοῦ Τίτου; Τίτον αὐτοκράτορα θεὸν θεοῦ Οὐεσπασιανοῦ υἱὸν Σεβαστόν).[135] Domitian was also acclaimed as "son of god Vespasian" (θεοῦ Οὐεσπασισανοῦ υἱός).[136]

Kim argues that none of the emperors who followed Augustus officially claimed to be called *divi filius* (or θεοῦ υἱὸς), and "this seems to support the view that *divi filius* (or θεοῦ υἱὸς) was not a title that could be applied to the Roman emperor in general."[137] Mowery, however, shows that this title was employed to designate Roman emperors such as Augustus, Tiberius, Nero and Domitian.[138] Levin also argues that "like Julius Caesar, Vespasian too was deified posthumously, making his sons Titus and Domitian into *divi filii*."[139] Therefore, it is likely that "the term υἱός θεοῦ would have been familiar to the Gospel's Gentile readers."[140]

In the Gospel of John, the basis for such an indication is particularly revealed in the passion narrative. The Jewish leaders accuse Jesus because he has claimed to be the Son of God (John 19:7). In addition, the Jewish leaders cry out that they have no king except Caesar (19:15; cf. 19:12; 18:36–37). In this context (18:28–19:16 – the trial of Jesus before Pilate), the Son of God is clearly revealed in the image of a king like the Roman emperors. At his trial, Jesus clearly states that he is a king, but that his kingdom does not belong to this world (18:36–37), while the Jewish leaders regard him as a rebel against the Empire. The narrator reports that when Pilate heard from the Jewish leaders that "Jesus made himself out to be (the) Son of God," he was the more afraid (19:8),[141] perhaps because this title reminded him of that of the emperor. Then, the narrative shows

---

134. *IGRR* III 690; IV 211; cf. *IGRR* IV 845; McCrum and Woodhead, *Select Documents*, no. 199.

135. *SEG* XXXIX 1388; *IGRR* IV 211; McCrum and Woodhead, *Select Documents*, no. 111, 138(b), 136.

136. *SEG* XXVII 1009–1010; McCrum and Woodhead, *Select Documents*, no. 121, 123, 436. cf. *IGRR* IV 1939; See also θεοῦ υἱός in Burnett, Amandry, and Repolles, *Roman Provincial Coinage*, II, 1727–28, 1746–49, 1752–56, 2598–2601, 2603–2605, 2610, 2615, 2619, 2657, 2667, 2671–78, 2694–2713, 2721–33, 2735, 2771–74, 2777–81; cf. also 2652, 2775–76.

137. Kim, "Anarthrous," 234–35.

138. See Mowery, "Son of God," 100–110.

139. Levin, "Jesus," 420–21; see also Scott, *Imperial Cult*, 1–60; Davies, *Death and the Emperor*, 22—"*Senats Populusqe Romanus Divo Tito Divi Vespasiani F. Vespasiano Augusto* (The Senate and People of Rome to the deified Titus Vespasian Augustus, son of the deified Vespasians)."

140. Levin, "Jesus," 419.

141. Now when Pilate heard this, *he was more afraid than ever* (Ὅτε οὖν ἤκουσεν ὁ Πιλᾶτος τοῦτον λόγον, μᾶλλον ἐφοβήθη).

that the Jewish leaders directly compare Jesus with Caesar in order to push Pilate (19:12, 15) to sentence Jesus to death.

In this narrative, the crucifixion plays the clearest role in revealing the universal kingship of Jesus.[142] The narrative reports that Pilate wrote an inscription on the cross, "Jesus the Nazarene, the king of the Jews," in Hebrew, Latin, and Greek (19:19-20). Ironically, when the Johannine readers read this statement they would see more clearly that Jesus was the true king to follow. It is likely, therefore, that John employs the title "the Son of God" in order to transfer to Jesus this title that belonged to Augustus and the other emperors so that his readers would reconsider who was their real king. In confessing Jesus as the Christ and the Son of God, the Gospel shows more clearly that God, not Rome, sent him into the world for a specific purpose: to reign as king. In short, it is quite probable that the title "the Son of God" which represents a hybridized concept from a multitude of cultures is, among other purposes, used in the Gospel to reveal the kingship of Jesus.

The Christ and the Son of God in the Gospel of John

Thirdly, in order to clarify the identity of the Johannine Jesus, it is important that the titles "the Christ" and "the Son of God," are used together twice in the Gospel of John (11:27; 20:30-31) to indicate the identity of Jesus.[143] What is the role of this phrase in this Gospel? Is there any special meaning attached to the phrase, "the Christ, the Son of God," given in this Gospel when the titles are used together? In other words, how would the contemporaries of the Johannine community as the readers of the Gospel, and living under Roman rule understand the title "the Son of God" in relation to the title "the Christ"?

The title "the Christ" seems to be used as a synonym for "the Son of God" in when applied to Jesus in the Gospel of John (11:27; 20:30-31).[144]

---

142. Koester, *Symbolism*, 125.

143. See Matt 26:63; Mark 14:61; cf. Luke 22:66-70.

144. De Jonge, *Jesus*, 2-3; Ashton, *Understanding*, 260-61. Ashton argues that "in all probability this title . . . Son of God, originally indicated messiahship," that is, the title, the Son of God, would seem a natural one to use of the Messiah because the king is addressed by God in Ps 2:7 and of the assurance to David that God would continue to favor his descendants (2 Sam 7:14). He concludes, "The term 'Son of God' was, at least in its early Christian usage, a messianic title." In addition, van Bruggen argues, "The *name* 'Son of God' came into the world after the incarnation. Only then can we understand how for Jesus' contemporaries the terms 'Christ' and 'Son of God' virtually coincide" (van Bruggen, *Son of God*, 146). De Jonge argues, "In the Fourth Gospel 'Son of God' and 'Son' are the most important titles, and that also the title 'Christ' is explained in terms of divine sonship" (de Jonge, *Jewish Eschatology*, 81; see also de Jonge,

Although the use of the term "the Christ" clearly presupposes the Jewish use of the term, it can be shown that it does not fully encompass the identity of the Johannine Jesus to readers in a multicultural society.[145] It is likely, therefore, that the two titles were employed together to clarify further the identity of the Johannine Jesus. As de Jonge argues, "these two designations belong together, and the second helps to determine the meaning of the first (cf. also Mark 14:61–62)."[146] In addition, it is not only in the Hebrew Bible, but also in the New Testament, that the title "the Christ" relates closely to the designation of the Son of God.[147] Cassidy remarks,

> This title [the Christ, the Son of God] may well have delineated an aspect of Jesus' sovereignty that was particularly meaningful to Jewish readers of the Gospel (that Jesus is the Christ, the long-awaited Messiah) and an aspect that would have been especially meaningful for those readers from a Gentile background (that Jesus is the exalted Son of God).[148]

These two titles, therefore, could be used together for a variety of readers from diverse backgrounds, to reveal the fuller meaning of the identity of Jesus as king in the Gospel.[149]

In addition, as the messiahship of Jesus has been presented in connection with the kingship motif, another series of titles, "the Son of God, and the King of Israel,"[150] as confessed by Nathanael, shows more directly

---

"Jewish Expectations," 246–70).

145. See de Jonge, *Jewish Eschatology*, 73.

146. de Jonge, "Christology," 216.

147. de Jonge, *Jewish Eschatology*, 135–44; van Bruggen, *Jesus*, 142. For example, in the Gospel of Matthew, Peter confessed Jesus as the Christ, the Son of the living God (Matt 16:16; cf. Matt 26:63; Mark 15:31–32—Jesus is the Christ, the Son of God by the high priest).

148. Cassidy, *John's Gospel*, 72.

149. Ashton, *Understanding*, 241–44. Ashton remarks that "[Within] Messiah and Son of God, lies a rich and complex range of meaning." He continues his argument that John and the Johannine community are "the right inheritors of the whole biblical tradition," and "so it is important to insist that the Fourth Gospel shares this intelligibility, this rootedness in a rich cultural heritage. This is where the study of Jesus' messianic titles belong, since with their necessary emphasis upon fulfillment they balance out the ideas of strangeness, alienation, and unbridgeable distance that have to be included in any complete account of Johannine Christology." Schnackenburg remarks, that "he is the *Messiah*, the Son of God, that is, he is Messiah to the extent that he is the Son of God, and the Son of God in his messianic ministry" (Schnackenburg, *Gospel*, 3:333). On the close relationship among the titles of Christ and Jewish messianism, see Horbury, *Jewish Messianism*, 140–52.

150. This title would also be a synonym to the Messiah in the Gospel (See Dahl, "Johannine Church," 127).

3. KINGSHIP AND THE JOHANNINE CHRISTOLOGICAL TITLES 95

the kingship of Jesus and carries messianic overtones. Jesus is the king of the new world.[151] De Jonge argues, "the title 'king of Israel' is not rejected as unsuitable but, again, reinterpreted."[152] Therefore, to understand Jesus as the Son of God and the King of Israel, gives new insight into him as the king whose kingship is not of this world (18:36). Jesus acknowledges himself a king before both a Jew, Nathanael (the Son of God and the King of Israel) and a gentle, Pilate (the Son of God and the King of the Jews), although his kingship holds a different meaning from that of the world's view.

In summary, it is quite probable that Jesus is designated as the king through the use of these titles in the Gospel and regarded as such by John's first century readership, which combined both Jewish and Roman points of view.[153]

Son of Man and Kingship

The Johannine usage of the title "Son of Man"[154] can also be regarded as, at least in part, a product of a hybridized society in the first century. Burkett[155] categorizes three basic views advocated by scholars concerning the background or origin of the term "Son of Man" as used in John: (1) the designation is completely explicable from its usage in Jewish apocalyptic literature, specifically Dan 7:13, *1 Enoch* 37--71, and *4 Ezra* 13 (Bernard; Smalley; Moloney); (2) the expression is derived from some background other than Jewish apocalyptic literary use (Abbott; Cullmann; Bultmann; Borsh; Lindars); (3) the designation itself is derived from Jewish apocalyptic, but the

---

151. In this passage, the author of the Gospel connects them with the designation "Son of Man." This connection shows all of the titles are related to one another to identify Jesus more fully.

152. De Jonge, *Jesus*, 60. "Obviously the true meaning of Jesus' kingship can only be understood . . . after his glorification, that is, after his death, resurrection, return to his Father, and the sending of the Spirit (see 12:23; 7:1; cf. 2:22; 7:39; 14:26; 16:13–15; 20:9)."

153. The Jewish readers as well as the non-Jewish readers could associate the kingship of Jesus with the Johannine Christological titles because of their royal and imperial backgrounds.

154. For a discussion of the Johannine Son of Man, see Higgins, *Jesus*, 153–84; Freed, "Son of Man," 402–06; Smalley, "Johannine Son of Man," 278–301; Lindars, "Son of Man," 43–60; Maddox, "Function," 186–204; Moloney, *Johannine Son of Man*; Burkett, *Son of the Man*; Kovacs, "Now Shall the Ruler," 227–47; Casey, *Is John's Gospel True?* On the general discussions of the Son of Man, see Schweizer, "Son of Man," 119–29; Black, "Jesus," 4–18; Vermes, "'Son of Man,'" 19–32; Casey, "General, Generic and Indefinite," 21–56; Casey, "Method," 17–43; Goulder, "Psalm 8," 18–29; Casey, "Aramaic Idiom," 3–32.

155. Burkett, *Son of the Man*, 16–37.

ideas associated with it have been modified under the influence of some non-apocalyptic figure (Kümmel; Dodd; Higgins; Talbert; Burkett). Many scholars have made their own connection of the Johannine Son of Man with other cultural backgrounds. This point shows that the use of the Johannine Son of Man, which could be linked to a variety of origins and backgrounds, seems to be one of the author's strategies for his multicultural readers of the first century. Lindars insists, "the use of the title is not accidental, because it provides him with the means to express the relationship of Jesus to God."[156] In addition, Dodd comments that John has entirely refashioned this title as a specific Son of Man Christology.[157] Maddox also says that the Gospel of John "will show us how Jesus' teaching about himself as Son of Man looked from John's perspective."[158]

In addition, there has been a "Son of Man debate" among scholars about its origin and meaning. As Black comments, there has been "no consensus of New Testament scholars that 'son of man' can be a substitute for the first person pronoun in Aramaic, and consequently the source of this enigmatic Gospel locution, and eventual messianic title."[159] It seems that we can state two main positions, which we may call the concept theory and the Aramaic theory,[160] although there have been a variety of other views regarding the origin of the title.

In particular, Vermes argues and "a/the son of man" was a periphrasis for "I,"[161] and many scholars follow his view with their own different emphases. For Lindars[162] "a/the son of man" could be used for a category of people of whom the speaker was one, but from whom he wished to distance himself. In addition, Casey says, "A Greek-speaking audience would understand it as indicating that Jesus was the outstanding member of mankind, and with 'son of God' . . . the understanding of 'son of man' as a reference to Christ's human nature could not fail to occur eventually."[163] They argue that *bar nasha* is a self-designation, when applying a general statement to himself in everyday Aramaic use, but they seem not to agree whether the Son of Man is a title. However, Dodd argues,

---

156. Lindars, "Son of Man," 44.
157. See Dodd, *Interpretation*, 231–49.
158. Maddox, "Function," 189.
159. Black, "Jesus," 8–9.
160. Lindars, "Son of Man," 642; Goulder, "Psalm 8," 18.
161. Vermes, "'Son of Man,'" 19–32.
162. Lindars, *Jesus*.
163. Casey, *From Jewish Prophet*, 54; see also, Casey, "Aramaic Idiom," 3–32.

> [I]n many of the sayings, "Son of Man" could be replaced by "I" or "me" without apparent change of meaning. . . . If Jesus thus employed a familiar way of speaking, not just casually but in circumstances which made it the vehicle of a partly veiled assertion of his vocation, then "Son of man" came to be something like a self-designation replacing the traditional title of "Messiah." That is how the writers of the gospels seem to have understood it.[164]

In these circumstances, it is necessary to examine the meaning of the Johannine use of the designation Son of Man for Jesus, because the title has been reshaped "to serve the Evangelist's distinctive emphases."[165]

The Son of Man and the Son of God in the Gospel of John

The title "the Son of Man" (ὁ υἱὸς τοῦ ἀνθρώπου), is used to express the identity of Jesus in all the canonical Gospels.[166] The title "the Son of God" is the determining christological title, which is clarified by its association with "the Christ" (20:31) in the Gospel of John. It is used to refer to both the anointed king in the Jewish tradition and as the Imperial royal title. Nevertheless, in the context of the Gospel, and certainly after John 1:18, it must have a deeper meaning in relation to the cognate title "the Son of Man."[167]

Its deeper meaning is linked with Jesus' reference to himself as the Son of Man who has come down from heaven, who will be in permanent contact with God in heaven, and has the ultimate authority (1:18-51; 3:13; 9:35). Brown comments,

---

164. Dodd, *Founder*, 111, 112, 113-14. Fitzmyer and his followers (P. Owen and D. Shepherd) argue that in the first century this term was not a common expression for generic man (Fitzmyer, "Contribution," 382-407, 397, n. 1; Shepherd and Owen, "Speaking Up," 81-122). The Son of Man debate is still ongoing among the scholars without any obvious agreement.

165. Lincoln, *Gospel*, 66.

166. Casey, *From Jewish Prophet*, 47; see also Casey, "Aramaic Idiom," 3-32. Van Bruggen argues, "The self-referential term 'Son of Man' belongs to the way Jesus referred to himself while on earth. . . . The phrase is simply part of Jesus' way of referring to himself in reaction to the way others saw him and rejected him as the Son of God" (Van Bruggen, *Jesus*, 112-13). In fact, the difficulty of interpretation of the title, the Son of Man, is that "only Jesus ever uses the expression, always of himself, with an air of mystery but without explanation" (Goulder, "Psalm 8," 19).

167. de Jonge, *Jesus*, 59. Moloney argues that the important Johannine characteristic of the Son of Man, which makes different meaning from the traditional idea as the reinterpretation of Dan 7:13, is that Jesus as the Son of a Man is "the incarnate revelation of God among men" (Moloney, *Johannine Son of Man*, 216).

[S]ignificantly, in 1:51 Jesus uses "the Son of Man" as a deepening improvement of the titles given by his disciples throughout the chapter (Messiah, the one described in the Mosaic Law, and the prophets, Son of God, King of Israel), but none of those titles is repudiated.[168]

The titles "the Son of Man" and "the Son of God" in this Gospel are closely related, that is, they are used interchangeably in some cases.[169] The Son of Man is found where Jesus is also identified as the Son of God in the Gospel of John (3:13–21; 5:19–29; cf. 1:50–51; 12:34[170]). Both terms, for example, could be related with that of "the Son"[171] which is used to designate Jesus as the Son of the Father in terms of Father-Son relationship (3:35; 5:21, 23, 26), and could be interchangeable in the Gospel of John. Jesus as the Son (of the Father) (1:14, 18, 3:16–17) is co-equal with the Father (10:30), has the power and authority to grant eternal life to those who believe (3:35–36; 5:24–26). He also has authority to execute judgment (5:27). In this way, Jesus as the Son of Man is the judge (5:27), and the life-giver (3:14–15; 6:27; 6:53). In addition, Jesus both as the Son of Man (12:23; 13:31) and the Son of God (11:4) will be glorified, even by the Father (14:13). Likewise, these titles are employed to clarify the identity of the Johannine Jesus. The Gospel presents Jesus as both the life-giver and the judge, using the Son (of God/of Man).

---

168. Brown, *Introduction*, 257.

169. Kim, *The "Son of Man"*, 5; Burkett, *Son of the Man*, 95–99; Barrett, *Gospel*, 73. De Jonge argues that as the very unusual Greek expression, and as a Semitic idiom, this title "the Son of Man" would become an unsuitable designation to explain the identity of Jesus to non-Jewish readers (de Jonge, *God's Final Envoy*, 87). So, another title would be needed to give fuller understanding of the Johannine Jesus, as Smalley argues that "the use of two titles for Jesus at this point indicates the 'double' nature of John's audience (Jewish as well as Greek)" (Smalley, *John*, 215–16); For research on *Theios Aner* from Hellenistic texts, see Painter, *Quest*, 10–16; Holladay, *Theios Aner*.

170. Here, the Son of Man is used to indicate the Christ.

171. It is likely that it is not simply an abbreviated form of "the Son of God" (see Burkett, *Son of Man*, 97). Freed suggests the synonymy of the Johannine Christological titles. Particularly, Freed argues, "The title Son of man is only a variation for at least two other titles, namely, the Son of God and the Son. And this means, therefore, that there is no separate Son of man Christology in the fourth gospel" (Freed, "Son of Man," 403). Lincoln also argues, "Son of Man language tends to become assimilated to the more dominant Son of God or Son terminology. . . . Son of Man can also take on some of the connotations of this Gospel's distinctive Son of God Christology" (Lincoln, *Gospel*, 66).

The Son of Man and the Christ in the Gospel of John

In addition to interchangeable usage between these titles, the Son of Man and the Son of God, it is obvious that the two terms, the Son of Man and the Christ, are used to clarify the identity of the Johannine Jesus.[172] Martyn pursues John's attitude toward the identification of Jesus as the Mosaic Prophet-Messiah, which recalls kingship as well as the Son of Man in different stages of the drama, in "a two-level drama."[173] According to Martyn, the identification of Jesus as the Son of Man occupies the central stage in the Gospel of John.[174] In John 12:34, these titles "the Christ" and "the Son of Man," in particular when "the Son of Man" comes after "the Christ," are used together to identify Jesus. Dodd argues, "the evangelist has brought together here most of what he has to say in reply to Jewish objections against the messianic claims made for Jesus."[175] In addition, de Jonge argues, "John wants to make clear that the Jewish Messiah-concept is fixed—it is connected with the expectation of the Davidic king."[176] Schnackenburg also remarks that the questions about the Son of Man by the people show that the contemporaries of the Gospel might have known that the Son of Man

---

172. There also are many different views on the understanding of the Son of Man in terms of Messiah. Moloney contends that the Johannine Son of Man is "not a convenient messianic term"; rather, he views the Johannine Son of Man as a product of "the continuation of a dynamic growing interpretation of Dan. 7.13." Moloney accepts the possibility of John's link with the traditional Son of Man and the humanity of the Johannine Son of Man (see Moloney, *Johannine Son of Man*, 217–20). Higgins argues that the Johannine Son of man tradition is of Palestinian origin, but there are also affinities with the Hellenistic idea of the heavenly Man (Higgins, *Jesus*, 153–84; see also Dodd, *Interpretation*, 243). Smalley also emphasizes the humanity of Jesus in relation to this title. He argues that the title designates Jesus as the ideal Man, saying, "The Son of Man in this theology is not a superhuman figure with supernatural trappings" (see Smalley, "Johannine Son of Man," 278–301; Smalley, *John*, 212–14). However, Bousset argues that the Johannine Son of Man is a "comprehensive designation of the preexistent and eternal glory of Jesus, which surpasses everything earthly, in comparison with which the earthly sojourn of Jesus is only an episode" (Bousset, *Kyrios Christos*, 213). Cullmann also concludes that the Son of Man Christology in John is a basic way of expressing their faith in Jesus (Cullmann, *Christology*, 187); see also Higgins, *Jesus*, 155.

173. See Martyn, *History and Theology*, 101–43

174. Martyn emphasizes the shift of the titles in order to clarify the identification of Jesus through the change of the historical situations of the Johannine community (Martyn, *History and Theology*, 128).

175. Dodd, *Interpretation*, 346.

176. De Jonge, *Jesus*, 95. On the occurrences of the two terms, Messiah and the Son of Man, together in Jewish literature, see De Jonge, "Χρίω," *TDNT* 9:514–6. Dan 7:13, 1 Enoch 37–71, and 4 Ezra 13 are the background of the term, the Son of Man, in Jewish apocalyptic literature.

is closely related to the Christ.[177] The term, the Son of Man, in John 12:34 is indirectly linked to John 8:28. It will not be until after the Jewish leaders have lifted up the Son of Man that they will realize the truth of Jesus' claims. It is also in this Gospel that Jesus is identified in terms of a complex relationship between the titles, the Christ and the Son of Man.

The Ascending and Descending Motif of the Son of Man as an Expression of Jesus' Kingship

Thirdly, the thirteen uses of the title[178] in the Gospel of John are employed to explain the identity of Jesus. The following terms in the Gospel are employed to describe the descending and ascending motif with reference to Jesus[179] (lifted up,[180] raised, glorification of Jesus as king); to describe him as the judge,[181] the life-giver (6:27), and furthermore as the object of belief and worship (9:35–39[182]). In short, the title "the Son of Man" is employed in connection with Jesus' suffering and glorification as the process of the enthronement of the king (his return to the kingly throne),[183] and his

---

177. Schnackenburg, *Gospel*, 1:531.

178. Schnackenburg remarks, "All thirteen texts in John which speak of the Son of Man form a consistent and well-knit whole" (Schnackenburg, *Gospel*, 1:532).

179. 1:51; 2:22; 3:13–14; 6:33, 38, 62; 8:28; 12:34; 13:31; 20:9, 17. Meeks argues, "There is a curiously close connection throughout the Gospel between this title and the descent/ascent language" (Meeks, "Man from Heaven," 52); see also Higgins, *Jesus and the Son of Man*, 153–84. On the background of the descent motif, see Reinhartz, *Word in the World*, 105–31.

180. Lindars links this verb, lifted up, to the suffering servant prophecy in Isa 52:13 (LXX: the servant of the Lord will be lifted up and glorified (ὑψωθήσεται καὶ δοξασθήσεται) (Lindars, *Jesus Son of Man*, 146).

181. 5:27 (cf. 9:39); 3:13–21; 5:22; 8:15–29; 12:31–36.

182. Here, the worship of the man born blind of Jesus as the Son of Man clarifies his kingship. The Son of Man is the final, central title in chapter 9.

183. Petersen, *Gospel of John*, 70. Petersen remarks, "Jesus' death is a part of the process of the Son of Man's return whence he came, which is a metaphor for the reintegration of the Other." Kovacs ("Now Shall the Ruler," 244–46), Meeks (*Prophet King*, 61–81), and Schnackenburg (*Gospel*, 3:268) interprets the glorification of Jesus/death of Jesus as the enthronement of the king in the Gospel of John. Borgen's research on Philo and the Revelation of John in terms of the kingship of Jesus gives another important point. He argues, "To Philo the people of God was the Jewish nation, while John the Seer expressed the conviction that this role had been transferred to the multinational people of God who had been established through the death of Jesus Christ" (see Borgen, "Moses," 145–59). The death of Jesus implies his universal kingship in the Gospel, and the non-sectarian feature of the Gospel (on this, see chapter 6 of this book). Lindars remarks that the crucifixion of Jesus as the Son of Man "refers to exaltation in an honorific sense" and "includes the idea of the healing effect of the passion, even supplying

authority in judgment and the granting of eternal life. The title, the Son of Man, therefore, which "embraces the total work of Jesus,"[184] is the only title Jesus applies to himself in the Gospel.[185]

It is now necessary, therefore, to investigate the relationship between the kingship motif of Jesus and the motif of the ascending and descending of the Son of Man in the Gospel of John.[186] The latter motif is well defined and developed throughout the Gospel. First, for example, the purpose of the descending of Jesus is described in the Prologue through the coming of the Incarnate Logos. Secondly, Jesus reveals himself as the Son of Man on whom the angels of God ascend and descend (1:51). Thirdly, in the dialogue with Nicodemus, he declares that although no one has ascended into heaven, the Son of Man who has descended from heaven must be lifted up just as Moses lifted up the serpent in the wilderness in order to give eternal life to those who will believe (3:13–15).[187] In the early part of the Gospel, the purpose of the descending of the Son of Man is emphasized, but gradually that of the ascending of the Son of Man becomes the center of emphasis.[188]

The motif of Jesus' descending and ascending is closely related to the open door of his kingdom and the gathering in of his people (10:16), and to his return to the realm above where his throne is (14:1–4).[189] This scheme explains why the death of Jesus is not a failure of his mission but it is the way

---

the notion of giving life" (Lindars, *Jesus Son of Man*, 145–47). Therefore, according to Lindars, Jesus' death is as an act of union with the Father's will as well as the cosmic victory over the power of evil. Koester comments on the death of Jesus as the revelation of his own love for others as well as God's love for the world (see Koester, *Symbolism*, 42).

184. Cullmann, *Christology*, 137. Cullmann emphasizes the significance of the Son of Man Christology for the Fourth Gospel rather than that for the Synoptics, making the connection with esoteric Judaism, Jesus, the Hellenists, and the Gospel of John (See Cullmann, *Christology*, 181–88).

185. Casey, "Aramaic Idiom," 3. Brown raises curious features about the title: "no person addresses Jesus by this title, and Jesus never explains its meaning. When the question comes up as to who Jesus is, 'the Son of Man' is never suggested by others as an identification of him" (Brown, *Introduction*, 253).

186. For research on this motif in the Gospel of John, see, Borgen, *Logos*, 133–48; Nicholson, *Death as Departure*.

187. In the dialogue, the role of Nicodemus must not be underestimated. Meeks links Nicodemus' confession of Jesus as the one who has come from God with that of the man born blind healed by Jesus in chapter 9:16–17 and 20–33 (Meeks, "Man from Heaven," 54). In addition, Nicodemus defends Jesus before the Jewish leaders (7:50–51). Lastly, he buries Jesus in a new tomb in a garden with Joseph of Arimathea (19:39).

188. This motif, the ascending and descending of the Son of Man, is shown from the early stage of the Gospel of John (1:51).

189. Kovacs, "Now Shall the Ruler," 244–46; on the house of the Father as the new kingdom of Jesus, see chapter 6 of this book.

of the establishment of his kingdom which is not of this world (18:36). In addition, the lifting up of Jesus like that of the exposure of the bronze snake (Num 21:8-9), implies the crucifixion of Jesus (12:32), and the revelation of the identity of Jesus as the king (19:17-22), which results in his drawing all men (πάντας) to himself (12:32-33). Therefore, it is closely linked to "the hour" of the glorification the Son of Man (12:23; 13:1; 17:1).[190]

In short, Jesus comes into the world to save by being lifted up and gives eternal life to those who will believe. He will gather all his people into his kingdom and they will be with him. Anyone can enter into his new world through him because he is the gate to the new world (cf. John 10:9). He shows the way through his descending from heaven into the world and ascending to the world above by being lifted up. It is possible to defend the claim, therefore, to say that the title "the Son of Man" can be linked to Jesus' kingship with other royal christological titles.

The Son of Man and the Man in the Gospel of John

In the Fourth Gospel, Jesus is the king greater than the Jewish Messiah whom both Jews and Samaritans were expecting, and even greater than the Roman governor Pilate is. He can be understood as king because he is the Messiah,[191] the Son of Man (= the Christ, 12:34) and the Son of God as well (19:7). Strikingly, in the trial of Jesus (John 18:28-19:16), the term "the Man"[192] in John 19:5 (ὁ ἄνθρωπος), which is used by Pilate to designate Jesus (cf. this Man (τοῦ ἀνθρώπου τούτου) in John 18:29), is equivalent to the Son of Man. It is striking that the Jews accuse Jesus (the Man) as the evildoer (οὗτος κακὸν ποιῶν) in 18:30, which is not a specific term

---

190. In John 5:25, the hour is related to the Son of God.

191. In John 1:35-51, Jesus is the Messiah, the Son of God, the king of Israel, and the Son of Man; in John 4:25-26, the Messiah and "I am He" are given; in 8:12-30, the Son of Man and "I am He" are presented together to designate Jesus.

192. On the relation between the Son of Man and the Man, see Schnackenburg, "'Son of Man,'" 529- 542. The LXX reads "man" (ἄνθρωπος) for scepter, and Philo interprets this "man" as a warrior, who "leading his host to war, will subdue great and populous nations" (see Philo, *Praem.* 95; Borgen, "'There Shall Come Forth a Man,'" 341-61). The Gospel of John frequently calls Jesus "the man," which appears to have some Christological significance (Higgins, *Jesus*, 153-54; Sidebottom, *Christ of the Fourth Gospel*, 96). Dodd comments that the author was aware that "the proper equivalent of the primitive Christian term for Christ, which was presumably *bar nasha*, was ὁ ἄνθρωπος.... The statements about the Son of Man which are actually made in the Fourth Gospel recall the figure of the heavenly ἄνθρωπος as we have met it in Hellenistic documents" (Dodd, *Interpretation*, 243). Dodd's argument also shows the possibility of the mixture of the concepts of the term from various origins.

3. KINGSHIP AND THE JOHANNINE CHRISTOLOGICAL TITLES 103

for a specific charge punishable by crucifixion.[193] Pilate, however, directly questions this Man, Jesus, as to whether he is "the King of the Jews" (John 18:33). In this context, the narrative does not give an explanation for the reason why Pilate uses the phrase "the King of the Jews" when questioning the identity of Jesus, while the narrative shows that Jesus is accused just as an evildoer in a general sense. It is evident that in the narrative, the title, the King of the Jews, is closely linked to the Man (the Son of Man) rather than to that of the evildoer. It is clear that the reason for his death is not the Jewish leaders' accusation but his willing death in order to save the world (18:32), as is recorded in previous passages in the Gospel: Jesus as the Son of Man will be lifted up (3:14; 8:28; 12:32). More strikingly, in John 19:14, the narrative shows that the Man (ὁ ἄνθρωπος) referred to by Pilate[194] in John 19:5 is the King of the Jews ("behold the king of yours" [ἴδε ὁ βασιεὺς ὑμῶν]; cf. "behold the man" [ἰδοὺ ὁ ἄνθρωπος] in John 19:5). It is in the Gospel of John that there is the relationship between the Man and the Son of Man, and that they are employed to show the kingship of Jesus.

In addition, it is shown that as the narrative proceeds further, the identity of Jesus as king becomes clearer through the change in Pilate's response to the Jewish leaders. In the narrative, the Jews accuse "the Man" in connection with the title, the Son of God,[195] when they know that Pilate finds no guilt in him (19:4). They accuse Jesus of claiming himself to be the Son of God (19:7), namely making himself to be a king, which is one of the titles of the Roman emperors. It is quite probable that Pilate begins to regard Jesus as one of the rivals to the emperor when he hears the Jewish leaders accusing Jesus of claiming to be the Son of God.[196] The narrative shows that because this claim was meaningful to him, Pilate became *more feared* when he heared it (Ὅτε οὖν ἤκουσεν ὁ Πιλᾶτος τοῦτον τὸν λόγον, μᾶλλον ἐφοβήθη in 19:8). That shows the possibility that Pilate as the Roman governor was seriously beginning to consider Jesus' kingship in terms of the title, the Son of God. He inquires into the origin of Jesus (πόθεν εἶ σύ;)[197] in John 19:9 immedi-

---

193. Lincoln, *Gospel*, 460.

194. Rensberger argues that this passage is ironic. That is, Pilate could well have used this term as an insult in this narrative, whereas for John's readers it has a deeper meaning, the kingship of Jesus (see Rensberger, *Johannine Faith*, 92–95; see also Meeks, *Prophet-King*, 69–76).

195. They accuse the Man as an evildoer at first to Pilate, but here, the Man as the Son of God. It is not clear that accusing someone as an evildoer means an accusation of a revolt; however, it is clear that the title, the Son of God, disturbs Pilate more when Jesus is charged with this title in the narrative.

196. Keener, *Gospel of John*, 219–94, 1125.

197. This is one of the ironically ambiguous themes in the narrative, Jesus gives no answer because the narrative shows that the Jews think that they know Jesus' origin

ately after this statement, indicating that he is in fact questioning his kingship. In this dialogue, death by crucifixion as a specific punishment from the lips of Pilate ("authority I have to crucify you"/ἐξουσίαν ἔχω σταυρῶσαί σε) shows the seriousness of the case, because earlier in the narrative Pilate clearly states that he does not find any guilt in Jesus to pass a sentence of death on him. This is before he listens to the accusation that Jesus claims to be the Son of God. As it gathers force, the accusation against Jesus by the Jewish leaders intensifies in their attempts to persuade Pilate; nevertheless, the narrator reports that Pilate does make efforts to release him (19:12). However, the narrative shows that he is gradually changing in his attitude moved by the increasing strength of the Jewish leaders' accusation against Jesus, because he could not ignore the title, the Son of God, nor the political pressure of the Jewish leaders (If you release *this man*, you are no friend of Caesar). As a result, Pilate can no longer reject their accusations. In the narrative the identity of Jesus as king is clearly seen, as the seriousness of the case reaches the point when the Jewish leaders accuse Jesus of claiming to be the Son of God in sharp contrast to Caesar (19:12). In John 19:13, the narrator reports that after listening to this accusation, Pilate publicly and officially puts this case on trial, and condemns Jesus to death by crucifixion (19:13–16). The narrative then shows that Jesus is killed as the King of the Jews (19:19–20) and the Jewish leaders, confessing their loyalty to Caesar as their king, deny Jesus' right to kingship (19:15). The account of the trial before Pilate shows that the title, the Man, as a possible equivalent of the Son of Man, the Son of God and king of the Jews, is used to designate the kingship of the Johannine Jesus.

In summary, the title "the Son of Man" which to a certain degree is used to indicate the kingship of Jesus that can be linked with other major christological titles in the Gospel of John, in order to identify Jesus as king.

Prophet and Kingship

I also contend that, as another example of hybridity of concepts, the title "Prophet" can connote kingship in both Jewish and Graeco-Roman traditions. In particular, there is a close connection between the concept of the Prophet and miracles.[198] Nicol points out, "occasionally in the dense forest of Jewish eschatological expectations, traces are evident of popular

---

(7:27), but the narrator and the readers only know that the origin of Jesus is the beginning, from heaven, from above, and from God the Father who sent him (1:1; 3:3, 13, 31; 6:23–33, 38, 41–42, 51; 7:28; 8:14, 23, 42; 9:29–30; 13:3; 17:14, 16).

198. Nicol, *Semeia*, 80–94.

expectations of some prophetic figure, and unlike the Messiah, this figure is frequently associated with miracles."[199] Vermes also remarks, "'Prophet' ... reflects the spontaneous admiration of people convinced of having witnessed a miracle."[200] The relationship between the concept of the prophet and miracles appears to point to hybridentity. Not only Jewish readers but also Graeco-Roman readers could link the prophet with the miracle worker, when they meet the description of Jesus as the prophet who performs miracles in the Gospel of John. Tiede shows that the literature of early Christianity is a microcosm of the non-Christian Hellenistic process, "both reflecting and contributing to the confluence of traditions [Jewish and Hellenistic]."[201] Moreover, miracles similar to those in the Gospel were ascribed to a rabbi, the emperor, and a magician by other ancient sources.[202] For example, healing a boy at a distance (John 4:46–54) is ascribed to Rabbi ben Dosa (*b. Ber.* 34b), whom some thought was a prophet. Healing blind eyes with a spittle was attributed to Vespasian.[203] Lucian told of a magician reputed to walk on water (cf. John 6:16–21), "call mouldy corpses back to life" (cf. 11:43–44) by spells, and of a man who was healed, picked up his mat, and walked away (cf. John 5:9).[204] Particularly, Georgi argues that the Imperial cult "as a prophetic one deserves more attention."[205] In addition, Fortna argues that the Johannine narratives portray Jesus as a wonder-worker fulfilling the traditional Jewish expectations of a Messiah.[206] Accordingly, we can associate the title "the Prophet" with kingship.

---

199. Nicol, *Semeia*, 81.

200. Vermes, *Jesus the Jew*, 87.

201. Tiede, *Charismatic Figure*, 292.

202. See Koester, *Symbolism*, 80.

203. Tacitus, *Hist.* 4.81 (Moore, LCL); Suetonius, *Vesp.* 7.2 (Lolfe, LCL); cf. Dio Cassius, *Roman History*, 56.8.1 (Cary, LCL).

204. See Lucian, *Philops.* 11, 13; cf. 26 (MacLeod). On ascriptions of magic to Jesus, see Justin, *Dial.* 69.5; Justin, *1 Apol.* 30; *b. Sanh.* 43a. The charge that Jesus was a deceiver and possessed by a demon seems to echo these debates (John 7:12, 20–21, 47; 8:48–52; 10:20–21; see also, Martyn, *History and Theology*, 76–83). The use of miracles in imperial propaganda was an innovation (see Tiede, *Charismatic Figure*, 91–92).

205. Georgi, "Who Is the True Prophet?," 36; see also Scherrer, "Signs and Wonders," 599–610.

206. See Fortna, *Fourth Gospel*.

The Prophet in Jewish Background

It is clear that the two terms "the Prophet" and "Elijah" are linked to the identification of the messianic figures.[207] In the Gospel of John, the Jews want to know the identities of John the Baptist and Jesus because of their miraculous signs (cf. 11:47). In the Hebrew Bible, Elijah is a prophet who performed miracles so that he could be regarded as a typical wonder worker by the Jews.[208] It is important also to note that prophets in the Hebrew Bible sought to validate their claim by announcing the judgment and redemption of Israel. They were anticipating the Messiah who would come and redeem Israel. The Jewish anticipation of the Messiah is closely related to the coming of Elijah who, in popular Jewish belief, is to be recognized as the forerunner of the Messiah and the beginning/arrival of the messianic times.[209]

Furthermore, the ultimate source of the idea of the Messianic king apart from Davidic Messianic kingship in Judaism may be found in the ideas about Exodus and Moses.[210] The Prophet like Moses[211] is sometimes called

---

207. In the Synoptic Gospels, Jesus is recognized as either John the Baptist, Elijah or a prophet (Mark 8:28; Matt 16:14; Luke 9:19). However, in this Gospel, Jesus is never identified with Elijah.

208. There are some examples concerning him in the Rabbinic works, although these are admittedly very late sources: *Pirqe Mashiach* 72, Elijah would show Israel seven signs as Moses did to convince them to believe, among other things by bringing people back to life and showing them the manna; *Mekh. Ex.* 16:33, Elijah will restore to Israel and the manna and the flask with oil which would remain undiminished until he anoints the Messiah with it; *Sotah* 59b, *pirqe Scheq.* 47c, Elijah would play a part in the resurrection of the dead (See Nicol, *Semeia*, 81–82). Vermes argues that the Synoptic Gospels, especially in Luke 24:19, in Mark 6:5, and in Matt 13:58, suggest that the terms, prophet, and miracle-workers were used synonymously by Jesus and his followers (see Vermes, *Jesus the Jew*, 88–89).

209. See Mal 3:23–24, 4:5, 5:5–6; Sirach 48:1–12; 1 Macc 2:58; *Martyrdom of Isaiah* 2:4; *1 Enoch* 89:52; *2 Baruch* 77:24; *4 Ezra* 7:109; 4Q558. On the background of the theme, see Vermes, *Jesus the Jew*, 86–102; Ohler, "Expectation of Elijah," 461–76. On the argument that the concept of Elijah as forerunner is new in the New Testament, see Faierstein, "Why Do the Scribes Say?," 75–86.

210. Horbury, *Jewish Messianism*, 31; Klausner, *Messianic Idea*, 18. In the case of the Samaritan tradition, it seems to be same, because the Samaritans kept only the Pentateuch as inspired Scripture; therefore, they had to depend on the Pentateuch alone as a basis for their eschatological hopes (see Boismard, *Moses or Jesus*, 4). In the Jewish literature, Mic 7:15; Isa 48:2; *1Pesiq.* 67b; *Tanch.* 7b—the oldest rabbinical instance of the Moses-Messiah typology; *Qoh. R.* 1.8—as the first redeemer was (Moses), so shall the latter Redeemer be; *Pirqe Mashiach* 72—Elijah appears with the Messiah and shows the Israelites seven signs "like Moses."

211. Many scholars believe that Jesus is the Prophet like Moses. See Teeple, *Mosaic Eschatological Prophet*, 84–94; Hill, *New Testament Prophecy*, 36, 57; Glasson, *Moses in the Fourth Gospel*, 27–31; Meeks, *Prophet-King*, 246–50; Martyn, *History and Theology*, 96.

king and will destroy the opponents of God.[212] In Deut 18:15, a prophet like Moses will be raised up and in Deut 18:18 he will declare all that God has commanded.[213] Moses is also regarded as a prophet-king in Deut 34:10 (cf. 33:5). It seems clear that there is a connection of ideas between the prophet, the Messiah, and kingship.[214]

There are also some records in Jewish literature, which refer to a prophet. First, *1 Macc.* 4:46, the story of the purification and rededication of the temple, predicts the coming of a prophet some day (cf. John 2:13–22). Secondly, *1. Macc.* 14:41 predicts a faithful prophet who would arise in the future. In *1 Macc.* 14:41 (cf. John 4:46) it is implied that this prophet is connected with Moses who would convey God's command. Thirdly, in *the Testament of Levi* 8:14–15,[215] the prophet of the Most High alludes to a Messianic

---

212. Meeks, *Prophet-King*, 249, 251.

213. See 1QS 11, 9ff—the Qumran community had to keep all the commandments "until the prophet and the Messiah of Aaron and Israel come"; 4Q Test. 5ff—the expectation of the prophet was based on Deut 18; Samaritans expected Moses to return; Josephus, *Ant.* 18, 85–86.; *Ant.* 20, 97/20, 167–68; 20:169–20; 20, 188—a deceiver; *B.J.* 7, 237ff. Boismard argues that the Gospel of John, in portraying Jesus as the Prophet like Moses predicted in Deut 18, is closely dependent on the Samaritan traditions (see Boismard, *Moses or Jesus*). In addition, the Johannine Jesus is the light of the world, like the Samaritan Moses who is depicted as a pre-existent primordial light who came to illuminate the world and as the one like Moses who would come to restore the world (see Anderson, "Samaritans," 946).

214. The kingship motif in the concept of the prophet is found in relation to the works of Moses. Porter argues that Moses in the Hebrew Bible has been shaped in terms of the model of the Israelite king (Porter, *Moses and Monarchy*). Particularly, in Isa 63:11 (the shepherd of the flock) and Exod 4:20 (he receives his scepter from God), a royal image of Moses is linked with the kingship of Jesus as the Good Shepherd. In addition, in Philo Moses is represented as a king (Horbury, *Jewish Messianism*, 31). In Philo, in particular, in *the Life of Moses* (*Mos.* 2: 66, 187, 269, 280, 292), Moses is mainly identified as both king and prophet (see *Mut.* 103, 125; *Somn.* 2: 189; *QG* 1:86; *Decal.* 175; *Virt.* 218; see also Cho, "Jesus as Prophet," 72). Freed also argues that in Rabbinic literature "the Messiah would be a second deliverer who would correspond to Moses the first deliverer; therefore, the miracle of manna would be repeated" (Freed, "Samaritan Influence," 585). In the Gospel of John, "When at the feeding of the five thousand the crowds acknowledge Jesus as "the Prophet who is to come into the world" (John 6:14), there is a strong desire to "make him king" (John 6:15). . . . The people realize that the promised judge/prophet must be given authority in Israel" (van Bruggen, *Jesus*, 119).

215. The problem of whether the Testaments are Jewish or Christian has been debated for a long time. Recently, scholars seem to agree that the Testaments were originally Jewish, but had Christian interpolations. However, it is still debatable among scholars (see Charles, *Apocrypha and Pseudepigrapha*, 2:309, 358; de Jonge, *Jewish Eschatology*, 231–43; Charlesworth, *Old Testament Pseudepigrapha*, 1:775–78). Charlesworth estimates the Maccabean period as the date of origin of the Testaments apart from the Christian interpolations. While he argues, "in the parenetic passages of the Testaments in particular, Hellenistic and Hellenistic-Jewish terms play an important

figure.²¹⁶ This prophet of the Most High in *the Testament of Levi* 8:15 is the one beloved by the Most High just as Jesus the Son is beloved by God the Father in the Gospel of John (John 1:18; 3:35; 5:20). Finally, the prophecy in *the Testament of Benjamin* 9:2-4 resembles the titles and life of Jesus in the Fourth Gospel. "The salvation in the visitation of an only-begotten prophet" in *the Testament of Benjamin* 9:2-4 is reminiscent of the incarnation and salvific ministry of the Johannine Jesus. In particular, because the concept or meaning of "an only-begotten prophet" was in relation to the Messiahship of the Jews, it is not an excessive interpretation to say that the concept or meaning of "the only begotten Son" and "the Prophet" in this Gospel are closely related to the Messiahship of Jesus.

In addition, in the Synoptics Jesus is also referred to as a/the prophet (Matt 14:5; 16:14; 21:11, 21, 46; Mark 6:1-4, 15; Luke 7:16; 9:8, 19; 8:27-28; 13:35; 24:19).²¹⁷ Furthermore, it is in Peter's second sermon in the Jerusalem temple in Acts 3:22-23 (cf. 7:37) that Jesus is presented as the prophet like Moses, foretold in Deut 18:18.²¹⁸ It is clear that Elijah and the prophet are meant as eschatological Messianic figures,²¹⁹ and it seems that the prophet is the one mentioned in Deut 18:18-19.

---

part," de Jonge stresses that the parenesis of the Testaments "cannot be called 'typically' Jewish or 'typically' Christian" (de Jonge, "Main Issues," 155, 158). About the present *the Testament of Levi*, de Jonge concludes, "the present *T. Levi* is thoroughly Christian, but at the same time it acknowledges the special position of Levi and his tribe . . . in the time before the arrival of Jesus Christ. It sees clear parallels between Levi and Jesus Christ, but does not establish a link between the new priest and the tribe of Levi" (de Jonge, "Testament of Levi," 259).

216. Young along with Charles interprets "a prophet of the Most High" as John Hyracanus who was regarded as the Messiah (see Young, "Jesus the Prophet," 289-91; Charles, *Apocrypha and Pseudepigrapha*, 2:309). Charles dates this verse under John Hyracanus, "who alone of the Maccabees is credited with the gift of prophecy." Josephus (*B. J.* 1.2.8.) regards "him," John Hyracanus, as the only one to unite three highest offices: kingship, high priesthood, and prophecy.

217. On the topic of Jesus as the New Moses, see Teeple, *Mosaic Eschatological Prophet*; Allison, *New Moses*. On the Moses-Messiah typology and references to expectations of a prophet in the New Testament, see Mark 6:14-15; 8:27-8 (Is Jesus John the Baptist, Elijah or a prophet like one of the prophets? (cf. Luke 9:7—one of the old prophets?). All three possibilities are prophetic figures; Mark 13:2 and Deut 13:22 (false prophets' signs; Matt 24:26); Rev 11:3-12 (two witnesses or prophets have the power to shut up the sky so that no rain falls like Elijah and to strike the earth with many plagues such as turning water into blood like Moses. Finally, like Elijah they will be taken up into heaven) (See Nicol, *Semeia*, 84-87).

218. Boismard, *Moses or Jesus*, 6; Nicol, *Semeia*, 84-87.

219. See *1 Macc* 4:46; 1QS 9:1-11; Pryor, *John*, 119.

3. KINGSHIP AND THE JOHANNINE CHRISTOLOGICAL TITLES

The Prophet and the Christ in the Gospel of John

The title "the Prophet" as applied to Jesus occurs five times in the Gospel of John, where this designation is used together with other christological terms to identify who Jesus is (in John 7:40–44 the Prophet and the Messiah are presented together; in John 6:14 the crowd refer to him as the Prophet who is to come into the world, and this is clearly connected with the title of king by the narrator in John 6:15; Jesus is designated a prophet by the Samaritan woman in John 4:19[220] and by the man born blind in John 9:17[221]; in John 1:21 (the Prophet), 25 (the Christ, Elijah, and the Prophet which is used to identify John the Baptist). In addition, in John 4:44, John records that Jesus regards himself as a prophet. Moreover, the Jews not only ask John the Baptist whether he is the Christ, the prophet or Elijah, but they also argue among themselves as to whether or not Jesus is the prophet. It is clear therefore that the terms, "the prophet," "the Messiah," and "the king" are also closely linked with the identity of Jesus in the Gospel of John.

First, because Jewish eschatology had developed rapidly, and this had affected every other Jewish concept under colonization by different empires through the centuries, the meaning of prophet had become hybridized, particularly eschatologically. It is therefore important to indicate that prophetic movements could be significant to contemporaries of the Johannine readers who were under Imperial rule. Consequently, in the Fourth Gospel, it is justifiable to say that the questioning of the identities of Jesus and John the Baptist in relation to the term "the Prophet," means more than that the Jews wanted to determine whether they claimed messianic status. For example, considering the various origins of the Gospel's readers, this title "the Prophet" could be employed to identify the Johannine Jesus in different ways. Jesus is often identified as a prophet before being called Messiah or king (4:19, 29; 6:14–15; 7:40–41; 9:17, 22). In particular, Jesus' role as a prophet is combined with his identity as Messiah during his dialogue with Pilate. This term is here replaced by the title "King of the Jews," but "Pilate's questions about Jesus' kingly status draw the theme of messiahship toward its climax."[222] Meeks argues that a study of the combination of the prophetic and royal motifs is useful "to clarify the way in which the motifs represented by the two terms 'prophet' and 'king' in the Fourth Gospel not only are

---

220. In this narrative, Jesus is finally acknowledged as the Savior of the world, which is the concluding title of the narrative, namely, the true king over the Roman emperors.

221. Like God or king, Jesus as the Son of Man was worshipped by the man born blind who confessed Jesus as a prophet, and was excommunicated from the synagogue.

222. Koester, *Symbolism*, 224–25.

interrelated, but interpret each other."[223] Just as in the case of the Johannine use of "the Christ," whose further definition is clarified with other terms (the Son of Man and the Son of God), the term "the Prophet" is explained by the use of other christological titles. In this respect, I contend that it is employed, in part, to identify the Johannine Jesus as king.

Secondly, as the title "the Messiah/Christ" is mainly related to the Davidic Messianic king in the Gospel of John (7:42), the title "the Prophet" is not understood as a different one in John 6:14–15. That Jesus is "the Prophet who is to come into the world" means that he is the one whom they had been anticipating for a long time. Because of the miraculous sign of the feeding of five thousand people recalling the "manna miracle" in the time of Moses,[224] the multitude's reference to Jesus as the Prophet, is reminiscent of the Mosaic prophet.[225] Moreover, a similar structure[226] is employed to designate Jesus in the Gospel: the Prophet who comes into the world, by the multitude (6:14); the Christ and the Son of God, who comes into the world, by Martha (11:27) (cf. the savior of the world by the Samaritans [4:42]). Usage in similar literary structures confirms the association of the titles "the Prophet," "the Christ," and "the Son of God." Further in 1:21–22,

---

223. Meeks, *Prophet-King*, 1. He clarifies his book through noting on the discourse of the Good Shepherd in John 10 and on the dialogue between Jesus and Pilate in John 18:33–38a: "In both passages—and in the whole Fourth Gospel—kingship is being radically redefined. The remarkable thing is that it is being redefined in terms of the mission of the prophet" (Meeks, *Prophet-King*, 67). In addition, Vermes argues that "the common assumption held by the New Testament interpreters appears to be that the prophetic image of Jesus was conceived by friendly outsiders, but that, not being good enough, not sufficiently suitable within the circle of his closer companions, it was replaced by more fitting titles" (Vermes, *Jesus the Jew*, 88).

224. Boismard, *Moses or Jesus*, 10. The miracle of the multiplication of the loaves also recalls the precedent of the prophet Elijah (2 Kgs 4:42–44; cf. 1 Kgs 17:8–16). Nicol also concludes that the New Testament adds strong evidence that the Jews of the first century expected the coming of an eschatological prophet who would be authenticated by signs, and that the early Christian preachers made use of the possibility in Jewish thought of connecting this expectation with Messianic ideas by proclaiming Jesus, the Messiah, as the final prophet, especially in the Gospel of John (See Nicol, *Semeia*, 87).

225. This motif is linked to Jesus as the bread of Heaven in John 6. Strikingly, in chapter 6, Jesus as the Son of Man (6:18) is the bread of God. Borgen argues that the Johannine Jesus is not just the Prophet like Moses in John 6:1–21, that He is the Son of Man as the Manna-bread from Heaven (See Borgen, "John 6," 268–91). This is another use of the combination of the titles in the Gospel. In addition, in Graeco-Roman tradition, Demeter, the goddess of grain, gave people bread as a gift, and those who ate the bread knew her as its divine source (Epictetus, *Discourses*, 2.20.32 [Oldfather, LCL]). "John's Gospel agrees that those who ate bread should recognize the divine giver, but transforms the way this is usually understood: True bread comes from God and the crucified Christ" (Koester, *Symbolism*, 102).

226. See Boismard, *Moses or Jesus*, 6–8.

parallelism between the titles "the Christ" and "the Prophet" is also found. It seems, therefore, that the structural similarity points toward association of the titles as a Johannine literary device, filling out the understanding of the kingship of Jesus in the Gospel of John.

There is some evidence to suggest that the title "the Prophet" is employed in the Gospel to highlight Jesus' kingship. It is clearly commented upon by the narrator that, at the feeding of the five thousand, the crowds acknowledged Jesus as "the Prophet who is to come into the world" (John 6:14),[227] and they had a strong desire to "make him king" (John 6:15). In addition, in John 7:40–52, there is a controversy about Jesus which shows the conflicts which existed among different groups in Jewish society in relation to these titles. An assertion of Jesus being the Prophet by some people is again rejected by the Jewish leaders (7:52) because of Jesus' Galilean origin.[228] John 7:40–52 clearly shows that the title "the Prophet" is related to the title "the Christ," because in the narrative the Jewish leaders rejected Jesus as the prophet for the same reason, namely, Jesus' Galilean origin, which is the reason given for the Jews' denial of Jesus in relation to both titles.

Therefore, although they are different from each other in meaning, these titles, "the Christ" and "the Prophet," are associated with the kingship of the Johannine Jesus in the literary structure of the Gospel. The title "the Prophet" is on the one hand linked to the one who had been anticipated for a long time (4:19–26[229]; 6:14), and on the other hand, to their rejection of him as the Prophet with the same reason as that of him as "the Christ," namely, his Davidic royal descent. As a result, these two terms are used interchangeably in this sense in the Gospel of John. Likewise, it is likely that

227. It is true that he retreated into the mountain because the crowd sought to make him king by force, but he did not deny the possibility of being the prophet who is to come into the world. Van Bruggen remarks, "He could not readily go along with that idea because the people continued to make a distinction between this prophet and the Christ (compare John 1:19–25; 7:40–41), while Jesus' coming and the course of his life make it clear that, while Elijah is indeed a separate figure (John the Baptist), 'the judge/prophet' and 'the Christ' are one. In addition, his juridical role as the prophet would be implemented at his return—not during the time of his humiliation" (van Bruggen, *Jesus*, 119).

228. Boismard points out that "since no OT text treats the origin of this Prophet, we must conclude that there was a transference of the theme of the Judean origin of the Christ, according to Mic 5:1 (7:41–42), to 'the Prophet' spoken of in 7:40 and 7:52. This transference would have been impossible if it had been a matter of any prophet whatsoever, and not of the Prophet par excellence who, in 7:40–41, is put parallel with 'the Christ'" (Boismard, *Moses or Jesus*, 8).

229. Here the definite article is omitted. Therefore, the Samaritan woman designates Jesus as a Prophet; however, Jesus designates himself as the Messiah (the Christ) in relation to the concept of prophet.

various titles used by the Gospel as "'king' and 'prophet' as well as other motifs overlap and concludes that there is a 'package' or confluence of motifs that are used to discuss or connote kingship."[230]

Savior of the World and Kingship

The Relationship between Samaritan Tradition and the Gospel of John

Research into the relationship between the Gospel of John and Samaritan literature[231] is helpful in understanding the kingship of the Johannine Jesus in relation to the term, the Savior of the World, and the background of reconstruction of the Johannine community as its readers. In this Gospel, the Samaritans are generally described in a positive light.[232] For example, John the Baptist baptizes in Aenon near Salim in Samaria (3:23), and the Samaritans come to believe in Jesus as the Savior of the World (4:1–42). After hearing of the conspiracy by the Jewish leaders to kill him, Jesus withdraws to the country near the wilderness and enters into a city called Ephraim (11:54), which is located in Samaria.[233]

This comparatively positive description of the Samaritans shows that a number of distinctive elements of the Gospel are also linked to the concepts of Samaritan tradition (hybridentity). It also explains one of the reasons why in this Gospel various titles are employed to designate Jesus. It is possible that some Samaritans were already members of the Johannine community, furthermore, that the community attempted to win the Samaritans in order

---

230. Reinhartz, *Word*, 110.

231. On research of Samaritan traditions, see Bowman, "Samaritan Studies," 298–327; Freed, "Samaritan Influence," 580–7; Freed, "Did John Write his Gospel?," 241–56; Buchanan, "Samaritan Origin," 148–75; Purvis, "Fourth Gospel," 161–98; Cullmann, *Johannine Circle*, 51; Brown, *Community*, 36–37; Samkutty, "Samaritan Mission." Meeks argues that the secondary aim of the Gospel is to win Samaritan converts (Meeks, *Prophet-King*, 313–19; Meeks, "Galilee and Judea," 159–69; Meeks, "'Am I a Jew?,'" 63–86; exp. 178). In addition, Cullmann points out that the Gospel was written from the standpoint of Samaritan Christian Mission by the Stephen/Philip group (Cullmann, "Samaria," 185–92; see also Scobie, "Origins," 390–414; Scobie, "Use of Source," 339–421, esp. 421; McDonald, *Theology*, 32–34; Brown, *Community*, esp. 36–40, 166–67; Olsson, *Structure and Meaning*, 254–56).

232. In comparison, according to John 8:48, the Jews (or the Jewish leaders) have a negative perspective on the Samaritans when they criticize Jesus (you are a Samaritan and demon-possessed?; Σαμαρίτης εἶ σὺ καὶ δαιμόνιον ἔχεις;).

233. Purvis, "Fourth Gospel," 168; Brown, *Gospel*, 441; Freed, "Samaritan Influence," 581.

to accomplish their mission. Purvis's endeavour to reveal the heterogeneity of Palestinian intellectual history during the Roman period is helpful to research on this topic.[234] Purvis remarks, "the Samaritan traditions were not in uniform theological perspectives from the early period."[235] Moreover, Bowman argues that the Gospel of John may have been written, "to make a bridge between Samaritans and Jews in Christ."[236] Regarding this viewpoint, it is quite acceptable that the Gospel of John describes the Samaritans in a positive light in order to win them. It is also probable that the author might have adapted and reflected some Samaritan concepts in his writing when he composed the Gospel, keeping in mind that the Samaritans were possibly one group among his readers.

The Samaritan story in the Gospel also shows how John relates Jesus to Samaritan tradition, Graeco-Roman conventions, and Jewish religious tradition. Various titles[237] are employed throughout the dialogue between Jesus and the Samaritan woman (lord/sir, a prophet, Messiah/Christ) and in her confession of the identity of Jesus (the Christ) to other Samaritans, and in the Samaritans' own confession of the identity of Jesus (the Savior of the World) in chapter 4. When the Samaritan woman addresses Jesus in differing terms during her conversation with him in chapter 4, each title demonstrates her growing realization of who Jesus really is. The more the dialogue proceeds, the deeper the level of her understanding of Jesus appears. Finally, the Samaritans' confession of Jesus as "the true Savior of the World" is the highlight of this account,[238] and reveals the identity of Jesus as king, an identity that is reminiscent of the titles of the Roman emperors.[239] Koester remarks,

234. Purvis, "Fourth Gospel," 161–98.

235. Purvis, "Fourth Gospel," 168. On the variety of Samaritan traditions and the complexity of Samaritan thought, see Bowman, "Samaritan Studies." The Samaritan literature also contains a wealth of traditions concerning the Hebrew Bible patriarchs, Abraham, Jacob, Joseph, Moses, and Joshua as well as the eschatological figure, namely the *Taheb* (Purvis, "Fourth Gospel," 164).

236. Bowman, "Samaritan Studies," 302; Freed suggests some additional evidence to confirm Bowman's argument (see Freed, "Samaritan Influence," 580–87).

237. For example: you (σὺ) in 4:9; lord (κύριε) in 4:11, 15, 19; a prophet (προφήτης) in 4:19; Messiah being called Christ in 4:25, cf. in 4:26, Jesus declared "I who speak to you am he"; in 4:29, "Could this [man] be the Christ?" (μτΤι οὗτός ἐστιν ὁ χριστός;); in 4:42, this man is *really the Savior of the World* (οὗτός ἐστιν ἀληθῶς ὁ σωτὴρ τοῦ κόσμου).

238. Jesus' identity reveals more clearly and fully when the Samaritans confess Jesus as the Savior of the world. Dodd argues that, for a certain dramatic propriety, the author purposely puts this title in the mouth of Samaritans (see Dodd, *Interpretation*, 239).

239. This title, the Savior of the World, is an important element in the kingship of Jesus, which can be associated with the issue of Roman sovereignty (Koester, "Savior,"

> [T]he narrative subsumes Samaritan expectations under the Jewish expression Messiah, since Samaritans did not use the term Messiah or await the coming of someone like David, who was a Jewish king, but expected a prophet like Moses to appear.[240]

Koester's remark seems to explain, at least partly, the hybridentity of the concepts of Jewish and Samaritan traditions, which results in the creation of a new character. Koester also remarks, "the interconnections between the particular and the universal aspects of Jesus' identity are also integral to John's Christology."[241] Cassidy also remarks,

> [I]t is well to explicate two aspects of the powerful meaning that John has achieved in positioning this title as the memorable culmination of this episode. As used here this title extends *universally*. At the same time, this title is also used *exclusively*. The titles of "Prophet" and "Messiah" appear earlier in this episode and disclose aspects of Jesus' identity that are especially significant within a Jewish context. Both of these aspects are then taken up into a more universal frame of reference when Jesus is acclaimed as Savior . . . *of the World*.[242]

Accordingly, the Samaritans' use of the title "Savior of the World" for Jesus is an important element in the theme of Jesus' kingship in its association with Roman imperial titles.[243] In this account, John might use this

---

677). In particular, the kingship motif, which is directly stated from chapter 1 of the Gospel ("the king of the Israel" in 1:49), is revealed more eminently in the trial of Jesus ("the king of the Jews" in 19:12, 15, and 21). The comparison of Jesus with Caesar in the trial makes the readers challenge and make them decide who the real king is.

240. Koester, *Symbolism*, 43.

241. Koester, *Symbolism*, 42.

242. Cassidy, *Christians and Roman Rule*, 45.

243. For example: 1. Julius Caesar, in an official inscription in Ephesus, he was spoken as "the god made manifest, offspring of Ares and Aphrodite, and common savior of human life" (τὸν ἀπὸ Ἄρεως καὶ Ἀφρπδε[ί]της θεὸν ἐμιφανῆ καὶ κοινόν τοῦ ἀνθροπίου βίου σωτῆρα) (*SIG*, no. 347); Σωτὴρ τῆς οἰκουμένης in *SEG* XXVII.

2. Augustus was honored as a savior and god (Θεὸς Καῖσαρ Σωτὴρ Σεβαστός) in *SEG* XXXIV 486; (. . . Δία Σωτῆρα καὶ θεὸν Καίσαρα Σεβαστὸν . . .) in *IGRR* IV 251 (Smallwood, *Documents*, no. 33); according to Deissmann, the combination of these two titles is dedicated to the honor "of Ptolemy the savior and god," (Πτολεμαίου τοῦ σωτῆρος καὶ θεοῦ). Deissmann argues, "The double form 'God' and 'Savior' afterwards became important in early Christian usage" (Deissmann, *Light*, 348).

3. Tiberius is also bestowed as god, savior, and son of god (θεοῦ Καίσαρος θεοῦ υἱοῦ Σεβαστοῦ Σωτῆρος in *SEG* XI 922–3; Ehrenberg and Jones, *Documents*, 87–89); (Τιβέριον Κλαύδιον Καίσαρα Σεβαστὸν Γερπανικὸν θεὸν ἐμιφανῆ σωτῆρα) in Smallwood, *Documents*, no. 136).

title, which truly belongs to Jesus, because the Samaritans receive him in a manner appropriate for a king.²⁴⁴ The reception of Jesus by the Samaritans is similar to the description given of the entrance of both Vespasian and Titus, later to become emperors, as each was acclaimed as Savior as they entered into the cities, which they had liberated.²⁴⁵ In addition, the entrance of Jesus into Jerusalem is also reminiscent of these victorious entrances of Vespasian and Titus. It is therefore clear that John uses this title to portray Jesus as the true king in order to encourage his readers never to be swayed or intimidated by the claims of the Roman emperors who styled themselves as saviors.²⁴⁶

Savior of the World in the Gospel of John

As I argued above, in the Samaritan story various titles, e.g., lord, a prophet, Messiah (Christ, the One who comes), the Christ, and the Savior of the World, are employed to designate the character of Jesus. In other words, although the admission of Jesus himself to be the Messiah (4:26) and the

---

4. This title was mainly used for the Roman emperor Domitian, who would be presumed a contemporary with John: for Statius, Domitian was "ruler of the nations and mighty sire of the conquered world, hope of man [sic] and care [beloved] of the gods" (*Silvae* 4.2.14-15; Carter, *Matthew and the Margins*, 25); for Martial, Domitian was "SURE savior of our state, the world's glory, Caesar" (*rerum CETRA salus, terrarum Gloria, Caesar* in *Epigrams* 2.91.1 [Ker, LCL]), "blest guardian and savior of the state" (*rerum felix tutela salusque* in *Epigrams* 5.1.7 [Ker, LCL]), and "our chief [savior] and only ward [Caeser]" (*rerum prima salus et una Caesar* in *Epigrams* 8.66.6 [Ker, LCL]).

244. In John 4:39-42, *going out* of the town to meet Jesus, *inviting him* into their town, and *calling him* "Savior of the world," are similar ways of welcoming as those granted to visiting rulers (see Koester, "Savior," 666). In addition, John 12:12-13 shows more dramatic similarity and reveals the kingship of Jesus: the great multitude in Jerusalem took the branches of the Palm trees and *went out* to meet Jesus, and *began to cry out*, "Hosanna! Blessed is He who comes in the names of the Lord, even *the King of Israel.*"

245. On the welcome that Vespasian received, see Josephus, *J.W.* 3.459 (Vespasian: went to city, upon which the citizens open to him their gates, and *met him with acclamations of joy*, and *called him their savior and benefac*tor); 7.70-71 (styled him their *benefactor and savior*, and the only person who was worthy to be ruler of the city of Rome). On Titus, see *J. W.* 4.112-3 (the people opened their gates to him, and *came out to him*, with their children and wives, and made *acclamations of joy* to him, as to one that had been their *benefactor*, and had delivered the city out of custody); 7.100-103, 119 (these were not the men only, but a multitude of women also, with their children, did the same and when they saw him coming up to them, they *stood on both sides of the way*, and *stretched out their right hands, greeting him, and making him all sorts of acclamations to him*, and returned back together with him).

246. Cassidy, *Christians and Roman Rule*, 46; see also Catchpole, "'Triumphal' Entry," 319-34.

use of the terms "the Messiah" and "the Christ" show that Jesus fulfills the hopes of both Samaritan and Jewish traditions,[247] the narrative goes further in referring to the identity of Jesus as the universal king assigning to him the title "the Savior of the World" on the lips of the Samaritans.[248]

The title "the Savior of the world" (4:42) appears only in the Gospel of John.[249] As I argued, it is not a typical messianic designation in first-century Jewish and Samaritan thought, but was often used for Caesar, who had dominion over the entire world in the New Testament era. In the Gospel, the author presents the Samaritans' claim that Jesus is the Savior of the World in a way that could never be rivalled by an emperor.[250] It seems that within the context, the title "the *true*[251] Savior of the World" denotes an extremely high level of sovereignty.[252]

Surely, it is Jesus to whom the real role in the "saving" of the world is attributed, not to the Roman emperors.[253] As a climactic title, the term "Savior of the World" in the Samaritan story, "tends to gather the aspects of meaning associated with such previous titles as 'prophet' and 'messiah' and indicates that Jesus' real identity is still greater."[254] In short, it is likely that

---

247. De Jonge, *Jesus*, 102–06.

248. Koester comments, "Jesus was Messiah, but when the Samaritans called him 'the Savior of the world,' they used a title that was associated not with Samaritan or Jewish messianic expectations but with worldwide dominion. They recognized that Jesus transcended national boundaries; like Caesar, he was a figure of universal significance (Koester, "Savior," 668).

249. John does not use the title, savior, outside the Samaritan story, but the concept is revealed clearly through the Gospel of John (3:17—God sends his only Son into the world to save the world; 12:47—Jesus came to save the world). In addition, this image is present in John 1:29; 3:16; 6:33; 6:51.

250. "Savior of the world" was bestowed with a range of variations (σωτὲρ τῆς (ὅλης) οἰκουμένης, σωτὴρ τοῦ κόσμου) in the Greek Julius Caesar, Augustus, Claudius, Vespasian, Titus, Trajan, Hadrian, and other Emperors in inscriptions of the Hellenistic East. Particularly the exact Johannine term is especially common in inscriptions for Hadrian (See Deissmann, *Light*, 369; Koester, "Savior," 667). Koester lists various forms of the title used for Roman rulers: Σωτὴρ τῆς οἰχουμένης (Julius Caesar, Claudius, Hadrian); σωτὴρ τῶν Ἑλλήνων τε καὶ τῆς οἰχουμένης πάσης (Augustus); εὐεργέτης καὶ σωτὴρ τοῦ σύμπαντος χόσμου (Augustus, Tiberius); σωτὴρ καὶ εὐεργέτης τῆς οἰχουμένης (Nero, Titus); σωτὴρ καὶ εὐεργέτης χόσμου (Vespasian); σωτὴρ τοῦ παντὸς χόσμου (Trajan); ὁ παντὸς χόσμου σωτὴρ καὶ εὐεργέτης (Trajan); σωτὴρ τοῦ κόσμου (Hadrian).

251. "Truly" shows Jesus' exclusiveness of the title in the Johannine Gospel.

252. Cassidy, *John's Gospel*, 35; Koester, *Symbolism*, 43.

253. See Barrett, *Gospel*, 244; Carson, *Gospel*, 232; Beasley-Murray, *John*, 65. The implication of the trial is that "the disciple will always have to decide vis à vis the empire whether Jesus is his king or whether Caesar is" (Meeks, *Prophet-King*, 64).

254. Cassidy, *John's Gospel*, 35. Barrett argues that John's terminology is drawn

3. KINGSHIP AND THE JOHANNINE CHRISTOLOGICAL TITLES

Jesus, in the narrative, is no longer the Jewish or Samaritan Messiah, but instead the Savior of the world as universal king.

Lord, "My Lord and My God," and Kingship

Background of the Title Κύριος

The title "the Lord," which was used directly of God in the LXX,[255] was employed specifically to indicate Jesus in the New Testament.[256] Hengel remarks, "the development from 'rabbi' or 'mari', used as a respectful form of address to Jesus, to the fully developed Κύριος can be shown to have as stringent an intrinsic consistency as the development in the use of the term Son of God."[257] In addition, Cullmann affirms, "the title 'King' (*basileus*) is a variant of the *Kyrios* title."[258] Cullmann argues that to exclude the political aspect in the christological titles, John subordinates the title "King" to the title "Κύριος." He assumes that "the expression [King of the Jews] is used in the political sense by the Zealots, whereas the first Christians attributed to it a non-political meaning related to the *Kyrios* title."[259] However, Κύριος, as a royal title, may have a political meaning for the Johannine readers, because

---

partly from Greek sources, but mainly from the Hebrew Bible, and that John definitely represents Jesus as the Messiah of Judaism in this chapter, however, John insists here that this term, and all others, must be understood in the widest sense (Barrett, *Gospel*, 244). In addition, Koester emphasizes that this title transcends the traditional meanings associated with Samaritan or Jewish messianic expectations and attributes a universal significance to Jesus like that of Caesar (see Koester, "Savior," 668). Moreover, Carson points out that the true Savior of the world was not any god or the Roman emperor "but the Lamb of God who takes away the sins of the world (1:29, 34)" (Carson, *Gospel*, 232).

255. For research on the background of this term, see Deissmann, *Light*, 353–66; Vermes, *Jesus the Jew*, 103–28; Fantin, "Lord of the Entire World." In the Septuagint, this term, κύριος, is used 8,543 times, primarily as a translation for Yahweh and God (Fantin, "Lord of the Entire World," 142–43).

256. Hengel, *Son of God*, 77. In the early centuries of the Christian era, the tetragram, YHWH, which is pronounced in Hebrew *Adonai* (LORD), was rendered as Κύριος in Greek (See Vermes, *Jesus the Jew*, 110). Bousset argues that this title originated and developed in Hellenism, or through Diaspora misuse of the LXX (See Bousset, *Kyorios Christos*, 128).

257. Hengel, *Son of God*, 80. Bousset also argues, "the evangelist sums up in the concept of the *huios tou Theou* all that is included in the title *kyrios* in Paul and in Hellenistic popular Christianity" (See Bousset, *Kyorios Christos*, 215).

258. Cullmann, *Christology*, 220.

259. Cullmann, *Christology*, 221.

it had Jewish royal implications[260] as well as Roman imperial titles.[261] Therefore, it is debatable that the titles "king"[262] and Κύριος are associated with Jesus without any political meaning in the Gospel of John.[263]

This title is associated with the Roman Emperors (Κύριος/*Dominus et Deus noster*) from the time of Gaius Caligula (37-41 CE) onward,[264] especially from Domitian (81-96 CE) onward, this title ("lord," or "our lord") was used as the first name of the Roman emperors.[265] In the East, however, this title was bestowed on the emperors much earlier.[266] Deissmann remarks, "[i]t is therefore in accordance with Egyptian or Egypto-Semitic custom that in numerous Greek inscriptions, papyri, and ostraca of the ear-

---

260. "My lord" (*adoni*; κυριὸς μου) is a common designation for the king in Samuel and Kings (*Adoni*—75 times in Samuel and Kings with reference to the king) (Strauss, *Davidic*, 42-43).

261. For example: 1. Tiberius and his mother Livia were spoken as "the lords Augusti" (τῶν κυρίων Σε[βασῶν]) in an inscription from Abila in Syria (*OGIS*, 606). 2. Caligula allowed himself to be called "lord" (Diessmann, *Light*, 358). 3. Claudius (41-54 CE) in *AOPetr* 209, *POxy* 37. 4. Nero (54-58 CE) in *PLond* 1215, *POxy* 246, *GOA* 1038, OPetr 288. 5. Vespasian (67-79 CE) in *POxy* 1493; *SB* 1927; *GOA* 439; SC 3563 (See Millar and Segal, *Caesar Augustus*, 171-75). In particular, Vespasian was commonly called *kyrios* in the east (Cuss, *Imperial cult*, 61). 6. Titus was called "of our lord Emperor Titus Caesa" (Τοῦ [κυρίου ἡμῶν] Αὐτοκράτορος Τ[ίτου Καί-]σαρος) in *IvE* (Die Inschriften von Ephesos = IGS 11.1-17.4) 2.421 1. 1-6; Friesen, *Imperial Cults*, 100). 7. Domitian was addressed "lord of the earth" (*Silvae* 2.4.20; Carter, *Matthew and the Margins*, 25), and called Κύριος Αὐτοκράτωρ Δομιτιανὸς Καῖσαρ Σεβαστὸς Γερμανικός in *SEG* XXVIII 758.

262. Carter remarks that "the term, *basileia*, . . . commonly refers to empires like Rome's, just as the term, *basileus*, usually translated 'king,' is used to denote emperors." So, "To call Jesus 'king' or 'emperor' presents a challenge to the Roman emperor" (See, Carter, *Matthew and Empire*, 5).

263. Rensberger argues the possibility in relation to Christology and politics (Rensberger, *Johannine Faith*, 87-100).

264. See, Vermes, *Jesus the Jew*, 106.

265. Deissmann, *Light*, 355-56, 360.

266. In Egypt, the Pharaoh was usually addressed with "O King, our lord": in a Munich Papyrus, King Ptolemy IV Philopator (221-205 BC) was called "lord of the diadems" (κύριος βα[σιλειῶν]) as one of the official titles (Deissmann, *Light*, 356); Ptolemy V. Epiphanes (205-181 BC) in the Rosetta Stone (*OGIS*, 90); Ptolemy XIII was called "the lord king god" (τοῦ κυρίου βασιλ[έ]ος θεοῦ) (*OGIS*, 186); Ptolemy XIV and Cleopatra are called "the lords, the most great gods," (τοῖς κυρίοις θεοῖς μεγίστοις) (*Sitzungsberichte der Kgl. Preuss. Akademie der Wissenschaften zu Berlin* (1902), 1906; re-quoted from Deissmann, *Light*, 356); the same title applied to the Herods in Greek inscriptions of Palestine (*OGIS*, 415 (Herod the Great - [Βα]σιλεῖ Ἡρώδει κυρίῳ), no. 418 (41 AD, Herod Agrippa I. - σωτηρίας κυρίου βασι|λεώς Ἀγρίππα), no. 423 (Βασιλέως Ἀγρίππα κυριόυ), no. 425 (βασιλεῖ μεγάλῳ Ἀγρίππα κυρίῳ Ἀγρίππας υἱὸς), no. 426 (Herod Agrippa II - βασιλέως Ἀγρίππα κυρί[ου Μ]αββογαρῖος Φίλω[νος καὶ οἱ] υἱοὶ οἰκοδόμησαν).

liest Imperial period the title 'lord' is attached to the Caesars by Egyptians and Syrians."[267] Moreover, under Nero this title is first found in an inscription in Greece (ὁ τοῦ παντὸς κόσμου κύριος Νέρων, τοῦ κυρίου Σεβαστοῦ [Νέρωνος]).[268] "This important inscription shows how far the East had already penetrated on its march of conquest into the West."[269] In addition, according to Josephus, Jewish rebels in Egypt refused to call the Caesar "lord" soon after the destruction of Jerusalem.[270] Evans' comment on the Gospel of Mark gives us a good insight into understanding the title "Lord" in relation to other Johannine christological titles:

> In my view, the Markan evangelist presents Jesus as the true son of God and in doing so deliberately sets Jesus over against Rome's quest to find a suitable emperor, savior, and lord. All of the features that made up the emperor cult and the various customs associated with the office and title of emperor in various ways find expression in the New Testament theology. . . . It is clear that early Christians fully well understood that their confession that Jesus was "Lord," "Savior," and "Son of God" directly competed with and challenged the Roman Emperor and the cult that had grown up around the office.[271]

It is safe to say, therefore, that the title "lord" was applied to the Caesars so that the author and the readers of the Gospel could have taken into account of the imperial meaning of this title, when they met it in the narrative, particularly where it implies his kingship.

Lord in the Gospel of John

As an ascription to or a title of Jesus, Κύριος (Lord) is found some 44 times in the Gospel.[272] The title "the Lord (ὁ Κύριος)" is rarely used in the first 19 chapters of the Gospel; however, in the account of the resurrection it is the ascription most commonly used (20:2, 18, 20, 24; 21:7, 15, 16, 17: 21:21; cf. "my Lord" in 20:13; "my Lord and my God" in 20:28)[273] in portraying Jesus

---

267. Deissmann, *Light*, 357.
268. Dittenberger, *SIG*, no 376.
269. Deissmann, *Light*, 358.
270. Josephus, *J. W.* 7.10.1 ("Caesar was their lord").
271. Evans, *Mark 8:27–16:20*, 59.
272. The meaning of the Johannine Lord mostly varies in its usage. On a useful classification of the usage of the term, see Pryor, *John*, 143.
273. Bousset, *Kyrios Christos*, 211.

as the risen and glorified Lord, the sovereign who is beyond the limitations of both time and space.[274]

It is necessary to investigate some passages in this Gospel where this term is imployed to portray Jesus in terms of kingship. First, the title "Lord (Κύριος)" is particularly used to address Jesus by those who truly believe in him.[275] It is important to recognize that the occurrences of this title are "unmistakably to convey and enhance the meaning that Jesus is a figure of exalted standing, someone whose sovereign power extends even to the limits of life and death."[276]

It is also acknowledged that the title "Lord" is significantly employed to identify the Johannine Jesus more fully alongside other christological titles. In John 9:38, for example, the blind man worships Jesus as the Son of Man, confessing him "Lord,[277] I believe [you are the Son of Man]." In addition, Martha confesses "Yes Lord! I believe that you are the Christ, the Son of God who was to come into the world" in John 11: 27.[278] Mary also falls at the feet of Jesus and replicates Martha's exact confession, Lord (11:32). The verb "to fall" (πίπτω), is used three times (11:32; 12:24; 18:6) in the Gospel.[279] In John 11:32 and 18:6, this verb is used in the context of the revelation of Jesus' authority. Mary falls down before Jesus after running to him and admitting that Jesus has the authority over life and death[280]; the Roman cohort and officers draw back and fall to the ground as one does before a king, when they hear that Jesus is the one ("I am He"). This scene shows the authority of Jesus over his opponents and over Roman military power.[281] In

274. Cassidy, *John's Gospel*, 37.

275. Peter (6:68; 13:6, 9, 36–37; 21:15, 16, 17, 21); Beloved disciple (13:25; 21:7; cf. 21:20); Mary Magdalene (20:2, 13, 18); Thomas (14:5); Philip (14:8); Judas not Iscariot (14:22); the disciples (11:12; 20:25); the official of Capernaum (4:49); the invalid man (5:7); the crowd (6:34); the man born blind (9:36, 38); the Samaritan woman (4:11, 15, 19); Narrator (4:1; 6:23; 11:2; 20:20; 21:7, 12); cf. Jesus' self designation (13:13–14).

276. Cassidy, *Christians and Roman Rule*, 44. See also Cassidy, *John's Gospel*, 36.

277. The vocative case of Κύριος, κύριε, is used here; not the full designation, the Lord (ὁ Κύριος).

278. Carson points out that it is a rich combination of the titles (Carson, *Gospel*, 414); Schnackenburg notes that it is the same combination of words in 20:31 (Schnackenburg, *Gospel according to St. John*, 2:332).

279. Particularly, this verb is used together with "to worship" in other New Testament passages. See Matt 2:11 (πεσόντες προσεκύνησαν); 18:26 (πεσὼν οὖν ὁ δοῦλος προσεκύνει), 29 (ἐσὼν οὖν ὁ σύνδουλος αὐτοῦ παρεκάλει); Rev 5:14 (ἔπεσαν καὶ προσεκύνησαν).

280. In John 11:41–44, Jesus is addressed and reverenced as "Lord" throughout this episode, then authoritatively and sovereignly offers the resuscitation of Lazarus (See Cassidy, *Christians and Roman Rule*, 44–45).

281. Jesus' authority over his opponents, and also over life and death in references

addition, in John 4:46–54, the healing of a royal official's son, the royal official addresses Jesus as Lord when Jesus' authority over disease is revealed, and it is also linked with the belief motif (the man believed the word that Jesus spoke to him in John 4:50). Finally, it is the same response when Thomas confesses and believes Jesus as "My Lord and My God" in John 20:28–29. In the direct context, Jesus in his response to Thomas mentions the matter of belief, which also clearly shows that the title "Lord" is closely linked with the belief motif. That Jesus is addressed as "Lord" makes him the object of belief and worship in these passages. It is safe to say, therefore, that the use of the title, Lord, is another example of the combination of the titles in the unique Johannine way as it relates to the kingship motif.

My Lord and My God

The combination of the titles "my Lord and my God" is found in the LXX to designate God as king in Psalm 34:23 (ὁ θεός μου καί ὁ κύριος μου).[282] So, this combination could be understood as pointing to the kingship of Jesus by the readers who were from a Jewish background, and who might understand it in relation to God as their real king in the Hebrew Bible.[283] On the other hand, this combination could be understood as a royal imperial title because it could be linked to that of the Roman imperial cult. In particular, Domitian insisted on the title *dominus et deus noster* ("our lord and god").[284] The Gospel of John implies many similarities with the political ideology of the Roman Empire as contained in the New Testament. Moreover, the Johannine readers and his contemporaries were familiar with the full force

---

of the term, Lord, is reminiscent of that of Roman emperors who were referred to by the same title, lord. On the Roman power over the world, see Carter, *Matthew and the Margins*, 17–24.

282. See also Ps 29:3; 87:2 (κύριε ὁ θεὸς); 85:15 (σύ κύριε ὁ θεός); cf. 2 Kgs 7:28; 2 Kgs 18:39; Jer 38:18; Zech 13:9 in LXX. For helpful discussion of the Hebrew Bible instances, see Schnackenburg, *Gospel*, 3:333, 475; Bultmann, *Gospel*, 695.

283. The combination of Lord and God is very common in the Hebrew Bible (Gen 24:3, 12; Exod 3:15; 5:1; Lev 18:4; Num 22:18; Deut 26:13); see Chennattu, *Johannine Discipleship*, 165.

284. Suetonius, *Domit.* 13.2; see also Barrett, *New Testament Background*, 19–20; Ferguson, *Backgrounds*, 38; Cassidy, *John's Gospel*, 14–16. Although Suetonius obviously has a disdain for Domitian, because his report that Domitian referred to himself in a formal degree as "our lord and our god" (*Dominus et Deus Noster*) is not total fabrication, his statement is important: "Suetonius supplies this account regarding the decree Domitian published arrogating 'lord and god' to his own person" (Barrett, *New Testament Background*, 14). Furthermore, this statement is paralleled with Thomas' confession in the Gospel of John, which might have been written under Domitian. On the general discussion about Domitian, see chapter 1 of this book.

of the customs and terminology of the Roman imperial cults, which saw the Roman emperors as gods more than as political figures.[285]

The following are some examples of the Roman emperors as gods more than political figures. First, Julius Caesar was the first figure who was consecrated a *divus* after his death[286] and hailed as god, particularly according to eastern sources.[287] In an official inscription in Ephesus, he was spoken of as "the god made manifest, offspring of Acres and Aphrodite, and common savior of human life" (τὸν ἀπὸ Ἄρεως καὶ Ἀφρπδε[ί]της θεὸν ἐμιφανῆ καὶ κοινόν τοῦ ἀνθρωπίου βίου σωτῆρα).[288]

Secondly, Julius' adopted son, Octavian, received the title Augustus and was honored as a god in the East during his reign and hailed as both god and son of god,[289] and ultimately was formally designated as *divus* in Rome after his death.[290] Augustus was specifically given the title "god of god" (θεοῦ ἐκ θεοῦ) in an inscription from Stetopaei Nesus in the Fayûm.[291] In addition, the calendar inscription of Priene speaks of the birthday of Augustus simply as the birthday "of the god" ([ἡ γενέθλιος] τοῦ θεοῦ; cf. ἥτις ἐστὶν γενέθλιος ἡμέρα τοῦ Σεβαστοῦ).[292]

---

285. During the first century BCE the cults of the deified emperors became common, especially in the eastern Roman Empire. Price attempts to discover why the Roman Emperor was treated like a god. He contends, "Christianizing assumptions and categories have proved a major stumbling block in interpretations of the imperial cult, and of these the most pervasive is our assumption that politics and religion are separate areas." He argues that Christianizing assumptions and categories had led to the cult being considered simply as a form of political honors. He examines how the Greek cults of the Roman Emperor located the Emperor with their subjection to the external power of Rome (see Price, *Rituals and Power*; Price, "Rituals and Power," 47–71).

286. See Weinstock, *Divus Julius*, 364–41.

287. *IGRR* IV 7, 1718; *SEG* XXXVII 1007.

288. *OGIS*, 347; see also Καῖσαρ Θεός in *SEG* XXXII 847; Καῖσαρ ὁ σεβαστὸς θεός in *SEG* XXXII 1135; Θεὸς Σεβαστός in *SEG* XXXII 1613; Θεὸς Σεβαστὸς Καῖσαρ in SEG XXXV 612 Θεὸς Καῖσαρ Σωτὴρ Σεβαστός in *SEG* XXXIV 486; Θεὸς Αὐτοκράτωρ Καῖσαρ Σεβαστός in *SEG* XXX 1627; Αὐτοκράτωρ Καῖσαρ Θεὸς Θεοῦ υἱὸς Σεβαστὸς in *SEG* XXXIII 1055.

289. *IGRR* I 853; *SIG* III 778; *SEG* XXXIX 752.

290. See Mowery, "Son of God," 101–05.

291. *OGIS*, 655. Deissmann remarks, "This formula is Ptolemaic (cf. the Rosetta Stone in honor of Ptolemy V. Epiphanes, in *OGIS*, 90, ὑβάρχων θεὸς ἐκ θεοῦ καὶ θεᾶς καθάπερ Ὧρος ὁ τῆς Ἴσιος καὶ Ὀσίριος υἱός, 'he is god of god and of goddess, as Horus the son of Isis and Osiris') and becomes very important later in Christianity" (Deissmann, *Light*, 349).

292. *Inschriften von Priene*, no. 105. Gaius Julius was also honored as the neokoros of goddess Rome and of god Augustus Caesar (Οἱ νέοι ἐτίμησαν Γάιον Ἰούλιον Σακέρδωτα, τὸν νεωκόρον θεᾶς Ῥώμης καὶ θεοῦ Σεβαστοῦ Καίσαρος) (*IGRR* IV 454; Friesen, *Imperial Cults*, 31). In addition, in the letter of Claudius to the Alexandrians,

3. KINGSHIP AND THE JOHANNINE CHRISTOLOGICAL TITLES 123

Thirdly, the other Roman emperors were also called gods: Tiberius (θεοῦ Καίσαρος θεοῦ υἱοῦ Σεβαστοῦ Σωτῆρος; Τιβέριος Καῖσαρ θεοῦ Σεβαστοῦ υἱὸς Σεβαστὸς);[293] Gaius Caligula is described as a new god,[294] and was the only emperor to make extensive use of divine attributes because he wished to be considered a god;[295] Claudius;[296] Nero as the good god (ἀγαθῷ θεῷ) of the inhabited world, the beginning of all good things;[297] Vespasian;[298] and Titus (Θεὸς Τίτος).[299]

Finally, an inscription at Stetopaei Nesus in the Fayûm, 17th of March in 24 BCE speaks of "to the god and lord Socnopaeus" (Τῶι θεῶι καὶ κυρίῳ Σοκνοπαίωι);[300] also an inscription of the Imperial period at Thala in the Province of Africa is consecrated to "the god lord Saturnus" (*deo domino Saturno*).[301]

Hence, it is likely that, within a Roman context, the Gospel of John compels its readers to decide who is a real king, and then to admit that Jesus is the real king and is challenging the Roman emperors. From this point of view, it is apparent that the affirmation of Thomas to Jesus as "my Lord and my God" plays a climactic role in revealing Jesus' kingship.[302] The climax is reached with this statement, "my Lord and My God," which refers back to the beginning of the Prologue (1:1-3). Cassidy remarks, "in John's literary structure, Thomas' acclamation of Jesus' majesty and divinity thus powerfully complements the Gospel's opening themes in a way that is particularly significant in the context of the imperial ruler cult."[303] It is also clear that Jesus is described as the exalted Lord after his

---

Augustus was spoken of as god ([ὁ] θεὸς Σεβαστὸς) (LCL; *Select Papyri*, 2:82).

293. *SEG* XI 922-3; Ehrengberg and Jones, *Documents*, 75-76, 87-89.

294. *IGRR* IV 1094; cf. as a new Ares in *CIA* III 444.

295. Price, *Rituals and Power*, 184; see also Josephus, *J.W.* ii. 184-7.

296. *PSI* 1235; *POxy* 713; *POxy* 808; *POxy* 1021; *PMich* 244.

297. *POxy* 1021; cf. Mark 10:18; Luke 18:19, there is no man good, but one, that is God.

298. *POxy* 257; *POxy* 1112; Millar and Segal, *Caesar Augustus*, 171-5.

299. *SEG* XXX 1308.

300. *OGIS* 655.

301. Deissmann, *Light*, 366.

302. If at the pregnant words "God" and "Lord" all manner of sensations of protest were roused in the Christian worshipper against the cult of the Caesar, this was of course also the case with the still more impressive combination κύριος καὶ θεός, "Lord and God," which as the confession of Thomas, is one of the culminating points (originally the climax and concluding point) of the Gospel of John (Deissmann, *Light*, 366). See Brown, *Gospel*, 1047; Barrett, *Gospel*, 573; Lindars, *Gospel of John*, 615, 675; Carson, *Gospel*, 659; Bultmann, *Gospel*, 695; Schnackenburg, *Gospel*, 3:333.

303. Cassidy, *Christians and Roman Rule*, 47; see also Cassidy, *John's Gospel*, 38-39.

resurrection and that this combination uitimately shows the sovereign status of Jesus as the Lord and God of the universe.³⁰⁴

In summation, it is clear that the confession of Thomas is another example of a Johannine combination of titles, which could be contrasted with those used for the Roman emperors, and which reveals the kingship of Jesus in the Gospel.

The Kingship Motif in the Johannine Christology

The kingship of Jesus is a more prominent theme in the Gospel of John than is usually acknowledged and John regularly emphasizes it. Of the many and various designations, portrayals, and titles³⁰⁵ it is difficult to suggest one as the key of Johannine Christology. However, the kingship of the Johannine Jesus might qualify as such a key.³⁰⁶ Rowland points out that "in the Gospel of John messianism and kingship sit alongside the dominant theme of Christ as the revealer of the divine glory who is sent from the Father."³⁰⁷ De Jonge's remark also exemplifies this book: "The reinterpretation of Jesus' kingship is given in terms of divine sonship, understood in a typically Johannine way. Jesus is prophet and king because he is the Son sent by the Father, and as the only Son of the Father."³⁰⁸

Although three christological titles in the Fourth Gospel, "Christ," "Son of God," and "Son of Man," are the major ones, they can be understood more fully in the light of other christological titles used in their immediate and wider context in the Gospel. So, how does this Gospel really reveal the identity of Jesus? To answer this question, it is also important to keep in mind that the kingship motif permeates all these titles.

First, various titles used throughout the Gospel emphasize Jesus' identity and tasks as king. In this Gospel, the unique Johannine Jesus is created by an unparalleled literary use of the christological titles, namely, by putting them in series, by synonymy or by the employment of the various christological titles in the same context.³⁰⁹ For example, John the Baptist

---

304. This is the climactic exemplification that the Son will be honored like the Father is honored (Carson, *Gospel*, 659).

305. On the various designations, portrayals, and titles as a key to Johannine Christology, see Brown, *Introduction*, 251–63.

306. See Rowland, "Christ," 474–96.

307. Rowland, "Christ," 484.

308. De Jonge, *Jesus*, 69.

309. Putting the Christological titles in series, for example, is "the Messiah and the Son of God," "the Son of God and the King of Israel," and the employment of the various Christological titles in the same context, for example, is the Lamb of God and the Son

3. KINGSHIP AND THE JOHANNINE CHRISTOLOGICAL TITLES 125

refers to Jesus as *the Lamb of God*, and *the Son of God* (1:29, 34, 36), which point to Jesus as the Messiah in the following context. Then, Andrew confesses to Simon that he has found *the Messiah* (1:41; cf. 1:45); when Philip finds Nathanael he says ("We have found the one Moses wrote about in the Law, and about whom the prophets also wrote—Jesus of Nazareth, the son of Joseph."), Nathanael doubts who Jesus is, saying, "Nazareth! Can *anything good* come from there? (ἐκ Ναζαρὲτ δύναταί τι ἀγαθὸν εἶναι;)"; however, he confesses later directly to Jesus that he is *the Son of God and the King of Israel*,[310] and Jesus does not rebuke him or deny his identity (1:49–51). Moreover, Jesus emphasizes his identity using the title, *the Son of Man* (1:51), in a statement which is reminiscent of Jacob's dream of the ladder at Bethel in Genesis 28:12.[311]

Furthermore, Jesus admits himself to be *the Messiah* to the Samaritan woman (4:26) and she witnesses to his Messiahship to the Samaritans (4:29). Consequently, the Samaritans confess that Jesus is *truly the Savior of the world* (4:42), a term which was used of the Roman emperors. In addition, after feeding five thousand men, the people confessed that Jesus is *surely the Prophet who is come into the world* (6:14). About this sign, the narrator comments that the crowd's intention is "to come and make him *king* by force" even though Jesus rejects this understanding (6:15). In the dialogue between Jesus and his disciples, Simon Peter confesses directly to Jesus that he is *the Holy One of God* (6:69). Moreover, during a controversy in the crowd, there is a question as to whether Jesus is a good man or a deceiver (7:12). In the following dispute, some of them confess that Jesus is *the Christ* or *the Prophet* (7:40–44), and, in relation to his origin, Jesus reveals it as from above (7:28; 8:23; cf.1:1–18). More strikingly, the man born blind confesses publicly that Jesus is a prophet (9:12); however, when he meets Jesus after his excommunication (9:35) and Jesus reveals himself as *the Son of Man*, he worships Jesus (9:38) in a way that people might worship (bow down to) one

---

of God, which are employed to designate Jesus by John the Baptist; the Son of Man and the Son of God in chapter 3; a prophet, lord, the Messiah (the Christ), the Savior of the world in chapter 4, etc. (see Koester, *Symbolism*, 40).

310. On this, see chapter 4 of this book.

311. On the relationship between Gen 28:12 and John 1:51, see Neyrey, "Jacob Allusions in John 1:51," 586–605; Rowland, "John 1:51, Jewish Apocalyptic and Targumic Tradition," 498–507; Collins, *John and His witnesses*, 92–97. Jacob's ladder in his dream at Bethel (the house of God) recalls the place of God's presence or the place of the gateway to heaven. John 1:51 is related to ascending and descending motif of the Son of Man (3:13–14; 8:28; 12:23, 34; 13:31) as king's enthronement. This motif is also related to the function of Jesus as the universal king, that is, as he is the only way to come to the Father (14:6), this verse implies that the Johannine Jesus is opening his new world to his followers (14:2).

who is God and King.[312] His kingship is revealed more clearly as the narrative proceeds to its climax. When the Jews ask him to reveal plainly if he is indeed the Christ (10:24), Jesus reveals himself implicitly as *the Christ* who has power to control life and death and clearly reveals himself as *the Son of God* (10:36). Martha confesses directly to Jesus that he is *the Christ, the Son of God* (11:27) when she meets him before her brother's resuscitation. The multitudes welcome Jesus when he enters Jerusalem, confessing him to be *the King of Israel* (12:13). John is the only evangelist to include this detail. When the Roman soldiers come to arrest Jesus in the garden, they draw back and fall to the ground when Jesus identifies himself to them (18:6) reminiscent of the way in which people fell down before God or a King.[313] At the trial by Pilate, the Jewish leaders accuse Jesus as an evildoer, and also as claiming to be *the Son of God* (18:30; 19:7). Furthermore, when Pilate asks him if he is the king of the Jews, Jesus identifies himself as a *king* (18:33, 36-37), although his kingdom is not of this world (18:36). Pilate refers to Jesus as *the Man* (19:5) as well as *the King of the Jews* (18:39; 19:14-15). When he is crucified, the inscription, "Jesus of Nazareth, the King of the Jews," written in Hebrew, Latin, and Greek, is put on the cross (19:16-22) to show ironically his universal kingship.[314] After death, he is buried in a new

---

312. In the Hebrew Bible, we can also find out the usage of this verb: to worship (bow down to) God (Gen 24:26, 48; Exod 4:31; 12:27; 24:1; 33:10; 2 Sam 12:20; 2 Chr 20:18; 29:30; 32:12; Neh 8:6; 9:3) or kingly figures: 1) Joseph in Gen 42:6; 43:26; 47:31; 2) Judah in Gen 49:8; 3) Pharaoh in Exod 11:8; 4) King David in 1 Sam 25:23; 25:41; 2 Sam 1:2; 9:6, 8; 14:4, 22, 33; 16:4; 18:28; 24:20; 1 Kgs 1:16, 23, 31, 47; 5) Samuel in 1 Sam 28:14; 1 Chr 21:21; (cf. in 1 Chr 29:20 the LORD and the king were worshipped by the people) 6) King Solomon in 1 Kgs 1:53; 7) Elisha in 2 Kgs 2:15; 4:37; 8) King Jehoiada in 2 Chr 24:10; 9) Haman in Esth 3:2; 10) Daniel in Dan 2:46; 11) King Nebuchadnezzar in Dan 3:6, 7, 10-15, 18). In the Synoptic Gospels, Jesus is the object of worship (Matt 2:2, 8, 11; 8:2; 9:18; 14:33; 15:25; 18:16; 20:20; 28:9; Mark 5:6; 15:19; 24:52). In Revelation, God and Lamb are the object of worship: 4:10; 5:14; 7:11; 11:1, 16: 14:7; 15:4; 19:4). In the Gospel of John, the appropriate use of the verb, to worship, shows the divinity of the Johannine Jesus as king in the broader Johannine context (4:20-24; 12:20-21) including the Johannine Christology (1:1, 18: 20:28) (Keener, *Gospel of John*, 795). Lincoln remarks, "After the acclamation of Jesus as Lord and in the context of this Gospel's conception of Christ as one with God, it may well be that the man's worship is meant to be understood in the strongest sense of the word, so that the accompanying act makes his confession equivalent to the later one by Thomas: 'My Lord and my God' (20.28)" (Lincoln, *Gospel*, 287).

313. The reaction of the soldiers recalls the typical human reaction to a theophany in the Hebrew Bible (Gen 18:2; 19:1; 24:52; Num 22:31; Ezek 1:28; Dan 10:9). John 18:8 reveals "the ultimate powerlessness of the massed representatives of this world's powers (the Roman forces, the Jewish guards and the disciple turned betrayer)" before the presence of "the unique divine agent who is one with God" (Lincoln, *Gospel*, 445).

314. Various titles that are employed to designate Roman emperors in Inscriptions and papyri are written in Greek or Latin.

tomb in a garden (20:41-42) like the burial of Jewish kings (19:40-42). After Jesus' resurrection, Thomas makes the climactic confession to Jesus that he is *"My Lord and My God,"* (20:28), a phrase applied to Roman emperors. Finally, the author reveals Jesus' identity as *the Christ and the Son of God* for which purpose this Gospel had been written (20:31).

Secondly, in the Gospel of John, Jesus' explicit avowals of his kingship are found (4:26; 10:24-25; 18:33-37). He is described as the king who wants to liberate the margins from the yoke of the Jewish religion as well as from the oppression of the Roman imperial power; he wants to lead them into the new world in which they can live together in harmony with less nationalism and without competition and struggles. It is necessary in connection with this viewpoint to say that there is a number of passages in which people convey their beliefs about Jesus in the Gospel.[315] It is evident that "representative people (disciples, ordinary people, the crowd, Jewish leaders, Samaritans) express representative beliefs and raise representative objections"[316] about Jesus. Furthermore, this shows that the various terms and motifs from the various backgrounds are used in the Gospel for the identification of Jesus.[317] Therefore, it seems that the various terms employed by the people to confess the identity of Jesus are related to Jewish expectations of the coming of the Messianic King, while other terms allude to royal titles in the Graeco-Roman world. Various titles (the Son, the Son of God, the Son of Man, Prophet, teacher sent by God, king, or Messiah) could not correspond completely with the real status and authority of Jesus, although they are not wrong but insufficient; and they need further definition to understand their full meanings in the contexts where they are used.[318] In addition, as van Bruggen remarks, "there was not just one Judaism but many kinds of Judaism existing side by side, and each kind generated its own messianic notions."[319] If his view is correct, it is a possible explanation as to why there are many Johannine christological titles that were linked with differing messianic expectations. Whether the Gospel was written in the surroundings

---

315. De Jonge argues, "In this process an important role is assigned to controversies with Jewish opponents. . . . The result is a specific, very characteristic Johannine Christology of a community that sees itself as standing in the tradition of the disciples in the Gospel" (de Jonge, "Christology," 214-15).

316. De Jonge, "Jewish Expectations," 248.

317. Painter, "Point," 231-52. Painter argues that "rather than seeing tensions between different traditions in this we may recognize the evangelist's use of a variety of motifs in the development of the Christology of the Gospel."

318. See de Jonge, "Jewish Expectation," 246-70. See also de Jonge, *Jesus*.

319. Van Bruggen, *Jesus*, 130.

of many kinds of Judaism which separately generated their own messianic notions,[320] or written in the surroundings of various ideas of the messianic expectations in one kind of Judaism,[321] it is clear that various kinds of titles (Elijah, the Prophet, the Christ, etc) were used to designate messianic figures by the contemporaries of the Johannine Gospel, and were also employed by the author to designate the identity of Jesus.[322] It is important to know, therefore, that John presents all aspects of the identity of Jesus using various titles without negating any one of them. The author also uses diverse christological titles, weaving them together to express an overall view of the identity of the Johannine Jesus.

It is important, then, that the titles employed to designate the identity of Jesus are able to reveal their fuller meaning when they are interpreted together in consideration with the meanings of other terms. Whether some terms were preferred by one group and others by another group, or whether the terms used imply conflict between the groups,[323] the successive locations of the titles in the Gospel, i.e., the Messiah/Christ and the Son of God, the Son of God and the King of Israel, etc. show that the author carefully put them together in order that the readers could come to know his identity without any misunderstanding caused by their different ethnic, cultural, or religious backgrounds.

---

320. See Neusner, Green, and Frerichs, *Judaisms and Their Messiahs*.

321. Van Bruggen, *Jesus*, 130.

322. For example, according to Matt 17:10–12, the scribes expected that Elijah must come first to restore all things. Jesus admitted their notion that Elijah must come first, saying that Elijah had already come. In order to draw out the fuller meaning of the royal terms, therefore, it is necessary to investigate them in both backgrounds.

323. De Jonge's explanation about this point emphasizes that the different titles are the result of the conflict between the Jews and the Christians (See de Jonge, "Christology," 209–29). However, if existed, the conflict of the Johannine community is not only between the Jews, but also between the Imperial power and the Christians.

4. The Kingship of Jesus in the Use of the Title Βασιλεύς and the Term Βασιλεία

IN THE PREVIOUS CHAPTER, I discussed a variety of christological titles that reveal the kingship of the Johannine Jesus. They contain many contact points with the political, religious, economic, cultural, or societal ideology of both the Jewish and the Graeco-Roman traditions. Particularly, the titles attributed to the royal Messiah and/or to the emperors "are often given an explanation in the text which brings them closer semantically: Jesus as a king who receives this authority from God."[1] Consequently, these titles applied to Jesus also often evoke Jewish and Graeco-Roman traditions that serve to contest Jewish messianic hope and Roman power, and present Jesus as one who is an alternative and superior to the Jewish messiah and the Roman emperor.[2] The title, "king of Israel/the Jews (ὁ βασιλεὺς τοῦ Ἰσραήλ/ὁ βασιλεὺς τῶν Ἰουδαίων)," is not exceptional in its usage in the Gospel. This term can deliever deeper meaning and understanding of the Johannine Jesus in with the light of backgrounds, as do other christological titles.

In this present chapter, therefore, in order to investigate further the kingship of the Johannine Jesus I will survey, firstly, the terms "king/kingdom (βασιλεύς/βασιλεία)," examining their general meaning in both Jewish and Graeco-Roman texts. Then, I will discuss the usage of the term "king" when it is attributed to Jesus in the Gospel.

---

1. Van Tilborg, *Reading*, 26.

2. Carter, *John and Empire*, 177 (–184). The titles, the Messiah/Christ and the Son of Man, were not used to indicate the Roman emperors; however, they are interlinked with other royal Christological titles in the Gospel to give a deeper understanding of Jesus' identity as king. That is, they evoke Jewish traditions challenging imperial claims.

A Survey of the Meanings of King/Kingdom

King in the Jewish Background

In this section, I will briefly deal with the Hebrew terms, *Melek/Malkut*,[3] in order to understand better the kingship of the Johannine Jesus in relation with the term, "the king (of Israel/of the Jews)." Generally, these terms, *Melek/malkut*,[4] were used for an earthly monarchy (1 Kgs 2:21; 1 Chr 12:23; 2 Chr 11:17; 1 Sam 20:31; 2 Sam 7; 23:1–7; Pss 2; 20; 21; 45; 72; 101; 110; 132; Jer 49:34; Dan 9:1), the Davidic redeemer-king in Jewish Eschatology,[5] or God as king (Isa 6:5; Ex 15:18; 1 Sam 12:12; Pss 145:11–21; 146:10; Isa 23:23; 33:22; Zeph 3:15; Obad 21; Zech 14:6–7; Pss 47; 93; 96; 97; 99) to show his eternal and universal rule in the Hebrew Bible. It is necessary to refer to three points about the use of this term in the light of its Jewish background, which are related to this book.

Firstly, "God as king" is observed in the lengthy and central tradition in the Hebrew Bible. The primary meaning of the Hebrew *malkut* is abstract and dynamic, that is, "sovereignty" or "royal rule" when it is applied to God in the Hebrew Bible and Jewish literature.[6] Thus God is described as "the King of Israel" and as "the King of the world" who rules the world and controls history (Jer 10:7, 10–16; Zech 14:9, 16–17; Mal 1:14; Pss 22:28; 24:1–10; 47:2, 7).[7] In other words, "human kingship was limited and conditional, under the continuing divine kingship of Yahweh

---

3. "Βασιλεύς" is the Greek form of the word "king," while its Hebrew form "*Melek/Malkut.*"

4. The term *Malkut*, which can be rendered "kingdom" or "kingship," has several meanings: secular sense of a political kingdom/empire (1 Sam 20:31; 1 Kgs 2:12); God's sphere of power (Pss 103:19; 145:11, 13; Dan 3:33; cf. Ps 22:28); kingdom of God (Dan 7; cf. the final kingdom of the believers, Dan 2:44; 4:22; an eternal kingdom, Dan 7:27). Particularly, when it refers to "kingdom of heaven," it "can never mean the kingdom of God in the sense of territory ruled by Him." Thus, it "denotes the fact that God is King, i.e., His kingly being or kingship" (see von Rad, "βασιλεύς," 570–71).

5. This expected king was of the house of David (2 Sam 7; Amos 9:11–15; Isa 9; Mic 5:1–5; Jer 23:5–6; Ezek 17:22–24; 34:23–24; 37:24–5; Isa 45:1–25; Zech 6:9–15). "The whole complex of religious and political ideas linked with the empirical king . . . all these form the soil for Messianic belief" (von Rad, "βασιλεύς," 566–67).

6. Caragounis, "Kingdom of God/Kingdom of Heaven," 417. His kingship or kingdom is manifested on earth where it is accepted and obeyed by humanity (Bruce, *Gospel*, 82).

7. The declaration of the Jewish leaders before Pilate, the representative of the Roman imperial power, "we have no king but Caesar" (in John 19:15) shows that they disavow God's kingship and his sovereignty over the world, while they submit their exclusive loyalty to the Roman emperor, not to God in order to deny Jesus' kingship.

(1 Sam 8; 19:17–27)."[8] Thus, knowing the origin and authority of a king is crucially important for his genuine kingship. In terms of origin and authority, the Fourth Gospel shows clearly the nature of Jesus' kingship. From the beginning of the Gospel, John clearly shows that Jesus' origin is from above (heaven, from God) (1:1–18; 3:2, 13, 31; 7:16; cf. 8:58). Furthermore, in John 19:10–11, the Johannine Jesus clearly affirms that the authority comes from above (heaven), namely from God, not from any earthly power. In this sense, John shows that the kingship of Jesus is linked closely with the matter of authority from God.

Secondly, the king from the house of David who rules in the kingdom of God (2 Sam 7:11–17; 1 Chr 17:14; 28:5; 29:23; 2 Chr 9:8; 13:8), and the expectations of the Davidic Messiah had been developed in Judaism (Isa 11:1–9; 9:2–8; cf. Mic 5:2–5; Jer 23:5–6; Amos 9:11–15; cf. Gen 49:8–12). Thus the title "the King of Israel" is closely related to the Davidic Messiah in the Jewish background (Pss 2:6; 72:1; Jer 32:5; Ezek 37:24; Zech 9:9; *Pss. Sol.* 17:21, 32, 42). In the Gospel of John, just as various Christologcial titles are interwined to portray Jesus as a royal Messiah,[9] it is precisely the title "the king of Israel/the Jews" that is employed to work in the same way. In fact, the christological terms in John seem to work more than that: they are used to portray the Johannine Jesus as the universal king beyond the Jewish messiah. The term "the king of the Jews" is used to show his universal kingship in the passion narrative (in particular the ironical proclamation on the cross in three languages, "Jesus of Nazareth, the king of the Jews").[10]

Thirdly, in the Jewish messianic theology of kingship, the kingly role of God is combined with that of the expected Davidic Messiah.[11] Thus, the earthly kings are kings only because and in so far as God allows. Therefore, "kingship is linked with the question on whose authority one is a king."[12] In this sense, the idea that God has real authority and only appoints the kings in this world is a penetrating and central theme throughout the Hebrew Bible. Thus, it is generally believed in Judaism that the kings who are appointed by God are able to have real kingship and a real kingdom. Accordingly, "in the later Judaism the thought of the Messiah is always the expression of a hope for the last times which knows God primarily as the King of Israel, as

8. Horsley, "Jesus and Empire," 87.

9. On this, see chapters 2 and 3 of this book.

10. See the section, "The King of the Jews in the Passion Narrative," of this chapter.

11. Klappert, "King," 374; Carson comments, "The coming ruler was . . . differentiated from the LORD, and in other passages identified with him—just as the Word is both differentiated from God, and identified with him (John 1:1)" (Carson, *Gospel*, 188). On this title, see chapter 3 of this book.

12. Van Tilborg, *Reading*, 52.

the goal of God's plan of salvation, with the Messiah as a king to whom all other peoples will be subject."[13] In other words, the Davidic Messiah rules the entire world with authority, representing the kingly rule of God.[14]

It is meaningful, therefore, to say that the relationship between the Messiah and God in terms of kingship is similar to that between Jesus and God in the Gospel of John. The question of God's kingship is not raised in the Gospel because the Johannine God is described as the Father of Jesus rather than as king. God's position as king is probably pressupposed in the Gospel, but it is not explicitly addressed and plays no central role. Whereas, Jesus, the Son of the Father (of God) who was sent by God, is the central figure in terms of kingship in the Fourth Gospel, because the very fact that Jesus who came from above has the same authority as God implies his kingship. The kingship of Jesus is no secret in John's Gospel, because from the very beginning, "John proclaims Jesus' position as king and the question of his kingship is kept warm throughout his story in a much more explicit and prominent way."[15] In John, Jesus has authority and power to rule the world as the agent of God. Jesus as king came to the world to save and judge as God the Father commissions him (3:18–21; 5:22, 27; 9:39; 12:48).

King in the Graeco-Roman Background

In this section, I will also deal briefly with the term, "king," to the extent that it is meaningful to interpret the Johannine text in terms of kingship. Firstly, the title "king" was employed to indicate important figures, mainly royal families, from the past in the Graeco-Roman world. Moreover, some of them had an ideological role in the first century context.[16] Thus, in the Greek world, the term βασιλεύς was used widely to refer to earthly, divinized kings, or to ancient gods like Zeus.[17] The Hellenistic kings, for example, combind the elements of both regal traditions, the Macedonian and the Egyptian and Persian.[18] Particularly, the concept of the rulers as "sons of god"

13. Kuhn, "βασιλεύς," 574.

14. Klappert, "King, Kingdom," 374.

15. Kvalbein, "Kingdom," 230. On this, see chapter 3 of this book. The climactic question and confirmation of his kingship is in the Passion narrative.

16. Van Tilborg, *Reading*, 25, 33–38.

17. Brown, *Gospel*, 880; Kleinknecht, "βασιλεύς," 564–65; Klappert, "King, Kingdom," 373.

18. "The Ptolemies adopted the traditional titles and other accoutrements of the Pharaohs and were welded into the Pharaonic tradition of kingship" (Grabbe, "Terminology," 232). Brown also comments, "Although the imagery may have had its roots in pagan (Egyptian) parallels where it was thought that a god sexually begot the king of

4. THE KINGSHIP OF JESUS IN THE USE OF βασιλεύς AND βασιλεία

was developed, and succeeded in the imperial cult, which had built up the incarnation of divinity in the emperor.[19] Consequently, "the Hellenistic idea of divine kingship originating with Alexander the Great was revived again in the Roman emperor cult."[20] In addition, according to the New Testament[21] and Josephus,[22] this term in general was attributed to the emperors. In short, the word "king" (βασιλεύς) was one of the titles of the Roman emperor employed particularly in the eastern part of the Empire, to indicate his ambiguous position between gods and mortals.[23] Thus, "this title contributes to the mosaic of references that suggest that the Fourth Gospel repeatedly implies a comparison between Jesus and the emperor."[24]

Secondly, the term βασιλεία "commonly refers to empires like Rome's, just as the term βασιλεύς, usually translated 'king,' is used to denote emperors."[25] In this point, to the first century readers, it is highly probable that to call Jesus "king" presented a challenge to the Roman emperor.[26] In addition, "entering the kingdom of God" also challenges the readers that the actual kingdom they pursue is God's kingdom/sovereignty, from where Jesus' kingship originated, not from Roman Empire/sovereignty.

---

a human mother, the specific Israelite concept associated sonship with the anointing which made a man king" (Brown, *Gospel*, 139).

19. On the usage of the term Son of God, see also chapter 3 of this book. Some scholars suggest that there might be possible connections between the contents of the Gospel and the language and the ideology of the imperial cult. Thus, scholars have attempted comparative study between them. On this, see Salier, "Jesus, the Emperor," 284–301; van Tilborg, *Reading*; Carter, *John and Empire*; Thatcher, *Greater than Caesar*.

20. Klappert, "King, Kingdom," 372–73; on the successors of Alexander called kings and the presence of kings in the Augustus-Trajan era, see van Tilborg, *Reading*, 34–36. Grabbe says, "Beginning with Alexander and continuing under the Diadochi, other aspects of the Hellenistic monarchies developed that were not characteristic of the Macedonian kings" (Grabbe, "Terminology," 232).

21. 1 Tim 2:2; 1 Pet 2:13, 17; Rev 17:12.

22. Josephus, *J.W.* 3.351; 5.563, Ῥωμαίων βασιλεῖς; cf. 4.596, to the Flavian line of Vespasian and his sons; 5.58–60, to Titus.

23. Aune, "Roman Emperors," 234; cf. Dio Chrysostom, *Kingship* 1.22 in *Dio Chrysostom, I, Discourses 1–11* (Cohoon, LCL), to Trajan, the king is to be a father to the people.

24. Salier, "Jesus the Emperor," 297. John 19:12–16 shows the explicit comparison between Jesus and the Caesar in terms of king. Thatcher argues, "John believed that Christ is in every way superior to Caesar, and his gospel communicates this vision by reversing the normal public meaning of Jesus' encounters with various agents of the Roman Empire" (Thatcher, *Greater than Caesar*, ix).

25. Carter, *Matthew and Empire*, 5.

26. Carter, *Matthew and Empire*, 5.

Thirdly, in the Roman world, it was a convention that the Roman emperors appointed the client-kings, who had played an important role to maintain the Empire. These kings "are kings only, because and in as far the Roman emperors allow them to be. Kingship is linked with the question on whose authority one is a king."[27] When they were told that Jesus was "king" in the Fourth Gospel, the readers living in the Roman Empire could understand him as one of the kings who ruled a part of the Empire in the Emperor's place. On this point, van Tilborg says,

> When Jesus is called "king" in the Johannine Gospel, the readers in [Ephesus] will link that to other kings who played and play a role in the city. Jesus is king next to other kings. The effect of this is reinforced, because his kingship is linked to the name of a country (Israel) or to the inhabitants of a country (king of the Jews), the same as other kings from far away regions: from Pontus, Armenia, the Commagene. Johannine history is about such a king from a far country.[28]

More importantly, we should ask the question, "From whom did he get his kingship?,"[29] because the Gospel of John presents a Jesus who comes from above, is sent by God (5:23, 24, 36, 37; 6:38, 57; 7:16, 29; 8:16, 18, 29; 12:45, 49; 16:15; 17:18, 21, 23), whose kingdom is not of this world (18:36), and who is greater than the Roman emperors (19:11) on the textual level.[30] Moreover, reading the Fourth Gospel from a postcolonial perspective, we can appreciate the power of John's vision, looking beyond this world to the new world where Jesus reigns as king, and living alongwith its ruling ideologies, which are love, service, freedom, forgiveness, and peace.[31] Therefore, the kingship of Jesus in the Fourth Gospel needs to be read in comparison with that of the Roman emperors in terms of the question: "Who is the real king (of Israel/of the Jews)?"

---

27. Van Tilborg, *Reading*, 52.

28. Van Tilborg, *Reading*, 52.

29. Van Tilborg, *Reading*, 53.

30. About the general survey on this, see Thatcher, *Greater than Caesar*; Carter, *John and Empire*.

31. See chapters 5 and 6 of this book.

King in the Synoptic Gospels

In the Synoptic Gospels, Jesus also bears the title, "king (of the Jews/of Israel),"[32] while earthly kings including the Roman emperors are explicitly or implicitly compared with God or the Messiah as king.[33] For example, the title "King" (βασιλεύς) was also the same word used for king Herod (Matt. 2:1, 3; cf. Herod as "King of the Jews" in Josephus, *Ant.* 14. 34–36; 15.373–379; 16.311).[34] However, in the Fourth Gospel, Herod the king does not appear, while the Roman Emperor and his representative Pilate appear as one part of the major antagonists of Jesus. This may indicate John's particular interest (and/or the particular context/need of/for the Johannine community). That is, as a resistant document[35] against Imperialism, and as a challenge for its first century readers who lived in the multicultural societies in Rome (particularly its first readers in Ephesus), it seems that the Gospel explicitly used the representative of the imperial royal figures rather than that of regional kings.

The term βασιλεία also signifes the "being," "nature," and "state" of the king, and denotes the king's dignity or power, namely kingship, royal rule, or reign. This kingship is expressed in the realm ruled by a king, i.e., in his kingdom, territory, empire, or dominion. In this sense, this implies that the essential meaning of the term βασιλεία is "reign" rather than "realm," and that this reign is the one that comes down by divine intervention.[36] Marcus claims, "it is not God's *basileia* as the abstract fact that he rules, but the force of his personal self-assertion that manifests his kingship by overpowering the resistance to it in the earthly sphere."[37] However, other scholars suggest the translation "dominion of God" in order to combine the two meanings of

---

32. Jesus is also regarded as "the king" in the Synoptics: "the King of the Jews," Matt 2:2; 27:11; 29:37; Mark 15:2, 9, 12, 18, 26; Luke 23:3; 37–38; "the King of Israel," Matt 27:42; Mark 15:32; cf. Luke 19:38, the anointed king; Luke 23:2, Jesus as the Messiah King in an antithesis to the Roman Emperor.

33. Schmidt, "βασιλεύς, βασιλεία," 576–77; Ferguson, *Backgrounds*, 46.

34. This title may have been a specific title first used by the Hasmonean priest kings, the last independent rulers of Judea before the Roman occupation of Palestine. "Perhaps the title was alive during the Roman governorship as a designation for the expected liberator" (Brown, *Gospel*, 851).

35. Thatcher, *Greater than Caesar*, 16, 33–41.

36. Just as in the case of the usage of the term, *Malkut*, in the Jewish literature: see BDAG, 168; Schmidt, "βασιλεύς, βασιλεία," 580–82; Louw and Nida, *Greek-English Lexicon*, 80; Marcus, "Entering into the Kingly Power," 663–75; Beasley-Murray, *Jesus*, 74; Ladd, *Theology*, 74; Chilton, *God in Strength*.

37. Marcus, "Entering," 664.

"reign" and "kingdom."[38] Kvalbein argues, "The actual use of a phrase in its context determines its meaning, not a preconceived opinion of its meaning as fixed, unchangeable concept."[39] That is, it also could emphasize the teritorial aspect of βασιλεία, the state or area over which a king reigns in some texts. Thus, the meaning of the phrase "the kingdom of God" in the Gospels can broadly be divided into two main senses: "God's decisive intervention in history and human experience and the final state of the redeemed, to which this intervention is designed to lead, including statements about entering the kingdom and the receiving the kingdom."[40]

In the Synoptics, moreover, the term is mainly used in the form of ἡ βασιλεία τοῦ θεοῦ,[41] which has a special and particularly close connection with Jesus Christ himself.[42] Particularly, the kingdom of God in the Gospels "denotes God's eternal rule rather than an earthly kingdom and its scope is universal rather than limited to the Jewish nation, and it was imminent and potentially present in [Jesus] rather than a vague future hope, being inextricably connected with his own person and mission."[43] Therefore, the term provides the Johannine readers with the possibility of a deeper understanding.[44] Although this term apparently has a messianic meaning in Jewish tradition, in the Fourth Gospel it goes beyond a Messiah of traditional expectation to reinforce the point that John is representing Jesus as the universal king with a variety of titles. The Gospel of John looks to Jesus to assert his kingship in order to overcome Roman imperial domination and to lead his followers into the Johannine new world.[45] Accordingly, in

---

38. On the argument for the local significance of the term, see Witheringon, *Christology*, 192–98; Kvalbein, "Kingdom of God," 215–32; Aalen, "'Reign' and 'House,'" 215–40; O'Neill, "Kingdom of God," 130–31; Buchanan, *Jesus*; Witherington, *Jesus, Paul*, 49–74; Sanders, *Historical Figure*, 171–75.

39. Kvalbein, "Kingdom of God," 219.

40. Marcus, "Entering into the Kingly Power," 664; Perrin, *Kingdom of God*, 168–85.

41. In the Gospel of Matthew, ἡ βασιλειά τῶν οὐρανῶν is employed, while in the other three Gospels, ἡ βασιλεία τοῦ θεοῦ is used.

42. See Matt 13:41; 16:28, the Son of Man and his kingdom; Luke 1:33; 22:30; 23:42, the implication of Jesus as king; cf. twice employment of "my kingdom" in emphatic form (ἡ βασιλεία ἡ ἐμή) in John 18:36; Matt 21:9; Luke 19:38, the actual identity of the kingdom with Jesus; Mark 10:29; Matt 19:29; Luke 18:29, the name and message of Jesus, or Jesus himself, are equated with the kingdom of God. These show that there are no references to the βασιλεία of Christ apart from that of God.

43. Caragounis, "Kingdom of God/Kingdom of Heaven," 417.

44. Schnackenburg, *Gospel*, 1:316.

45. Thatcher argues that Jesus as a new king overcomes and secures victory over the imperial power, Pilate, the Jewish authorities and the cross (see Thatcher, *Greater than Caesar*, 11–17).

4. THE KINGSHIP OF JESUS IN THE USE OF βασιλεύς AND βασιλεία   137

the following section, we move on to investigate the usage of the terms, βασιλεύς/ἡ βασιλεία Τοῦ θεοῦ, in this Gospel.

King/Kingdom in the Gospel of John

The titles for Jesus are not always interpreted in the same way in different texts.[46] Sometimes the Johannine titles are interpreted differently from the titles in the Synoptics. That is to say, different interpretations might come from the authors' more or less different composition purposes; from different emphases on the life and teaching of Jesus for the necessity of the different contexts, namely from different communities' situations which might cause different portrayals of Jesus;[47] and/or different people and authority figures and/or different plots involved in the narrative world which produces a different understanding of the story,[48] more specifically a different identification of Jesus. Thus the title, "king,"[49] which is used to designate Jesus mostly in John, may be employed to create the kingly identification of Jesus (his universal kingship) more clearly.[50]

There are several passages which reveal explicitly the kingship of Jesus using the term "the king (of Israel/the Jews)" in John.[51]

Firstly, in John 1:18–51, John employs this term as the climactic title to reveal Jesus' identity in 1:49: "You are the Son of God; you are the King of Israel (σὺ εἶ ὁ υἱὸς τοῦ θεοῦ, σὺ βασιλεὺς εἶ τοῦ Ἰσραήλ)."[52] The unique point in this passage is that only John puts these two major christological titles together in series to clarify the identity of Jesus.[53] That is, John

46. Barrett, *Gospel*, 71; Beasley-Murray, *John*, lxxxii.

47. Ridderbos, *Gospel*, 10–11.

48. For example, the Gospel of John "has Jesus recognized by his followers as Son of God from the outset of his ministry and then develops this category as the key to understanding Jesus' true identity" while the Synoptics employs it in the later part of them (Mark 15:39; Matt 14:33; 16:16; 27:54) (Lincoln, *Gospel*, 121).

49. John uses the term "king" sixteen times, which refers to Jesus on almost every occasion: King: 6:15; 12:15; 18:37 (x2); 19:12, 15 (x2); the King of Israel: 1:49; 12:13; the King of the Jews: 18:33, 39; 19:3, 14, 19, 21(x2); the Kingdom of God: 3:3, 5.

50. Caragounis, "Kingdom of God," 125: except "no king but Caesar."

51. It is striking, by using this term, John emphasizes Jesus' kingly role more often than the Synoptic Gospels do (see Reinhartz, *Word*, 110–12; Thompson, "Gospel of John," 378).

52. About this, see chapter 3 of this book. Carter argues that "Nathanael's ascription of the title 'King of Israel' to Jesus (John 1:49) evokes this sort of kingship, as does the people's welcome to Jesus as he enters Jerusalem (John 12:15). Kingship is God-given . . . and cannot be enacted by the people (6:16)" (Carter, *John and Empire*, 192).

53. Ridderbos comments that "the notion that . . . 'Son of God' completely

emphasizes Jesus' kingship by putting these titles together. This term confessed by Nathanael in John serves to reveal the kingship of Jesus, as does the term "King of the Jews" spoken by the Magi in Matthew 2:2.[54] However, by adding the other christological title "the Son of God" John clarifies the kingship of Jesus. This implies an attempt to reveal Jesus' identity as king more explicitly in the Gospel.[55]

Secondly, only in John 3:3, 5, does John say that Jesus reveals clearly how to see/enter the kingdom of God.[56] In this narrative, the term, "king," does not appear. However, it is necessary to investigate "the kingdom of God" with reference to Jesus' kingship.

Thirdly, in John 6:14–15 the narrator explicitly uses the term "king" when the crowd[57] attempts to make him "king" by force after he feeds them.[58] This narration implies that at least the first century readers could easily understand Jesus' kingly role because of Jesus' benefaction.

Fourthly, in the story of Jesus' triumphal entry into Jerusalem, the crowd welcomes him and hails him as "the King of Israel." The story reveals explicitly the kingship of Jesus (12:13, 15). The triumphal entry of the Johannine Jesus could be read as the revelation of his kingship to the readers both in Jewish and Graeco-Roman backgrounds.[59] Particularly in this passage, many points can be used to denote the establishment of God's rule by the Johannine Jesus: his entry into Jerusalem with people waving palm branches in John 12:13 as symbols of national victory (1 Macc 13:15;

---

overshadows 'King/Messiah,' thus proving that in Johannine Christology the typically Jewish categories are blurred, is in conflict with all that has preceded in vss. 35ff, . . . which in fact depicts all these initial encounters in colors derived from Old Testament and Jewish future expectation" (Ridderbos, *Gospel*, 91).

54. This is the only occurrence of the term in the Synoptic Gospels outside the passion narratives.

55. Koester, "Messianic Exegesis," 27; Lincoln, *Gospel*, 121. It is striking that the Fourth Gospel refers the term to Jesus more than twice as often as the Synoptics (Morris, *Gospel*, 147).

56. Caragounis argues that although the Fourth Gospel and the Synoptics share several common aspects in their presentation of the Kingdom of God, there are significant differences between them because of the Johannine ideology (Caragounis, "Kingdom of God," 125–34).

57. The crowd confesses Jesus as "the Prophet who is to come into the world" (6:14). This shows that the close relationship of the terms, the Prophet and the king, in the semantic field of the Gospel of John.

58. On this, see chapter 3 of this book. The first century readers could read the Johannine Jesus as a benefactor in the Graeco-Roman world because of his food supply, and also as the Mosaic king (Lierman, "Mosaic Pattern" 210–34).

59. see Carter, *John and Empire*, 162–89; Koester, "Savior"; Kinman, *Jesus' Entry*, 25–65; Carter, *Matthew and the Margins*, 413–18.

4. THE KINGSHIP OF JESUS IN THE USE OF βασιλεύς AND βασιλεία

2 Macc 10:7); the shouts of "Hosanna" or "Save us, O King"; the use of the title "King of Israel" from Zephaniah 3:15–16; the quote in John 12:13 from the royal Psalm 118, which gives thanks for victory over enemies; and the citing in John 12;15 of Zech 9:9, which anticipates God's victorious entry into Jerusalem as king of the nations. Carter comments,

> [I]t is an antitriumphal entry into Jerusalem, evoking and mocking Roman displays of greatness and conquest while proclaiming God's victory, which is taking place in Jesus even now. ... Jesus theologically confirms this momentum by declaring his death in accord with God's purposes.[60]

Lastly, and most importantly, in the passion narrative, Jesus' kingship is explicitly revealed through this title. Unlike the passion narratives in the Synoptics, in the Fourth Gospel there is a long trial between Jesus and Pilate on the kingship of Jesus, where the term, the king of the Jews, is mainly employed.

In this section, we shall focus on two Johannine passages, John 3 (particularly, 3:3, 5, 12, 13, 15 and 16) and the passion narrative (18:33; 38, 39; 19:1–5, 12, 13–15; 19:19–22, 38–42), which are not fully dealt with in the previous chapter, to clarify the kingship of the Johannine Jesus.

The King of Israel/the King of the Jews

John employs two expressions, "the king of Israel," and "the king of the Jews," to designate Jesus.[61] However, it is not clear that "the king of the Jews" is to be distinguished from "the king of Israel" in the Johannine narratives. Bauckham argues that "the king of the Jews" is merely expressing the same idea in "Gentile or Gentile-friendly terms."[62] For example, Nathanael as a true Israelite who has no deceit (1:47) admits and confesses Jesus as "the Son of God and the King of Israel" (1:49), and the large Jewish crowd (12:13–14) hail Jesus as "the King of Israel"[63] in the triumphal entry story, whereas Gentiles including Pilate and Roman soliders (18:33, 39; 19:3, 19) speak of "the King

---

60. Carter, *John and Empire*, 167.

61. Carson comments that "both expressions were in the popular mind largely tied to expectations of a political liberator" (Carson, *Gospel*, 162).

62. Bauckham, "Messianism," 60; Carson, *Gospel*, 162; Ridderbos, *Gospel*, 593; van Tilborg argues that the term "Israel" has positive connotations in the Johannine text while this is certainly not so with "the Jews" (van Tilborg, *Reading*, 26; see also Lincoln, *Gospel*, 474).

63. Cf. Matt 27:41–42; Mark 15:31–32 (the chief priests with scribes and elders).

of the Jews"[64] to address Jesus. In addition, when Palestinian Jews speak to or write for Gentiles, they prefer to use "the Jews," so do the chief priests to Pilate (19:21).[65] Accordingly, it is fair to deal with the two terms, "the king of Israel" and "the king of the Jews," as synonyms in John.

Furthermore, this term, "the king of Israel," is employed to reveal the identity of Jesus by significant figures in the Gospel. In chapter 1, this term is used when Jesus' kingship is confessed by Nathanael as a representative of the true Israelites (believers). Likewise, in chapter 3, the term "the kingdom of God" which is slightly differernt in form, but almost the same in meaning, is used, when Jesus as the representative of the kingdom of God shows firmly the kingdom of God[66] to Nicodemus, a representative of the Jewish leaders. Finally, the term, "the king of the Jews," is used several times in the Passion narrative, when Pilate, a representative of the Gentiles and of the Imperial power, is inquiring the identity of Jesus with this term. In the Passion Narrative, John reveals that Pilate proves ironically the kingship of Jesus in the trial; Jesus himself does not deny his kingship; and that his suffering and death is the ultimate decision by the king for the world.[67] Finally, on the cross, the universal kingship of Jesus is approved ironically in the trilingual titulus, "Jesus of Nazareth, the King of the Jews."

The Kingdom of God in John 3

Here, I will investigate the term "the kingdom of God" in John 3 in relation to the kingship of Jesus.[68] Firstly, in the beginning of the dialogue in John 3, Nicodemus acknowledges who Jesus is, using the expression, "a teacher who has come from God." Here, Nicodemus "wants to set up criteria by which to access who Jesus is." That is, "Nicodemus claims he can 'see' something of

---

64. Cf. Matt 2:2 (by the Magi); 27:11, 29, 37 (by Pilate and Roman Soldiers); Mark 15:2, 9, 18, 26; Luke 23:3, 37, 38.

65. Kuhn, "Ἰσραήλ," 359–69; Bauckham, "Messianism," 59. Tomson, "'Jews,'" 176–212.

66. Jesus brings his followers into it. In this sense, Jesus is the king.

67. In this sense, Jesus is not a victim of the Imperial power. He is the king who controls the situation and has authority of life and death (to give life and a right to withdraw life); for a contrasting view on this, see Orchard, *Courting Betrayal*. John shows that Jesus himself takes his life into death for the sake of his sheep (10:15–18; see also Thatcher, *Greater than Caesar*, 97–122).

68. Because of the saving sovereignty of God manifest in Jesus through the whole Gospel, John is concerned with the kingship of God in Jesus, although the term "kingdom of God" occurs in John 3:3, 5 (Beasley-Murray, *John*, 330).

4. THE KINGSHIP OF JESUS IN THE USE OF βασιλεύς AND βασιλεία

who Jesus is in the miracles."[69] However, his claim is only partly acceptable in the narrative world, because the revelation of the identity of the Johannine Jesus does not end with an agreement of Nicodemus' understanding of the identity and role of Jesus (a *teacher* who has come from God) in John 3:1–21. "That Jesus is 'a teacher come from God', for example, is true beyond the comprehension of Nicodemus (3:2), for Jesus is the Revealer from Heaven to bring the ultimate truth of God to man."[70] Similarly, the Johannine Jesus is not a typical prophet in the Jewish tradition, but "the prophet who should come into the world."

> He performs greater works in a great exodus for redemption unto life in the kingdom of God (3:14–15; 6:32–58). While the related terms "Messiah," "King of Israel," "Son of God" are all rooted in Israel's religion and eschatological hope, they acquire deeper dimensions in the Fourth Gospel; so also the significant variants of Messiah, "Lamb of God," "the Holy One of God" (6:69), and "the Savior of the world" (4:42). "The King of Israel" is expounded in terms of the king who has come into the world to bear witness to the truth (18:37).[71]

Thus, the passage shows that the identity of the Johannine Jesus goes beyond Nicodemus's limited understanding.[72] John reveals that Jesus is more than a teacher of Israel through the scene of Jesus' response to Nicodemus in this passage.[73] It is in his answer that the term "the kingdom of God" is used to reveal the identity and role of Jesus.[74] Therefore, John reports that Jesus insists no one can "see"[75] the kingdom (saving reign) of God at all, unless

---

69. Carson, *Gospel*, 187.

70. Beasley-Murray, *John*, lxxxii.

71. Beasley-Murray, *John*, lxxxii.

72. In the narrative world, "the tactic of the Johannine discourse is always for the answer to transpose the topic to a higher level" (Brown, *Gospel*, 138). About the Johannine usage of this tactic, see John 3:4; 4:11; 8:22; 11:13; 13:36–38; cf. 7:35; 7:41–42; 8:56–57 (Barrett, *Gospel*, 208).

73. Jesus' answer is meant to show Nicodemus that Jesus has not come from God in the sense that Nicodemus thought (a man approved by God), but in the unique sense of having descended from God's presence to raise men to God (see Brown, *Gospel*, 138).

74. "The kingdom of God" is closely related to reveal who Jesus is in the context, although "kingdom of God" (John 3:3, 5) can be rendered as "the royal reign or kingdom of God" in terms of a chiefly eschatological concept. Many scholars argue that John puts more emphasis on the realized eschatology then the futuristic, although this view is quite disputed. On more discussions, see Caragounis, "Kingdom of God," 125–34; de Jonge, "Radical Eschatology," 481–87; Caragounis, "Kingdom of God/The Kingdom of Heaven," 473–80.

75. There is no essential difference in meaning between them (see Barrett, *Gospel*,

"born from above"[76] (3:3).[77] In particular, in John 3:5, Jesus repeatedly insists that one must be born of water, that is, the Spirit,[78] who comes "from above," to enter the kingdom of God. Here, Jesus states that the Spirit is the instrument of regeneration, namely of entering the kingdom of God. Then, in John 3:34, John reveals that Jesus is the dispenser of the Spirit without limit to humanity (οὐ γὰρ ἐκ μέτρου δίδωσιν[79] τὸ πνεῦμα; cf. 14:26; 15:26; 20:22). In

---

209; Lindars, *Gospel*, 152—merely stylistic; Morris, *Gospel*, 189; cf. "entering the kingdom of God" in the Synoptics: Matt 5:20; 7:21; 18:3; 19:23–24; 23:14; Mark 9:47; 10:15, 23–25; Luke 18:17, 25). Bruce comments, "To a Jew with Nicodemus's unbringing, seeing the kingdom of God would mean participation in the age to come, the resurrection of life. In this Gospel as in the others 'the kingdom of God' in this sense is interchangeable with 'eternal life'" (Bruce, *Gospel*, 83; see also Carson, *Gospel*, 188). Caragounis also argues that John replaced "the kingdom of God" sayings in Synoptics with an emphasis on "eternal life" (Caragounis, "Kingdom of God," 125–26).

76. "Ἄνωθεν" can be translated into "again," "anew," or "from above" (see Keener, *Gospel of John*, 538–39; Carson, *Gospel*, 188; Morris, *Gospel*, 189). This word is one of the Johannine uses of the words in double meaning. We can find many words of double meaning in John. They are "this man" (19:5); "again/from above" (3:3, 7); "to die for" (11:50–51; cf. 18:14); "king" (19:14–15, 19, 21); "to give thanks" (6:11, 23); "sit/appoint" (19:13); "seize/understand" (1:5); "water" (3:5; 4:10); "go up" (8:21; 13:33); "sleep" (11:13); "lifted up" (3:4; 8:28; 12:32, 34) (see Barrett, *Gospel*, 208; Carson, *Gospel*, 189). In this passage, it is better to translate this word as "from above," because "Just as the Redeemer 'comes from above' (3:31; 3:13), so also the redeemed must be born 'from above'" (Ridderbos, *Gospel*, 125).

77. The earthly things (Judaism, water-baptism, or Roman order etc.) are inadequate for the kingdom of God where the Johannine Jesus reigns; "men must be prepared by a radical renewal of themselves, a new birth effected by the Spirit who comes as the advance guard of the new age" (Barrett, *Gospel*, 209; see also Morris, *Gospel*,189). In this sense, Johannine ideology is very radical. On its ideology of the Johannine new world (love, service, freedom, forgiveness, and peace), see chapter 6 of this book.

78. The regeneration of which Jesus speaks is not a physical birth, but a spiritual birth (3:6, 8; cf. 7:39). Thus, although there are some possible alternatives, the expression "born of water and Spirit (γεννηθῇ ἐξ ὕδατος καὶ πνεύματος)" can be translated as "born of water, that is, the Spirit," "since both nouns are anarthrous and are governed by a single preposition and the "καί" likely functions here epexegetically" (see Keener, *Gospel of John*, 546–52; esp. 550; Carson, *Gospel*, 189–95; esp. 194). As there is no great difference in meaning between "seeing" the kingdom of God and "entering" the kingdom of God, so there are no great difference in meaning between "born from above" and "born of water and spirit." However, the phrase "born of water and spirit" echoes the Hebrew Bible phraseology (Ezek 36:25–27; 37:9; 1QS 4:19–21) and "might have been calculated to ring a bell in Nicomdemus's mind" (Bruce, *Gospel*, 84; Lincoln, *Gospel*, 150).

79. The subject of this verb could be Jesus or God as well. However, the point that Jesus is the giver of the Spirit to humanity is not changed, because the Father gives Jesus the Spirit to carry out God's works in Johannine theology ("all things into his hand," 3:35; 13:3). We can find similarity in Johannine theology that "Jesus is the giver in 4:10; 6:27; 14:27, and the Son indeed exercises delegated authity to carry out God's works" (Keener, *Gospel of John*, 582).

this sense, we can also say that Jesus is the king in terms of the only giver of life to humanity in the kingdom of God.[80] Thus, the employment of the term "Kingdom of God" is a crucial key to understand the character of Jesus' own kingship (the identity and role of Jesus as king) in John 3, just as the titles, the Son of God and the King of Israel, as the clmactic titles are used for the clear revelation of the Johannine Jesus in John 1:19–51.[81]

Secondly, it is necessary to say that origin affects identity. Jesus' origin could be a clue to recognize his identity in the Gospel of John.[82] The first century readers might easily comprehend that his divine origin implies his kingship like kings who were appointed by God in the Hebrew Bible or like the emperors in the Roman Empire who were also recognized by their subjects as divinised kings. In John 3:2, Nicodemus also acknowledges that Jesus has come from God/from above (cf. 1:1–18; 3:31; 8:23; 18:37; 19:11). Nicodemus' stating of Jesus' origin, i.e., from God, can be one of the factors to reveal Jesus' kingship, although it is used to refer to Jesus' credentials as a teacher. That is, "in the reply to his unspoken question, Jesus states the kingdom of God is open only to those who have the same origin. For to be born from heaven is equivalent to being born from God (cf. 1:13; 3:5, 34)."[83] In addition, in order to show more magnified understanding of his identity, particularly to describe Jesus as the new king of the new world in the new age beyond the Messiah in Judaism,[84] a variety of christological titles attributed to Jesus (the μονογενής Son [3:16, 18; cf. "his Son" in 3:17] or the Son as the giver of life [3:15–21, 35–36] and the Son of Man [3:13–14]) are employed together in the passage. Particularly, the Johannine Jesus emphasizes that the lifting-up of the Son of Man[85] is the starting point of entering

80. The kingdom of God has "in certain respects already been inaugurated in the person, works and message of Jesus" (Carson, *Gospel*, 188). Thus, there is in this Gospel the implicit comparison between Jesus as the true life-giver and the Roman emperor as a rival life-giver in the contemporary culture. Sailer argues that whereas "the claims of the emperor are challenged and shown to be false," "John's claim is that Jesus alone is the true life giver" (Salier, "Jesus, the Emperor," 299).

81. Collins regards "the King of Israel" as the final and climactic designation of Jesus in the literary unit (Collins, *Jesus and His Witnesses*, 91).

82. That Jesus has come from God is a crucial issue in John (3:31; 8:23).

83. Lindars, *Gospel*, 151.

84. In addition, in terms of history, "Jews in Jesus' day best anticipated the coming of the Messiah when they most wanted to be transformed in line with the promise of life under the messianic age—to enjoy a new heart for God, cleansing and the fullness of the Spirit (e.g., Jer 31:28–39; Ezek 36:25–27)" (Carson, *Gospel*, 188). In John, however, Jesus is presented as the universal king more than the Jewish king (on this, see chapter 3 of this book).

85. On the discussion of "the Lifting up or glorification of the Son of Man" (John 3:14; 8:28; 12:32, 34) in terms of a king's enthronement, see chapter 3 of this book.

heaven (3:13–15).[86] The believers' entering the kingdom of God is possible because of the lifting-up of the Son of Man who descended from above in the Fourth Gospel.[87] In other words, "only Jesus as heavenly Son of Man and the man from above (cf. 8:23) can give the birth from above allowing a human being to 'enter the kingdom of God.'"[88] Jesus, the Son of Man, has authority over life and death (5:24–29; 11:24–25).[89] In addition, the Son (of God), particularly the μονογενής Son, is the unique and sole basis for the eternal life in the Gospel (3:16–18; cf. 5:25–29). Therefore, it is clear that the kingship of Jesus is well interwoven in this narrative with various elements, which have royal implications.[90]

Thirdly, John has a clear emphasis on "having (eternal) life"[91] through Jesus as the same meaning of "entering the kingdom of God."[92] If we admit

86. It is also alluded in the concept of the descending and ascending motif of the Son of Man (1:51; cf. Wis 16:6–7). In John, it is clear that God's power to save is mediated through and attributed to the crucified Son of Man (Lincoln, *Gospel*, 153). "The Lord by his death and resurrection has achieved a once-for-all cleansing and sent the Spirit of the kingdom: he who is baptized in faith in the Son of Man, exalted by his cross to heaven, becomes a new creation by the Spirit, "sees" the kingdom, and in Christ has life eternal" (Beasley-Murray, *John*, 49).

87. "The kingdom of God is seen or entered, new birth is experienced, and eternal life begins, through the saving cross—work of Christ, received by faith" (1:12; 3:16) (Carson, *Gospel*, 202). Thus, the eternal life means life of the age to come, namely the resurrection life, which Jesus accomplished in the end in John. In John, Jesus is the owner of life (1:4; 6:63; 11:25; 14:6), and he gives life to humanity (3:1–35; 5:26; 6:57; 10:1–18; the passion narrative).

88. Kvalbein, "Kingdom of God," 223. Ridderbos comments, "This surely ties in the fact that John focuses everything on the *person* of Christ. All the more prominent in the Fourth Gospel, therefore, is the 'personal' concept that corresponds to the concept of 'the kingdom of God,' that of 'the Son of Man' as the fully empowered Revealer and Bringer of the kingdom of God" (Ridderbos, *Gospel*, 125).

89. In the same sense, we can say, "entering the kingdom of God" as "entering the eternal life" corresponds to the description of a believer as one who has crossed over from death to life through the Johannine Jesus, the life giver (John 5:24).

90. On the royal implications of the titles, see chapter 3 of book.

91. On (eternal) life in John, see John 3:15, 16, 36; 4:14, 36; 5:24, 39; 6:27, 40, 47, 54, 68; 10:28; 12:25, 50; 17:2, 3. In Matt 19:28, the term "basileia" is replaced by "regeneration," which is equivalent of "new world" or "new age" (Beasle-Murray, *John*, 48).

92. Kvalbein, "Kingdom of God," 222. "As the Kingdom (or reign) of God in Jewish thought belongs to the Coming Age, so eternal life, i.e., the Life of the Age, is another way of describing the same thing" (Lindars, *Gospel*, 158). On Jesus' explanation of how God works to bring people into God's kingdom (3:1–10; βασιλεία, 3:3, 5) through him, see Carter, *John and Empire*; Marcus, "Entering into the Kingly Power," 663–75. The noun βασιλεία refers to Babylonian, Median, Persian, and Hellenistic (Alexander's) empires in Dan 2:37–45 (LXX); to the empires of Alexander in *1 Macc.* 1:6 and Antiochus Epiphanes and the Seleucids in *1 Macc.* 1:16, 41, 51; and to Rome's empire in Josephus, *J. W.* 5.409. Whereas, "the use of 'kingdom' language is quite unusual in John and

4. THE KINGSHIP OF JESUS IN THE USE OF βασιλεύς AND βασιλεία

that "entering the kingdom of God" means "receiving eternal life" in John's Gospel,[93] we can say that the dialogue between Jesus and Nicodemus reveals the kingly role of the Johannine Jesus.[94] In other words, because John stresses "receiving eternal life" as having the same meaning of "entering the kingdom of God," entering the kingdom of God could refer to entering the realm of salvation, life, and light from now to then, as well as to entering the kingdom of God invisible or/and visible. John simultaneously emphasizes eternal life as a present gift, but does also confirm it as a future gift linked to judgment and resurrection (11:24–29).[95] It also means to enter the realm of the kingship of Jesus whose ideology is love, peace, freedom, service and forgiveness, as well as to enter the place Jesus has prepared for his followers (John 14:3). In addition, the present acknowledgment of the ruling power of God gives a guarantee of the final stage of entering the kingdom of God in the future. Entering the kingdom of God means the full acceptance of the kingship of Jesus, that is to say, entering the realm of his present ruling power, regardless of whether it is present or futuristic. Entering the kingdom of God means fully belonging to the kingdom of God, where Jesus as king reigns. Therefore, the language of "entering the kingdom of God" creates a strong emphasis on Jesus' kingly role and on its totally different quality from that of the world, e.g., Rome.[96] Furthermore, "Those who enter into God's manifestation of kingly power (βασιλεία) do so not as equal partners with God but as holy warriors caught up in 'the tidal wave of the divine

---

is a synonym for the Gospel's preferred term, 'life of the age' (3:15, 16)" (Carter, *John and Empire*, 160–61). In Mark 10:17–31 (cf. Matt 19:16, 19, "enter life"), we also find that the phrase, "enter the kingdom of God" (10:23–25) is used as a synonym of "inherit eternal life" (10:17) and of "be saved" (10:26) (Kvalbein, "Kingdom of God," 221).

93. In John, "eternal life" is first mentioned after the only references to the kingdom of God (3:3, 5). Although the concept retains something of its original eschatological connection, it may equally be thought of as a present of gift of God. Thus, what "is properly a future blessing becomes a present fact in virtue of the realization of the future in Christ" (Barrett, *Gospel*, 214).

94. Whereas there is a reminiscence here of God's earlier display of kingly power in leading his people out of Egypt and into Canaan (cf. Exod 12:21–22), those who are born from above/born from God enter into the kingdom of God, namely the demonstration of kingly power of God through the Johannine Jesus.

95. Kvalbein, "Kingdom of God," 223; Caragounis, "Kingdom of God," 125–34. "The eternal life" or "the life of the Age" carries with it a sense of timelessness of an abiding fellowship with God, and this is uppermost in John's thought" (Lindars, *Gospel*, 158).

96. In the Gospel of John, Jesus is the giver of the eternal life. This theology might challenge the readers of the first century readers, because the Gospel proclaims that it is Jesus whose origin is above who has the authority of life and death (which is kingly role), rather than the Roman emperors.

victory' over Satan and his dominions."[97] This shows the radical stress on the dependence of Jesus' followers, who were born again/from above[98] to enter the kingdom of God, namely to live the citizens of the new world where Jesus as king reigns.

In summary, the concept of the kingdom of God is to be understood as a typical Johannine term, which stands for "(eternal) life," in John. Although many scholars have argued for the meaning and concept of the kingdom of God in terms of its present or futuristic features, and its dynamic ruling or territorial aspects, one thing is clear in the Gospel of John: it is the Johannine Jesus who has the exclusive role as the giver of eternal life to the believers. That is, the Johannine Jesus functions as king in the kingdom of God in terms of the giver of life. Therefore, it is safe to say that in the Gospel, the phrase "the Kingdom of God" is used to reveal the identity and role of the Johannine Jesus in his kingdom.

"The King of the Jews" in the Passion Narrative

It is clear that the kingship of Jesus is one of the main themes in the Passion Narrative,[99] which is elaborated in a unique way.[100] A reference to the kingdom of Jesus ("my kingdom"[101] in 18:36) appears once, but "king" and

---

97. Marcus, "Entering," 669.

98. Brown, *Gospel*, 143-44. On this, Marcus comments, "Entering the *basileia* is not an autonomous human action that transfers the disciple into another world, but rather an incorporation of him into God's powerful invasion of this world" (Marcus, "Entering," 674).

99. Schnackenburg, *Gospel*, 3:241; Beasley-Murray, *John*, 327; Carson, *Gospel*, 592; Barrett, *Gospel*, 530. John enhances Jesus' passion story for the sake of his theological purpose: Jesus is the majestic figure who controls his destiny and accomplishes his mission. Thus, in the Passion narrative, no taunts by the peoples, no mention of the darkness at noon, no cry of dereliction, but a pervading calm shows Jesus' control over the trial and his voluntary death to save the world (Lindars, *Gospel*, 572-73).

100. Moloney, *Glory not Dishonor*, 136; Kvalbein, "Kingdom of God," 228-32. Many scholars regard the passion of Jesus as the enthronement of a king (Salier, "Jesus, the Emperor," 297-301; Lindars, *Gospel*, 533; Brown, *Gospel*, 912; Beasley-Murray, *John*, 342). John holds up Jesus as the model king to his audience, a king who turns the concept of glory and honor (Ford, "Jesus as Sovereign," 110-17).

101. It is probable that "my kingdom," a personalized form of the kingdom of God, is closely linked to the kingdom of God in 3:3-5. It is a Johannine literary adaptation in order to amplify Jesus' kingship. This term, "my kingdom," is sharply contrasted with the earthly kingdom, Rome. This contrast implies to the readers that Jesus is the real king to follow who challenges them to live their lives according to his kingdom's ruling ideology: love, peace, service, freedom, and forgiveness. Thus, John challenges the readers through the passion narrative not to fear Roman power, not to be cowed

4. THE KINGSHIP OF JESUS IN THE USE OF βασιλεύς AND βασιλεία

"the king of the Jews" occur frequently (18:33, 37, 39; 19:3, 12, 14, 15, 19, 21),[102] showing the centrality of the kingship of Jesus in the Narrative.[103] That is, the kingship of Jesus is developed much more fully and continues to play a dominant part in the Passion Narrative.[104] In order to elaborate the kingship of Jesus,[105] on the one hand, only John includes a dialogue on the character of Jesus' kingship (18:34–38),[106] a dialogue on the authority of Pilate (19:8–11), and a dramatic confrontation where the Jews at the end reject their own king and prefer the Emperor in Rome (19:4–7, 12–15).[107] On the other hand, there stands the much longer and detailed narrative of Jesus' crucifixion and his royal burial (19:16–42).[108] Finally, Jesus' kingship is concluded in the trilingual public notice on the cross (19:19). Moreover, in the Passion narrative John describes Jesus' authority and his actions in complete control of the situation, which implies the true meaning of his kingship.[109] The Johannine passion narrative reveals that Jesus' death is intended to accomplish God's plan (18:32). For example, the demanding of the crucifixion by the Jewish leaders is associated with the deliberate intention of fulfilling Jesus' words about his death (the lifting-up motif; John

---

by imperial ideology, and not to be seduced by "the everyday fabric of the cult that proclaimed an inferior rival to the God and Father revealed in Jesus Christ." Moreover, John encourages them "to remain friends of Jesus and not desire to become Caesar's friend" (Salier, "Jesus, the Emperor," 301).

102. Lincoln, *Gospel*, 441. The title βασιλεύς is applied to Jesus twelve times in the Passion narrative.

103. In John, the title "the King of the Jews" is somewhat ambivalent in the Passion Narrative, however, very definitely was employed to bring out the supreme royalty of Jesus. On the one hand, this term is employed to mock Jesus on the surface of the narrative; on the other hand, it shows ironically his genuine kingship in the deeper level of the meaning (19:7; cf. 10:32) (Brown, *Gospel*, 848). Ironically, the readers see that Jesus in the Passion narrative was slain, but this does not detract from his majesty.

104. Lierman, "Mosaic Pattern," 216. Salier argues, "[I]n the passion narrative, the imperial presentation of Jesus in imperial terms comes into greater focus, as a final cluster of scenes resonate with imperial theology. One of the keystones of the presentation of Jesus' death is the stress on kingship" (Salier, "Jesus, the Emperor," 297; see also van Tilborg, *Reading*, 165–73; 213–18).

105. Carson, *Gospel*, 593.

106. Reim argues that Jesus' utterance before Pilate is a fulfillment of Ps 45 (Reim, "Jesus as God," 159).

107. Kvalbein, "Kingdom of God," 228–29.

108. Lincoln, *Gospel*, 458. John ties in the theme of suffering with that of kingship. Thus, John shows Jesus' innocence and Jesus as the true Judge who puts his adversaries on trial (Brown, *Gospel*, 863).

109. Keener, *Gospel of John*, 1109; Brown, *Gospel*, 787; Bacon, *Gospel of the Hellenists*, 226–27; Thatcher, *Greater than Caesar*.

12:32-33).¹¹⁰ In addition, John presents more examples in the Gospel: 1) Jesus' willing entrance into Jerusalem as king to accomplish his mission – John "has timed the death of Jesus to coincide with the slaying of the Passover (the Lamb of God). By this means he not only has overt motif of kingship, but the hidden motif of the death of Jesus as the paschal sacrifice".¹¹¹ 2) In John 18:1-11 and John 18:36, Jesus does not need servants with violence and does not want to be defended with swords. "Jesus goes voluntarily and in full freedom to his death. Neither his own disciples nor Pilate are allowed to stop him" (John 10:17-18).¹¹² It reveals that Jesus fulfills his mission as king, that is, the witness to the truth. 3) That the world power of Pilate is shown up to be derivative from God and subject to his will (9:11) shows Jesus' control over the situation. In addition, the arrest is the moment of the arrival of "the ruler of this world" who has no power over Jesus (14:30; 19:10-11).¹¹³ "So in the arrest Jesus gives himself up to the representatives of both ecclesiastical and secular power, and his real supremacy in regard to both is established from the first."¹¹⁴ 4) Finally, Jesus' control of events is triumphantly completed on the cross (19:28-30; "It is finished"). The passion is the hour for Jesus to be gloried and the time of the judgment of this world (12:31; cf. 3:14; 8:28; 12:32, Jesus as master over his own life and death (cf. 10:17-18) has determined his way to the death on the Roman cross, using the term "being lifted-up."¹¹⁵

In short, the further the trial proceeds in the Passion narrative, the more remarkably his kingship is revealed. It is clear that John uses and stresses the Roman trial more effectively to expound the kingship of Jesus. It is necessary, therefore, to investigate the use of the terms "king" and "the king of the Jews" in the Passion narrative in order to clarify Jesus' kingship.

Firstly, in the dialogue between Jesus and Pilate,¹¹⁶ we find the explicit conflict between the kingdom of Jesus and that of the world, Rome, and between Jesus the king and the Emperor (18:33-37; 19:8-11). The comparison between Jesus and the Emperor and Jesus' superiority provides

---

110. "By the crucifixion Jesus would be literally 'lifted up from the earth'" (Bruce, *Gospel*, 352).

111. Lindars, *Gospel*, 356-37.

112. Kvalbein, "Kingdom of God," 231.

113. Bultmann, *Gospel*, 639.

114. Lindars, *Gospel*, 539-40.

115. Lincoln, *Gospel*, 461; Brown, *Gospel*, 850. Thus, the passion is "the moment when unbelief is exposed as resistance to God himself, and those who condemn Jesus in fact condemn themselves (19:15)" (Lindars, *Gospel*, 535).

116. Pilate as a representative of Rome has to be asked to decide between the world and the truth, namely Jesus.

4. THE KINGSHIP OF JESUS IN THE USE OF βασιλεύς AND βασιλεία 149

a counterpoint to the presentation of Jesus as king.[117] In Pilate's first question,[118] "Are you the king of the Jews?" (18:33), the term "the king of the Jews" is used in an emphatic way to interrogate Jesus' royal status. In his answer to Pilate's question,[119] Jesus goes on to give a christological definition of his kingdom/kingship.[120] Admitting that his βασιλεία is not of this world (18:36),[121] Jesus does not deny his kingship (18:37) and responds that he was born a king and for this came into the world from above, i.e., from

---

117. Salier, "Jesus, the Emperor," 301. Because Jesus proclaims that he has conquered the world (16:33), his kingship affects the world, although his kingship does not belong to this world, but comes from above (18:36; 19:11).

118. Pilate's question, "Are you the king of the Jews?" is employed to draw attention to the necessity of crucifixion in the passion narrative, even though his position is ambivalent (cf. 19:12, 22), because "any one who claimed kingship in a Roman province denied the sovereignty of Caesar and was guilty of sedition against him" (Bruce, *Gospel*, 352). Thus, in the narrative, this point is implicitly given to the readers: After declaring Jesus guiltless, if Pilate was sincere, he should have released "the king of the Jews" rather than suggesting the release of the rebel, Barabbas (18:39–40); then Pilate took Jesus and had him flogged (19:1–3), and finally handed Jesus up to be crucified after obtaining the Jewish leaders' acknowledgment of Caesar to be their king (19:12–16). It seems that Pilate negotiated with the Jewish leaders in order to get their submission to the Roman power (Rensberger, *Johannine Faith*, 92–95; Bruce, *Gospel*, 359). After the Jewish leaders' acknowledgment of Caesar to be their king, finally Pilate handed Jesus over to them to be crucified (19:16). To imply the necessity of crucifixion, John also decribes Pilate's position, sitting on the tribunal, executing the sentence by soliders under his command, and his initiative in the matter of the title on the cross (20:19), which was the charge on which he was originally brought before Pilate.

119. In 18:37, Pilate's question (οὐκοῦν βασιλεὺς εἶ σύ;) and Jesus' answer to him (σὺ λέγες ὅτι βασιλεύς εἰμι. ἐγὼ εἰς τοῦτο γεγέννημαι καὶ εἰς τοῦτο ἐλήλυθα εἰς τὸν κόσμον, ἵνα μαρτυρήσω τῇ ἀληθείᾳ) affirm Jesus' kingship fundamentally, although other possible translations have been suggested (see Morris, *Gospel*, 680–81; Brown, *Gospel*, 869). Thus, this verse ironically reveals Jesus' kingship that the Jewish leaders rejected.

120. Kvalbein, "Kingdom of God," 228; Schnackenburg, *Gospel*, 3:249; Carson, *Gospel*, 594. The emphatic employment of the pronouns in 18:26–37 implies that Jesus denies his kingship in terms of politics (18:34–47), but approves his kingship in different sense shadowing his messianic kingship, namely in the spiritual meaning of his kingdom (see John 10:10, 16, 27). That is, his kingship can only be established by God, not by human means (Lincoln, *Gospel*, 462).

121. This phrase, "my *basileia* is not of this world," indicates not only the origin but also the nature of what is involved (Brown, *Gospel*, 854). That is, Jesus' *basileia*, which finds its origin from God, is not to be understood in terms of this world, while earthly kingship preserves it by force and violence. Thus, Jesus' answer reveals that his kingship is nothing to do with that of the world, because it will not be defended by the world's means (18:10–11:36), because Jesus' *basileia* means mainly his kingship, his sovereign rule, i.e., "his action in his capacity as the king who brings salvation" in John (Beasley-Murray, *John*, 330; Schnackenburg, *Gospel*, 3:249; Carson, *Gospel*, 594).

God (18:37-38; cf. 6:15; 3:13; 5:19; 8:23, 26).[122] It shows clearly that Jesus' universal kingship is emphasized. That is, in terms of his mission (witness to the truth) his kingship "has permanent and universal validity, and confers genuine liberation on those who acknowledge it."[123] It also shows the non-violent feature of his kingdom, which is an opposite ideology to the Roman Empire.[124] Salier's analysis of the passion narrative gives more clear understanding on this:

> The shadow of the emperor and the imperial cult . . . comes into relief as Jesus stands before Pilate, in confrontation with the representative of Roman power. Two competing stories are to be compared and contrasted. The imperial story presents the reign of the emperors, particularly in the light of Augustus' achievements, as an eschatological phenomenon promising peace and a new beginning for the world, in the context of absolute power and the family of the Roman Empire. The competing story is of the new beginning brought about by the death and resurrection of Jesus, which brings a peace the world cannot give, marks a return to the true beginning of all things, and enables participation in the true life of the family of the one true God. In the end the contrast is clear. Christ is the true God, the true bringer of a new order of reality, true life and peace.[125]

Thus, John represents the Johannine Jesus as a quite different "king of the Jews."[126] That is, while he describes that Jesus does not intend to undermine the Roman authorities, John portrays Jesus as a king of truth who is superior to the world (cf. 18:36; 19:11).[127] In this verse, Jesus also reveals his kingship

---

122. To the first century readers, the claim that authority comes from God could be strong evidence to prove his kingship. Thus, Jesus' response to Pilate implies strongly his kingship (18:37).

123. Bruce, *Gospel*, 354.

124. Cf. 18:9, 32. Crossan, "Roman Imperial Theology," 59-73; Carter, *John and Empire*. In addition, Ps 45:5 speaks of the peaceful task of the Messiah, which is to advocate the truth (Reim, "Jesus as God," 159).

125. Salier, "Jesus, the Emperor," 298.

126. Because this title, the king of the Jews, was not a Christian messianic formulation in the first century (Brown, *Gospel*, 867-68), it was employed to reveal Jesus' kingship beyond the political aspect in the Fourth Gospel, that is, his universal kingship.

127. Most significantly, Jesus redefines the nature of his kingship in the light of his mission to be a witness to the truth, while the Jewish leaders present him as a threat to Rome (19:12). Thus, Jesus always claims that he says and does nothing on his own and that the Father has granted him his identity and function as the Son (5:19, 20, 26; 10:35-38).

4. THE KINGSHIP OF JESUS IN THE USE OF βασιλεύς AND βασιλεία

in terms of the testimony to the truth,[128] which is used to represent the relationship between Jesus and his followers in John. 1) In John 17:14-21, Jesus' kingly mission and his followers' mission are closely related to the truth, which is God's word (17:17), while John 14:6 reveals that Jesus is the truth. 2) As Jesus' kingdom is not of this world, neither are his followers (17:16).[129] 3) In spite of the rejection and persecution of the world, Jesus sent them into the world like Jesus himself (17:18; cf. 20:21). Thus, Jesus came to the world as king from above (from the Father; 8:23) to set his followers free when they know the truth (8:31-32) and his task is to testify to the truth and to gather those who belong to the truth (18:37; cf. 3:16-21; 10:3, 16, 17). Thus, it is natural that everyone on the side of truth listens to Jesus (5:25; 8:45-47; 10:3-4,[130] 26-27). In addition, in John 18:36-37, Jesus' kingship is also revealed, when Jesus states that the people of the kingdom of God are those who are of the truth, namely those who respond to Jesus' voice, "see", and "enter into" the kingdom of Jesus (cf. John 3:3, 5).[131] In short, we see that the concept of the truth is closely linked to the concept of discipleship as well as to his own kingship. Thus, in the first scene of the interrogation, the dialogue between Jesus and Pilate portrays Jesus as the king.

Secondly, in Pilate's question to the Jews, Jesus' kingship is intensified.[132] Pilate says to the Jewish leaders, "do you want me to release 'the king of the Jews'?" (18:39). Then, the Jews shout back "No, not him [this man], give us Barabbas!" Their clamour for Jesus' death on the cross is ironically used for the revelation of his kingship.[133] Their shouting is more strongly

---

128. It is closely related to the kingship of Jesus in the Fourth Gospel, because his heavenly origin and his mission are employed to reveal his kingship in John. For example, in John 1:14, Jesus has entered this world with full of grace and truth; in John 9:39, Jesus says, "For judgment I came into this world"; in 5:33, John the Baptist had testified to the truth, which is Jesus (14:6; cf. 1:7). Jesus came for the purpose of witnessing to the truth, "that is to the eternal reality which is beyond and above the phenomena of the world, and, in particular, to the true and eternal kingdom of God which is the fount and pattern of all human authority (19:11)" (Barrett, *Gospel*, 537). Truly in John Jesus is the embodiment of the truth so that the deeds and words of his ministry constitute testimony to the truth.

129. Brown, *Gospel*, 852, 869.

130. The shepherd motif as the portrait of the king in the Hebrew Bible has its background. In John 18:37, that Jesus is answering a question about his kingship intensifies Jesus' kingship motif (cf. 8:47; Meeks, *Prophet-King*, 67).

131. Moloney, *Glory not Dishonor*, 198.

132. Just as the dialogue on kingship between Jesus and Pilate was a commentary on the charge in 18:33, so the dialogue between Pilate and the Jews over who has the royal power in 19:1-16 functions to intensify Jesus' kingly state.

133. Ford, "Jesus as Sovereign," 114.

expressed in John 19:6, "Crucify! Crucify!,"[134] when Pilate introduced Jesus, "[Behold] Here is this man!"[135] In John 19:14, in addition, the kingship of Jesus is more clearly revealed, when Pilate says, "[Behold] Here is your king!"[136] This significant change of words, which is a taunt to the Jewish leaders rather than mockery of Jesus, brings the irony of the whole affair to the point. Thus, "John's formulation of Pilate's mockery . . . employs the words used of Israel's very first king [1 Sam 9:17] and thereby reinforces Jesus' true identity as 'King of the Jews.'"[137] In this way, "Behold the man" in John 19:5 anticipates Pilate's explicit acclamation, "Behold your king" in John 19:14 as a coronation in irony.[138] Furthermore, the Jews' shouting for crucifixion, which was chiefly a Roman execution of revolutionaries,[139] shows that the Jews regard Jesus as a royal pretender against Rome.[140] In John 19:7, the Jewish leaders accuse Jesus with their religious evidence, when they say, "according to their law Jesus must die, because he made himself (the) Son of God."[141] However, it is not sure that Pilate understood their accusation as

134. Ford argues that "'crucify him, crucify him' (19:6) is the antithesis to acclaiming him as monarch" (Ford, "Jesus as Sovereign," 115). In Pilate's response, "Shall I crucify your king?," the word "king" is in an emphatic position. The emphatic use of the term "king" in the Passion narrative is used to reinforce Jesus' kingship.

135. In irony, John discerns a deeper significance of this phrase. It is probable that at least John intends "the man" to evoke memories of Jesus' self-designation (Moloney, *Johannine Son of Man*, 207). It is probable that John introduces Jesus as the Man sent from God and the bringer of the kingdom of God for all humankind (cf. 1:14) (Beasley-Murray, *John*, 337, 598). This term also was a title of honor used among Hellenistic Judeans under a messianic title (Brown, *Gospel*, 876). On the royal implications of the term "this man" in relation with "Son of Man," see chapter 3 of this book; Zech 6:12; Num 24:17; Meeks, *Prophet-King*, 70–71.

136. Pilate's use of the term in a formal but dramatic way to mock Jesus and the Jewish leaders shows that Jesus has no kingship in the surface level of the scene, but for John the kingship is real on the deeper level of the scene. John wants us to see Jesus as king who voluntarily takes this way for his people (Beasley-Murray, *John*, 342).

137. Lincoln, *Gospel*, 466.

138. In addition, in John 19:13, the image when Pilate brought Jesus out and sat down on the judge's seat (regardless of whether he sat on the real judge's seat or not) implies that Jesus is the one to whom the Father himself entrusted all judgment (5:22) (Beasley-Murray, *John*, 603).

139. Bruce, *Gospel*, 351; Brown, *Gospel*, 849–50.

140. John 18:31 and 19:6–7 (cf. 11:47–53) imply that the Jewish leaders accused Jesus as a political pretender against Rome rather than as a religious criminal. Even though they could kill him because of his blasphemy according to their law, they asked for Jesus' crucifixion (Bruce, *Gospel*, 351; about the execution of violators of the sanctity of the temple by the Jewish authorities, see Josephus, *J.W.* 6.124–126; cf. Mark 14:57–59; Acts 6:13–14; 24:6).

141. The title, the Son of God, is in an emphatic position. Two titles, the King of Jews and the Son of God, have emerged in the trial, in which they have royal implications.

4. THE KINGSHIP OF JESUS IN THE USE OF βασιλεύς AND βασιλεία

a religious one.¹⁴² It is highly probable that when Pilate heard of the title, he felt more afraid because this title might remind him of the emperor.¹⁴³ That is, the accusation by the Jews is not only religious, but also political;¹⁴⁴ thus, he needed to clarify whether Jesus is a royal pretender. He asked Jesus about his origin because origin reveals his identity (19:9).¹⁴⁵ Furthermore, in John 19:12, 15 the Jewish leaders reveal their political intention,¹⁴⁶ relating the term "king" to Caesar by confessing Caesar as their king.¹⁴⁷ Indeed, the Jews declared Caesar to be their *only* "king," denying Jesus' kingship. It is a strong irony. That is, John shows in this narrative that the Jewish leaders present Jesus' kingship as a rival to Caesar's power. In order to obtain Jesus' death, the Jewish leaders confessed their loyalty to Caesar, which ended up in their renouncing God as their King (Judge 8:23; 1 Sam 8:7). By their rejection of Jesus' kingship, they ironically rejected the way of deliverance from oppression. Indeed, their confession, "We have no king but Caesar" turns out be a profession of allegiance to the oppressor.¹⁴⁸ In the Gospel of

---

Because the claim to be king of the Jews was a capital offense against Roman law (cf. 19:12), and because the claim to be Son of God was a capital offense against Jewish law (cf. 19:7), Jesus' kingship, which is not of this world, is condemned in both traditions (Bruce, *Gospel*, 360).

142. For the usages of the term, the Son of God, as the title of the Roman emperor, see chapter 3 of this book.

143. Some argue that the reason for Pilate's fear comes from his religious reaction when he heard that Jesus has made himself the Son of God. However, there is no implication that he has religion in mind in the text; rather, it is more probable that because the trial has an issue that is more political in it, it shows that his fear comes from his political understanding of the term (Carter, *John and Empire*, 307; Morris, *Gospel*, 704).

144. Lincoln, *Gospel*, 462.

145. The question of Jesus' origin cannot be separated from the question of the source of his authority. Pilate's exertion of his authority is sharply contrasted with that of Jesus, whose authority comes from above, that is from God (19:11; 3:31, 35). Ancient readers, who acknowledged that a ruler's authority was ultimately derived from the sovereign authority of God, may quite well recognize Jesus' kingship in this dialogue. In addition, Jesus' remark on the authority also shows that his authority is superior to that of Pilate. "You would have no power over me" is grammatically emphatic, which implies that, without divine support, Pilate would collapse before Jesus (cf. 15:30; 16:33).

146. Bruce, *Gospel*, 363.

147. The Jewish leaders' challenge to Pilate shows vividly the conflict between Jesus and Caesar and the Kingdom of Jesus and the Roman Empire. Through this, John deepens the kingship of Jesus in the narrative. In John 19:14–15, John reports that Pilate has no alternative to condemning Jesus to death, but through Pilate's negotiation with the Jewish leaders, John reveals Jesus' kingship in more strongly in his comparison between the two figures, Jesus and Caesar. Thus, this scene challenges the readers to make their real confession of their loyalty between Christ and Caesar.

148. The confession of Jewish leaders' acknowledgment of Caesar's sole sovereignty, "We have no *basileus* but Casesar," also reveals that "their status and privileges depended

John, however, it ironically testifies that Jesus is the real "King of the Jews" (19:19–22). Thus, the term, king, and the title "King of the Jews" are used in the most part for the revelation of Jesus' kingship and his superiority in authority to Pilate and the Jewish leaders as the representatives of this world, because John proclaims that Jesus conquered the world through the cross and the resurrection.

Thirdly, John 19:1–3, the crowning and homage of Jesus as king,[149] is the central scene to show the theme of Jesus' kingship with irony,[150] when Jesus is dressed in mocking fashion as an emperor by the soldiers.[151] It is probable that the readers will notice that Jesus actually is the King of the Jews, despite all appearances.[152] John reveals Jesus' kingship through the irony of the soldiers' taunting remark, "Hail the King of the Jews,"[153]

---

on their collaboration with the imperial power" (Lincoln, *Gospel*, 471; Bruce, *Gospel*, 365; Brown, *Gospel*, 895; on the Jewish leaders' collaboration to the Imperial power, see chapter 5 of this book). Furthermore, "this is the ultimate evidence in support of the Prologue's pronouncement. 'He came to that which was his own, but his own did not receive him' (1:11), and of terrible blindness depicted in 12:37ff" (Beasley-Murray, *John*, 606).

149. On the mocking of King Agrippa in Alexandria after he was appointed the king of the Jews by the emperor during political disturbances in 39 CE, see Philo, *Flacc*, 36–43, where the mocking is described with details almost identical with that of Jesus. It probably implies that in comparison to Philo's description, Roman authority treated Jesus' case as a political issue.

150. John has transformed this mocking into a matter of deep theological impact in irony (Duke, *Irony*, 11–12; Lindars, *Gospel*, 565; Lincoln, *Gospel*, 458, 465; Brown, *Gospel*, 889; Beasley-Murray, *John*, 598). In particular, to the readers who know Jesus' resurrection, the fall of Jerusalem, and the disgrace of Pilate, this story gives an ironical conclusion: the victims of John's irony are Pilate, and the unbelieving Jewish leaders (Ford, "Jesus as Sovereign," 114; Lincoln, *Gospel*, 468).

151. A crown of thorns based on a ruler's adornment and a cloak of royal purple worn by the emperor are probably representative of kingship (Carter, *John and Empire*, 305; Brown, *Gospel*, 875; Beasley-Murray, *John*, 336).

152. "For it is precisely in that suffering, culminating in the cross on which he hung, that Jesus revealed his royalty and the glory of a love that gives itself to the uttermost for the redemption of a world that knows not what it does" (Beasley-Murray, *John*, 336–37).

153. The soldiers mocked Jesus in some formal manner; however, the image of the description of this scene may well be employed to contrast with their acclaiming royalty ("Hail the King of the Jews" vs. "Hail Caesar"). Thus, this scene implies that the one whom they so mocked is indeed "the King of the Jews" in the real irony (Morris, *Gospel*, 700–701; Brown, *Gospel*, 875). It is striking that Jesus' kingship is revealed in the contrast between faith and unbelief in the Fourth Gospel. For example, in John 1:35–51, christological titles are given to Jesus as the expression of the faith of the disciples (Son of God, King of Israel, and Son of Man) on the one hand; in the Passion narrative, Jesus is mockingly called "the king of the Jews (18:38), "the man" (19:5), and "the Son of God" (19:7) in the mood of disbelief, which imply his kingship in irony, on the other

4. THE KINGSHIP OF JESUS IN THE USE OF βασιλεύς AND βασιλεία

because "only this Gospel has the soldiers use the definite article in addressing Jesus as 'king.'"[154]

Fourthly, the second question of Pilate to Jesus, "where do you come from?,"[155] intensifies the identity of Jesus as king in terms of authority.[156] In John 19:8-11,[157] Jesus asserts that all authority comes from above which denotes a heavenly derivation (cf. John 3:3, 7, 31; 10:17-18). Jesus' tracing of all authority back to God also shows his kingship, because his origin shows his identity as king.[158] In this dialogue, Pilate might claim that his authority was

hand (Brown, *Gospel*, 891).

154. Moloney, *Glory not Dishonor*, 137. At the deeper level, ironically the Gentiles speak better than they know just as the Jewish leaders did (11:49-52), for Jesus is in truth the king of Israel (cf. 1:49; 3:3, 5; 18:36).

155. In John 18:37, Jesus already gives the answer: "he came into the world" (cf. 1:1-18; 3:34; 6:14, 33, 41-42; 7:25-29; 9:39; 11:27; 16:28—Jesus came into the world from God), which implies his heavenly origin (on the sending motif, see chapter 2 of this book). The discussion of kingship and authority is hardly possible to separate from each other. "The discussion of ἐξουσία provides a counterpart to the discussion of βασιλεία in 18:33-8" (Barrett, *Gospel*, 542-43). While Pilate uses the word "authority" in an un-theological sense, but Jesus holds and exercises his kingship in bearing witness to the truth.

156. This has been one of the ironically ambiguous themes in the narrative (7:27-28; 8:14; 9:29-30). Although Jesus' birth is nowhere else explicitly mentioned (1:13), "it is synonymous with his entry into the world" (Barrett, *Gospel*, 537). Jesus' heavenly origin is revealed to the people, but is acknowledged only by the believers. John has led the readers to reach the conclusion that Jesus' origin was heavenly throughout the Gospel. Thus, the readers know that the appropriate answer to Pilate's question is "from above, from God," while the world would not know because they did not listen to him.

157. Jesus' statement on authority is the core of this dialogue. Jesus speaks to Pilate of genuine power. In other words, Jesus' authority over the world, comes from above, from God, just as Pilate's authority was given to him from above (see ἄνωθεν in 19:11; cf. 3:3, 5). Carson argues that Judas, Caiaphas, and Pilate all acted under God's sovereignty (Carson, *John*, 600-602) which leads to intensify Jesus' kingship in the following episode (19:12-16). The more the Jewish leaders added the crimes of Jesus using a variety of titles, and pushed Pilate to recognize Jesus as the opponent to Caesar, the more the ideal readers can clarify the kingship of Jesus in irony from the narrative.

158. Jesus' affirmation that authority does not come from the earthly world, namely the emperor in Rome, but from heaven, reveals that God is over all and that an earthly governor can act only as God permits him. In addition, John reveals Jesus' authority over all through the whole Gospel. Thus, readers may well understand that Jesus' kingship has divine authority. For example, in John 18:5, 7, when the detachment of the Roman soldiers and officials from the chief priest came with Judas Iscariot to arrest Jesus, they state twice that they are seeking "Jesus of Nazareth." The crucial point is that they draw back and fall to the ground when they heard Jesus identify himself as "I am." This image shows that Jesus is King and God (This scene is reminiscent of the scene in Gen 17:3. "When Abram met God Almighty, he fell on his face." See also Dan 10:9; Acts 9:4; 2:7; 26:14; Rev 1:17), who has absolute authority and power. Furthermore, in chapter 9, when the blind man meets Jesus (Jesus identifies himself as the Son of Man [9:35])

delegated to him by the emperor. However, "Jesus discerns behind Pilate's discretionary power a higher authority than the emperor's."[159] Furthermore, Jesus' claim that Pilate has no power over him implies that Caesar cannot have the principal place, but God (from above) has.[160] It challenges the readers to choose "Christ or Caesar" as the real king to follow.[161] Thus, Jesus claims his superiority to Pilate and to the emperor in his kingdom.

Fifthly, in John 19:19 the author records that Jesus died as "the king of the Jews."[162] His kingship is ironically confirmed by the title in the trilingual notice that the Roman representative, Pilate, caused to be written.[163] This trilingual titulus, "JESUS OF NAZARETH, THE KING OF THE JEWS,"[164]

---

after his eyes had been opened, he believed in Jesus and worshipped (προσεκύνησεν; Cf. Mark 5:6, where a man with an unclean spirit worshipped Jesus) him (9:38) just as people worshipped God or the Emperors.

159. Bruce, *Gospel*, 362.

160. Jesus' words (19:11) echoes Jesus' statement of 14:30, "the prince [ruler] of this world . . . has no hold on me" in sense of Jesus' giving himself to die (10:11, 17–18), and ultimately, of Jesus' overcoming him in his resurrection (Carter, *John and Empire*, 290).

161. In John 10:17–18, Jesus says that no one can take his life from him, rather he alone has power to lay it down. In John 12:27, Jesus has voluntarily entered "the hour" appointed by the Father when he will lay down his life. In this context, the Father has permitted men to have power over Jesus' life (cf. 11:51–52) (Brown, *Gospel*, 892–93). Thus, John "sees in the death of Jesus by crucifixion God's way of fulfilling his purpose to 'lift up' Jesus in the glory of divine love to enthronement with himself; thereby the saving sovereignty is opened for all the world, and the exalted Lord can draw all who will into the eternal life of the kingdom of God (12:31–32)" (Beasley-Murray, *John*, 328; see also Thatcher, *Greater than Caesar*). For John, the crucifixion does not contravene the authority of God but lies within his purpose (Barrett, *Gospel*, 543).

162. In the Passion narrative, the kingship motif is continued from the beginning to the end. Thus, the crucifixion can be also read as an enthronement of Jesus, when his royal title is proclaimed trilingually and thus intentionally (see Brown, *Gospel*, 912–19). Brown comments, "The real enthronement comes now on the cross when the kingship of Jesus is acknowledged by heraldic proclamation ordered by a representative of the greatest political power on earth and phrased in the sacred and secular languages of the time."

163. John's report of trilingual titulus is unusual, because "the Romans did not normally give such permission in the case of people excuted for sedition" (Morris, *The Gospel*, 729; Brown, *The Gospel*, 901). Thus, that John employs that titulus in his Gospel may quite well point out that he intentionally reports this to emphasize Jesus' universal kingship. In addition, trilugal languages themselves also reveal the universality of his kingship, because Aramaic was the language of the Jews, Latin the official language, and Greek the common language of communication throughout the Roman Empire.

164. John uses this term as stated by Philip at the beginning of the Gospel as well as toward the end of it as a literary device in order to reveal Jesus as the King. This title reflects the combined confessions of Philip ("Jesus of Nazareth") and Nathanael ("the King of Israel"). It reveals also an element of ironic contrast or tension in the combination of the two titles. Nathanael confesses his kingship when he meets Jesus, saying,

4. THE KINGSHIP OF JESUS IN THE USE OF βασιλεύς AND βασιλεία

implies ironically that the title was true and unalterable, and is retained, not only as the grounds for crucifixion, but also as the proclamation of the Gospel.[165] Carter comments, "Pilate's trilingual death notice proclaims his kingly identity to all people, suggesting overtones of coronation (19:17–22) and echoing Jesus' words of universal appeal in 12:32."[166] Thus, the description of the trilingual titulus in John, which does not exist in the Synoptics, implies that John wants to reveal Jesus' universal kingship.[167]

Finally, the narrative of Jesus' burial is also employed to project the idea of Jesus' kingship.[168] The description of the procedure of Jesus' burial in John is unique and "would also be in line with the portrayal of Jesus in both his trial and his death as the true King of the Jews."[169] John employs and reveals terms and contents which are different from those in the Synoptics or delivers in details in John: 1) "Linen[170] with the spices" (19:39–40; cf. 20:6–7) implies Jesus' royal burial. John implies that the preparation of this great weight of spices for Jesus' burial by Nicodemus, who came to Jesus at night and heard of the kingdom of God/Jesus' kingship (3:1–3), reminds us of Jesus' kingship and consequently his burial is a royal one.[171] 2) Jesus was buried in accordance with Jewish burial customs in "a new tomb in the

---

"You are the Son of God; the King of Israel." Hence, the kingship of Jesus of Nazareth is revealed through these terms, the Son of God and the King of Israel. In the titulus on the cross, the sentence, "Jesus of Nazareth, King of the Jews," is echoing Jesus' kingship which is revealed in chapter 1. Thus, for John, "the action of Pilate is the climax of the whole series of events that culminated in the crucifixion of Jesus" (Beasley-Murray, *John*, 346).

165. Even though Pilate dedicated the trilingual titulus with the purpose of annoying the Jewish leaders, it holds a deeper theological meaning. That is, the hour has come for the Son of Man to be glorified. The titulus delivers the ironical message to the readers that "the Crucified One is the true king . . . because it is he who is stretched throne of glory and 'reigns from the tree'" (Bruce, *Gospel*, 369).

166. Carter, *John and Empire*, 168.

167. Beasley-Murray, *John*, 611; Hoskyns, *Fourth Gospel*, 628; Bruce, *Gospel*, 369.

168. Brown, *Gospel*, 912, 960; Lindars, *Gospel*, 592. Ford, "Jesus as Sovereign," 116.

169. Lincoln, *Gospel*, 485.

170. Cf. John 11:44, where linen was not used in the description of the wrapping of the body of Lazarus. In addition, the Synoptics report that the body was only wrapped in a shroud (Matt 27:59; Mark 15:46; Luke 23:53).

171. Brown, *Gospel*, 943; Bruce, *Gospel*, 379; Morris, *Gospel*, 729. The record of the use of a great quantity of spices for funerals is found in Josephus' writings. According to Josephus, five hundred servants carried the spices for Herod's burial (cf. *B.J.* 1.173; *A.J.* 17.199). In addition, large quantities of spices are reminiscent of the royal burials of Jewish kings (2 Chr 16:14; Jer 34:5). On the burial of Gamaliel the elder with eighty pounds of spices, see Beasley-Murray, *John*, 359.

garden" (19:41)[172] which also implies Jesus' royal burial.[173] Jesus received a regal burial. This is also an irony. It would be expected that because Jesus was crucified on the charge of being a revolutionary against Rome, he could not have received a regal burial. However, John reports Jesus' regal burial in order to emphasize his kingship.

In summary, ironically, Jesus was condemned and crucified, but John proclaims that he is the real king in the Passion narrative. As Barrett argues, "John has with keen insight picked out the key of the passion narrative in the kingship of Jesus, and has made its meaning clearer, perhaps, than any other New Testament writer,"[174] John stresses the kingship right to the end, because the kingship of Jesus is a significant motif particularly as the narrative draws to its clamax.

Summary of the Chapter

In this chapter, I have researched the concept, meaning, and usage of the terms, βασιλεύς/βασιλεία, including ὁ βασιλεὺς Τοῦ Ἰσραήλ/ὁ βασιλεὺς Τῶν Ἰουδαίων, in the Gospel of John. I have argued that these titles are employed to reveal explicitly the kingship of Jesus throughout the Gospel, particularly through the Passion narrative. Thus, for the Johannine readers, the Gospel continues to demonstrate Jesus' kingship with the aid of many christological titles, most crucially with the terms, βασιλεύς/βασιλεία, in order to proclaim Jesus' identity as the king who represents the new Johannine world, namely the kingdom of God. In addition, John challenges them to decide whom they believe and follow: either King Jesus or the earthly king, the Emperor, forming a sheer antithesis of royalties.

---

172. Matthew and Luke record a new tomb in Jesus' burial story, but only John addresses "the Garden," which is reminiscent of the royal burial of the Jewish kings in the Hebrew Bible. It indicates that the one who is buried is in fact Israel's king. Thus, "the theme that Jesus was buried as king would fittingly conclude a Passion Narrative wherein Jesus is crowned and hailed as king during his trial and enthroned and publicly proclaimed as king on the cross" (Brown, *Gospel*, 960).

173. On the burial of kings in the royal garden in the Hebrew Bible, see 2 Kgs 21:18, 26; 2 Chr 33:21, 24; Neh 3:16 (cf. Acts 2:29); on royal corpses next to the Sanctuary, see Ezek 43:7–9. In addition, the crucifixion of Jesus, his death on *the tree*, is also reminiscent of his kingship. On the relationship between kingship, gardens, and trees, particularly, kings as trees and trees as kings, see Num 24:6–7; Judg 9:8–15; Ezek 17:3–10; 28:12–19; Dan 4; and on tree motifs, tree imagery, fertility, and dynasty including "Branch" and "Shoot" designations, see Isa 6:13; 11:1; 56:3–5; 61:11; Jer 23:5; 33:15; Ezek 17:22–24; Zech 3:8; 6:12. In John 15, Jesus as the true vine is linked to this motif (Na'aman, "Death Formulae," 245–54; Nielsen, *There Is Hope for a Tree*).

174. Barrett, *Gospel*, 531.

PART II

A Postcolonial Reading of the Kingship of Jesus in the Gospel of John

5. Identity Matters of the Groups in the Gospel of John

IN THE FIRST PART of my book, I have investigated the kingship motif of the Johannine Jesus in relation to christological titles by researching the use of the various titles, their backgrounds, and their distinctiveness in the Gospel of John. Furthermore, I have argued that the concept of kingship is a key theme that runs through the christological terms.

Jesus is identified as king in the Gospel, which made me ask why the author described him as such. What prompted him to write his Gospel? Why did he characterize Jesus as king? In order to discover a possible answer, in part two of my book, under the presupposition that the Johannine community of readers lived in a hybridized society and in conflict with other groups at that time, I will argue that the author needed to write the Gospel for them in order to consolidate them in their faith. Furthermore, on a more positive note, the aim is to motivate them to evangelize the world, and to inspire them to seek as their goal the new world where Jesus as their king reigns in love and freedom.[1] To verify this, in the present chapter, I will attempt to identify and categorize the various groups in the Fourth Gospel. Then, in the following chapter, I will attempt to describe the message of the Gospel by considering the function and message of Jesus.

To this end, I will attempt to demonstrate that the Johannine Jesus needed to be characterized as the king so that he would be seen as the one through whom a solution could be found to the conflicts that they faced. His kingship also helps clarify their identities as followers of Jesus and gives them a hope that will enable them to face persecution in the years to come. I will then deal with the unique message of Jesus in this Gospel as providing the answer to each and every situation.

---

1. See chapter 2 of this book.

A Perspective of a Korean Reader on Conflict and Identity Matters

A Brief View of Korean Colonial History

To begin with, it is necessary to refer briefly to my view of Korean colonial history in attempting a postcolonial reading of the Gospel of John. Colonization and post/neo/colonization in Korea has not been well known outside Korea, despite the wide growth of interest and concerns in postcolonial studies in many other contexts. One of the reasons is that Korea was colonized by a non-western country, namely Japan. Therefore, not only have the critics not paid attention to colonization in Korea, but also the Koreans themselves have not been able to properly explain their colonial situation to the world.

My view is that Korea was colonized by two foreign powers in the twentieth century, Japan and the USA, so that Korean society has been a kind of hybrid of the West and the East, similar to Jewish society in the first century. First, Korea was occupied by Japan, which was pursuing a global empire during the 35 years from 1909 to 1945.[2] Most Koreans admit that Japan bitterly exploited Korea. It attempted to assimilate Korea into itself in political, economical, cultural, and geographical terms. They compelled Koreans to worship their gods (Shintoism; the Shinto Shrine Worship), to change Korean names into Japanese, and they prohibited the use of the Korean language in public. They drafted many Korean males into the Japanese army during World War II and also drafted many Korean females into the army to give physical, in particular sexual, consolation to Japanese soldiers during the war. They educated Koreans in the Japanese educational system so as to enforce the view that the Japanese were a superior race and they attempted to erase all Korean cultural and racial originality (identity) from their minds.

Secondly, following their emancipation from Japan a different type of colonization came into being, although most Koreans have not admitted it as such, in that the occupation by the USA was very different. After the end of World War II, the United Nations decided that the Korean Peninsula should be divided into two distinct nations.[3] The USA as victor was to lead

2. On the aggressive nature of the Japanese toward Korean society and the independent movement of the Koreans, see Mckenzie, *Korea's Fight for Freedom*.

3. On the division of the Korean Peninsula into the North and the South, and the American interim regime of South Korea, see McCune, *Korea Today*, 61–92, 221–50; Macdonald, *Koreans*, 37–66; Kim, *Division of Korea*. On international relations and the geographical circumstances, and the Korean War and armistice, see Kim, *Foreign Intervention in Korea*.

South Korea in its independence from Japan and help in the reconstruction of its society. This has resulted in Korea becoming increasingly under the domination of the US government.

Conflict and Collaboration Matters in Korean Society

The experience of colonization in Korea under the Japanese, as well as by the US, has greatly influenced social changes in many ways, from both minor issues to major ones, resulting in a radical mixture of cultures. In particular, americanization in Korea has been quite different from japanization. Despite existing and increasingly negative issues (such as the submission of the Korean government to the US, acceptance of American culture without resistance, no independent military actions without the approval of the US, the impossibility of legal action by the Korean authorities against American soldiers who break the law in Korea, and so on), most Koreans consider that Korean society has developed positively under the influence of the US.[4]

It is necessary to say again that during the last century, Korea has experienced colonization by two influential foreign powers, one from the East, the other from the West. This kind of experience is unique and rare in the colonial history of the world, in that most colonization and post/re/colonization has been carried out by the West. Through the process of resistance to, and acceptance of foreign influence, Korea has produced a modified identity, which is different from that of her tradition. Under the rule of Japan especially, many people adopted a resistance to colonization as their means of survival, although some did collaborate with Japan, and these are called "the collaborators with Japan," whom I will compare with the Jewish leaders as depicted in the Gospel of John. Most of these were the political, economic and military leaders. Some of them were in the elite group of society and co-operated fully or partly with Japan in praising the nation and its king, and in seeking to persuade the people to become Japanese. This has been one of the biggest issues in Korean society because most of the collaborators and their sons still possess riches, political influence and high social ranking, and have a grip on Korean society in many areas. Some also became collaborators with the US. Thus, Korea has not been totally free from Japanese influence, and hatred and resentment have been rife in society. In short, in comparison with Japanization most Koreans accept that

---

4. On the American influence on Korean Society, see Kim and Shin, *Korea and the World*.

the influence of the US has been a positive one and although another type of colonization, it is very different from that of Japan.

Conflicts Facing Christianity in Korea

In this section, I will look at Christianity in Korea, particularly that of the Protestant church, from the same perspective. The introduction of Christianity into Korea and the development of the Korean church have been more closely related to the missionary activity of the US than to anywhere else. From the onset of the Japanese occupation, the Korean church led the way in resisting Japanization and worked ceaselessly for independence from Japan. However, there arose a conflict between inner groups in the church in relation to Shintoism.[5] The Japanese government in its desire to erase Korean identity compelled them to worship their gods. Most of the leaders of the Korean church accepted and co-operated with the Japanese in this matter teaching that worshipping Japanese gods was not idol worship.[6] This decision by Korean church leaders caused conflict and resulted in division in the church. Similarly, conflict and division occurred in whole areas of society while under Japanese rule, and the lasting ill effects of this are still affecting both church and society today.

Following the Korean War and the collapse of society, the people were resigned to living out their lives in whatever way they could. Communism and anti-communism swept through the whole Korean Peninsula. The Korean church then took the lead in reconstructing society and co-operating fully with the Korean government that was now under US government control. The end result of this is that, due to friendly relations between the two countries, Korea has become more americanized.

---

5. For example, in 1938, the Japanese colonial government launched the so-called Assimilation Campaign between Japanese and Korean churches to make the Korean church a Japanese religious institution (Park, *Protestantism*, 156). Secondly, in the same year, in the 27th Presbyterian Assembly in Pyeung-yang, Korean Christian leaders passed the Shinto Shrine worship as the legitimate ceremony (see Lee, *English Sourcebook*, 301–3, 304, 541–43, 552–53, 544–45; Clark, *History of the Korean Church*, 193–204; Kang, "Church and State Relations," 97–115). Thirdly, in the case of Korean Presbyterian denominations, they were completely under government control while they were brought into one Christian group (Park, *Protestantism*, 156).

6. Likewise, emperor-worship and sacrificing to the pagan gods are factors of importance in the persecution of the Christians (Croix, "Why Were the Early Christians Persecuted?" 210–49, esp. 216–17), Korean Christian persecution under Japanese colonization was similarly related to worship of Japanese gods, even though it was not separated from political issues. Many Christians accepted it as a national ceremony, but some regarded it as idol worship and apostasy, which caused conflict among Christians.

The Korean church has played a very great part in seeking to provide answers to the psychological and emotional pain of society as a whole. For example, one major, central group portrayed Jesus as the only way to heaven. They are called evangelicals. They have offered Jesus as the way to the better world so that many on the fringes of society could receive spiritual comfort through believing in him. These people could then endure their present circumstances, knowing that after death they would enjoy the kingdom of God eternally. However, this means that they have a tendency to avoid facing up to their earthly troubles.

Another group on the margin of Korean Christianity has insisted that Jesus is an alternative way to social righteousness. They are called radicals. Their desire is to rid society of social evils, and have done much to improve things for the better. One of their ideologies, Min-Jung theology[7] (theology for people/Korean liberation Theology), has its emphasis on the liberation of the lower classes. As such it appears to reject the influence of the US as they regard them as colonizers.

Both groups, evangelicals and radicals, are never free from their theological ideology. As Culpepper points out, "[t]he influence of the perspective, the culture, and the social location of the interpreter is being recognized. No text, no interpretation, is ever completely unbiased or neutral."[8] They act according to their dogma, which has been produced by their own theological perspectives. Historically speaking, it is by and large the US missionaries who have evangelized the Korean peninsula, so the evangelicals have became the major grouping in the Korean church. As a result, Korean Christianity is similar to US Christianity.

With this historical background, I was born into one of the lower middle classes in Korean society. I converted to Christianity at the age of 13 and became a Presbyterian pastor when I was 32 years old. I belong to a Korean Presbyterian denomination called "Pure Presbyterian," which is evangelical, very conservative and fundamentalist in keeping to the authority of the Bible. The origin of my denomination goes back to the time of the Japanese occupation, and the compelling of everyone to worship their gods. Some Korean Christians regarded such worship as idolatry and so resisted and fought against the Japanese government.[9] This active show of rebellion led to some being jailed and their suffering at the hands of Japanese

---

7. Suh, *Minjung*, 73–81. On Min-Jung Theology, see Na, *Criticism*, 128–41; Kim, "Minjung Theology's Biblical Hermeneutics," 221–37.

8. Culpepper, "Gospel of John," 118.

9. On the persecution of Korean Christianity by the Japanese colonial government, see Song, *History*, 217–27; on the history of the struggle of the Korean Presbyterian Church against Shintoism, see Pak, *Millennialism*, 173–220.

torturers resulted in the death of some of them. The Korean Presbyterian General Assembly, however, regarded the worship of the Japanese gods as a national ceremony and not idolatry and so it remained. Other groups left the General Assembly, and as such have not associated for a long time with other Korean churches.

In terms of church life, I was educated in evangelical, conservative dogma, and grew up and worked in that environment until I began to study theology at the seminaries. I learned many other perspectives on the Bible and a variety of viewpoints of interpretation. This opportunity opened my eyes to see Jesus' concern for the margins. I, as a pastor in Korean evangelical Christianity, which generally focuses on the spiritual life of Christians, have acquired the perspective of liberation theology as well. This is ambivalent, but co-existing well within me.

In terms of social life, I have received a good education in a well-adjusted society. However, I have experienced troubles among the groups whose ideologies differ; democracy opposing dictatorship; those on the margins of society who have been outcast for too long struggling for a better life.[10] Although I have only observed these conflicts in Korean society, and not positively participated in them, they have made me ask myself the fundamental question: "Is there any solution, or alternative in this world to solve these conflicts?"

I contend that the Gospel of John presents a positive answer to this question. In order to argue this point, I shall briefly describe the similar situation between the Johannine community and Korean society under colonialism. First, the image of the Roman Empire in Palestine seems to me to be that of Japan in Korea in the last century. Just as the Jews resisted the Roman Empire at the beginning of her Imperial expansionism, most Koreans chose resistance to the foreign power (Japan). However, after a series of failures to gain independence from the Roman Empire, many of the Jews, particularly the Jewish leaders, acknowledged Rome as the ruler. Many Koreans also negotiated and compromised with Japan and accepted her as their ruler.

Secondly, another parallel with the Roman Empire in the Gospel of John seems to be that of the US in Korea. As many Jewish people waited in anticipation for their promised savior who would liberate them from colonization, many Koreans also prayed and awaited the independence of Korea from Japan. At last, after the end of World War II, Korea was liberated from Japan by the UN, and in particular by the US in South Korea, whose image is similar to that of the savior of the world. Most Koreans welcomed the US

---

10. On Christianity and Struggles for Democracy, see Chang, "Carrying the Torch," 195–220; on from dictatorship to democracy in Korea, see Chung, "From Development Dictatorship to Civilian Democracy," 151–68.

5. IDENTITY MATTERS OF THE GROUPS IN THE GOSPEL OF JOHN

and have adopted her culture, and thus the image of the US as a savior of the world is still very real for many Koreans. So americanization in Korea has become more deeply ingrained. It seems that the US still remains an image of the savior of the world for many Koreans.

After this series of colonization by both Japan and the US, Korean society seems to be a hybridized society, which has been able to embrace the characteristics of both Eastern and Western culture. Although Koreans are one of the Asian peoples, they accepted Christianity from a Western culture as one of their religions along with other indigenous religions. However, they rejected Shintoism and Japanese culture, which, as one of the Oriental religions and culture, permeated into Korean society and still influences Korean thought today. That is why Korean society is ambivalent and can be identified as a hybridized one. As a member of Korean society, I in a sense am ambivalent and identify myself as a product of hybridentity. Although I can understand something of both Eastern and Western cultures, as well as the mixtures of the two, I prefer Western culture and choose Christianity as my religion from which, I believe, I can find the solution to my fundamental question, "Who is the real alternative to the conflicts?"

In short, just as the japanization or the americanization of Korean society never gives an alternative for social integration nor a solution to social conflicts, so the Romanization of Jewish society never offered an alternative. When I attempt to read the Gospel of John using a postcolonial analysis, my experiences allow me to see Jesus as a decolonizer for liberating both the suppressed and the margins in the Roman Empire and for freeing them from both spiritual and worldly darkness. The Johannine community at the margins had eagerly hoped to live in a liberated world; the Jewish leaders were the collaborators with the Roman Empire; and Rome was the center of the earthly world. Thus, the some of Korean churches and the collaborators with Japan are reminiscent of the Jewish leaders in the Gospel of John who seem to acknowledge Rome as an unavoidable reality for their survival and positions.

Now, I will attempt in this chapter to identify the major groups in the Johannine Gospel, namely, Rome, the Jews/the Jewish leaders, and the Johannine community as the basis for identifying the Johannine Jesus and his function.

Identification of the Groups in the Gospel of John

Resistance and/or accommodation could be the main ways of response to colonial oppression, although these two are not either/or alternatives, but both/and options in many cases.[11] Mbembe argues,

> In short, the public affirmation of the "postcolonized subject" is not necessarily found in acts of "opposition" or "resistance" to the *commandment*. What defines the postcolonized subject is the ability to engage in baroque practices fundamentally ambiguous, fluid, and modifiable. . . . These simultaneous yet apparently contradictory practices ratify, de facto, the status of fetish that state power so forcefully claims as its right. And by the same token they maintain, even while drawing upon officialese (its vocabulary, signs, and symbols), the possibility of altering the place and time of this ratification.[12]

It is also found that this tendency existed among the Palestinian Jews, including Christians, under Roman rule.[13] Alexander points out that there was a wide diversity of early Christian attitudes to Rome in line with the variety found among their Jewish contemporaries.[14] In addition, Goodman demonstrates that within Palestine there was room for a wide variety of ideological stances toward the Roman Empire in the pre-70 period.[15] Horsley also contends the existence of complexity and conflict in Palestinian Jewish society under Rome.[16] It is likely, therefore, that "there existed the potential differences in interest and outlook between the priestly aristocracy [the center/the collaborators], who controlled the society as client rulers for the Romans, and the mass of peasants [the margins], who were taxed to support the aristocracy."[17]

To survive in colonial circumstances, the margins could accept the reality of the Empire and her power, and cooperate with its logic, because an

---

11. Carter argues, "often accommodation and resistance coexist" (*Roman Empire*, 136).

12. Mbembe, "Intimacy of Tyranny," 67.

13. On the wide diversity of Palestinian views concerning the Roman Empire, see Alexander, "Rome," 835–39; on the polarity between the center and the margins, see Alexander, *Images of Empire*; particularly for a positive view of the Empire, Griffin, "*Urbs Roma, Plebs* and *Princeps*," 19–46; Goodman, *Ruling Class*; Rajak, *Josephus*; for a negative view, see Bauckham, "Economic Critique," 47–90.

14. Alexander, "Rome," 835–39.

15. Goodman, *Ruling Class*, 76–108.

16. Horsley, *Jesus and the Spiral of Violence*.

17. Horsley, *Jesus and the Spiral of Violence*, ix.

ideology of expansion and imperialism takes on diverse forms and methods, and because it "seeks to impose its languages, its trade, its religions, its democracy, its images, its economic systems and its political rule on foreign nations and lands."[18] Accordingly, the margins are apt to be persuaded by the logic of imperialism and to collaborate with it. Dube argues that "the colonized do not always resist their oppressors: they also collaborate and imitate the imperial power at various stages of their oppression."[19]

For example, the Jewish leaders in the Gospel of John are a typical model of collaboration with Imperialism.[20] In *B. J.*, Josephus shows his Gentile readers that Jews of the richer class like himself were just like other aristocrats in the Eastern part of the Empire, and that they should be entrusted again with the Jerusalem Temple and the flourishing Judean society of which they had lost control in 70 CE[21] It is also interesting to point out that Diaspora Judaism saw Rome positively as a protective power.[22] This positive view of the Empire shows that there was a high possibility of collaboration by the margins after their acceptance of its reality.[23] Brooke shows clearly that "Roman power was a fact of life even for minority groups on the fringes of the empire, and that one way to make it manageable was to locate it within the group's indigenous traditions."[24]

On the other hand, the margins could resist the Empire's campaigns in a variety of ways, e.g., violent and non-violent, concealed and opened, directly confrontational or more concerned with the distinctive practices and ideology (theology) of an alternative community.[25] Using

18. Dube, "Reading for Decolonization," 51.

19. Dube, "Savior of the World," 119.

20. Rajak argues that Josephus is one of the examples of the collaborators with Rome. She points out that Josephus recognized himself as a Jew, particularly as one of a former governing class of the Jews, but distinguished himself from the Jewish populace. According to Rajak, Josephus was always ready to come to an understanding with the government of Rome. Consequently, "it is natural that he should ascribe to the misdemeanours of that populace most of the blame for the destruction of Jerusalem" (Rajak, *Josephus*, 103). Rajak concludes that Josephus sought some integration into the world of Greek culture, and an accommodation with Rome.

21. Goodman, *Ruling Class*, 6; Rajak, *Josephus*, 104–73.

22. In *m. Abot* 3.2, the imperative, "pray for the peace of the ruling power" (regularly and habitually), shows their positive view on the Roman Empire as a protective power.

23. Smallwood, *Jews Under Roman Rule*, 356–58.

24. Brooke, "Kittim," 159; see also Alexander, "Introduction," 15.

25. For discussion on the complex and diverse ways of accommodation and resistance in the New Testament, see Alexander, "Rome," 835–39; Carter, *Roman Empire*, 118–36.

anti-language or symbolic language could be one way to resist.[26] For example, Alexander points out,

> Empires can physically coerce their subjects, but they cannot easily compel the imagination or storm the citadel of the mind. The Heikhalot mystics doubtless believed literally in their vision of the world, with its reversal of visible relationships, and that belief may have saved them from despair and helped them to remain true to their own traditions and culture. Their vision can, consequently, be seen as an effective strategy for resisting the imperialism of "wicked Rome."[27]

In the same way, John and his community seem to pursue a similar outlook of faith, and the Fourth Gospel seems to function as resistant literature, in persuading its readers to remain in faith and encouraging them to invite other margins to the Johannine world in which Jesus reigns as the king. This Johannine strategy is very similar to that of the Heikhalot mystics in terms of resistance to Imperialism. In most cases, the use of anti-language and symbolic language is found in this Gospel, particularly in Johannine Christology.[28] In addition, we can trace it in the structures of these conflicts in the Gospel. Analysis of conflicts between individuals and/or groups could help to identify them in the text. Thus, we find some individuals and groups that are for the power, while some are against it.

In general, groups, whether ancient or modern, can be categorized as both/either the center (the colonizer) and/or the margin (the colonized).[29] If so, it is important to identify groups as the center (the colonizer) or the margin (the colonized) in attempting a postcolonial reading of the Gospel of John because different identifications result in different interpretations.

It is obvious that the Johannine community, Jewish society, and other marginal groups in the first century were under Imperial domination, resulting in immense conflicts and competition among the marginal groups.[30] These conflicts could be crucial clues in identifying the individu-

---

26. See chapter 3 of this book.

27. Alexander, "Family of Caesar," 296–97.

28. Karris contends that the Gospel of John consequently encourages believers to remember that the Messiah to the marginalized was himself marginalized (Karris, *Jesus and the Marginalized*, 9–10).

29. This kind of categorization is based on the theoretical concepts of postcolonialism, e.g., mimicry, ambivalence, and hybridentity. For the theoretical concepts of postcolonialism, see chapter 2 of this book; Samuel, "Postcolonial Reading," 48–53; Segovia, "Interpreting Beyond Borders," 11–34; Segovia, *Decolonizing Bible Studies*; Reinhartz, "Colonizer as Colonized," 170–92.

30. For example, the conflict between the Johannine Jesus and the Jewish leaders,

als or the groups in John's Gospel, and seem to occur mainly between Jesus and the Jews, in particular the Jewish leaders (ch. 1, ch. 2, ch. 5, ch. 9, ch. 10, and in the passion narrative). We can also find conflicts between the Jewish leaders and other Jewish people (ch. 7; ch. 9), and between the Jews and the non-Jewish people (ch. 4). In addition, we read of conflicts between Jesus and the Roman authority (Passion narrative), and implicitly between the Jewish leaders and Rome (ch. 11). Therefore, in this chapter, my main concern is to investigate and categorize three major groups: Rome, the Jewish leaders and the Johannine community as to whether they function as the colonizer (the center) or the colonized (the margins). It is necessary to categorize these groups in order to clarify what kind of king the Johannine Jesus is and what his role is.

Rome as Center/Rome as the Colonizer

In this section, I attempt to identify Rome as center in the first century in order to read the Gospel of John from a postcolonial perspective; in order to deal with the matters of conflicts in the groups and the identification and role of Jesus as given in this Gospel.

Rome as the Center from a Historical Perspective

First, historically speaking, the Roman Empire may be identified as the colonizer and as the center in terms of modern postcolonial perspective.[31] Roman expansionism compelled the subordination of the margins.[32] The groups implied in this Gospel, which were at the margins of the Empire in terms of political, geographical, economic, and cultural differences, had been occupied by the Roman Empire. These groups at the time the Gospel

---

and the conflict between the later followers of Jesus and other Jewish groups (see Bieringer, Pollefeyt, and Vandecasteele-Vanneuville, "Wrestling with Johannine Anti-Judaism," 20).

31. Reinhartz, "Colonizer as Colonized," 172; Moore, *Empire and Apocalypse*, 63. It is clear that Rome is center, and that the other groups including the Johannine community are the margins in the context of the Roman Empire.

32. On the oppressiveness of Roman rule, see Goodman, *Ruling Class*, 9–11, 51–73; Cassidy, *Christians and Roman Rule*, 7–11; Carter, *Matthew and Empire*, 9–34. The Roman Empire subordinated the margins by compulsion and harshly ruled them on the basis of her military power: Imperial cult, Roman taxation, construction projects, relative peace and order by military power, the effective utilization of the regional and municipal elites, and the dissemination of convincing propaganda on behalf of imperial rule.

was written would have been compelled to bow to the Imperial power and to worship the Emperor.[33] Roman provincial rule was a common experience for John and his readers. Price emphasizes the importance of the imperial cult in terms of power.[34] While he points out the interconnection between religion and politics in terms of power, Price argues, "the imperial cult, along with politics and diplomacy, constructed the reality of the Roman empire."[35] In addition, since the provincial elite became imperial clients as well as the principal sponsors of the imperial cult, "the political-religious institutions . . . were virtually inseparable from the local social-economic networks of imperial society."[36] It is obvious, therefore, that the Roman Empire was the center of the world in the first century.

Rome as the Center of the Darkness

Secondly, as we read the John's Gospel we see Rome as belonging to the center of the darkness or the collaborator with the darkness, because the Gospel shows a conflict between the light (the Johannine Jesus) and the darkness (the world, which includes the Jewish leaders and their groups, and a hostile Roman governor, Pilate).[37] The Gospel of John implies that the darkness is the major opponent of Jesus. The darkness is in the world (1:5, 11).

According to the Prologue, the *Logos*[38] created the world by his creative power (1:3). After the creation of the universe, the *Logos* (the life[39] as the light[40] of the people) appears/shines (φαίνει) in the world (1:4–5), but the world in the darkness does not comprehend (κατέλαβεν) it.[41] The

---

33. See Cassidy, *John's Gospel*, 3–5; Frend, *Martyrdom and Persecution*, 31–35.

34. See Price, *Rituals and Power*.

35. Price, *Rituals and Power*, 248.

36. Horsley, "Introduction," 11.

37. Light: 1:4–5, 7–9; 3:19–21; 5:35; 8:12; 9:5; 11:9–10; 12:35–36, 46; Darkness (eight times in the Gospel): 1:5; 3:19; 8:12; 12:35, 46. See Culpepper, *Anatomy*, 190–92; Koester, *Symbolism Gospel*, 123–54.

38. The concept of *Logos* could be one of the evidences of the hybridentity of the multi-culture in the time of the Johannine community. This term could be connected with Jewish conceptions of Wisdom and Torah and with those of Hellenism of a divine and universal power (Keener, *Gospel of John*, 333–63).

39. The term appears thirty-six times in the Gospel.

40. Keener argues that "John identifies 'life' with 'light' (1:4; 8:12), and 'light' contextually refers to Christ (1:9–10), we must understand that on a functional level 'life' is ultimately Jesus himself (11:25; 14:6; cf. 3:15; 5:24)" (Keener, *Gospel of John*, 382); In 1 Enoch 48:4, the Messiah is called the light.

41. "The light *shines* (φαίνει) in the darkness, and the darkness did not overcome it (κατέλαβεν)" (1:5) could be translated as "the light *appears* in the darkness, and the

5. IDENTITY MATTERS OF THE GROUPS IN THE GOSPEL OF JOHN

Gospel shows that the tendency of the world in the darkness is to reject its creator.[42]

The Prologue shows that it was the same in the time of the Roman rule. The world, in particular Jewish society, was in darkness, and in spite of the testimony of John the Baptist about the light (1:6–8), the contemporaries of John the Baptist did not comprehend it. In these circumstances, the Johannine Jesus (the Logos who has the creative power) as the *true*[43] light "came (ἐρχόμενον) into the world"[44] (1:9, 10) to enlighten/shine in (φωτίζει) the world; however, the world in the darkness, including Christ's own people, did not recognize the light nor receive (παρέλαβον[45]) him (1:10; cf. 1:4–5), they even became hostile to him (15:18–19). However, any who did receive (ἔλαβον) him would be given the power to become the children of God (1:12).[46] This statement shows the openness of the Gospel from its beginning: the universality of the Gospel.[47]

The darkness has gripped and dominated the world with its power. In the first century at least, in the view of the Gospel (11:48), this is what Rome did. Rome, on her part, as well as Jewish society typifying the world in the grip of darkness, did not comprehend Jesus nor receive him. Particularly, the darkness of the world hated Jesus and his disciples, persecuted, and even killed them (15:18–20; 16:33; 18:1–6). Moreover, Rome was an object of fear to the Jewish leaders because they knew that when rebellions broke out against Rome, they were ruthlessly put down and the rebels executed.[48] From this perspective, Rome could be regarded as the darkness itself or at least the collaborator with the darkness because she had invaded, grasped, exploited, and suppressed the fringes of society, and even destroyed by means of military power those who were against her. As a result, for the marginal groups who were suppressed and colonized, it meant that they lived their lives in the darkness.

---

darkness did not *comprehend* or *understand* it."

42. Ridderbos, *Gospel*, 45.

43. The adjective, *true*, mainly applies to Jesus in the Gospel to indicate his genuineness (5:31; 6:32, 55; 7:18; 8:14; 15:1).

44. "Coming into the world" in John (1:15, 27; 3:31; 6:14; 11:27; 12:13) is an appropriate depiction of Jesus. Jesus was sent into the world to complete the Father's mission (3:17; 10:36; 12:47; 17:18); he came into the world as light (3:19; 12:46; cf. 8:12); he was the prophet "coming into the world" (6:14).

45. Morris argues that the aorist tense in 1:10, 11 "points to the decisive action of rejection" (Morris, *Gospel*, 86).

46. Keener, *Gospel of John*, 349.

47. About the openness of the Gospel, see chapter 6 of this book.

48. See John 18:1–6 and the crucifixion of Jesus.

Rome as the Center in the Passion Narrative

Thirdly, in the account of the plot by the Jewish leaders[49] to kill Jesus and in the passion narrative, most people seemed already to accept that domination by Rome was to be their lot.[50] In their hastily convened council meeting (11:47–57) after the raising to life of Lazarus, it is obvious that the main concern of the chief priests and the Pharisees (11:47)[51] was that Rome would intervene and deprive them of their positions of authority as long as the Jesus movement continued to grow (11:48). Beasley-Murray argues that the fears of the Jewish leaders in John 11:47–8 show that what they fear is not that "the Romans will come and *destroy* both our holy place and our nation," but that "the Romans will come and *take away from us* both the place and the nation."[52] Bammel well points out the psychological state of the collaborators with the Empire: "the consideration that 'the Romans might take away from us . . .' must continually have been in the minds of those who collaborated with them."[53] Keener also remarks, "plotting seems to have characterized Jewish as well as Roman aristocratic politics in the first century."[54] It is quite probable that most Jewish people accepted Roman domination after the failure of Jewish independence movements over a period of the time.[55] According to Josephus, this was the attitude of the Jewish leaders in Jerusalem who were desperate to prevent any movements

---

49. As a rejection of Jesus' whole public ministry (cf. 1:11), "The Romans would not stand by indifferent if there were popular tumult stirred up by messianic expectations" (Morris, *Gospel*, 502). According to Josephus (*Bell*, 6.288ff), it is clear that the political leaders would not have tolerated anything that looked as if it were provoking disorder.

50. The historical background of the narrative is in the time of Jesus' earthly ministry, but it seems to reflect on the historical situation of the time of the Johannine community.

51. Morris argues, "The separate articles with chief priests and Pharisees possibly point to two groups combining for the purpose" (Morris, *Gospel*, 501). It is interesting that from this narrative of plotting to kill Jesus, the chief priests are the main opponents of Jesus, while the Pharisees are the major opponent group in the early chapters of the Gospel. The alliance of the Jewish leaders to eliminate Jesus is eminent in the Gospel.

52. Beasley-Murray, *John*, 196. He also points out that "the fears of the members of the Sanhedrin show that they had as little understanding of Jesus as the people who tried to compel Jesus to be king and from whom he fled (6:15)."

53. Bammel, "EX illa itaque die consilium fecerunt. . .' (John 11:53)"; Recited from Beasley-Murray, *John*, 196.

54. Keener, *Gospel of John*, 852; see also, Goodman, *Ruling Class*, 6; Rajak, *Josephus*; Smallwood, *Jews Under Roman Rule*, 120–43, 356–58.

55. Crises in the relationship of the Jewish people to the Roman government mostly ended with the fall of Jerusalem (Goodman, *Ruling Class*, 1). For the history of Jewish revolts and accommodation, see Smallwood, *Jews under Roman Rule*, 144–79, 256–330, 356–58; Horsley, *Jesus and the Spiral of Violence*, 3–19, 28–58.

that were likely to provoke Rome.[56] The Jewish leaders desired peace under Rome. It seems to me that they were persuaded, in a sense, by the Roman campaign, *PAX ROMANA*,[57] and that they only desired to save their lives and to maintain their positions under Rome.[58]

In particular, in John 11:49–50, the utterance of Caiaphas, who was *one of them* (εἷς δέ τις ἐξ αὐτῶν) as well as the *high priest that year* (ἀρχιερεὺς ὢν τοῦ ἐνιαυτοῦ ἐκείνου), concerning Jesus was "the establishment's attitude,"[59] just like that of king Herod, who put John the Baptist to death in order to "prevent any mischief he might cause, and not bring himself into difficulties."[60] He seems to regard Jesus as the leader of one of the groups dramatically opposed to the Jewish leadership and to Rome. According to the Gospel, Caiaphas pursues public peace in a manner that satisfied both Rome and the populace, as well as securing his own position.[61]

Accordingly, the phrase "high priest that year" alludes "to a Roman insistence on an annual confirmation of the Jerusalem high priest."[62] This view seems to explain why John employed the statement "high priest that year" three times in the Gospel (11:49, 51; 18:13; cf. 18:24) in the manner of the emphatic Johannine use.[63] That is, it is used in a more emphatic way to

56. Josephus, *War* 2.237.

57. The relative peace and order, *pax atque quieta*, within the conquered territories was achieved by military campaigns or the threat of such campaigns (Cassidy, *Christians and Roman Rule*, 9; Carter, *Matthew and the Margins*, 36–40).

58. In my reading, the response of the Jewish leaders is very similar to that of the Korean collaborators with Japan in terms of maintaining their positions and power under colonial situation.

59. Vermes, *Jesus and the World of Judaism*, 12.

60. Josephus, *Ant* 18:118; see Vermes, *Jesus the Jew*, 50.

61. Stauffer, *Jesus and His Story*, 100–105, esp., 102. Keener's comment on him shows the attitude of political and religious leaders who made it their object to keep the peace for personal interests: "Yet it is reasonable to suppose that, even given the purest of concern for their people's welfare—on which their own rose or fell—the priestly aristocracy would regard unrest, hence the popularity of Jesus, as a threat" (Keener, *Gospel of John*, 853). According to Mark 14:60, Caiaphas stands up from the judge's seat. It is unusual because the accused man stands, while the judges sit on the seat. Stauffer points out that when Caiaphas arises, the whole council of the seventy-one stands up, as required by the rules of the court. Stauffer argues that Caiaphas has an intention, that is, he wants to make Jesus lose his composure (*Jesus and His Story*, 101). Stauffer emphasizes the manner of the Jewish leader who manipulated the situation to gain what he wanted.

62. Grundmann, "Decision," 304; Bultmann, *Gospel*, 410, n. 10.

63. Morris, *Gospel*, 503. Carson argues that "in reality the office had long been a political football, high priests being appointed and deposed at the will (or whim) of the overlord. Caiaphas, in fact, displayed extraordinary sticking power for the times (eighteen years). John's remark may therefore reflect his intimate knowledge of the

reveal the high priest's position in relation to Rome (11:48). In addition, the high priest in Jerusalem no longer had the authority to issue the death sentence (John 18:31). This implies that Caiaphas collaborated well with Rome at this time not only to safeguard his own position, but also to secure the death of Jesus. Although the Jewish leaders attempted to persuade Pilate to execute Jesus for the sake of their place/position and the land/people (John 11:48), their work resulted in the accomplishment of the Roman ideal (*pax romana*) as well as the securing of their own position.[64] In other words, the Jewish leaders had Jesus executed for the same reason as Rome did when they showed no mercy on any leaders of a rebellion against them.[65] Therefore, that Caiaphas was the high priest that year shows that he obviously cooperated well with Rome,[66] and that he as a representative of the Jewish leaders acknowledged Rome to be the guardian of the peace and the means of their survival and ownership in Jewish society. This attitude of the Jewish leaders toward anti-groups and Rome in the Gospel shows that Rome was the center of the world and exercised dominion over them.

Rome as the Center with Military Power

Fourthly, Roman intervention into the margins, especially by their use of military power, seems to be the thing most dreaded by the Jews and any other marginal group (11:48). In the Gospel of John, Rome as the center of the world, which is symbolically described as the darkness (1:5), is characterized in negative terms. This description of darkness is more clearly revealed in the narrative of the arrest of Jesus (18:3; cf. 18:12).[67] Hoskyns points out that "[I]n the Johannine account the forces of darkness, the Roman and the Jewish authorities, and the apostate disciple are arrayed against the Christ from the beginning."[68] Bultmann also comments that the arrest is

---

tenuousness of the office" (Carson, *Gospel*, 421).

64. Cassidy points out that "with respect to the Roman province of Judea, various members of the Herodian dynasty and various members of the priestly families who dominated the Jerusalem Sanhedrin are examples of local rulers who functioned effectively within the Roman system and profited thereby" (*Christians and Roman Rule*, 10).

65. In the passion narrative, the Jewish leaders have shown their character as part of the world, which did not receive Jesus nor understand, but rejected (John 1:5, 11) and killed him (11:47–57; ch. 18–20).

66. There might be good relations between Caiaphas and Pilate by the implication of the text (Morris, *Gospel*, 657).

67. It is probable that the employment of a Roman cohort in the passion narrative also has symbolic meaning: the confrontation of Jesus with the power of this world.

68. Hoskyns, *Fourth Gospel*, 509.

the moment of the arrival of "the ruler of this world," who nevertheless "has no power" over Jesus (14:30).⁶⁹ Barrett also points out that Roman involvement "seems to be due to John's desire to show that the whole κόσμος was ranged against Jesus."⁷⁰ Bultmann says,

> It becomes plain that the struggle between light and darkness cannot simply be played out in private, nor in the discussions that take place in fraternities and official religion. The world has been shaken to its foundations by Jesus' attack, so it seeks help from the power set over it to maintain order.⁷¹

Lindars also argues,

> In the trial narrative the world's power over Jesus is incarnated not in the Jewish leaders, but in the Romans (cf. 19.10-11). So in the arrest Jesus gives himself up to the representatives of both ecclesiastical and secular power, and his real supremacy in regard to both is established from the first.⁷²

Carson also comments, "the combination of Jewish and Roman authorities in this arrest indicts the whole world . . . and suggests that Pilate may well have been tipped off to the imminence of the arrest before Jesus was actually brought into his court."⁷³

The formation of an alliance between the Jewish leaders and the Roman cohort demonstrates the fact that Rome is the inevitable and undeniable power in Jewish society to maintain social order and to crush any opposition.⁷⁴ The theme of light versus darkness is further illustrated by the fact they came to Jesus with lanterns and torches and weapons (φανῶν καὶ λαμπάδων καὶ ὅπλων), which are symbolic, demonstrating the darkness in comparison the light of the world (Jesus is the true light).⁷⁵

---

69. Bultmann, *Gospel*, 639.
70. Barrett, *Gospel*, 516; cf. Ridderbos, *Gospel*, 575.
71. Bultmann, *Gospel*, 633.
72. Lindars, *Gospel*, 539-40.
73. Carson, *Gospel*, 577.
74. As the collaborators with Rome, the Jewish leaders work to accomplish the Roman campaign. The reality of Rome was not far from them, rather, was in them as the decisive, grasping, and seductive power just like the darkness, which is employed symbolically in this Gospel to indicate the opposition against Jesus, the light.
75. As a symbolic and ironic meaning, "the agents of darkness prove completely unaware that they are approaching the light of the world" (Keener, *Gospel of John*, 1078). The author "may have intended by means of these feeble lights to stress the darkness of the night in which the light of the world was for the moment quenched" (Barrett, *Gospel*, 519). In addition, the trial of Jesus by the Jewish leaders was done at night.

These situations in the Gospel show that Rome as the colonizer and the center of the world have exercised their power to rule the margins. Furthermore, it is evident that the Fourth Gospel implies that the Jewish leaders use the power of Rome for their own purpose, i.e., the elimination of Jesus. Although this description of the Jewish leaders' use of Roman power could imply the author's hostility to them, it shows obviously that Rome had absolute power to kill or spare lives at its own discretion.

In this situation, the Jewish leaders plot to kill Jesus. They urge the Roman governor, Pilate, to kill him. The Roman soldiers arrest him. Jesus is judged in the Roman court. These show tacitly that the power of Rome has already deeply permeated into Jewish society as the dominant force, the colonizer. It would be one of the reasons why the author adapted and employed the allusive and symbolical expressions against Rome in the Gospel of John. In short, it is acceptable that through the situations which I argued above, I identify Rome as colonizer and colonized.

Jews/Jewish Leaders as Colonizer as Colonized

In this section, I will identify "the Jews"[76] in the Gospel of John, particularly "the Jews of Jerusalem," as the Jewish leaders, who are one of the conflicting parties.[77] This Gospel demonstrates the complexity of interest between the Jewish leaders and other groups. It is necessary therefore to define the identity of these Jewish leaders.

Identification of the Jews

It seems that the term "the Jews" (οἱ Ἰουδαῖοι) has a diversity of usage in the Gospel of John, when we examine its some seventy occurrences.[78]

---

76. On the identification of "the Jews," see Culpepper, *Anatomy*, 123–32; Motyer, *Your Father the Devil?*, 46–57; Bieringer, Pollefeyt, and Vandecasteele-Vanneuville, *Anti-Judaism and the Fourth Gospel*; Elliott, "Jesus the Israelite," 119–54.

77. Particularly, the term "the Jews" refers mainly to the Jews as a group (Culpepper, *Anatomy*, 128; Motyer, *Your Father the Devil?*, 46), which is the subject of conflict with Jesus within the textual level in the Gospel of John. For Reinhartz, the Jews represent the negative one of two opposing poles of his narrative, which shows the conflict between Jesus and the Jews (Reinhartz, "'Jews' and Jews in the Fourth Gospel," 214).

78. A variety of usage: 1. Neutral – John 2:6 (used by the Jews for ceremonial washing); 2. Positive – John 4:9 (Jesus is a Jew, in addition, most disciples and followers were Jews); John 4:22 (salvation is from the Jews); John 8:31; 11:45; 12:11 (many Jews believe in Jesus); cf. 19:19 – the king of the Jews; 3. Geographical – John 7:1 (the people of Judea); 4. Most commonly, it refers to the Jewish leaders (1:19), who actively opposed

Furthermore, the use of the term has caused contradictory arguments among scholars: 1. Can this term be used as an evidence for anti-Semitism?; 2. Does it refer primarily to Jewish leaders, not to the people at large?; 3. Does it reflect geography (a Galilean might well refer to his fellow Israelites from Judea as "Judeans")?; 4. Or is there diverse usage of this term in the Gospel of John?[79]

This term "the Jews" is simply the most prominent one within a variety of social designations in the Gospel.[80] Opinions about the meaning of "the Jews" vary greatly from "the Jews" as "Judeans or the Jewish leaders" to "the Jews" as "the representatives of unbelief" because of the ambiguous use of the term in the Gospel.[81] Fortna points out, "the phrase *hoi Ioudaioi* obliterates virtually all distinctions within first century Palestinian society by speaking of the Jews in an external, monolithic way.... John's phrase gives the impression of a stereotype."[82] Therefore, it is important to indicate that, "the Jews" in this Gospel, as one of the characters within the narrative "play a central role in its plot."[83] Now, it is necessary to discuss briefly two scholarly views on "the Jews" in the Gospel in relation to their identification, 1) the Jews as the representative of the unbelieving world, 2) the Jews as the Judeans.

The Jews as the Representatives of the Unbelieving World

First, Bultmann argues that the term means the representatives of unbelief and thereby it represents the unbelieving world in general.[84] This view of "the Jews" presupposes that the term does not mean "'real' Jews but only about 'Jews' as a symbol or metaphor."[85] Culpepper also points out that "in their unbelief the Jews are 'symbols, types of universal human condition.'"[86]

---

and killed Jesus; 5. Exceptions to the negative descriptions of the Jewish leaders – Nicodemus and Joseph of Arimathea (3:1–21, 7:50; 19:38–42).

79. See von Wahlde, "Johannine 'Jews,'" 33–60; Lowe, "Who Were the ΙΟΥΔΑΙΟΙ?" 101–30; Bassler, "Galileans," 245–57.

80. Motyer, *Your Father the Devil?*, 50.

81. Motyer, *Your Father the Devil?*, 52–53.

82. Fortna, "Theological Use," 90; see also Culpepper, *Anatomy*, 128–29; Motyer, *Your Father the Devil?*, 50; Bassler, "Galileans," 243–44.

83. Bieringer, Pollefeyt, and Vandecasteele-Vanneuville, "Wrestling," 19.

84. Bultmann, *Gospel*, 86; Bultmann, *Theology*, 2:5, 26.

85. Reinhartz, "'Jews' and Jews in the Fourth Gospel," 213.

86. Culpepper, *Anatomy*, 129.

Although he emphasizes the universality of the human condition (hostility of the people toward the Johannine Jesus), Culpepper's commentary gives a clearer indication of the identity of "the Jews." He says, "the pathos of their unbelief is that they are the religious people, some even the religious authorities, who have had all the advantages of the heritage of Israel."[87] Moreover, Reinhartz argues, "the Fourth Gospel does not merely speak about 'the Jews' as a symbol for the unbelieving world but also sees the historical community of Jewish nonbelievers as the children of the devil and sinners destined for death."[88]

However, it is necessary to distinguish the Jewish leaders from "the ordinary Jews" in the ethnic sense (3:1, 25: 4:9) or from generalization of the term.[89] It is revealed more clearly in the Gospel that "the Jews" stand for the opponents of Jesus who reject his claims (6:41; 7:11; 8:22), particularly the Pharisees in their opposition to Jesus (9:13–22; 10:24, 31; 11:8, 45–47; 18:14, 36, 38; cf. 12:42; Pharisees and the high priests in 7:32, 45; 11:47; 12:42).[90] Bassler argues,

> Though the Fourth Gospel refers to the "Jews" in a variety of contexts and ways, a characteristically Johannine usage emerges in which the term loses its nationalistic meaning and comes to designate unreceptivity—even hostility—toward Jesus. Already at this point in the narrative the term has acquired these negative connotations.[91]

Von Wahlde says that the term means "the Jewish leaders," arguing, "if the term refers only to authorities, it hardly provides evidence that the gospel is an attack on the attitudes of all Jews."[92] Therefore, the term οἱ Ἰουδαῖοι refers mainly to the Jewish leaders in Jerusalem with whom Jesus and the Johannine community were in conflict, though they are characterized as the representatives of the unbelief of the world.

---

87. Culpepper, *Anatomy*, 129.
88. Reinhartz, "'Jews' and Jews in the Fourth Gospel," 225.
89. See, Beasley-Murray, *John*, 20; and Brown, *Gospel*, lxxi.
90. Beasley-Murray, *John*, lxxxix; von Wahlde, "Johannine 'Jews,'" 41–42; Dodd, *Historical Tradition*, 242 n. 2; Rensberger, *Johannine Faith*, 27, 34 n. 64; Brown, *Gospel*; Brown, *Community*, 41; von Wahlde, "Johannine 'Jews,'" 33–60.
91. Bassler, "Mixed Signals," 636–37.
92. Von Wahlde, "Johannine 'Jews,'" 33.

The Jews as the Judeans

Secondly, "the Jews" could be regarded as the Judeans. The relation of the term "the Jews" to Jerusalem or Judea is revealed distinctively in the Gospel of John (1:19; 2:18, 20; 2:23–3:1; 3:22–25; 7:1, 11, 13, 15, 35; 11:7–8, 54, 55; 18:14; cf. 4:9). Lowe identifies "the Jews" as the Judeans "either in reference to the Judean population in general or (less frequently except after Jesus' arrest) to the Judean authorities."[93] Elliott agrees with Lowe, contending, "Ioudaioi has a more inclusive sense and identifies persons, who according to birth, ethnicity, cult, Torah observance, and loyalty to Judea and its Temple are 'Judaean,' wherever they reside."[94] Bassler reinforces this view by arguing, "Galilee is the land of acceptance, refuge, and belief in Jesus, while Judea is the land of rejection, hostility, and disbelief."[95] Some scholars, however, argue against this view, because the term, the Jews, "has a fundamental religious significance which is not represented by "the Judeans" as a definition of its primary sense,"[96] and because the Gospel also reports that there is unbelief in Galilee (6:36) and faith in Judea (11:45).

It is hardly surprising, therefore, that the term "the Jews" usually stands for the ordinary Judeans. However, in many cases it means the Jewish leaders who dwelt in Judea, especially in Jerusalem.[97] They had power to excommunicate people out of the society (9:22; 11:47–57). The marginal people, including the Jewish people in Judea, are afraid of "the Jews" (7:13; 9:22: 19:38; 20:19), who oppose and reject not only the identity of Jesus but also deny their own identity as the people of God (19:14–42).[98] In short, the meaning of this term in the Gospel seems to be more political and religious than geographical and ethnic.[99]

---

93. Lowe, "Who were the ΙΟΥΔΑΙΟΙ?," 128; Elliott, "Jesus the Israelite," 137–38.

94. Elliott, "Jesus the Israelite," 138; see John 2:13; 4:22; 5:1; 6:4, 41, 52; 7:2; 18:35; 19:40, 42.

95. Bassler, "Galileans," 250.

96. Motyer, *Your Father the Devil?*, 49, see also Ashton, *Understanding*, 134.

97. Brown, *Gospel*, lxx–lxxv, 42–44; Lindars, *Gospel*, 102.

98. Particularly, John 19:15, "We have no king but Caesar." Culpepper comments, "at the last festival, Passover, instead of celebrating how God spared them and delivered them from a foreign oppressor, they seize Jesus and deliver him to the Romans for execution. Having now no king but Caesar, the world's king, they kill in order to defend their nation and their holy place" (*Anatomy*, 129).

99. Von Wahlde, "Johannine 'Jews,'" 47.

The Jews of Jerusalem in John 1:19

It is necessary, therefore, to identify the term "the Jews"[100] more clearly. All possible explanations hinge on the identification of "the Jews of Jerusalem" in John 1:19.

First, I will discuss a point of debate found in John 1:19 and John 1:24 in order to identify "the Jews of Jerusalem." In John 1:19, "the priests and Levites"[101] are sent by the Jews of Jerusalem to inquire into the identity of John the Baptist. Who would have had the authority to send "the priests and Levites"? The leaders of the Jews had that authority, or, more precisely, the leaders of the Sanhedrin (11:47), because "the Sanhedrin was largely controlled by the family of the high priests and so it was natural enough that the envoys be priests and Levites."[102]

Secondly, it is important to know that this verse is closely linked to John 1:24,[103] where John the Baptist and the priests and Levites are still in the dialogue. So, possible different manuscripts and/or translations of John 1:24 show differing aspects of the identity of the Jews of Jerusalem. For example, one translation of this verse (RSV: they had been sent from the Pharisees) has considerably more support than others (KJV: they which were sent were of the Pharisees).[104] Verse 19 indicates that the Jews of Jerusalem sent the priests and Levites, but how could they be the Pharisees or be sent by the Pharisees in John 1:24? It is unlikely that those sent by the Jews of Jerusalem are simultaneously the priests and Levites (1:19) as well as the Pharisees (1:24).

At the textual level, rather, it is accepted that the Jews of Jerusalem (1:19) stand for the Pharisees (1:24). However, it is difficult to explain how the Pharisees could send the priests and Levites.[105] Then, how could the

---

100. This expression is rare in Synoptic Gospels except referring to "the King of the Jews." In comparison with the Synoptic Gospels, the Gospel of John employs this expression, the Jews, more frequently.

101. This expression is used in this verse only in the Gospel as well as in the New Testament. Barrett sees it as a familiar Hebrew Bible phrase that was simply borrowed to describe Jewish functionaries (See, Barrett, *Gospel*, 172). Morris says this expression points to an official embassy from official Judaism (See Morris, *Gospel*, 116).

102. Carson, *Gospel*, 142. In addition, Levites served as the temple police and assisted in temple worship in Jesus' day (see Brown, *Gospel*, 43; and Barrett, *Gospel*, 172; Beasley-Murray, *John*, 112).

103. In the Gospel of John, the term "the Jews" needs to be identified, because in most cases it refers to the Jewish leaders.

104. REB: "Some Pharisees who were in the deputation asked him"; Phillips: "Now some of the Pharisees had been sent to John."

105. Bernard, *Critical and Exegetical Commentary*, 1:38. Phillips considers that

Pharisees send the priests and Levites, if the Sanhedrin, most of whom were Sadducees, were the Jews of Jerusalem in John 1:19? Although there is no consensus among scholars that the priests and Levites held Pharisaic convictions, Lagrange contends that some priests sided with the Pharisees.[106] Moreover, Lindars views that "in fact many priests and Levites belonged to the Pharisaic party, because of their concern for strict observance of the Jewish Law."[107]

Bruce claims that the deputation in John 1:19 and in John 1:24 is the same because the question in John 1:25 presupposes John's answers given in verses 20–23. He says, "If the deputation who was sent by the Sanhedrin, then the Pharisees, who formed an influential minority in that body, could insist on having some of their own number including among those who sent."[108] However, there is no hint that some Pharisees were part of the deputation in John 1:19.

Thirdly, it is important to recognize that the Sadducees are not mentioned in the Gospel of John but instead the chief priests. It suggests that they may no longer have been a significant power at the time of the Johannine community/of the writing of the Gospel, but it may mean that they were still a significant power in society, but not the only one any more.[109] Accordingly, it is possible that the collaboration between the Pharisees and the chief priests existed to maintain their power and position, because the Pharisees had become more powerful at the time of the writing of the Gospel.[110] According to Brown, the Pharisaic influence was stronger in Judaism

---

these were some of the Pharisees in a second deputation that was different from those in John 1:19. However, his view is given out of context. How could they abruptly interfere into the dialogue? If they were some of the Pharisees, they had to be in the dialogue from the beginning, however, there was no record of it. Carson's view is that some Pharisees were in the deputation from the beginning because they were sufficiently influential to send their members with the priests and Levites, although they did not control the Sanhedrin (*Gospel*, 144). However, if the Pharisees were not a strong party in the Sanhedrin and in society, how could they collaborate with the chief priests to eliminate Jesus? It is more possible that the Pharisees were one of the major powers in society at that time of the composition of the Gospel, and that their influence might be very influential in the decision of the Sanhedrin (see Frend, *Rise of Christianity*, 23–24). Martyn argues that the employment of the two terms simultaneously in the Gospel is to reflect the two levels: the chief priests as the reflection of the time of Jesus, and the Pharisees as that of the composition of the Gospel (*History and Theology*, 86).

106. Lagrange, *Evangile selon Saint Jean*, 37; Brown, *Gospel*, 44.

107. Lindars, *Gospel*, 105.

108. Bruce, *Gospel*, 49.

109. Motyer, *Your Father the Devil?*, 52; see also Nicol, *Semeia*, 144–45; Martyn, *History and Theology*, 84–85.

110. Brown, *Gospel*, lxxii. Even though the influence of the Sadducees was stronger

after the destruction of the Temple (70 CE), so "for a Gospel written with this situation in mind 'Pharisees' and 'Jews' would be the most meaningful titles for the Jewish authorities."[111] It is probable, therefore, that John attempts to reveal the identity of the major opponents of Jesus to his readers by saying that the Pharisees could send the priests and Levites to John the Baptist with the (tacit) approval of the High chief priests.[112]

Furthermore, as one of the characteristic features of the Gospel, the term "the Jews" is employed to refer to the political and religious leaders in Jewish society in conjuction with other terms (*Pharisaioi, archiereis,* and *archontes*) with no attempt to distinguish between them.[113] Among the 70 usages of the term, "the Jews," 38 refer to the Jewish leaders who were hostile to Jesus. The term is employed reciprocally with other terms for religious and political leaders in Jewish society (1:19–24; 7:32–46; 9:13–41; 18:3–14).

It is probable, therefore, that "the Jews of Jerusalem" refers mainly to the Jewish leaders, the members of the Sanhedrin, which consisted of the chief priests, and the Pharisees. This is in harmony with the description of the Pharisees and the chief priests who were the main opponents of Jesus in this Gospel.[114] Now, I will deal with "the Jews" as the Jewish leaders in the Johannine text.

---

at the time of Jesus' earthly ministry, the influence of the Pharisees could not be ignored (See Bruce, *Gospel*, 65). Then, after the collapse of Jerusalem, because the influence of the Pharisees was much stronger, its possibility is much higher (see Ferguson, *Backgrounds*, 515; Lindars, *Gospel*, 37, 105; Ridderbos, *Gospel*, 407). In addition, in the writing of Josephus (*Vita*, 21; *J.W.* 2:411), there are two instances of the combination of the Pharisees with the high priests. In the Gospel of Matthew, it is found twice, where it refers to Sanhedrin. It is distinctive that the combination of the Pharisees with the high priests in the Gospel of John occurs more frequently (7:32, 45; 11:47, 57; 18:3).

111. Brown, *Gospel*, 44. He also sees the possibility that the mention of Pharisees is the product of editing.

112. Motyer, *Your Father the Devil?*, 52; Martyn, *History and Theology*, 86. In the Gospel of John, the Pharisees are mentioned as the most influential leaders of the people, sometimes in conjunction with the chief priests, sometimes not (7:32, 45, 47; 9:13, 40).

113. For a good analysis of the terms, see von Wahlde, "Terms" 231–53; Martyn, *History and Theology*, 87–89. However, Martin views that the author refers to the secret believers among the Jewish leaders (12:42) as "rulers" (3:1; 7:26, 48; 12:42).

114. In the Gospel, the Jewish leaders, particularly the Pharisees, oppose and reject Jesus consistently. They attempt to lead the whole society to oppose and reject Jesus (9:22; cf. 5:15–16; 19:38–42). This opposition and rejection tendency toward Jesus by the Jewish leaders becomes clearer as the Gospel develops.

The Jews as the Jewish Leaders Who Are Hostile to Jesus

In the Gospel of John, "the Jews" as the Jewish leaders are described as those who desire to persecute Jesus (5:10, 15, 16, 18; 18:12, 14, 36), as those who decide to excommunicate any who confess Jesus as the Christ (9:18, 22a, 22b), as those who still caused fear in people regarding the consequences of talking about Jesus (7:13; 9:22; 20:19). I will examine some major passages concerning "the Jews" as the Jewish leaders in John chapters from 5 to 9 and in the Passion narrative.

"The Jews" in John 5

In chapter 5, after Jesus heals a man who had been an invalid for thirty eight years, "the Jews" of Jerusalem (5:10), who are obviously not the ordinary Jewish people, accuse the man of breaking the law of the Sabbath. When they realize that it was Jesus who had healed him, they persecute Jesus and seek to kill him (5:16). It is worthy of notice that the event happens in Jerusalem. Why then should the man go and tell "the Jews" when he learns that it was Jesus who healed him?[115] If "the Jews" were some of the ordinary people in Jerusalem who had no power to charge him with being a Sabbath breaker, he had no reason to betray Jesus. However, "the Jews," who accuse him, have sufficient power over the healed man for him to report who it was who had healed him, and thus was responsible for his Sabbath breaking.[116]

Besides this, the healing account in chapter 5 is different from other healings in the Gospel, as they result in people believing in Jesus (9:35; 11:45). However, in this case, the healing results in the worse thing: unbelief (5:15), greater sin (19:11),[117] and the final judgment (5:29).[118] Furthermore, it results in the growth of the conflict between the Jewish leaders and Jesus, and in Jesus' first direct confrontation with them. In short, "the Jews" in

---

115. For the debate regarding the role the invalid, see Ridderbos, *Gospel*, 189–90, and Brown, *Gospel*, 209.

116. Morris argues that the negative attitude toward Jesus of the invalid obviously comes from that of the Jews. It shows that the influence of the Jews was so decisive (Morris, *Gospel*, 272–73).

117. What the warning of Jesus to the invalid is hinted at in the light of Jesus' saying (19:11: "You would have no power over me if it were not given to you from above. Therefore the one who handed me over to you is guilty of a greater sin."). Jesus gave him a chance to know who Jesus is and to believe in him, but he failed like the Jewish leaders who were given several chances to know the true identity of Jesus.

118. Carson, *Gospel*, 246; Barrett, *Gospel*, 255.

John 5 are the Jewish leaders in Jerusalem, who appear at the beginning of the Gospel (1:19; 4:1).

"The Jews" in John 6

Secondly, "the Jews" in John 6:41 are used to describe the negative response to Jesus' teaching. This episode begins with John 6:1. The Gospel narrates that a great multitude[119] (John 6:2) is following Jesus from Jerusalem (John 5) to the other side of the Sea of Galilee, because they see the signs which Jesus performed on those who were sick (4:46–54; 5:1–15). Moreover, a great multitude whose number is about five thousand men (οἱ ἄνδρες) (6:10) follow Jesus up a mountain (6:5). They are clearly distinguishable from "the Jews" (of Jerusalem) who react negatively to Jesus (5:18). The multitude keeps following Jesus from the other side of the sea and comes to Capernaum to seek him (6:24–25). The multitude even more eagerly pursues Jesus (6:34) when they hear that he is the bread of God (6:33).

In this context, when Jesus says to the multitude that he is the bread of life (6:35–40), the Gospel reports abruptly that a negative response comes from "the Jews" (6:41), and not from the multitude.[120] Here, John employs the term "the Jews" once again. He is clearly distinguishing between the multitude who are favourable to Jesus and the Jews who respond negatively to him. Who are these Jews? In terms of their knowing Jesus' family (6:42), some seem to be Galileans.[121] However, it is not impossible to regard "the Jews" as the ones who had opposed him in chapter 5, because the multitude followed Jesus from Jerusalem (6:2). Many commentators link "the Jews," not to those in John 5:18, but to the synagogue congregation in Capernaum or rather to the leaders of that congregation.[122] However, it is more likely that they are the Jews of Jerusalem (1:19), although there is some place for

---

119. This term which is distinguishable from "the Jews" appears here.

120. Von Wahlde convincingly argues that "the Jews," who showed hostility and stereotyped reaction to Jesus (John 6:41, 52) are common people rather than the authorities (von Wahlde, "Johannine 'Jews,'" 33–60). Some scholars suppose that the author slipped in Jesus' opponents in the discourses as his usual way (see Lindars, *Gospel*, 262). However, it is more likely that the Jewish leaders might already be amongst the multitude in order to examine Jesus because Jesus said these things in the synagogue and taught in Capernaum (6:59).

121. Some scholars support this view (Lindars, *Gospel*, 262; Brown, *Gospel*, 270).

122. Bruce, *Gospel*, 155; Carson, *Gospel*, 292; Ridderbos, *Gospel*, 231; Brown, *Gospel*, 270. However, there is no clear evidence that the Jews in 6:41 are the only synagogue congregation in Capernaum. Rather, it is likely that they are in the multitude as the dialogue partner of Jesus in chapter 6. That is, it is hard to exclude that the Jews are from Jerusalem, although they dialogue in Capernaum, Galilee.

the thought that they are Galilean leaders.[123] In short, it is highly probable that the Jews in 6:41 are the Jewish leaders whether they come from Jerusalem or Capernaum. The Gospel does not describe "the Jews" in the ethnic sense,[124] but uses the term to describe a group in power which is at the center of the society which opposes and rejects Jesus. Therefore, the negative description of "the Jews" in this Gospel can be read against the background of the conflict between the center and the margin, not in the ethnic sense, which is a cause of anti-Semitism.[125]

The conflict between Jesus and the Jewish leaders has reached a dangerous level.[126] They grumble (6:41) and begin to argue with one another because of Jesus' teaching (6:52). Moreover, this dangerous level of conflict is reinforced by the grumbling of many disciples of Jesus (6:61) and the fact that many now leave him (6:66) because of both his difficult teaching and their unbelief (6:60, 64). Furthermore, for the first time, John states that just the twelve remain with Jesus, including the one who is going to betray him (6:64), Judas Iscariot the son of Simon (6:71). As a result, the Jewish leaders are *publicly* seeking to kill Jesus (7:1, 11, 25; cf. 5:18). As the story unfolds, the Gospel describes ever more clearly the conflict between Jesus and the Jewish leaders, not between Jesus and the Jewish people. Therefore, in spite of its ambiguity, it is more acceptable that "the Jews" in John 6:41 represent the Jewish leaders.

"The Jews" in John 7

Thirdly, in chapter 7, the narrative is more complicated in its use of the term "the Jews" and so needs to be investigated in more detail.[127]

---

123. Morris, *Gospel*, 237.

124. This weakens an argument that refers "the Jews" just to the Judeans, because the term, the Jews, is not mainly employed geographically or ethnically. This tendency is clearer in chapter 7 of the Gospel. Concerning arguments that the reference is to "the Jews" as the Judeans, see the section, "Rome as the Center of the Darkness" of this chapter; Lowe, "Who were the ΙΟΥΔΑΙΟΙ?," 101–30; Ashton, "Identity and Function," 40–73. This also is the reason why we need to read the Gospel with the postcolonial perspective, the conflict between the center and the margin.

125. Cassidy, *John's Gospel*, 41.

126. Carson, *Gospel*, 292. Carson says, "The grumbling was not only insulting, but dangerous."

127. Here, the author uses the term, "the Jews," in the more restricted sense in the Gospel.

1. In John 7:1, the author reports that "the Jews" are seeking to kill Jesus and are continually on the look out for him (7:11, 25, 30, 32, 44).[128] These verses show that the tensions between Jesus and the Jewish leaders are growing in intensity,[129] and may help the readers to understand the seriousness of the conflict brought about by the rapid spread of the good news and the rumours about Jesus. This might have made the Jewish leaders react more forcibly than usual.

2. "The Jews" in John 7:11 apparently indicate Jewish leaders, as distinct from the multitude in 7:12–13. In John 7:11–13, the author reports that the Jewish leaders are seeking Jesus, while there is much whispering[130] among the multitude about him. However, no one is speaking openly of him for fear of "the Jews."[131] The division among the multitude shows the division of public opinion about Jesus. They "stand as an independent but uninstructed party between Jesus and the Jews (the Pharisees),"[132] and the role they play shows the growth of the conflict.

Why, then, is the multitude afraid of "the Jews," i.e., the Jewish leaders? It is likely that the multitude knows that the Jewish leaders have sufficient power to kill Jesus (7:25), to excommunicate those who confess Jesus to be Christ (9:22; cf. 16:1–4), and that they themselves could be harmed if they are regarded as being on the side of Jesus.[133] Furthermore, it is because the Jewish leaders are mixing among the multitude that the multitude are not openly expressing their opinions (7:13),[134] because of their fear of "the Jews." On the other hand, it may be that the multitude are gradually changing their minds and deciding to follow "the Jews" of Jerusalem as the safest option. In short,

---

128. Many scholars regard this narrative as the reference to John 5:18. See Barrett, *Gospel*, 310; Carson, *Gospel*, 305; Lindars, *Gospel*, 267–68; Bruce, *Gospel*, 169. Ridderbos, however, regards this as a continuation of Jesus' stay in Galilee in chapter 6 (Ridderbos, *Gospel*, 206). In short, whether it is directly linked to chapter 5 or a continuation of chapter 6, the important thing to focus on is that this verse shows that the tension grows and the conflict between Jesus and the Jewish leaders is not reconcilable.

129. That is why Jesus goes up to Jerusalem in secret during the Feast of Tabernacles. It is worth knowing that the events described in the Gospel are connected with the Jewish Feasts (2:13; 5:1; 7:2; 10:22; 12:1; 18:28).

130. This verb (γογγύζω) is employed in 6:41, 43, 61, which is rendered "grumble" to complain about Jesus; however here, its nuance is different: "it probably signifies quiet discussion" (See Morris, *Gospel*, 256).

131. Here, the role of the multitude is important. Most of them were residents of Jerusalem and those who came to join the Feast.

132. Barrett, *Gospel*, 314.

133. Bruce says, "The authorities did not wish him to be discussed at all, and anyone who disregarded their wishes was liable to feel their displeasure" (Bruce, *Gospel*, 174).

134. Barrett, *Gospel*, 313.

"apparently, the antipathy of the authorities has reached the point where they do not want Jesus discussed publicly,"[135] resulting in some seeing Jesus negatively while others view him in a more positive light (7:12).

3. When Jesus teaches in the Temple,[136] "the Jews," including the leaders, marvel at his teaching (7:15).[137] When Jesus questions their intention to kill him, the multitude denies the fact and treats Jesus as demon-possessed (7:19-20).[138] According to Ridderbos, "the Jews" here are the people in general.[139] It is likely, however, that "the Jews" are particularly the Jewish leaders.[140] Their amazement at Jesus' teaching is reminiscent of that of the Jewish leaders in John 5:28. In addition, the fact that Jesus' addresses the question, "Why do you seek to kill me?," (7:19) to "the Jews" must indicate that they are "the Jewish leaders," because in 11:47-57 it is the chief priests and the Pharisees (i.e., the leaders) who gather the council together and who from that day plotted to put him to death (11:53).[141] The reply of the multitude in John 7:20 would indicate that they were the section of the crowd in John 7:12 who claimed that Jesus deceived the people.[142] This is also echoed in John 8:48 and 10:19, 20.[143]

---

135. Carson, *Gospel*, 310.

136. The place where Jesus teaches has a similar function to that of the Feasts in the Gospel of John. Because Jesus teaches in the Temple, the readers infer that the issue about Jesus among the Jewish leaders has become a "hot potato," and that their intention to eliminate Jesus is revealed more clearly. This literary device is reinforced by the revelation of the Jews as the rulers, and the chief priests and the Pharisees in chapter 7.

137. Carson, *Gospel*, 311.

138. See 8:48; 9:19-20. In these verses, the Jews are linked to the Pharisees (8:13; 9:13).

139. Ridderbos, *Gospel*, 262

140. Bruce, *Gospel*, 174.

141. Carson, *Gospel*, 314.

142. Cf. John 8:44-47; Bruce, *Gospel*, 176. In Jewish law, this charge is a serious one that could lead to capital punishment (Deut 3:1-6) (Beasley-Murray, *John*, 107). In Revelation, the devil (the dragon, Satan) is referred to as deceiver (19:9; 20:3, 8, 10) (see Böcher, "Πλάναω," 100). More importantly, the author's employment of the negative view of the multitude on Jesus needs mention. According to Carson, the negative view of Jesus (you have a demon) "became dominant in some Jewish circles after the resurrection. The Evangelist is doubtless aware of it, and, seeking to win Jews and proselytes to the Christian faith, here attempts to explain it by tracing it to its origin" (Carson, *Gospel*, 310).

143. Carson, *Gospel*, 314; Barrett, *Gospel*, 319. In the Synoptic Gospels, Jesus was accused by the Jewish leaders of being possessed by Beelzebul (In Mark 3:19-22, the scribes accused him; in Matt 12:22-24, the Pharisees did; in Luke 11:14-16, some of the people who marveled did).

4. The response of Jesus to these accusations from the people is to declare that they must "judge with righteous judgment and not with appearance" (7:24). This statement brings a response from some of them from Jerusalem, "Is not this man whom they seek to kill?" (7:25).[144] The fact that these people know of the plot of the Jewish leaders to put Jesus to death indicates that they are clearly linked to the rulers (οἱ ἄρχοντες).[145] As the people become more and more inclined to believe in him (7:31), the Pharisees and the chief priests send officers (ὑπηρέται)[146] to seize Jesus (7:32; cf. 18:3, 12, 22; 19:6). Therefore, it is probable that some of the Jerusalemites in John 7:25 are the officers sent by the chief priests and the Pharisees.

In short, it is likely that "the Jews," namely, the Jewish leaders and officers of the chief priests and the Pharisees in chapter 7, are mixing[147] among the multitude so as to ascertain the trend of public opinion regarding Jesus and to stir up negative views about him. In addition, it is likely that the Pharisees and the chief priests are the group behind the scenes manipulating events and who then begin to occupy center stage (cf. John 8:13; 9:13).[148]

After the failure of the officers to seize Jesus (7:30, 44-49), the Pharisees in particular emerge as the front line of opposition to him. They are scathing in their verbal attack on the officers (7:47-49) and the content of their criticism ("he has deceived you also" in 7:47; "a prophet does not come out of Galilee" in 7:52) is similar to that of the multitude in John 7:23 and 7: 41, 42. In chapter 7, it seems that the mixed use of the terms raises a difficulty in identifying the Jews. However, it is more relevant that the Jews in chapter 7 are not the ordinary Jewish people but the Jewish leaders and their officers.

---

144. Ridderbos proposes that "verses 25-27 still presuppose vs. 14 as the scene of action and thus form the direct continuation of vss. 15-24" (Ridderbos, *Gospel*, 267).

145. This word is employed to describe Nicodemus in 3:1. This word means the Jews, particularly the Sanhedrin members (Brown, *Gospel*, 313). In John 7:48, the Pharisees distinguish themselves from the rulers.

146. Its literary meaning is "servants," however; their duty is guards (Morris, *Gospel*, 368). According to Bultmann, one of the duties of the "officers" is as a police force, that is, Temple guards (Bultmann, *Gospel*, 306; Beasley-Murray, *John*, 112; Lindars, *Gospel*, 295). "They were a picked body of Levites, and their commander (the 'captain of the temple') was an official wielding high authority, next only to the high priest, and he too was usually drawn from one or another of the leading chief-priestly family" (See Bruce, *Gospel*, 179; see also Carson, *Gospel*, 319-20).

147. Beasley-Murray, *John*, 112.

148. In John 7:45, one definite article governs "chief priests and Pharisees." It gives "the impression that they are very much together in this action" (Brown, *Gospel*, 325).

"The Jews" in John 8

Fourthly, in chapter 8, John links the Pharisees together with "the Jews." "The Pharisees" as a technical term is used as the direct opposition to Jesus for the first time in John 8:13. The Pharisees in John 8:13 are "the Jews" in John 8:22–59, and together are the counterpart in their verbal attacks against Jesus in the dialogue in chapter 8. They are among the multitude,[149] and are in controversy with Jesus. We read that many of the people believed in him (7:31) and it would seem that some of the Pharisees are included in the many in John 7:48–49: "Has any of the rulers or of the Pharisees believed in him? No! But *this* mob that knows nothing of the Law—there is a course on him." Again in John 8:31, we are specifically told that this included "the Jews" (cf. 12:42). Hence not only is there a division among the multitude but apparently amongst the rulers and Pharisees also.

It is noteworthy that when Jesus is talking to "the Jews" who believed in him (8:31), there are Jewish leaders (the Pharisees)[150] also in the multitude. They again accuse Jesus of having a demon in John 8:48 (cf. John 7:20) and pick up stones to throw at him in John 8:59 (cf. John 5:18). In the controversy in John 8:31–59, the description of the opponents of Jesus is striking. In chapter 5, negative descriptions of "the Jews" are given. They are described as those who do not believe in God (5:38), Moses, and the Scriptures (5:46–47). Moreover, in chapter 8, a worse description is given: they are the sons of the devil (8:44). "The Jews" in John 8 therefore are equated with the Jewish leaders who have negative views of Jesus.

"The Jews" in John 9

The fifth item of evidence is found in John 9.[151] Jesus heals a man born blind by making clay of dust mixed with his saliva, anointing the man's eyes with the clay and telling him to wash in the Pool of Siloam (9:6–7). This miracle takes place in Jerusalem because the narrative is continuous from John 8:59 to 9:1, and the Pool of Siloam is situated in Jerusalem.

In this story, the Pharisees and "the Jews" appear together (9:13; 9:16; 9:18). In addition, "some of the Pharisees" are mentioned in John 9:40. It is particularly striking that the division among the Pharisees (9:16) is

---

149. See John 8:2. They might be among all the people who came to Jesus, namely, the multitude. Furthermore, if it is a continuous story from chapter 7, they might be among the multitude: John 7:37 shows that it was the last day of the Feast and in Jerusalem (cf. 8:59).

150. See John 8:13.

151. See chapter 2 of this book.

reminiscent of the division of the multitude in chapter 7,[152] although this division is not caused by what Jesus has said but rather by his action of giving sight to the man. Furthermore, John reports that the Jews have already decided that anyone who acknowledges that Jesus is the Christ will be cast out of the synagogue (9:22). Who are "the Jews" in John 9:22? They also are not the ordinary Jews, but the leaders of Jewish society who have absolute authority. They are able to have people cast out of the synagogue at their command. In addition, because of Jesus' performance of miracles and his teaching, there arises a division again among the Jews and many of them treat Jesus as demon-possessed, while others deny his demon-possession (10:19–21). More strikingly, this division of "the Jews" comes from the restoration of the sight of the man born blind in John 10:19–21, and is closely linked to that of the Pharisees in John 9:16. Therefore, the Jews in John 9 are the Jewish leaders who have power to excommunicate the powerless, as they will.

"The Jews" in the Passion Narrative

Finally, we need to investigate the identity of "the Jews" in the Passion narrative. It is noticeable that the chief priests, the Pharisees and the officers all appear in this account,[153] along with the collective term "the Jews." The term "multitude" does not appear in the Johannine passion narrative, but in the corresponding narratives in the Synoptic Gospels, it is the chief priests, the rulers and the multitude[154] who cry out "crucify him" (Matt 27:11–66; Mark 15:1–47; Luke 23:1–49). However, in this Gospel, "the Jews" are the ones demanding his death (John 9:7, 12, 15). These are not the common people, but the Jewish leaders. Cassidy comments, "the group pressuring Pilate for Jesus' death is essentially an alliance of chief priests and Pharisees and is distinct from the Jewish populace of Jerusalem."[155] The officers from the chief priests and the Pharisees along with the detachment of troops who are sent to arrest Jesus are reminiscent of "the Jews" of Jerusalem who send priests and Levites (i.e., the officers) to John the Baptist (1:19). More explicitly, in John 7:32, 45, the Jewish leaders send their officers to seize Jesus. After the arrest of Jesus by the Roman cohort, the commander, and the officers of

---

152. The statement of the multitude who believed in Jesus in John 7:31 is reminiscent of that of the some of the Pharisees in John 9:16.

153. See the section, "Rome as the Center in the Passion Narrative" of this chapter.

154. Ὄχλος in Matt 27:20 and in Mark 15:8; λαός in Luke 23:13.

155. Cassidy, *John's Gospel*, 41.

"the Jews,"[156] they lead Jesus to Caiaphas. He is the one who had advised "the Jews" (18:14) that it was expedient for one man to die on behalf of the people (John 11:49–51). Therefore, "the Jews" to whom Caiaphas speaks in John 18:14 are the same as the chief priests and the Pharisees of John 11:47. In addition, after the trial by Caiaphas, "the Jews"[157] lead Jesus to Pilate (18:28). It is "the Jews" who are the loudest in their accusations of Jesus (18:31, 38; 19:7, 12). They are not the multitude, but are instead the chief priests and the officers (19:6; 19:15; 19:21). Pilate then delivers Jesus to the chief priests (19:15–16), and the chief priests and the officers take Jesus out and crucify him (19:16, 18).[158]

In addition, after the death of Jesus on the cross, two other Jewish leaders emerge, i.e., Joseph of Arimathea, and Nicodemus (19:38–42). Their appearance and actions are clearly distinguishable from those of the Jewish leaders who crucified Jesus. It is probable that their functions help the readers to have a more positive impression of the other Jews who also believed in Jesus. This episode also reinforces the fact that there are many of the Jewish people, including some of the Jewish leaders, who do believe in Jesus (7:31; 8:30–31; 10:42, 45; 12:11, 19, 42). In short, it is quite clear that "the Jews" in the Passion Narrative are the Jewish leaders.

In summary, I conclude that "the Jews" in the Gospel of John mainly stand for the Jewish leaders who are hostile to Jesus. In the next section, I will argue that "the Jews" can be identified as collaborators with the Imperial power.

Jewish Leaders as Collaborators

There is an ambivalent and symbiotic relationship between the colonizer and the colonized. This interdependence is formed by colonization and determines the character and behavior of the two.[159] These relationships seem to form in a colonized society through a lengthy repetitive cycle of resistance and also accommodation to the foreign power. Particularly, two minds in conflict with each other seem to co-exist in the attitude of the colonized toward the colonizer. In the mind of the colonized, there is extreme hatred of the colonizers, but there may also be fervent admiration

---

156. That the officers, in the other texts, are sent by the chief priests and the Pharisees means "the Jews" here stands for the Jewish leaders.

157. Cf. John 18:12

158. The soldiers crucified Jesus (19:23); however, the chief priests are responsible for his crucifixion.

159. Gandhi, *Postcolonial Theory*, 11; Dube, "Savior of the World," 119.

of them. In these complex conditions, through mimicry of the exercise of power by the colonized as the client rulers of the empire in the colonized society, these relationships are formed (hybridentity).[160]

After the colonizing power has established its domination over the colonized by means of military force, it seeks to promote a peaceful, stable, government which is in the best interests of both the parties concerned. In order to do this successfully, it needs the help of collaborators. For their part in this collusive arrangement, the collaborators can secure their own positions as local rulers ruling on behalf of the colonizer. The colonizer can thereby more effectively exert control over the colonized with far less resistance than would otherwise be possible. This collaboration between the two groups does however produce certain conflicts and divisions within the colonized society.[161]

These ambivalent and symbiotic relationships between the colonizer and the colonized can be found in the Gospel of John, and the Jewish leaders could be a typical example. They were suffering under the heel of the Roman Empire, but ironically, they could also be preserving their power and position under the supervision of the imperial power. The political structure had formed an interdependence between them. On the one hand, the Jewish leaders hated Rome, because the Romans occupied their land by force, usurped their positions and deprived them of their rights as an independent nation. On the other hand, they collaborated with Rome in order to survive, and maintain some semblance of their power and positions, and at least would envy the Romans in their exercise of power.

During the occupation of Palestine by Rome, the Jews had fought against Rome for their independence, but in most cases, they had failed. A result of these series of failures might be both an admission of the reality of Rome and the beginning of collaboration with her. Some of the Jewish leaders might have changed their attitude from resistance to cooperation and thus gradually elevated themselves to positions of power under the supervision of Rome. Ultimately, they might become powerful political elites in Jewish society. It is probable that they reached the belief that they could not exist without Rome, and they seemed to think that in cooperation with

---

160. Hybridentity occurs "as a result of conscious moments of cultural suppression, as when the colonial power invades to consolidate political and economic control, or when settler-invaders dispossess the indigenous peoples and force them to 'assimilate' to new society patterns" (Ashcroft, *Post-Colonial Studies Reader*, 137).

161. See chapter 2 of this book, and the section "The Perspective of a Korean Reader" of this chapter. In the case of Korean colonial history, I believe, the competition of the colonized and collaboration with Imperial power have resulted in conflict and division of the society.

Rome's absolute power, they could preserve their lives and live in Roman peace (11:49–50). They might even have wanted to become a real part of Rome. The reality, however, was different. They never became Romans and they never achieved the peace they desired.

These conflicts and competitions existed in Jewish society.[162] Furthermore, they seemed to occur not only in their political, economic, cultural, and religious spheres,[163] but also in their psychological identities. The groups who were anti-Roman still caused conflict with pro-Roman groups.[164] Smallwood argues that Rome's comparative generosity toward Judaism as a religion is embroidered with toleration and protection in the history of Rome's dealing with the Jews, while Rome was less generous to Christianity which lacked a national basis and pursued a much more vigorous missionary campaign for the first three centuries.[165] This argument implies that there would have been conflict and competition between Judaism and Christianity (between the margins) in the Roman world (in the colonial territories), because of the different policies of the ruling power to different marginal groups.

In this situation, the Jewish leaders as depicted by John might think that their positions were threatened when they saw Jesus' miraculous actions and heard his message, a message that challenged their thinking concerning Rome as the absolute power and authority and the one who could bring them peace. Instead, they were challenged to acknowledge that Jesus as the king who would reign universally, and that they needed to become the children of God through belief in Jesus as king. Furthermore, they might be afraid of Roman military intervention to solve the conflict between them, as the Jesus movement grew and became too serious to ignore. They had seen the rapid growth in the number of Jesus' disciples from various backgrounds and they might regard them as an anti-Roman force.

Gandhi's comment on ambivalent and symbiotic relationships between the colonizer and the colonized in the modern colonizing period could imply the same relationships between the colonizer (Rome) and

---

162. On conflict and competition within Jewish society, see the section "Rome as the Center" of this chapter; Goodman, *Ruling Class*, 12–25; Josephus, *B. J.* 7.260–1.

163. Horsley argues that the relations between the center and the margins can be understood in terms of interrelations of economic, political, and cultural dimensions (Horsley, *Jesus and the Spiral of Violence*, 5–6).

164. Major resistance of the Jews against Rome seemed to end mostly after the destruction of the Jerusalem Temple; however many resistances occurred afterwards including major revolts in 115, 135 CE (see Goodman, *Ruling Class*; Smallwood, *Jews*).

165. Smallwood, *Jews*, 539–43.

the colonized (the Jewish leaders) in the Gospel of John in terms of the exercise of power.

> They are ideologically interpellated by the restrictive confinement of knowledge and value to the sovereign map of Europe. The Europe they know and value so intimately is always elsewhere. Its reality is infinitely deferred, always withheld from them. Worse still, their questing pursuit of European plenitude, their desire to own the colonizer's world, requires a simultaneous disowning of the world which has been colonized.[166]

It is helpful to look into the attitude of "the Jews," in particular that of the Jewish leaders, toward Jesus in the Gospel: 1. The Jews had already agreed that if anyone should confess Jesus to be the Christ, he should be put out of the synagogue (9:22); 2. Jesus must be killed; if not, Rome would destroy them (11:48); 3. their attitude toward Rome in their confession: "We have no king but Caesar" (19:15); 4. their challenge to Pilate to crucify Jesus: "If you would let this man go, you are not a friend of Caesar" (19:12); 5. their persistent riotous clamours: "Crucify him! Crucify him!" (19:6, 15). This Gospel describes that the Jewish leaders are in a dilemma because of the popularity of Jesus. In particular, John 19:15 reports that the Jewish leaders, in order to obtain their objective, choose Caesar as their king, not God. These show clearly that they use their power for their own interests, to the extent that they abandon their national and religious identity as the chosen people of God.

We can see this more clearly in the arrest of Jesus. The Jewish leadership had Jesus arrested in conjuction with Roman military power, because the Temple police had failed to arrest Jesus on the previous occasion (7:44–52).[167] The Jewish leaders needed Roman power to be able to get rid of Jesus.[168] Therefore, Judas, the traitor, accompanied *the Roman cohort* and the officers/police from the chief priests and the Pharisees (τὴν σπεῖραν καὶ ἐκ τῶν ἀρχιερέων καὶ ἐκ τῶν Φαρισαίων ὑπηρέτας) in order to arrest Jesus. Roman involvement in the arrest seems striking in the Gospel. The term "cohort" refers mostly to Roman soldiers in the New Testament (cf. 18:12).[169] It is quite probable, therefore, that the high priests would have

166. Gandhi, *Postcolonial Theory*, 12.

167. Morris, *Gospel*, 657.

168. Robinson comments, "What was distinctive, and shameful, about the arrest of Jesus is that the Jews took the initiative, *and collaborated*. But then the exercise was, as John insists, collaborationist from start to finish" (Robinson, *Priority*, 242).

169. Brown, *Gospel*, 807–8; Bruce, *Gospel*, 340; Lincoln, *Gospel*, 443. Carson points out that the move of Roman troops to Jerusalem "not only ensured more efficient

informed Pilate, who had the responsibility for the dispatch of Roman troops, that there was a real risk of a riot occurring,[170] and would thus have secured troops to assist in the arrest of Jesus. This inference could also be made from two references in the Gospel.

First, the fact that the Jewish leaders already regard Jesus and his disciples as a threat (11:47–53) like a riot (12:19) is an evidence. After the arrest of Jesus, Annas the high priest questions him about *his disciples* and his teaching (18:19). Annas's inclusion of the disciples implies that they have been watching Jesus' movement as not simply a personal one, but one that had aroused considerable public support. In addition, the Jewish leaders choose Barabbas the robber (ληστής) to be released rather than Jesus, when Pilate asked them whom they wanted to be released according to the Jewish custom of the Passover (18:40). It seems that they think Jesus is a more serious threat to their security than the robber. In the Gospel of John, the term "the robber (ληστής)" is employed twice (10:1; 18:40), and is used in contrast with the kingship of Jesus, the sharp contrast between Jesus, the real king, and the robber/the revolutionary.[171] Robinson points out that the Romans would have arrested Barabbas the robber (ληστής) because only the Romans could arrest such a rebel, terrorist or freedom fighter, taking the precaution of doing it in strength.[172] Thus, the choice by the Jewish leaders of the robber reveals the darkness of the world from the beginning (1:5, 11).[173]

---

policing of the huge throngs . . . during the high feasts, but guaranteed that any mob violence or incipient rebellion, bred by the crowding and the religious fervour, would be efficiently crushed. That is probably the reason why they were called out to support the temple officials: the risk of mob response was doubtless rather high in the case of an arrest of someone with Jesus' popularity" (Carson, *Gospel*, 577). Bruce also points out, "The fact that Roman troops were there as well as temple police implies that the Jewish authorities had already approached the military command, probably indicating that they expected armed resistance to be offered" (Bruce, *Gospel*, 340).

170. Robinson, *Priority*, 242.

171. In John 10:1–18, the image of the good shepherd, with its kingly connotations, is sharply contrasted with that of thief (κλέπτης) and robber (ληστής). This kingly image is reinforced putting those of a thief and a robber together in the narrative. They *only* comes to steal, kill, and destroy (10:10), however, Jesus as good shepherd gives life and abundantly. Furthermore, in John 18:40, ironically, the identity of Jesus as king is revealed, by putting together Jesus the king side by side with Barabbas the robber (ληστής).

172. Robinson, *Priority*, 241–42.

173. In the Synoptic Gospels (Matt 26:55; Mark 14:48; Luke 22:52), in addition, this image is given in Jesus' saying, "As against a robber (ληστὴν) did you come out, with swords and clubs to seize me?" The presence of swords implicitly confirms that it was the Roman soldiers' job.

The second reference is when Pilate meets the Jewish leaders early in the morning (18:29) implying that there must already have been a certain kind of conspiracy between the Jewish leaders and Pilate to have Jesus arrested.[174] That Pilate is ready to meet the petitioners and to examine Jesus implies that Pilate already knows about the arrest of Jesus. It is probable that the author of the Gospel seeks to indicate that Pilate and the Jewish leaders together bear the responsibility for Jesus' arrest.[175] After the judgment is given, Roman soldiers mock Jesus (19:1–5) and crucify him (19:23).

This has serious implications for the logic of the colonized under imperial power. The Roman exercise of power was deeply rooted in the consciousness of the colonized. Furthermore, the collaborators, who were given power over inner groups by the colonizer, had copied Roman methods in the colonized spaces. If the exercise of power over the anti-groups by the collaborators, who themselves were once part of such groups, had been performed in the same way as by the colonizer, who never tolerated any rebellion, the conflicts within society would have become more and more serious. Just as Roman imperial power never allowed any challenge to her authority, so the Jewish leaders also might never approve of anything which threatened their position in Jewish society.

Exercise of power is frequently seductive, while the logic of power is fundamentally coercive.[176] The casual and diverse use of power is represented in complex ways by both compulsory military force and civilian action. In particular, the exercise of power in the civil arena causes collaborators to arise from among the colonized societies and because of this colonization permeates into society in a stronger and deeper way. Very similar phenomena are described in the Jewish society under the domination of the Roman Empire in this Gospel. The Jewish leaders already admit the reality of Roman Imperial power, which they fear. The Jewish leaders are afraid that Rome will destroy them if it recognizes the seriousness of the Jesus movement and their inability to deal with it in an appropriate way. These things show that the Jewish leaders accepted the reality of Rome and that collaboration with her was their only way of survival under this dominant Imperial power. In their eyes, Jesus could be considered as a revolutionary against both Roman imperial power and the collaborators' power in Jewish society. Jesus could be understood by them to be the one who attempted to overcome this kind of oppression. They never accepted Jesus and his movement. They arrived at the conclusion to kill Jesus themselves.

---

174. Bernard, *Critical and Exegetical Commentary*, 2:584; Lincoln, *Gospel*, 443.

175. Hoskyns, *Fourth Gospel*, 509; Beasley-Murray, *John*, 322.

176. Gandhi, *Postcolonial Theory*, 14.

In summary, while quoting Foucault's point: "such apparent 'collaboration' is really symptomatic of the pervasive and claustrophobic omnipresence of power," Gandhi argues that "power is best able to disseminate itself through the collaboration of its subjects."[177] In the Gospel of John, we can find this apparent collaboration between the Imperial power and the Jewish leaders ("We have no king but Caesar"). It means that the Imperial power has already pervaded deeply both inside and outside Jewish society. The Jewish leaders' attitudes show it well. They regarded Jesus as a serious threat to both the Imperial power and themselves. They also possessed both their positions and a semblance of a stable society under the domination of the Imperial power. That is the reason, according to the Gospel, why they killed Jesus. Their behavior is typical of those who are corrupted by power. They collaborated with Rome outwardly and maintained their power and positions inwardly by the elimination of the threat, i. e. Jesus. Therefore, the Jewish leaders could be identified as the collaborators with the colonizer, who themselves caused more severe conflict in the marginal society.

The Johannine Community as Margin

In this section, I will attempt to identify the Johannine community in terms of the readership of the Gospel. At a textual level, it is possible to reconstruct the Johannine community,[178] which is closely related to the recipients/readers of the Gospel, although it is almost impossible to reconstruct them as a historical reality. Accordingly, I will first argue that it is important to indicate three points in this section in order to reconstruct them: 1. the Johannine community under Rome; 2. the wide spectrum of the Johannine readers; 3. John's positive view of other marginal groups. Then, I will identify the Johannine community as a margin at the textual level.

The Johannine Community Under Rome

To begin with, it is again important to point out that the reading of the Gospel of John is more meaningful when we understand that the Johannine community was in the Roman Empire in the first century CE It is probable that there was another conflict between the two, which was an

---

177. Gandhi, *Postcolonial Theory*, 14.

178. See chapter 1 of this book. On the historical reconstruction of the Johannine community, see Culpepper, *Johannine School*; Martyn, *History and Theology*; Brown, *Community of the Beloved Disciple*, 14–17, 55–58, 59–91; Klink, *Sheep of the Fold*, 24–35.

unavoidable entity in the historical situations with which Johannine community was faced.[179]

Some scholars argue that the Johannine community has spoken about the conflicts between the Jews and the Johannine community and/or within the Christian community. There are three major views on the conflict in the Gospel in terms of the conflicting parties – the conflict as Christians;[180] the conflict as inner-Jewish;[181] the conflict as Christian-Jewish.[182] In short, the relationship of the Johannine community with contemporary Jews is complex and ambiguous. In addition, the relationship of the Johannine community and other (marginal) groups is more ambiguous. Furthermore, the relationship between the Johannine community and Rome is most ambiguous in this Gospel. However, it is quite clear that there must be conflict within the colonized society, with other colonized societies, and with the colonizer; and that we find these kinds of conflict in the Gospel. Moreover, most importantly, it seems undeniable that the conflict has its roots in the core of the Johannine Christology.[183] In this complex and ambivalent society, this Gospel was written, and Johannine Christology developed.

The Wide Spectrum of Johannine Readers

Secondly, it is widely accepted that the Johannine community was radically estranged, "not only from the wider society [Rome], but also from the society of the synagogue [Jewish Society], even perhaps from the society of other Christian groups."[184] It seems that this view has focused on the experinece

---

179. Stegemann and Stegemann, *Jesus Movement*, 237-47. Not only synagogue exclusions (9:22; 12:42) but also persecution (5:16; 15:20) and killing (16:2) are recognizable in the texts.

180. Dodd, "Behind a Johannine Dialogue," 42-47; de Jonge, "'Jews,'" 122, 125.

181. Dunn, "Embarrassment of History," 52; de Boer, "Depiction," 142, 155-56.

182. Martyn, *History and Theology*; Culpepper, "Anti-Judaism," 63; Tomson, "Names 'Israel' and 'Jew,'" 120-40, 266-89; Tomson, "'Jews,'" 211; Reinhartz, "'Jews' and Jews in the Fourth Gospel," 225.

183. Beieringer, Pollefeyt, and F. Vandecasteele-Vanneuville, "Wrestling with Johannine Anti-Judaism," 25; Painter, "Point," 213.

184. Barton, "Christian Community," 281; see chapter 1 of this book. Some scholars argue against Martyn and his followers. 1. Kimelman argues that the charge of expulsion was designed to persuade Christians to stay away from the synagogue, not to report the actual historical event (Kimelman, "Birkat Ha-Minim," 226-44). 2. Davies also claims "it is more likely that the Evangelist is not reflecting the practice of contemporary Jews at all, but is extrapolating from Scripture in order to justify the fact that the Christian community has nothing to do with the Jewish community" (Davies, *Rhetoric*, 299). 3. Reinhartz argues the possibility of the desertion of the Jews by the Johannine

5. IDENTITY MATTERS OF THE GROUPS IN THE GOSPEL OF JOHN 201

of estrangement, or on the reason of their estrangement from society. Moreover, most scholars, regardless of whether or not they agree with Martyn, seem to accept that the Gospel emphasizes conflict and separation between the Johannine community and other religious groups. However, if we consider that the Johannine community lived in a colonized society,[185] namely the Roman Empire, a hybridized, mixed, and complex society, and if we assume that they pursued peaceful coexistence with other groups in the society, we can say that the Johannine message focuses not on the estrangement nor on the separated life of the community from the world (13:35; 16:2, 33; 17:15, 18; 20:21), but on how to survive and live together in harmony with other groups (13:15, 34–35; 15:4–5;17:18; 20:21; cf. 21:15–17). Thus, in the situation of expulsion and persecution from society, the Johannine message might show to its readers how to overcome it and live in peace, and be reconciled with others in the Johannine Community.

We can explain this point in terms of "the spectrum of Johannine readers."[186] The Gospel of John gives examples of the spectrum of Johannine

---

community in order to believe in Jesus. She also argues that the expulsion texts (9:22; 12:42; 16:2), as a warning against returning to the synagogue constructing a world in which a return would be met with rejection, are more indicative of the ambiguity experienced by those who deserted the synagogue (Reinhartz, "Johannine Community," 111–38). 4. Conway argues that the view of Martyn on the Johannine community is, in its origin, the dramatic production of an outcast community which appealed especially to the radical sensibilities of the late 1960s and 1970s (Conway, "Production of the Johannine Community," 479–95). Conway continues that "it plays on the desire to align oneself with the marginalized over against the established institutional authorities" (Conway, "Production of the Johannine Community," 488). Although there are different views against Martyn, since Martyn argues that the Gospel reflects events in the life of particular community, his view has been accepted widely (Culpepper, "Gospel of John," 113–14). In terms that Martyn's goal is to say something as specific as possible about the actual circumstances in which John wrote, his view is valuable for my argument (Martyn, *History and Theology*, 27–29). In other words, Martyn's argument gives us a pivotal reason of the necessity of the composition of the Gospel. In this respect, Martyn's argument should not be ignored. At the textual level, it is safe to say that the Johannine community seemed to be in the dangerous stage of persecution from the outside of the community as well as conflict within the inner groups of the community (returning to Judaism; apostasy). That is, they were in conflict with both sides: imperial persecution and expulsion from Judaism, and as a result of it, they might be suffering side effects in the community, break down of the community (16:1). If it is acceptable that in order to give an alternative in this circumstance in which the Gospel was written, then, the next question is much more important to ask: which direction does the Gospel indicate to the readers? In other words, does the Gospel defend sectarianism and challenge its readers to break away from the world? Alternatively, is the Gospel an open text in order to show the readers how to live together in harmony in this tabulated world? On this argument, see chapter 6 of this book.

185. Koester, "Spectrum," 9.

186. Koester says that "literary and historical studies suggest that it may be better to

readers consisting of Christians of Jewish background including some expelled from the synagogue (i.e., the man born blind in chapter 9; 16:2), Samaritan Christians (chapter 4), and some Gentile Greeks (12:2–22, 32).[187] Moreover, in the Gospel Jesus came into the world to save it, not to judge it (1:9, 11; 3:16–17). This basic theme of the Gospel, the coming of Jesus into the world to bring salvation, does not justify the estrangement and expulsion of the Johannine community (the readers, the Christians) from the world, but rather it pursues their harmony and coexistence in the world from the beginning of the Gospel. The Johannine Jesus functions as the one who overcomes the conflicts with other groups (Jews, Samaritans, and Gentiles) and the tendency of the separation by/from the world.[188] For example, Jesus visits a Samaritan town and attempts to correct the Samaritan woman's misunderstanding, and she introduces him as the Christ to the Samaritans who then confess him as the Savior of the World. This development of the story shows how the Johannine Jesus takes on the role of the one who attempts to reduce the conflict between groups and thus to win the out-groups.[189] Furthermore, the healing stories, and especially his redemptive death for the world[190] highlight this literary strategy.

With this perspective, we can find both exclusiveness and inclusiveness in the Gospel of John.[191] In other words, a tension exists between the text of the, which formulates a clear limitation of the revelation of the kingship of Jesus to the margins (exclusivity of revelation of Jesus to the

---

envision a spectrum of readers when considering John's Gospel" (Koester, "Spectrum," 9). Okure also argues the mixed audience of the Gospel (See Okure, *Johannine Approach*, 280–81).

187. Koester, "Spectrum," 9–10.

188. The Gospel of John does not only describe an unworldly Johannine utopia, which seems to be revealed implicitly in John 14:2–3, the concept of the Father's house as a dwelling place, and in John 18:36, the kingdom of Jesus is not of this world. However, the unworldly point of view is not the sole point of view of the Gospel of John, because the Gospel of John introduces Jesus as an alternative to solve or to reduce the problems of the conflicting world.

189. Esler, "Jesus," 185–205.

190. See John 1:29, 35; 11:7–16; 18:1–11, 36, 37; 10:11, 30. On portraying Jesus as a sacrificial victim, for example, Isaac, the Suffering Servant of Isaiah, and the Paschal Lamb, see Orchard, *Courting Betrayal*, 224–46.

191. This is the literary device as the strategy to persuade the readers. Barton points this out from a different angle: "[Jesus] is the one who manifests 'the name' (i.e., presence) of God to believers and keeps them united in that name (17:6–26). Paradoxically, however, this radical claim about God's unique self-disclosure in his Son not only provides the communicative ground for the unity of a new people of God: it also provokes controversy, division, and 'judgment.' *Unity creates separation!*" (Barton, "Christian Community," 291).

margins) and unlimited proclamation toward other marginal groups who could come into the Johannine community (the Johannine readers). This is revealed on the basis of the new identity of the Johannine community. This combined exclusiveness and acceptance in the Gospel can be explained as consequence of the fact that the Johannine community (author as well as readers) seemed to have relations with readers from further afield: not only Palestinian Jews and Diaspora, but also with the Samaritan and non-Jewish groups. Koester points out, "Recent attempts to sketch a profile of the early readers of the Gospel also suggest that the Johannine community encompassed various sorts of people by the time the Gospel was completed."[192] Brown argues that the final form of the Gospel probably addressed a community of Christians from different backgrounds.[193] Culpepper also admits a heterogeneous readership of the final form of the Gospel.[194] In addition, Bauckham argues the purpose of the Gospels to be for general circulation around the churches and for the general Christian audience.[195] Although he rejects the community theory which presupposes that each of the Gospels was written for a specific church or group of churches, his argument is highly persuasive, "the implied readership is not specific but indefinite, namely any and every Christian community in the late-first-century Roman Empire."[196] His argument corresponds with the character of the Gospel of John as an open book, whose readers could be both Christians and non-Christians, namely the missionary purpose of the Gospel.

Regardless of whether scholars admit the theory of the existence of the Johannine community or not, they generally agree that the Gospel reveals conflict and the fact that the Johannine Jesus presents the solution to that conflict. For example, the Gospel reveals the message of life through love and forgiveness to the readers, regardless of whether they are members of the Johannine community, universal Christians, or non-believers, and regardless of whether the message comes from the author or the text itself. Although Martyn's view of a two-level drama is rejected by those who argue that the Gospel is not about the actual circumstances of a certain group in the first century, the important thing to point out is that conflict is revealed in the Gospel, whether it is the conflict in the time of Jesus or at the time of the composition of the Gospel, and whether or not it is about the real parties of the conflict. The Gospel throughout the whole presents

192. Koester, "Spectrum," 9.
193. See Brown, *Community*.
194. Culpepper, *Anatomy*, 221–25.
195. Bauckham, "For Whom?," 9–48.
196. Bauckham, "Introduction," 1.

to its readers how to reduce the conflict and solve it. It reveals, therefore, not only the exclusive life of the Johannine community in the world (staying away from the world; not returning to the world because they would reject them), which is partly true at the textual level, but as a whole, it invites the readers to come and belong to the Johannine world, a world in which Jesus reigns as the universal king. This is a world where the people can live as their king lives, their lives governed by the ruling principles of love, sacrifice, forgiveness, peace, and freedom.

John's Positive View of Other Marginal Groups

Thirdly, is it possible to attempt to find common ground on which the Johannine community and other marginal groups could stand together? One of the possibilities might be found in John's concern for the whole world in which Jesus reigns as King. Another possibility comes from an indication at the textual level that many sub-groups from different origins already existed in the Johannine community. To describe Jesus as the universal king enables every ethnic group to understand this concept when they read or heard the Gospel. John adopted, modified and used various terms, which included the kingship motif, to indicate Jesus as king for both Jewish and non-Jewish groups.

At the textual level, a relationship between the Johannine community and many other marginal communities seems to be implied in this Gospel. The Gospel shows a positive tendency: 1. a positive view of the Samaritans, which was different from that of the Jews, if we consider that for centuries, the Jews treated "the Samaritans as a despised out-group and subjected them to negative stereotyping"[197]; 2. a positive view of "the Jews" as the subject of salvation (4:22, the salvation is from the Jews; the belief of the Jews, even the Jewish leaders in Jesus), while it reflects a negative view of the Jewish leaders; 3. the "other sheep" concept (10:16), which shows the universal perspective of the Gospel; 4. the visit of the Greeks which inaugurates the time of Jesus' death and glorification (12:20–36), as an example of the positive role of non-Jewish people in the Gospel; 5. the universal expression of the inscription on the cross in Hebrew, Latin, and in Greek (19:19–20), which promotes understanding by its various readers.

---

197. Esler, "Jesus," 187.

The Johannine Community as Margin

Finally, then, how should we identify the Johannine community of the Gospel? Knowledge of the literary strategy of the author could be a contact point in identifying the Johannine community. It seems that the Gospel deals with various groups both inside and outside of the community. In considering these groups, my hypothesis on the Johannine community is that it consisted of various inner groups from various original backgrounds, Palestinian Jews, Diasporic Jews, Samaritans and non-Jewish people like Greeks, because the Gospel shows a positive attitude toward the marginal groups in terms of faith in Jesus. Koester argues, "If this scenario is correct, we cannot assume that all members of the Johannine community read the Gospel from the same perspective."[198] If Koester's argument is accepted, the universal tendency in the Gospel could be explained. It is also something that is linked to my argument concerning the kingship of Jesus, because the main concern of the Gospel is the identity of Jesus, and the author had to employ a variety of christological titles to identify Jesus as king, to avoid any misunderstanding by the readers. Unity in diversity can be found in the Gospel of John, as Koester points out,

> A common Christian faith would have helped to foster a strong sense of solidarity within Johannine Christianity, but we cannot assume that it expunged all the variations in outlook that people of Jewish, Samaritan, and Greek background would have brought with them into the community of faith. The likelihood of such diversity increases when we recognize that there were almost certainly a number of Johannine congregations rather than a single community with all members residing in the same place.[199]

The Johannine community seemed to have ethnic relations not only with Palestinian Jews and Diaspora, but also with the Samaritan and non-Jewish groups. In addition, relationships of the Johannine community and other marginal communities seem to exist in the Gospel. There might be a possibility, therefore, that many sub-groups from different origins had already existed in the Johannine community. If so, a variety of ways indicates Jesus as the king for both Jewish and non-Jewish groups, which every ethnic group could understand when they read or heard the Gospel. Therefore, to describe Jesus as the universal king, John adapted and used many terms, which contained the kingship motif.

198. Koester, "Spectrum," 10.
199. Koester, "Spectrum," 10; John 11:52.

Furthermore, encounters with Jesus, whether they were personal or in groups, in the Gospel display individual responses to him: some radically confess Jesus as their king, while others hostilely reject his kingship. Those who confess Jesus as their king come from several ethnic groups, and belong to several classes and status in the society: Jews, Samaritans, Greeks, royal servants, governors, male and female. Most of them are at the margins under Roman imperial power, while in some cases there are those who come from the center. These examples show the concern of the Johannine community to demolish the boundaries, which were located in political, religious, and cultural environments at that time.

However, the groups hostile to Jesus represented by the Jewish leaders are located at the center of power or in close proximity to it. The description of them is simplified and defined in a narrow way, while the pro-groups are described in more detail in the Gospel. Why did John use this strategy? In this regard, I am interested in John's brief comments about the believers in Jesus. The author several times refers briefly to the fact that many persons or groups believe in Jesus (2:11; 4:39, 41; 4:53; 7:31; 8:30–31; 9:38; 10:42; 11:27; 11:45; 12:11: 12:42). It is a possibility, therefore, that there were already several groups from different backgrounds in the Johannine community. Admitting the co-existence of several marginal groups in the Johannine community, it is also possible that the weakening of the intensity of the criticism of the Jews in general, narrows down to the persecutors among the Jewish leaders. Furthermore, this hatred does not correspond to the message of the Johannine Jesus who teaches them to live a life of love, forgiveness, peace, service, and freedom. John might therefore weaken this criticism of the inner groups from which believers came into the Johannine community, regardless of whether they were Jews or Gentiles, regardless of whether they came from any groups, which were for or against Jesus.

In short, the Johannine community might have a mission strategy. The function of such a writing tactic offers a basis for entering into the Johannine community when the readers, regardless of whether or not they belonged to any other group, read the Gospel. To accomplish the dual purpose of the Gospel,[200] the author magnified the pro-groups in favour of Jesus, while narrowing down the anti-groups into just the Jewish leaders.

In addition, we need to consider the historical situation with which the Johannine community was faced. Although Reinhartz argues that Rome was ignorant of the infant Christian movement,[201] the persecution of Christians

---

200. On consolidation of the readers and their missionary purpose, see chapter 2 of this book.

201. Reinhartz, "Colonizer as Colonized," 175.

by Rome was very severe in the late first century, and Roman response to Christianity was never deficient. These reasons explain the silence or indirect expressions against Rome in the Gospel. John never advocates imperial power, rather it resists by way of anti-language and symbol.

It seems acceptable, therefore, to locate the Johannine community as a margin in the Roman Empire, in contrast to the location of Rome as the center. In this circumstance, John might deliver an alternative vision to overcome the effects of expulsions and persecution by the Roman Empire and the Jewish leaders, and to reinforce the consolidation of the inner groups in the Johannine community. On a more positive note he challenges them to win (liberate) the world, emphasizing the importance of following the way of life of the Johannine Jesus.

Summary of the Chapter

In this chapter, I defined Rome as the colonizer, the center, which ruled over all the margins of the Empire at the time of Jesus and the Johannine community. From this perspective, "the Jews," in particular the Jewish leaders, can be defined both as the colonized (the margins) under the Roman Empire, and as colonizers, that is, collaborators with the imperial power in the marginal society. The Gospel shows that although they had once resisted the imperial power in an attempt to regain their independece, it seems that they had already admitted the imperial power of Rome as the absolute power of domination. Their ambiguity and ambivalence is well revealed in the Gospel. As the collaborators, the Jewish leaders eliminate Jesus in the same manner as their center, Rome, dealt with opposition; as the colonized, they kill Jesus so as not to be deprived of their position by the colonizer. Finally, I gave evidence that the Johannine community as the margin experienced conflict with both the center and the collaborators. The Fourth Gospel as a postcolonial text challenges this marginal people, the Johannine Community, to live in this colonized world with the principles of the Johannine new world: love, forgiveness, peace, service, and freedom.

Under these circumstances, Jesus in the Gospel could be represented as the decolonizing king who has resisted the imperial power and the darkness, and who has liberated the margins from the oppression of the imperial power and the darkness. I will deal with this in the next chapter.

6. Reading John as a Postcolonial Text
Jesus and His Function as King

IN THIS CHAPTER, I will deal with the function of the Johannine Jesus as king. I will contend that (the kingship of) Jesus in the Johannine Gospel is presented as an alternative solution to the conflict, a way of unifying divided marginal societies, and as a cure for those societies who, through exploitation, oppression, and persecution by the center, are suffering deep hurt and immense scarring.

First, in order to present the function of the Johannine Jesus as described above, I again claim that this Gospel is a type of postcolonial text.[1] In fact, the purpose of the Gospel can be more clearly understood when it regarded as a postcolonial text.[2] Young argues,

> [A]bove all, postcolonialism seeks to intervene, to force its alternative knowledge into the power structures of the west as well as the non-west. It seeks to change the way people think, the way they behave, to produce a more just and equitable relation between the different peoples of the world.[3]

Likewise, the Gospel has a similar concern of postcolonialism in that it suggests, as an alternative, Jesus as the universal king. This is to a world that is in conflict, and suffering oppression and exploitation under the hand of the Imperial power. It is quite acceptable that the Gospel attempts to change their way of thinking and behavior in order to see a better life and a better world. The life in Christ, which produces love, service, peace, liberty, forgiveness, and reconciliation, is brought to the readers to challenge them and teach them how to live in harmony with a variety of people, who come from different origins, in a hybridized society.

---

1. See chapter 2 of this book.

2. On the multipurpose of the Gospel, and on the relationship between the Gospel of John and postcolonialism, see chapter 2 of this book.

3. Young, *Postcolonialism*, 6–7.

In short, the Johannine Jesus can be read as the one who seeks to liberate the world (the margins) from the yoke of darkness;[4] who wants to lead the world into the light, i. e. the new world, in which they can live together in harmony free from these things which oppress them.

Identification of the Johannine Jesus

Moving the Center/From Center to Margin

For the sake of my argument, it is necessary to ask the question: how then did John communicate his message to accomplish these purposes? One of the best ways at the textual level would be to introduce Jesus as the center.

To clarify my argument, first, it is meaningful to refer to the fact that this Gospel presents a liberating way by "moving the center" from the world to Jesus. Ngugi argues that, in the world as a whole as well as at a national level, the existing power at the center should be moved to the margin in order to break down the walls between the center and the margin. Ngugi remarks,

> Moving the center in the two senses – between nations and within nations – will contribute to the freeing of world cultures from the restrictive walls of nationalism, class, race and gender. . . . For I believe that while retaining its roots in regional and national individuality, true humanism with its universal reaching out can flower among the people of the earth.[5]

The logic of Ngugi's "moving the center" can be found in John's Gospel: "moving the center" from the darkness to the Light of the world. This application is given from the very beginning of the Gospel.[6] Therefore, exploring the kingship motif in the Fourth Gospel is of benefit in pursuing a positive alternative to this world with a vision for a better future, which is one of the principal objectives of postcolonialism. The logic of the Gospel proposes that this objective can be realized by the life and teaching of Jesus.

---

4. Historically speaking, from the corrupt old (Jewish) tradition as well as the oppression of the Roman imperial power; spiritually, from the dark power of the ruler of the world, Satan.

5. Thiong'o, *Moving the Center*, 66.

6. See John 1:1–18; John 8:12–41. The Gospel presents Jesus as the center of the world and the focus for the future. The Jewish people had regarded themselves as "a guide for the blind, a light for those who are in the dark" (Rom 2:19), but in John, Jesus concentrates his function in *himself* when he calls himself "the light of the world" (John 8:12).

Some scholars raise a question about the language of the Johannine Gospel, particularly the way in which the Johannine Christology is described. Reinhartz argues,

> When I consider the language of Johannine Christology, which identifies Jesus as the Son of God and claims that he is the one and only path to salvation for all humankind, then Johannine Christianity becomes the center, and those groups whose views are challenged and delegitimized within the Gospel, such as the Jews and the Samaritans, become the margins.[7]

Dube also contends,

> "World" in these titles symbolizes the claim to unlimited access to foreign geographical spaces. "King" and "Savior" articulate the claims of power by certain subjects and their followers (races and nations) over unlimited geographical spaces—over the world and its inhabitants. While "king" implies dominion over space and people—which may be just or unjust—"savior" also implies power. But it carries an imperial ideology that came to a full-fledged maturity in modern centuries, whereby the violence of imperialism was depicted as a redeeming act for the benefit of the subjugated, or the so-called "duty of the natives."[8]

In a postcolonial analysis, it could be claimed that the language of Johannine Christology sees Jesus as a new colonial center who pursues the power to rule the world. However, this view might be lacking in consideration of the historical situation of the first century and of the readers of the Gospel, who were mostly marginal people in the Empire. Considering that the Gospel was written within the Roman Empire, it is more probable that the Johanine Jesus is not described as the colonizer with a desire for conquest and domination, but as the decolonizer who visits the margins to liberate them from the darkness. Culpepper argues that the Gospel "needs not to be read from the perspective of the empowered," and that "the Gospel challenges contemporary believers to oppose prevailing structures and social patterns that oppress the marginalized."[9]

For example, Jesus visits and liberates the marginal people (e.g., the Samaritans, the 38 year old invalid, the man born blind, Lazarus, and so on), who have waited for help from others/Messiah/liberator/Savior, and

---

7. Reinhartz, "Colonizer as Colonized," 172.

8. Dube, "Reading for Decolonization," 52.

9. Culpepper, "Gospel of John," 120–21. On the trace of the voice for the margins in the Gospel of John, see Cassidy, *John's Gospel*; Rensberger, *Johannine Faith*; Karris, *Jesus and the Marginalized*.

eventually who need to be liberated from the darkness. In the narrative of the entry into Jerusalem in John 12, the image of Jesus as conqueror is never found, but rather as the king of Israel he enters into Jerusalem seated on a donkey's colt (12:15). In terms of sacrifice, the image of Jesus in the narrative could be linked to that of Isaac who went with a donkey to Mt. Moriah to be sacrificed (Gen 22).[10] In addition, this image is overlapped with that of the king of humility in Zechariah 9:9. Moreover, the image can also be linked with that of the Lamb of God who takes away the sin of the world (1:29, 36). In particular, the entry of Jesus into Jerusalem does not make the crowds run for their weapons, but rather makes them cut down the palm branches with which to welcome him (John 12:12–15). In short, the Johannine Jesus (1:45, 49) functions as *the king of peace* not "by the short-term options of an anti-Roman mentality,"[11] but from the eternal perspective of world peace.

Peace in Jesus, therefore, is one of the most important ideological aspects in the Johannine new world, because no earthly political aspirations can give the margins a new world where they could live in peace (14:27). Likewise, this Gospel sings a song of peace, although this world is still seeing persecution and tumult. To those who are afraid of persecution and death, the Johannine Jesus shows what real peace is, and how to obtain it in this world. Peace in Jesus is the way of the consolidation of the Johannine community and its way of life in this world, while pursuing and declaring the world to come.

As a third example, the episode of footwashing (13:1–20) clearly shows an example of humility by the king, *the king of service* (service by the center to the margins).[12] In doing this, Jesus leaves an example to all his followers to encourage them to serve in the same way. This ideology is totally the reverse of that of this world. In this world, the only reason for the existence of the margins is to serve the center, but the converse is true in the new world where Jesus reigns as king; the center is for the margins, and the masters serve the disciples (13:16; 15:15, 20). Thus, the only way of accomplishing the healing of a society driven apart by conflict is by following the teaching of the Johannine Jesus i.e., the margins are being served by the center instead of vice versa. The

---

10. The appearance of donkey (22:2–3) and Isaac's taking the wood (LXX: τὰ ξύλα) of the burnt offering on his back (22:6) going up to Mt. Moriah can be compared with the entry of Jesus into Jerusalem. Jesus entered into Jerusalem (which was the place of offering) with a donkey to die, and went up to Golgotha bearing his own cross (John 19:17; τὸν σταυρὸν). On Jesus as a sacrificial victim, see Orchard, *Courting Betrayal*, 226–30.

11. Van Bruggen, *Jesus*, 45.

12. A variety of scholars view this aspect as the dominant theme in John 13:1–20. See Thomas, *Footwashing*, 12, n. 1.

end result of this is a new world in which love, service, forgiveness, peace, and freedom are the predominant characteristics. In summary, the image of Jesus as colonizer/conqueror is not found in the Gospel. Instead, the language used in Johannine Christology might be regarded as a literary device to decolonize the world, because the way Jesus is presented in the Gospel differs completely from that of worldly power.[13]

Secondly, for my argument, it is also necessary to say that the destination of the new group which is created in the process of hybridentity is "neither the one (the center) nor the other (the margin)."[14] Pratt says, "This need for interaction within radically asymmetrical conditions of power invariably produces an estrangement of familiar meanings and a mutual 'creolisation' of identities."[15] Pratt's perspective can be helpful to attempt a new understanding and interpretation of the various christological titles in this Gospel.

It is highly probable that a variety of special terms, which contained various different meanings before the era of early Christianity, seemed to have been undergoing a change of meaning (hybridized meanings) in the multicultural environment of the Roman Empire. One of the reasons for this change would be related to "asymmetrical conditions of power" at that time.[16] The center, which had absolute power, influenced the margins in every aspect of their society. The change of meaning(s) of specific terms through mutual transaction was no exception, but mostly through unequal exchange. It is the tendency of an imperial power as the dominant force at the center to force the change or modification of the meanings of the terms (hybridentity); and to choose their dominant meaning which correspond with the logic of the center (the domination of the center).[17]

---

13. In comparison, Imperial logic (the logic of power, Roman taxation, Imperial cult, Ruling on the margins with military power, utter punishment of the rebels, etc.) differs from Johannine logic of power (Jesus' teaching and life—love, peace, service, forgiveness, liberation).

14. Although he is talking about political matters, Bhabha's mention is meaningful to my argument: " the construction of a political object that is new, neither the one nor the other, properly alienates our political expectations, and changes, as it must, the very forms of our recognition of the moment of politics" (Bhabha, *Location*, 25).

15. Pratt, *Imperial Eyes*, 4–5.

16. The Palestine region as the background of the Gospel of John "was an unpromising, isolated land marked by asymmetrical relations of power" between the center and the margins, "which were the source of significant cultural contradictions" (Ling, *Judean Poor*, 84).

17. For example, Fredriksen remarks that the urbanization and Hellenization of Palestine, particularly of Galilee, was progressing in the areas, e.g., Greek language; Hellenized architecture—theaters, baths, stadiums, and so on (see Fredriksen, *Jesus of Nazareth*, 160–73. On the Hellenization of Palestine under King Herod, see Frend, *Rise*

Therefore, it is quite likely that the influence of the Imperial power is in every aspect of society, including the combination of languages and their meanings. Greek was used as the dominant language, and its influence among other language speakers must have been formidable. It was impossible to reject the Imperial influence or not to be influenced by it. As Sullivan comments: "[I]n regards to the Jews, there seems no question of 'Romanization' in spirit or attitude for the population at large."[18] This tendency influenced the composition of the Gospel under Rome. Thus, it is probable that in these circumstances, the terms employed in the Gospel to indicate the identity of Jesus might undergo a similar process of "meaning change," because the marginal societies including the Johannine community were in the world under asymmetrical conditions of power. Accordingly, it is probable that John might have needed to adapt a variety of the christological titles, which were commonly permeated/linked with the kingship motif, in order to clarify the identity of Jesus in terms of kingship. Furthermore, he might need to arrange them in the same passages as mutual complements of one another to declare the identity of the Johannine Jesus as king to avoid any misunderstanding by his readers. Culpepper argues, "The christological titles are intertwined in the Gospel. No one title can be understood apart from its narrative contexts and its conceptual relationship to other titles and to the presentation of Jesus in the Gospel as a whole."[19] MacRae also contends, "John's critical attitude toward his sources suggests . . . a concern on his part to incorporate as much as possible of the traditional even while creating his own gospel 'style.'"[20] Therefore, the christological titles, which had also been changed in meaning, might be adapted in the Johannine narrative in order to create its own meaning in a unique way, which seemed to differ from those outside of the Johannine Christianity. So, without linking this Johannine textual tendency with sectarianism,[21] the adaptation of the

---

of Christianity, 21–22).

18. Sullivan, "Dynasty of Judaea," 296–354, esp. 345–51.

19. Culpepper, "Christology," 85.

20. See chapter 2 of this book; MacRae, "Fourth Gospel," 17; see also Brown, *Community*, 57; Kysar, *John*, 40, 43.

21. On the sectarianism of the Johannine Community, see Meeks, "Man from Heaven," 44–72 (the Johannine community as a small group of believers isolated over against the world); Smith, "Johannine Christianity," 222–48 (the community as possessing "a sense of exclusiveness, a sharp delineation of the community from the world"); Culpepper, *Johannine School*, 287 (the community as an "embattled brotherhood" that with time "withdrew further from the world and clung to the teachings and new commandments of its Lord"); Segovia, "Love and Hatred," 258–72 ("the use and meaning of the relationship of love for and hatred toward Jesus in the Fourth Gospel confirm the recent and frequent opinion that the Gospel is a 'sectarian' document and

Johannine christological titles on the textual level can be explained in terms of authorial intention. It is quite probable that John "deliberately incorporates a variety of symbols, traditions, and perspectives into his Gospel in order to emphasize precisely the universality of Jesus."[22]

Consequently, it is quite possible that the Johannine readers could have discovered the kingship of the Johannine Jesus from his various royal titles. They could reach the conclusion that his kingship is displayed in the christological titles, even if the book had been translated into another language and was being read one century later.

For example, in John 1:19–51 there is an arrangement of christological titles in successive verses (Messiah, [Elijah], the prophet, the Lamb of God, the one announced by Moses and prophets, anything good, Son of God and king of Israel, the Son of Man). The intention of this arrangement is not only to show a variety of understanding of the christological titles, but also to show the particular identity of the Johannine Jesus as the universal king. MacRae also argues,

> In the Fourth Gospel we have a somewhat similar Hellenization of early Christianity insofar as John attempts to assert both the universality and the transcendence of the divine Son Jesus. In the end, John's message is that Jesus can be approached in many ways, but he can only be understood on Christian[23] terms, not Jewish or Greek, or Gnostic.[24]

In summary, to present the identity of the Johannine Jesus as king, the author might need to describe him by using a variety of the christological titles, which had royal connotations, and which might be one of the dominant concepts in the society at that time.

Thirdly, it is necessary for my argument to point out the openness of the Gospel. Although the terms had been produced by adding or changing the meanings, the Johannine christological titles were not very unconnected to previous usage of them in diachronic and synchronic terms.[25] The Johannine christological terms, therefore, might be employed to deliver new concepts both inside and outside the Johannine Christianity/

---

the Johannine community is a 'sectarian' group"). On the rejection of the sectarian nature of the community, see Cullmann, *Johannine Circle*; Nissen, "Community and Ethics," 194–212; Nissen, "Mission," 213–31; MacRae, "Fourth Gospel," 13–24.

22. MacRae, "Fourth Gospel," 15.

23. In my view, particularly, "on the Johannine terms."

24. MacRae, "Fourth Gospel," 24.

25. Loomba describes this tendency as "a sense of difference which is not pure 'otherness'" (see Loomba, *Colonialism*, 182–83).

community/readers.[26] Berger argues, "the Johannine language is characterized not by a 'closed metaphorical system' but by a 'semantic openness,' and that he speaks not only to 'insiders' but also to 'outsiders.'"[27] In addition, by employing christological titles, which acquire new meanings in the Johannine text, the author might create and deliver a new identity of Jesus to the readers[28] who were from a variety of backgrounds and were experiencing the mixture of meanings under the huge suppressing power of Empire. Under the circumstances, the change of terms might not only deliver new meanings to the inside readers of the Johannine Christianity/group, but also might make the outside readers of the Johannine Christianity/group better able to understand the meanings, because the terms were not totally changed (a basis of interconnection with outsiders/non-Christians/readers of various origins). Nissen remarks,

> The bewildering variety of Johannine "backgrounds" would thus lend a positive value to this interpretation. To be a community of Jesus the Son of God, the Johannine Community could not close itself off from human expressions of longing for wholeness and salvation. The community's openness and diversity were necessary features of its congruence with Jesus.[29]

Fourthly, it is necessary to remark that there seems to be linguistic resistance in John's Gospel against any colonizers.[30] However, it does not simply accuse colonialism nor resist it. Rather, it proclaims a considerably more than generous double consciousness over ethnicity and nationalism/Imperialism. That is, the Gospel proclaims a kind of postcolonial utopia, namely the kingdom of the Johannine Jesus, where Jesus as the universal king reigns (as the center). Moreover, it admits to and promotes the coexistence of various ethnicities and nations in the new world.[31] The Johannine positive view on the Samaritans, and the believing individuals and groups in the Gospel serves to illustrate the universality of the Gospel. The Johannine new world includes the whole world irrespective of race, gender, econom-

---

26. Nissen, "Community and Ethics," 197.

27. Berger, *Exegese des Neuen Testaments*, 230–31; recited in Nissen, "Community and Ethics," 197.

28. On the view that the Johannine community was in dialogue with a wide spectrum of groups and ideologies in the first century, see Senior and Stuhlmueller, *Biblical Foundations*, 280; Nissen, "Mission," 224; Koester, "Spectrum," 5–19; Culpepper, *Anatomy*, 221, 225; Brown, *Community*.

29. Nissen, "Community and Ethics," 197.

30. See chapter 3 of this book.

31. See chapter 5 of this book.

ics, politics, and religion, and pursues a new kind of hybridized society. It proclaims the kingdom/kingship of Jesus as a huge melting pot of cultures and ethnicities accepting a variety of different identities and consequently, their mixture (hybridentity), in pursuit of the postcolonial utopia.

Now, I will deal with the Johannine Jesus as the new center for the salvation/liberation of the world in the Gospel. To begin with, I will deal with the Johannine Jesus as a decolonizer who has come to liberate and integrate the whole world into himself.

Jesus as Decolonizer

The Johannine Jesus can be interpreted as the decolonizer who resists Imperialism and provides an alternative for a world where exploitation and oppression exist. Recent research on the Gospel throws light on this. Key terms and concepts of postcolonial studies describing developments in terms of liberation and decolonization can be related to the Johannine christological titles. These were employed to reveal the identity of Jesus as liberator or decolonizer to the Johannine readers. Dube gives a good definition of decolonization.

> Decolonizing . . . defines awareness of imperialism's exploitative forces and its various strategies of domination, the conscious adoption of strategies of resisting imperial domination as well as the search for alternative ways of liberating interdependence between nations, races, genders, economics and cultures.[32]

Staley also points out that "Jesus' statement . . . can sometimes have a totally different meaning when spoken by one victim of oppression to another,"[33] giving as an example the dialogue between Jesus and the Samaritan woman. He argues, "one victim of oppression can also say to another victim what Jesus says to the Samaritan woman, and it can be heard as a liberating voice."[34] In the same way, when I[35] read the Gospel of John from a postcolonial viewpoint, I view him as the one who has come to decolonize the world because I hear the voice of a liberator in him.

---

32. Dube, "Reading for Decolonization," 52.
33. Staley, "'Dis Place, Man,'" 46.
34. Staley, "'Dis Place, Man,'" 47.
35. See chapter 5 of this book. I have lived in a society that has experienced immense suffering under foreign powers during the last century. Korean society is a victim of oppression in the modern colonizing era.

Jesus as Sacred Space

The one major advantage of postcolonial reading in biblical studies is obviously related to a discourse of resistance and emancipation. This concept can be regarded as a multidimensional and conflicting phenomenon because it brings about the possibility of diversity in the coming world. On this, Segovia remarks that, "there is nothing more feared or disliked in any context of domination and oppression than the very possibility of diversity, of thinking and/or acting differently, away from the norm."[36]

The Johannine view of the new world evidently shows the possibility of diversity in the first century. Furthermore, the person of Jesus in the Gospel demonstrates by his thought and actions a different way of life to the norm of his era. The Johannine message through Jesus' teaching and his performance of miracles shows that it was fundamentally different from that of the Jewish and the Graeco-Roman world. Thomas remarks, "Jesus' action is unparalleled in ancient evidence, for no other person of superior status is described as voluntarily washing the feet of a subordinate,"[37] an action which was motivated by love. In addition, the Johannine Jesus is rejected by the Jewish leaders who lead the people (the margins) to accept the dominant power of Rome in their everyday lives (11:47–57; 12:19), because he resists this worldly trend. Likewise, Jesus comes to liberate people from this domination and oppression (Prologue; 3:15–7; 8:31–32). It is meaningful to quote Horsley's comments on the kingdom of God where Jesus reigns as king.

> The kingdom of God is somewhat analogous to the bipartite agenda of recent and current anticolonial (or anti-imperial) movements in which the withdrawal (or defeat) of the colonizing power is the counterpart and condition of the colonized people's restoration to independence and self-determination.[38]

The Gospel of John identifies Jesus as the true king of this world whom the margins should receive for their liberation/salvation (1:12; 3:16; 7:32).[39] He opens a new universal world into which every individual and group

---

36. Segovia, *Decolonizing*, 141.
37. Thomas, *Footwashing*, 59, cf. 187.
38. Horsley, *Jesus and Empire*, 14.
39. See the section, "The Coming of the King Into the World," of this chapter. Jesus came into his own (1:9, 11) as the Savior of the world (4:42), the Prophet who is indeed coming into the world (6:14); the Christ and the Son of God who comes into the world (11:27).

can come (1:12; 10:9[40]).[41] Jesus as the new sacred space in the Gospel also pursues a new world where diversity can be accommodated in him (10:16; 11:52; 12:32).

The persons and groups that Jesus meets in the Gospel are very diverse.[42] However, he never suppresses them by power, but rather liberates them from the darkness by his sacrificial love. He does not entrust himself to the people who only pursue earthly power, nor to the people who follow him for their own sake (2:23–25). This attitude is also clearly revealed in John 6:15, where the crowd attempts to make him king by force, Jesus *again*[43] withdraws himself to the mountain alone. Here, Jesus resists the earthly way to become king because his kingship is different from that of this world (18:36–37). Although his overcoming and liberating life results in diverse responses from the people,[44] the Johannine Jesus never attempts to overcome this world by violence and suppressive power. Rather he alter-

---

40. The sheep symbolizes humankind, often referred to metaphorically as the "world" in the Gospel of John (Reinhartz, *Word*, 38–41, 74).

41. Koenig remarks, "In certain passages Jesus not only provides a place, but also becomes the *entrance* to the place or even *the place* itself. In the Fourth Gospel we can speak of a 'hospitality Christology'" (Koenig, *Jews and Christians*, 133).

42. The diversity of the people whom Jesus meets in the Gospel must not be simply analyzed under one classification, i.e., of economics (the have and the have-not), religion (Judaism and Paganism), ethnicity (the Jews and the Gentiles), or politics (Sanhedrin, Pilate, and Ceasar). In the Gospel of John, however, a variety of people appears. Jesus meets the Jewish people (the Jewish leaders and the marginal people in the Jewish society) and non-Jewish people (Samaritans, Greeks, a royal official, and Romans [Pilate, Roman soldiers]); male and female; the rich and the poor; the healthy and the sick; officials and ordinary people; the center and the margins. This is evidence of their environment of a multicultural society under Imperial power.

43. His withdrawing (2:24–25; 4:1; 5:13; 6:1; 6:15; 7:1; 8:59; 10:40) to reduce conflict with others, particularly the center, the Jewish leaders in Jerusalem, until his hour has come, but his continuous meeting (2:13–25;4:3–42; 5:1–14; 7:10, 14, 37, 12; 9:1–12, 35; 10:22; 11:1,7–8, 16; 12:12–19) with the people under suppression to liberate them are described in the Gospel over and over again.

44. The various responses to Jesus appear in John 6 and following chapters more prominently. The grumbling of the Jews about Jesus, when they heard Jesus is the bread of heaven (6:41), (even his disciples ([6:60–70]), although they asked for a sign (6:30), show a variety of responses among the margins. This kind of a variety of opinions of Jesus is clearly revealed in John 7:12–52. From negative to positive, the Jewish people divided among themselves concerning the identity of Jesus (a good man? or the deceiver?) In John 7:12; the Prophet, the Christ as the king (the Son of David in 7:40–42; some Jews wanted to seize Jesus in 6:42; the division of the Jewish leaders in 7:45–52; cf. The Jews said he was a Samaritan and demon-possessed in 8:48). After his healing of the man born blind, the narrative states that the negative view of Jesus by the Jews who were mainly the Jewish leaders (9:22) led public opinion. Finally, the raising of Lazarus triggered the determination of the Jewish leaders to kill Jesus (11:47–57).

natively shows to the margins the life of self-sacrificial love and forgiveness as the way to liberation from domination and oppression.[45] Therefore, the Johannine new world might be the one, which accommodates the possibility of diversity in the world.

Is it then possible to attempt to find a common place, where inner groups of the Johannine community consisting of different origins and backgrounds and other groups outside of the community could stand together with one vision? One possible place might be found in John's concern for the universal space in which Jesus reigns as king. For this, the Johannine Gospel opens its narrative in a way designed to show the Johannine new world as an open space which receives those who accept Jesus' name/title[46] as members without any restrictions (1:12).[47] Since Jesus is also the gateway to the Johannine New world, i.e., to the Father for his followers (14:6), every other group can also come there, i.e., to God through this one true door (10:7–21; cf. 14:2–3).

A research on space in the Gospel from a postcolonial perspective or using an anthropological approach[48] gives hints about the kingdom/kingship as the space where Jesus reigns as king. Of the various ways of classification of space,[49] the classification of "fixed or fluid sacred space" could be linked to the Johannine Jesus as space. Smith also classifies the tension between "fixed or fluid space" as a tension between "locative and utopian space."[50] According to Smith, "locative (fixed) space" focuses on the central space as a closed space, and centripetal in direction[51] just as sects which have their own sacred spaces and languages to which out-groups may never

45. Van Bruggen, *Jesus*, 199.

46. This presupposes that the phrase "to believe in his name" (πιστεύω εἰς τὸ ὄνομα), means "to *believe in the name of someone*, i.e., have confidence that the person's name (rather in the sense of a title, cp. Phil 2:9) is rightly borne and encodes what the person really is (John 1:12; 2:23; 3:18; 1 John 5:13)" (BAGD, 572). In John 1:12; 2:23; 3:18, the name of Jesus/the title of the king is the object of faith (cf. 10:25; 12:13); in 14:13–14; 15:16; 16:23–24, in the name/title of Jesus, his followers can request anything and it will be given them from Jesus and God, even eternal life (20:31).

47. Although exclusivism could be found in the Gospel of John (14:6; 6:44, 45, 53; 15:6), it is a literary device of the Gospel to persuade the readers, and it does not mean that the Gospel is a sectarian text, because the witness to the world of Jesus as the king is still the foundation of its fellowship of love (13:34–35).

48. For more studies of space or territoriality, see Dube and Staley, *John and Postcolonialism*; Neyrey, "Spaces and Places," 60–74.

49. Neyrey classifies space under the following seven categories: public/private, sacred/profane, honorable/shameful, clean/unclean, fixed/fluid, center/periphery, and civilization/nature (Neyrey, "Spaces and Places," 60–74).

50. Smith, *Drudgery Divine*, 121–42.

51. Smith, *Map Is Not Territory*, 101, 186, 437.

enter without permission, nor know without explanation by them.⁵² On the other hand, "utopian (fluid) space" as an "open" society focuses on the margins, and is centrifugal in thrust.⁵³ This utopian space "is characterized by rebellion, freedom, and breaking of limits and boundaries by humankind."⁵⁴ Malina also remarks on fixed or fluid space,

> This situation of porous boundaries and competing groups stands in great contrast to the solid, hierarchical, pyramidal shape of strong group/high grid [fixed space] . . . as groups form and re-form anew, permanence is no longer to be found outside the group; and where the group is, there is stability. Sacred space is located in the group, not in some impersonal space like a temple.⁵⁵

Thus, just as the central location is important in the marginal group, the body of Jesus as the central location/space is important (2:21) in the Johannine Gospel.⁵⁶ In addition, in the message of the Johannine narrative, Jesus becomes "the mobile, portable, exportable focus of sacred place, in fact more important than the fixed and eternal sacred places."⁵⁷ That is, in the Gospel Jesus/the kingship of Jesus functions as the integration of the universal space into himself and the Johannine message becomes the ruling ideology of the space. While arguing "John neither spiritualizes the reality of earth (his incarnational theology would not permit it) nor makes it a literal object

---

52. In my view, the Johannine community does not belong in this category.

53. The Johannine community is more close to this category. Cf. Rensberger, *Johannine Faith*, 150.

54. Neyrey, "Spaces and Places," 61–62.

55. Malina, *Christian Origins*, 38.

56. The replacement of the Temple with the body of Jesus also reveals the kingship of Jesus. For arguments regarding replacement of the Temple with the Johannine Jesus and his new world (his followers), see Davies, *Gospel and the Land*, 28–318; McCaffrey, *House with Many Rooms*, 21, 247, 254–5; Hoskins, *Jesus as the Fulfillment*; Gundry, "In My Father's House," 68–72; Aalen, "'Reign' and 'House,'" 215–40; Coloe, "Households of Faith," 326–35; Coloe, *God Dwells with Us*; Kerr, *Temple of Jesus' Body*. The replacement of the Temple with the body of Jesus as the real/true new Temple seems to be more meaningful in comparing the implication of his kingship to the house of the Father (2:16; 14:2–3). The Father's house in the Gospel (2:16; 14:2) stands for the kingdom of God (Aalen); the Temple is the dwelling place of God (Coloe); Jesus as the real dwelling place of God (the new Johannine world) will go to prepare many places in the kingdom of God for his followers; This new Johannine world will be accomplished through the death, resurrection of Jesus (see Hoskins, *Jesus as the Fulfillment*, 147–81); finally, Jesus and his followers will be together where Jesus is (14:3, 17:24).

57. Malina, *Christian Origins*, 38.

of promise," Burge also emphasizes that "the Fourth Gospel reinterprets the promise of land in the historic presence of Christ."[58]

Therefore, it is quite probable that suggestive interpretations of the replacement of spaces by Jesus can be found in the Gospel. That Jesus is the replacement of the old system is, in fact, one of the principal themes of the Fourth Gospel. Now, I will demonstrate this by using four examples from this Gospel.

First, the Logos as a spiritual sacred space is the only space where all other spaces belong.[59] Using Philo's Hellenistic understanding of the Logos, Swanson argues that all the spaces in the Gospel are integrated into the Logos as the space.[60] The Logos is Jesus himself as space. He integrates all the spaces into himself, as well as connecting the earth with heaven (1:51; 8:35; 14:2–3).[61]

Secondly, Jesus in the Gospel of John is described as a unique being who gives a new interpretation to all the earthly spaces for his kingdom/kingship. This is revealed to the people by several christological titles within these spaces.[62] Burge contends, "John exploits territorial images of place, acknowledges their use in eschatology, and then absorbs them in christology."[63]

---

58. Burge, "Territorial Religion," 388.

59. Culpepper shows how the concept of the Logos as a universal phenomenon can be applied to the Johannine Jesus as the contact point for the readers in pluralistic culture. He remarks, "Wisdom belongs to the diversity of human pluralism, necessitating a pluralism in theological expression in the prolongation of the mystery of the incarnation, i.e., God becoming a human being absorbed into the cultures of all people of the world. Here there is a paradox in faith between the particularity of the Jesus of Nazareth and the universality of the cosmic Christ, the 'logos' of God" (Culpepper, "Gospel of John," 123–24).

60. Swanson, "To Prepare a Place," 16–17; Philo, *Confusion of Tongue*, 61, 95–96. Swanson points out, "For Philo, the founder of the Israelite nation [Moses] becomes a 'God-loved type' or embodiment of the Logos. . . . Consequently, the Mosaic spaces of this world . . . all become signposts to the true country, 'the place which is the Logos', where all physical divisions of the manifold world are left behind. It is within this broad framework of Hellenistic thought on unity and the nature of ethnic territories that the problem of attachment to sacred space presupposed by John will best be understood."

61. The concept of "the house" as the kingdom of God, the parable of the vine and branch, are good examples.

62. As the accomplishment of John 1:12, when Jesus reveals his kingship, the marginal people believe in his titles, and/or confess various Christological titles in terms of kingship, i.e., the king of Israel/Jews, the savior of the world, (believing verses: 2:11, 23; 4:39, 41; 7:31; 8:30; 10:42; 11:45; 12:42), the prophet who comes into the world; the Christ and the Son of God who comes into the world; My God and My Lord, etc.

63. Burge, "Territorial Religion," 391; Collins, *These Things*, 210. In the Gospel of John, we can see the Johannine use of the replacement motif for Christological emphasis: Jesus replaces festivals like the Passover (John 6) and institutions like the temple

Whilst arguing for Jesus' replacement of holy places, including the Temple, Davies concludes, "the Gospel is destined to personalize or Christify that space, or, rather, holiness is no longer to be attached to space at all."[64]

It is clearly described in the Gospel that Jesus goes beyond many spaces which have theological meanings in the Hebrew Bible, such as Bethel (1:52), the Temple (2:13–25), Jacob's well (4:1–15), Jerusalem (4:21), the sacred pool of Bethesda (5:1–19), and the waters of Siloam (9:17), and reinterprets their meanings in himself, and integrates them into himself. In particular, it is revealed more climactically in the Johannine presentation of the risen Jesus as transcending the limitations of time and space (John 20:19, 26).

In the dialogue between Jesus and Nathanael, for example, Jesus associates the Son of Man with Bethel as the place of Israel's sanctuary (Gen 12:8; 13:3–4; 28:10–17), and the place where the opening of the heavens takes place (1:51). In John 4:21–24, it is in Jesus that true worship of the Father takes place. Thus, "The functions which had primitively accrued to Bethel have finally been fulfilled in Jesus."[65] Jesus is the real Bethel, the authentic "dwelling place of God" (1:14). In the dialogue with a Samaritan woman, the water, which Jesus gives, is far superior to that drawn from Jacob's well (4:1–15). At the pool of Bethesda, Jesus' healing is greater than that of the pool itself (5:1–9). As the real "Sent One,"[66] Jesus overrides the Siloam pool when he heals the man born blind (9:7).

Thirdly, it is eminently emphasized that the new Temple which replaces the old is the Temple of his body (2:19–21) and his followers (19:25–30).[67] I will now investigate the idea that Jesus as the new Temple operates as the decolonizer of the world in the Gospel.

1) Again, it is necessary to point out that in the Gospel the new world is opened up through Jesus. In John 4:21–26, Jesus himself replaces the Samaritan place of worship, Jerusalem and the Temple. The Samaritans and

---

(John 2); Cleansing the temple means sweeping away of principal themes of traditional Judaism and the reinterpretation and replacement of their covenantal meaning; Jesus as living bread (6:35), living water (4:10; 7:38), and the light of life (8:12) replaces ritual sources in ceremony as being obsolete; Jesus as vine whose direction is to integrate other spaces (branches) invites readers to the vine.

64. Davies, *Gospel*, 290.

65. Collins, *These Things*, 210.

66. *Siloam* stands for Sent One in the LXX (see Burge, "Territorial Religion," 389).

67. Coloe, "Households of Faith," 327; see also Coloe, *God Dwells with Us*; Aune notes that the term "household of my Father" may in fact be the self-designation of the Johannine community (Aune, *Cultic Setting*, 130). In particular, the declaration of the Johannine Jesus in John 2:19 reveals the vision of the new world. The resurrected body (2:21) will be the accomplishment of the new world. In addition, he will the way to the new world, the Father's house (14:2, 6).

the Jews had worshipped in the wrong place, or in wrong ways. Through the Johannine Jesus, however, they can come to the right place and discover the right way. Finally, they can enter into the place, which Jesus will prepare for them (14:2–3). Therefore, in the Gospel of John, "Jerusalem was no longer a place of true worship, so the Land as holy place cannot be an avenue to the blessing of God."[68] Only Jesus as the new space is the way to the blessing of God (14:2–3, 6). Accordingly, Jesus in the Gospel functions as the decolonizer for the margins through leading them into the real place of worship and ultimately to God.

2) In addition, the notion that Jesus is the unifying center for the new people of God is seen in Jesus as the real Temple in John 2:12 (cf. 1:14; 4:21; 12:32).[69] In the narrative of the Temple purge (2:13–16), we can find Jesus' decolonizing process. I argued in chapter 5 that the Jewish leaders as the political and religious leaders were collaborators with the Imperial power.[70] They had been able to establish and maintain their political and religious positions and had predominance in the Temple under Imperial supervision.[71] The Temple was the core instrument for the establishment of their status in politics, economics, and religion in Jewish society.[72] It is likely that they could accumulate wealth by the raising of the Temple tax[73] and by

---

68. Burge, "Territorial Religion," 394.

69. Swanson remarks that because from the time of Exile to Babylon, traditional rituals lost their power to reestablish the center, "space threatened to become permanently emptied of meaning" (Swanson, "To Prepare a Place," 12). In the post-exilic Jewish traditions (Isa 56:6–8; 60:4–7; 66:18–21; Zech 14:16–19; 1 Enoch 90:33; Sib. Or. 3:702–718; 773–776; 808; 5:426–433; etc), thus, "the eschatological Temple was expected to function as the center of unity of the new people of God" (Collins, *These Things*, 208). In the Gospel of John, the coming of Jesus (the incarnation) becomes the new way of the reestablishment of the center, the new Temple, the house of the Father, the Johannine new world. As the real center of the people of God, there can only be one Temple, the Johannine Jesus (2:21). Moreover, the Johannine kingdom as the new center becomes meaningful, while not attaching to any particular space, except to Jesus (15:1–17).

70. See chapter 5 of this book.

71. The new economic, political, and religious, even cultural, concepts that the Empire(s) brought to Jewish society were bound to lead to sharp tensions between the Jewish leaders and the marginal groups in the society (see Fiensy, *Social History*, 177–79).

72. In 1 Sam 2:12–17, for example, the conduct of the two sons of Eli shows how the religious leaders could accumulate their wealth. On the details of the relation of the Jewish leaders in Jerusalem and their power, see Ling, *Judean Poor*, 62–97; Applebaum, "Judaea as a Roman Province," 355–96; Fiensy, *Social History*; Jeremias, *Jerusalem*; Hamel, *Poverty and Charity*.

73. On Roman taxation and its problems, and their relation to tithes and the question of the double taxation, see Applebaum, "Judaea as a Roman Province," 373;

their admittance of the merchants into the Temple under the guise of the fulfillment of the law of sacrifices.[74] Ling remarks,

> [i]t [Jerusalem] was the center for the cult and administration. It was where the elite Owners of the land lived; where land was appropriated in the courts; where legislation was formed to assist in the monetisation of the economy; and where taxes and tithes were accrued. It was the focus for both consumption and expropriation of revenues.... Jerusalem was a veritable parasite feeding off the rural populace of Judea.[75]

These phenomena show that access by the margins to the economics (to the Temple) was difficult or impossible. The Temple was gradually degraded into the house at the center of the economy.

The Temple purge by Jesus therefore meant the purification of the corrupt old (Jewish) tradition. It functions as a signpost to the new Temple, his body, which is the entrance door to the new world (2:21; 10:1–18; 14:2–4, 6). This episode shows that Jesus resists the center, which has collaborated with the darkness. Jesus comes to decolonize the margins who are enslaved under the old Temple system, the powerful center of religion, politics, and economics, and to replace it with a new Temple (himself).

Furthermore, the Jesus movement is raised to the spiritual sphere by the narrator as he links the Temple to Jesus' body (2:21).[76] Moreover, the Temple is linked to the House of the Father as the holy space (2:16; 14:2–3).[77] When Jesus says, "Get these out of here! How dare you turn *My Father's house* into a market!" (2:16), he links it to "my Father's house" in John 14:1–3

Hamel, *Poverty and Charity*, 145–49; Grant, *Economic Background*, 89; Fiensy, *Social History*, 161.

74. See Goodman, "First Jewish Revolt," 417–27, esp. 420; Fiensy, *Social History*, 21–74, 161; Jeremias, *Jerusalem*, 99, 224–26. Cf. John 2:16. Through their various interventions of rights and interests in the Temple, which was the center of religion, politics, and economics, the Jewish leaders could establish their positions and manipulated the people in the name of religion. The transaction of the animals in the Temple (some portions of the offerings would be given to the priests and Levites as well as they could get profits from the merchants for transaction) stimulated more offerings, and resulted in their accumulation of wealth.

75. Ling, *Judean Poor*, 83–84.

76. Swan, "To Prepare a Place," 14; Coloe, "Households of Faith," 327–28; Coloe, "Raising the Johannine Temple," 47–58.

77. Cf. in the Hebrew Bible, God himself had become the Temple (Ezek 10:18; 11:15–16; cf. Jer 17:12–13; Isa 8:14). The body of Jesus as the new Temple as well as the house(hold) of God (14:2), the Kingdom of God, integrates all sacred spaces into himself, so Jesus is the way to the Father (14:6), the Johannine new world, the kingdom of God.

which has many dwelling places as the ultimate space (the kingdom) where Jesus will go to prepare places for his followers. Jesus himself/ the kingship of Jesus itself is this holy space and the way to this holy space (14:6) as well as the door of the sheep (10:7).[78] The holy space, the Johannine new world, which Jesus pursues, is the space where no conflict for wealth and power ever exists amongst the individuals or the groups. He pursues a new world of light, which is very different from this world of darkness (17:15; 18:36), by his decolonization (liberating death) on the cross.[79]

Fourthly, another hint can be found in the concept of the vine as the space. The vine as the holy space in Judaism was metaphorically represented as both wisdom/Logos and the Messiah (the Anointed One). 2 Bar 39:7 says "And it will happen when the time of its fulfillment is approaching in which it will fall, that at that time the dominion of my *Anointed One* which is like *the fountain and the vine*, will be revealed. And when it has revealed itself, it will uproot the multitude its host." In addition, Sir 24:17 says, "*I* [*Wisdom* in Sir. 24:1] as a *vine* put forth grace, and my flowers are the fruit of glory and wealth." The vine, which stands for the Logos and Messiah, is Jesus in the Gospel of John. The Johannine Jesus could be understood as more than the fulfillment of the Logos and the Messiah in Judaism. Jesus is the *true* vine (15:1), not the realization [of image] of the vine, but the real accomplishment of the life-giver for his people (15:5).[80] As the true vine, Jesus emphasizes the mutual indwelling in order that his disciples become more fruitful (15:4-5, 7-8).[81] This image shows the direction of Johannine Christianity: from Jesus to the world (From the new center to the margins

---

78. Swanson remarks, "Most important, the opening of a spiritual place in 'the Father's house' seems to have required an end to the sacred topographies of this world" (Swanson, "To Prepare a Place," 14). Burge also contends, "Only one person, Jesus, is the way to such nearness to God. He alone is attached to God's vineyard. He alone is the way to God's Holy Space, to God's Holy Land. 'The Way' is not territorial. It is spiritual. It is to be in Father's presence (John 14:1-11)" (Burge, "Territorial Religion," 394).

79. Through his redemptive/liberating death to take away the sin of the world (1:29), his followers can dwell in the house forever (8:34-37; 14:2-3; mutual in-dwelling between Jesus and his followers; 20:17).

80. For example, in the parable of the good shepherd, Jesus as the good shepherd lays down his life for his sheep (10:11); in the parable of the true vine, Jesus as true vine, who tells that a greater love is to give one's life for one's friends (15:13), lays down his life for the world (11:50-52). In addition, Jesus calls his followers friends, not slaves (15:14). The friendship of Jesus and his followers (15:12-16) could be sharply compared with that of Pilate and Caesar (19:12) in terms of kingship.

81. The analogy of the Father-Son relationship and that of Jesus and his disciples implies that as Jesus comes into the world for mission in root of love (3:16), his believers should go to the world for the same mission (15:16-17).

for decolonization/liberation).[82] By remaining in Jesus and "loving one another" (15:13), they would clearly demonstrate his sacrificial love, even to the point of death. Thus the work he commenced to liberate the world will continue to be carried out by his people.

In short, I have argued that the Gospel presents Jesus as the new space replacing the old spaces and integrating all spaces into himself in order to liberate and decolonize the world in darkness. Now, I will deal with Jesus as universal king.

Jesus as Universal King: New Center

The Coming of the King Into the World

In this section, I will argue that the Gospel presents Jesus as the universal king who comes into his "own" world to liberate his people from oppression, exploitation, and death. This message can be the connection with the postcolonial, ideal world. It functions as the open door of invitation into Jesus' new world to all the readers of the Gospel of John.

Firstly, already the Prologue, the Gospel of John proclaims that Jesus is the true light (1:9: Ἦν τὸ φῶς τὸ ἀληθινόν; 1:4–5, 9; 8:12: 9:5; 12:46; 16:11) coming[83] into his "own" world (1:11: εἰς τὰ ἴδια ἦλθεν), enlightening every person (1:9: ὃ φωτίζει πάντα ἄνθρωπον, ἐρχόμενον εἰς τὸν κόσμον), and giving the right to become the children of God to all who will receive him and believe in him (1:12; cf. 20:17). Here, to make clear my argument, it is important to remark that from the beginning, the Gospel presents that this world is Jesus' own (τὰ ἴδια and οἱ ἴδιοι in 1:10–11),[84]

---

82. The mission of the followers of the Johannine Jesus, love and forgiveness, is given in John 13:34–35; 14:12; 17:14–18; 20:21.

83. For example, the coming of Jesus into the world from above/God (Journey motif of Jesus) in the Gospel of John reveals Jesus as the universal king (1:4–5, 9; 3:19; 4:25–6, 42; 12:47; 5:42; 6:14; 8:42; 11:27; 12:13, 46; 16:18). In addition, Jesus' visiting the margins who were in the darkness clarifies that Jesus is the light who came into the world to liberate them (chapters 4, 5, 9, 11; post-Easter visitations to his disciples; cf. 7:27—the Jews or the crowd did not know from where Jesus came).

84. This phrase means "person or thing associated with an entity" (see, BAGD, 369–70). A possible rendering is "his home/possessions and relatives." However, it has been seen as a disputed point in interpretation. For example, while some interpret τὰ ἴδια as the human world and οἱ ἴδιοι as humans, some interpret both as God's own people, Israel and Israelites. The literary meaning of them could be like this: the meaning of τὰ ἴδια is 'his own land' and that of οἱ ἴδιοι is 'his own people'. In the LXX, 15 occurrences refer to "home or homeland" ("to one's home" in Esth 5:10; 6:12, Macc 6:27; 6:37; 7:8); In the NT, "to one's home" in John 16:32; 19:27; Acts 21:6, 3 (see Pryor, "Jesus and Israel," 208–14).

because he as the Logos, a universal creating entity, created the world (1:3, 10). Accordingly, the identities of "his own world" (τὰ ἴδια) and "his own people" (οἱ ἴδιοι) in John 1:10–11 are crucial keys to reading the Gospel from a postcolonial perspective.

Before identifying them, it is necessary to say that interpretations of τὰ ἴδια and οἱ ἴδιοι are not agreed among commentators. Some interpret "his own" as Israel and "his own people" as Israelites.[85] However, it is not a correct rendering that "his own" stands only for Israel and the Jews in this Gospel. Because of its immediate context, it could mean the whole world and the people who dwell in it. We can find possible accounts to support this in the level of the literary structure of the Gospel.

In John 1:10 Jesus as the Logos made the world as a whole. Segovia comments that "at one level of reference, creation and world constitute synonymous concepts, as the ironic statement of the narrator in 1:10 indicates, 'and the world came to be through him' (v. 10b)."[86] Although Barrett refers to these terms as Israel and the Jewish people, in the wider references, in particular, in relation to John 1:10, he leaves open the possibility of the world which rejected Jesus.[87] Morris states that Jesus came home to Israel, emphasizing that Jesus did not come as an alien, but came to his own possessions.[88] Carson rejects the view that verse 11 is merely a repetition of verse 10. For him, the neuter might mean "his own property" or "his own home" (16:32; 19:27). He argues that "The former could be referring to the world as the Word's 'property'; the latter tilts the meaning in favour of a reference to the Jewish nation and heritage."[89] Therefore, this term should be rendered the world and the world of men, humankind in its entirety, not merely Israel and the Jews.[90]

In addition, those who receive Jesus in John 1:12 cannot only be the Jews. If it is correct that the term "his own" is rendered as Israel and the Jews in John 1:11, Jesus only comes into his own land (Israel) for his own

---

85. See Lincoln, *Gospel*, 102; Brown, *Gospel*, 10; Barrett, *Gospel*, 163; Meeks, "Man from Heaven," 61. Pryor concludes that τὰ ἴδια and οἱ ἴδιοι refer to Israel and her people, not to the cosmos and the wider world of humanity; that the Jews rejected him when he came to Israel (Pryor, "Jesus and Israel," 214, 218).

86. Segovia, "John 1:1–18," 39–40, n. 7.

87. Barrett, *Gospel*, 163.

88. Morris, *Gospel*, 85.

89. Carson, *Gospel*, 124. In addition, Bultmann (*Gospel*, 56–57) and Lindars (*Gospel*, 90) take τὰ ἴδια as a reference to the world as a whole and yet οἱ ἴδιοι as a reference to Israel. In addition, Schnackenburg does not agree that it refers exclusively to Israel, because it may represent Israel as a representative of the creation (see, Schnackenburg, *Gospel*, 1:258, 260; see also Lincoln, *Gospel*, 102).

90. Beasley-Murray, *John*, 12.

people (the Jews) and it is only the Jews who do not receive (παρέλαβον) him.[91] However, in the immediate context, it can be rendered that all who receive (ἔλαβον) Jesus are not only the Jewish people, and because of the universality of the Logos' creative work, "his own" in masculine stands for all people in the world. As the ultimate object of the love of God and of the mission of Jesus (3:16–17; 4:42; 6:33, 51; 13:1), the world could not only be Israel and the Jewish people. In addition, this interpretation is not matched by the purpose of the mission of Jesus nor that of the Johannine community. If we consider that many Diaspora Jews sought the conversion of the Gentiles[92] at that time, it is inappropriate to say that the mission of the Johannine community was restricted to Israel and the Jewish people in a multicultural society. In short, John 1:11 is closely related to the mission of Jesus, the incarnate Logos (1:14), to his people in the world. Jesus comes to his "own" world, but his "own" people do not receive him (1:10–11). He does not come to another world which is not his own.

From the beginning of the Gospel, therefore, the author proclaims that the world belongs to Jesus the king and to no-one else, that Jesus has already owned it from the beginning, and that he has authority and power to rule it without acknowledgment to any other. John 1:5 says that when he (the light) shines in the darkness, the darkness did not overpower (κατέλαβεν)[93] him.[94] Just as the world (κόσμος) means either people or the physical universe in the whole structure of the Gospel, it is the same when we consider the concept of darkness. We cannot apply this term narrowly in the interpretation of the Gospel. If τὰ ἴδια means Israel, then, does the darkness rule over Israel only? Furthermore, does the light shine on Israel only? John 1:13 says that flesh and blood have no place in the purpose of the coming of Jesus, although Jesus is a Jew (4:9). The territory of the ministry of Jesus must not be restricted to Israel only. The children of God who believe in Jesus in the Gospel are not only the Jews, but also non-Jewish people including Samaritans and Gentiles.

---

91. In the Gospel of John, it is the world that rejects Jesus. That is, Jesus is rejected by not only the Jewish leaders, but also the Romans (the death of Jesus on the Roman cross; trial by Pontius Pilate; execution by the Roman soldiers). On the contrary, he is mainly welcomed by the marginal peoples (Galileans, Samaritans, the marginal peoples in the Judea and Jerusalem), even the Greeks (12:20).

92. Josephus, *Ant.* 20.34–36; see Segal, "Universalism," 1–29.

93. In the Gospel, this word means "to cease" in John 8:3–4, and "to overtake" in John 12:35.

94. The aorist κατέλαβεν may be either gnomic (has/does never) or historic (referring either to creation or to the cross).

Secondly, the universal kingship of the Johannine Jesus is revealed in the image of the good shepherd in relation to his "own." Particularly, in John 10:2-4, the image of the good shepherd is linked to "his own"[95] in the manner in which they hear his voice. As the good shepherd, he will bring together two folds of sheep, namely Jewish and non-Jewish (10:16; cf. 11:52).[96] In the parable of the good shepherd, Jesus' "own" is redefined as his true flock, which is not restricted to the Jewish people. Although this word is employed to indicate the distinctive relationship between shepherd and flock, it is also used to strengthen the role of the shepherd in comparison to that of a thief.[97] Moreover, by his death, the good shepherd will unite in one his two flocks of sheep i.e., the Jews and non-Jewish people (10:11, 16). They shall be one flock with one shepherd because they were of his own people (1:11).

Thirdly, in John 13:1, this term, "his own," is used together with the other term, "in the world (τοὺς ἰδίους τοὺς ἐν τῷ κόσμῳ)," just as in the Prologue. Jesus loves his own people who are in the world right to the end, and when Jesus knows that the time has come for him to depart out of this world, he shows them the full extent of his love (cf. he came into the world [John 1:9, 11] to show the love of God [3:16]). Jesus came to his own world in order to save his own people who were in the world. Although they do not receive him (1:11), whoever does receive him become the children of God (1:12). As a result, many of them including the Samaritans (4:42), the Galileans (4:45), and other Jewish people did receive him. Furthermore, after his resurrection, when Jesus speaks to Mary Magdalene, he refers to his disciples as his brothers (20:17).[98] By calling them brothers, he indicates that Jesus has already gathered his sheep into one flock.

95. This phrase, τὰ ἴδια and οἱ ἴδιοι, is used once in John 1:11; cf. 4:44, his own homeland; 10:3, his own sheep; 10:4, all his own; 10:12, his own sheep; 13:1, his own loving ones; cf. his own father (5:18).

96. The reference to the Gentile mission may be found by its context (cf. 7:35; 12:20). Thus, particularly, "other sheep" in 10:16 are identified as Gentile believers (Brown, *Gospel*, 396; Martyn, *Gospel of John*, 117-21) rather than as the other Jewish Christians who separated from the Johannine community. On the argument of the other sheep as the other Jewish Christians, see Brown, "Other Sheep," 5-22; Schoeps, *Jewish Christianity*; Lincoln, *Gospel*, 298. Cf. 1 Enoch 89:35-40 describes a sheep, which was leading the flock. The sheep took some other different sheep together with them; he caused those sheep that went astray to return, and brought them back into their folds; and the sheep was transformed into a man and built a house for the Lord of the sheep, and placed the sheep in it.

97. The implication of the kingship of Jesus is given. Jesus is the real king whom the people are to follow rather than a thief (Roman emperors?), who is not a real king for their lives.

98. The relationship between Jesus as king and his followers as members of the

In short, this is an important point to indicate that Jesus is not a colonizer, but a decolonizer, that he came into *his own world* to liberate it from the darkness (Rome), the symbol of the grasping force for oppression of the margin, the colonizer (the center of the world). Therefore, it is evident that Jesus as the decolonizer came into the world to save it from the darkness and to judge the ruler of the world.

It is my argument, therefore, that in the Gospel Jesus is described as the decolonizing king of the world, particularly through the use of many christological titles which reveal his kingship.[99] In other words, these christological claims that Jesus is the king, uttered from the lips of individuals or groups, in describing Jesus' miraculous act, as well as the direct comments of the narrator, might be employed to liberate the margins from Roman oppression and, ultimately, from the darkness.

The Universal King for All People

The Gospel of John more clearly shows that Jesus came for all people, and this means the whole of the divided nation (1:9, 11). Individuals as major characters in the narrative, as compared to the crowd as a whole, reach out in faith to Jesus.[100] These included both the rich/the center and the poor/the margins. Van Bruggen argues,

> Jesus' concern for the poor is not based on a dislike of the wealthy. He does not side with any particular class, but he demonstrates God's precepts and mercy to everyone, rich and poor. Because the rich are more apt to bypass the kingdom of

---

new world is that of lifelong family.

99. For example, in John 1:49, Nathanael's declaration of Jesus being the Son of God and the King of Israel, and the similar declaration of Jesus as the King of Israel/Jews on the lips of the Jerusalem crowd (12:13) is shown as the fulfillment of biblical prophecy (12:14–5; Zech 9:9). In addition, although the title was modified, Jesus was declared the King of the Jews by Pilate in the passion narrative. Furthermore, right after Jesus fed the people with bread and fishes, the crowd wanted to make him their king in John 6:1–15. Particularly, this passage in John 6 deconstructs the idea of earthly kingship, but reconstructs new Johannine kingship, which is not of this world (18:36).

100. For example, the Disciples of Jesus including Nathanael, Nicodemus, the Samaritan woman, the Royal official, the man born blind, Martha and Mary, Joseph of Arimathea, and so on. The individuals who believed in Jesus in the narrative have a variety of identities (various ethnic, gender, economic, social status). There is one exception of this in the Gospel of John: the invalid man for thirty-eight years, who reported Jesus to the Jewish leaders. He was in Jerusalem where the Jewish authorities became increasingly hostile to Jesus, and collaborated with them in spite of the warning of Jesus (5:14).

heaven and to abuse their position, they receive relatively more admonitions. And because the poor, in their dependence, are sometimes quicker to seek shelter with Jesus, we notice how he accepts them and encourages them. That Jesus focuses his attention on the rich as well as on the poor only emphasizes the reality of Jesus' attention for *everyone*.[101]

Horsley also concludes that there is no evidence that Jesus either recruited or especially welcomed such social outcasts.[102] After all, because fewer of the rich followed Jesus in comparison with the poor, it seems that Jesus is regarded as the one for the poor in the Gospels. However, in the Gospel of John, not only the poor and the margins, but also the rich and the center believe in Jesus (Joseph, Nicodemus, royal official, 12:42, and so on). John's Gospel reveals to Jewish as well as to non-Jewish readers that there happened to be many people, including some people among the Jews of Jerusalem, who came to Jesus and believed in him. This strengthens the idea of kingship of Jesus for the whole universe. Now, I will demonstrate this from the Gospel.

1. One obvious example of those believing from the center is that of Nicodemus and Joseph of Arimathaea. North and other scholars regard Nicodemus as someone failing to grasp the essentials of Johannine truth,[103] in contrast to Joseph of Arimathaea who was a disciple of Jesus but secretly for fear of the Jews. It seems that he failed to come to faith in the Johannine Jesus. He comes to Jesus at night. However, he does not come to argue with Jesus like the Jews of the Jerusalem, but comes to Jesus in order to hear his teaching (3:2). In the dialogue between Jesus and Nicodemus, Jesus delivers his message to Nicodemus, and his teaching makes Nicodemus perplexed. The narrator never tells us in chapter 3 whether he believed in Jesus or not. However, when we read the Gospel as a whole, it seems possible that Nicodemus might well have believed in Jesus secretly. We can deduce that Nicodemus does eventually become Jesus' disciple (John 7:50 and 19:39). He defends Jesus (7:50–52) in the controversy with the Pharisees and at his burial comes with a mixture of

---

101. Van Bruggen, *Jesus*, 181.
102. Horsley, *Jesus and the Spiral of Violence*, 209–45.
103. North, *Lazarus Story*, 125–26; de Jonge, *Jesus*, 29–47; Bassler, "Mixed Signals," 635–46; Goulder, "Nicodemus," 153–68. Van Bruggen argues, "Nicodemus represents the world, and the Jewish authorities and the masses from whom he speaks are called "the world" elsewhere (8:23; 12:18–19). . . . The encounter is fraught with ambiguity and its conclusion leaves readers in suspense" (van Bruggen, *Jesus*, 47).

myrrh and aloes (19:39). Although he follows the Jewish law, Nicodemus does finally become one of the disciples, albeit a secret one.[104]

2. Another example is a royal official in chapter 4. The narrator reports that Jesus heals the son of a certain royal official in Cana of Galilee. In this passage, we discover that negative opinions about Jesus are not the only ones in Jewish society, because this official comes from Capernaum to Cana for the sole purpose of seeking Jesus out (4:46). However, Jesus' response to the royal official in John 4:48 clearly shows that there is conflict between Jesus and the Jewish leaders: "Unless you people (second person plural) see miraculous signs and wonders, you will never believe." Here Jesus is referring to the Jews of Jerusalem who demand from Jesus a miraculous sign in John 2:18. The narrative, therefore, not only shows that the conflict between Jesus and the Jews of Jerusalem is becoming more serious, but also that some leading groups outside Jerusalem were not always opposed to Jesus in the same way. Although Jesus is not pleased with the unbelief of the Jewish leaders, he heals the son of the royal official because the royal official demonstrates a different attitude to Jesus from that of the Jews of Jerusalem, in that he has faith. This story results in the official himself and his entire household believing in Jesus. The royal official emerges as a positive example of faith. Like the disciples, the man simply believes Jesus' word and acts upon it without seeing a miracle. Although the official's national identity is surprisingly ambiguous,[105] it is helpful as representing believers from any background.[106]

3. Finally, it is again necessary to point out that the fiercely negative attitude of the Jewish leaders in their opposition to Jesus is employed to describe Jesus' sacrificial death for his people, not to describe the possibility of their exclusion from entry into the Johannine new world.[107] Jesus came to earth to liberate the people who were suppressed and in bondage in darkness. Therefore, there must be no exception. The Johannine Jesus delivers the Good News to everyone without discrimination and invites them into the new world (1:12; 3:16; 7:37–38).

---

104. The Gospel of John adds that there are believers among the Jews, especially the Jewish officials (12:42). The more the narrative goes on, the more the believers from among Jewish leaders arise. This implies that Nicodemus becomes one of the disciples of Jesus.

105. He is called a *basilikos*, a term that usually designated officials and soldiers employed by the king (van Bruggen, *Jesus*, 52).

106. On the possibility of the non-Jewishness of the official, see Moloney, *Belief*, 182–83; Mead, "*Basilikos*," 67–72.

107. This functions as one of the purposes of postcolonialism: to see their colonial history with objective optics to overcome their coloniality.

Briefly, the Gospel of John reports that there was a division between the people who accepted him and the people who rejected him because of their love of the darkness (1:11; 3:19). Undoubtedly, the Gospel narrative shows that the opponents of Jesus, the Jewish leaders who were the center of political, religious, and economic power, were united in their opposition to him. Accordingly, the followers of Jesus were effectively marginalized. However, it does not mean that they are excluded from the purpose of the coming of the Johannine Jesus (1:12; 3:16; 6:39), but rather the Gospel retains the possibility of their salvation by showing that, finally, some Jewish leaders believed in him (12:49; 19:38–39; cf. 8:30).[108] It is safe, therefore, to say that the Johannine Jesus comes into the world of the darkness in order to liberate those who are both at the center and at the margins, and opens the door and invites them into his new world. However, the Gospel reveals that those who did enter the door were mainly at the margins.

Furthermore, the Fourth Gospel of John describes the death of Jesus as a willing sacrifice on his part, in order to save the world.[109] Jesus declares that he has come for the salvation of the world (3:14–17), on the cross he as the universal king,[110] completed his mission (19:30) and gave a message of forgiveness to his disciples (20:23).[111] "Thus he accepts his suffering, not as a powerless individual who trusts that God will do right by him or her, but as the Ruler who thinks it necessary to allow himself to be bound and killed."[112] This is another important point that Jesus came into the world for everyone. Although the Jewish leaders could not escape from the criticism that they

---

108. The attitude of the Pharisees toward Jesus was critical. As a result, their hostile oppositions killed Jesus. However, owing to their critical reactions to Jesus, there is no reason why the Jews as a whole should be condemned as the murderers of Jesus. The Gospel describes the suffering and death of Jesus as due by the Jewish leaders not by the Jews as a whole. Because the Gospel does not condemn the Jews as a whole as the murderers of Jesus, all readers including the Jews, might believe that they have been invited to come into the Johannine new world without condemnation, and that they can be privileged to be God's children when they believe in Jesus. The Gospel invites every one without any restrictions of ethnic, social, political, or religious differences.

109. This concept is implied in the title of "the Lamb of God" in John 1:29. Jesus' mission: 1:29, 36; 10:11; the "lifting up" of the Son of Man; 12:24–25, 27–28; the passion and resurrection of Jesus. Boyd comments, "The passion itself is Christ's true glory. The alliance of glory with suffering is confirmed in the description of Christ as the Lamb of God" (Boyd, "Ascension," 23).

110. That he was ironically declared as the king of the Jews in Hebrew, Latin, and Greek nevertheless points to his universal kingship in the Gospel of John.

111. Cf. in the Gospel of Luke, Jesus prays for forgiveness for those who execute him (Luke 9:52–56; 23:34).

112. Bruggen, *Jesus*, 159. It shows part of John's deconstruction of what kingship means.

killed Jesus for their own sakes, it does not mean that they themselves were excluded from the privilege of becoming the children of God by believing in Jesus, because one of the ideologies of the Gospel is forgiveness.[113]

Accordingly, it is important to state that the Gospel was written for everyone, although, at the textual level, it is more apt to be accessible to the margins rather than the center because of their rejection in the darkness. Therefore, in the Gospel, it seems that Jesus in the narrative reveals himself to the margins,[114] but contrariwise, hides his identity from the center[115] in order not to increase conflict but to win everyone without any restriction of gender, status, ethnicity, and so on. He comes into the world for everyone who is in the darkness, but, in order to accomplish his mission, he needs to hide his identity from the center of this world until his hour has come.

In summary, the Gospel of John seeks to portray Jesus as the universal king, over a new world order where everyone could live in peace and harmony. In order to do so, John puts Jesus at the center of the world so that every individual and group can reach the center (14:6), because Jesus as the center came to the world/the margins. By his death on the cross, the way has been opened to everyone, irrespective of race, religion, status, gender, etc. the Johannine Jesus could be interpreted as the decolonizer who breaks down territorial boundaries, showing that the Johannine community might

---

113. See John 20:23.

114. It was not the Jews of Jerusalem (who mainly consisted of Pharisees and chief priests) but the margins (who mainly consisted of Galileans and Samaritans in ethnic terms, or the ordinary people who did not have political power in social status under the Empire) who Jesus made them believe in him by performance of miraculous signs and of wonderful teachings, and by revealing himself (1:35–51; 2:13–22; 4:45–54 – Galileans; 4:1–42 – Samaritans; see chapter 3 of this book). In summary, Jesus might be recognized as the king of the Jews, the Samaritans, the Greeks and the Romans, when the readers read the Gospel.

115. In John 4:26, for example, Jesus' self-disclosure in Samaria is different from that in Jerusalem. Jesus never revealed himself when the Jews wanted Jesus to show a miraculous sign to prove his authority after Jesus cleared the courts of the temple. Jesus closed himself to the Jews in chapter 2, however, he revealed himself as the Messiah to the Samaritan woman. Jesus' avoidance of the Jews, the center in this world can be found in other passages. Firstly, when he knew that the Pharisees heard of his gaining and baptizing more disciples than John the Baptist, Jesus left Judea (where Jerusalem was) and went back once more to Galilee (4:1–3). Secondly, after curing the invalid of thirty-eight years, Jesus had slipped away into the crowd (5:13), otherwise, he would have had to be involved in an argument with the Jews. Thirdly, Jesus withdrew again when he knew that the crowd intended to come and make him king by force (6:15). Fourthly, the narrator added another comment in 7:1, "After this, Jesus went around in Galilee, purposely staying away from Judea because the Jews there were waiting to take his life." There also must have been Jews in Galilee. Nevertheless, Jesus stayed away from Judea because he knew that the Jews in Judea (not the Jews in Galilee), particularly of Jerusalem, were waiting to take his life. See also John 8:59; 10:39; Lazarus story.

be a group that has no territory restricting others' access. This territory-lessness functions to show an open community that pursues the new world, and that has no restriction of entry into it, apart from the condition of belief in Jesus. It declares that the Johannine new world is not an exclusive and unsociable group. The only key to open and enter into the new world is Jesus, the new center. His new world is one of love, freedom, humble service, peace, and forgiveness and it is open to all.

The Function of the Johannine Jesus

The Function of the Johannine Jesus as the New King: Over This World

The world, from the time of the composition of the Gospel, is a world where the margins are suffering from oppression, exploitation, and living in poverty. From ancient times, many empires have risen to power in order to establish their own ideologies but later were toppled by those who followed them. Many countries have claimed to stand for justice, freedom, peace, equality, wealth and happiness as their national foundations, but the accomplishment of their ideologies does not seem likely now or in the future. Particularly, it seems to be more difficult to realize these ideologies in regions where religious, ethnic, and ideological conflict has been deeply rooted. So, is it possible to realize the new world (utopia) in which the margins hope in this huge spiral of conflict and suffering?

It seems that this alternative world has never been fully realized. The Gospel of John, however, "contains a new horizon that takes us beyond the conditions of this factual world."[116] That is, the Gospel declares that this alternative world has been initiated in the coming of the king into the world (Prologue). Furthermore, this Gospel states that the expectation of the second coming of Jesus the king shows that the perfect place, the Johannine new world, will be given to all believers (14:2–3).

The Fourth Gospel presents a new way to overcome the present reality of this world, and a new ideological alternative to realize the better world, the new world. However, as Bieringer contends, "In this world we know the alternative world of God only by approximation and in the light of our own interpretation. Therefore, error and selfishness continue to mar our vision of the future."[117] The appropriation of the Johannine new world and its realization in our future is an ongoing community effort.

---

116. Bieringer, Pollefeyt, and Vandecasteele-Vaneuville, "Wrestling," 34.
117. Bieringer, Pollefeyt, and Vandecasteele-Vaneuville, "Wrestling," 34.

The time of the composition of the Gospel might have been a turbulent period. However, there have been similar situations throughout history. Although the specific situations faced by people at the time of the Gospel were different from those of other times, every era has had the margins and those who pursued utopia, in an attempt to present new alternatives to overcome their present limitations and problems. The Gospel of John represents one of these attempts in that it presents Jesus as an evident alternative in terms of pursuing utopia. It projects an alternative world of all-inclusive love and life. The Johannine Jesus has been given to the marginal people who have been caught up in oppression and conflict, violence and exploitation, persecution and death. He always comes as the liberator and gives them hope of the new world where he reigns as king. He opens the door to the new world while living in this world, and begins to reveal the ideologies of his rule. The Gospel delivers its message of the new world mainly through the kingship of Jesus, because in the Gospel he is described as the Lamb of God who takes away the sin of the world. In the passion narrative, he takes away the sin of the world on the cross, because he is the way to the Father; he went to the new world to prepare rooms for his followers and will return; he is the light to overcome the darkness of this world. Therefore, the Gospel invites every reader into the new world that transcends time and space.

Vision of the Johannine Jesus: To the New World

The Gospel of John projects an alternative world; it contains Jesus' vision for the future of humanity. In this Gospel, God gives his only Son to save the world, to give eternal and abundant life in the new world (1:12; 3:16–18; 10:10).[118] Particualrly, this vision for an alternative world is clearly revealed in the passion narrative.

1. On the night Jesus was arrested by the Roman soldiers, Jesus had taken on the role of a servant and had washed the feet of his disciples in order to deliver an important message to his disciples. The main message of this visual lesson is "serve one another with humble mind" (13:15); and from his last teaching is "love one another" (13:34–35; cf. 13:1). In this situation right before his arrest, he challenges his disciples to serve and love one another. The Gospel readers would surely have been surprised at Jesus' attitude and teaching. He does not seek to stir his disciples' hearts up to rebellion and anger. Rather, he clearly demonstrates the best and only way to overcome this worldly mighty power.

---

118. A universalist perspective is also found in John 1:7; 6:39; 10:16; 11:54; 12:32.

Someone might argue that he had already admitted the Imperial reality so that his disciples would not resist. However, the Gospel shows his unique way of resistance or decolonization (18:1–10, 36–37). The only way to overcome power conflicts is not by mightier power of the same kind, but by the mightiest and most superior power which people naturally do not have, that is the power of love and service. The Johannine Jesus is *the king of love and service* and his way is the way of "Moving the Center": from the world of hatred and exploitation of the margins by the center, to the world of love and service of the center for the margins.

In short, hatred among the people in the darkness provides evidence of the ruling of the darkness in the world. In this world, love is one of the most important ideological items to overcome the darkness. The vision of the Johannine Jesus was/is that his people should reveal themselves as his disciples by loving one another and in so doing to overcome this world and to bring about the new world (13:34–35; 15:12–13).[119]

2. This ideological term, "love," is never separated from forgiveness, because in the world of conflict, oppression, exploitation, and slavery, without love there can be no real forgiveness with which to open the Johannine new world.

After his resurrection, Jesus appears to his disciples several times, and he again gives a message, which functions as the most important one in the Gospel: peace and forgiveness (20:19–23). As he sends his disciples into the world with a mission, he encourages them to confront the world, which has persecuted their king with hatred and violent force, in an attitude of peace and forgiveness. Jesus in the Gospel is *the king of peace and forgiveness* who goes forth to decolonize the world.

Military power, violence, enmity and vengeance; these things have been regarded as viable ideologies by the contemporaries of the Johannine community living under the Roman Empire and in following eras. In order to achieve Roman peace the margins were kept down by military force and by heavy taxation and had to be chained to the oar. In this situation, resistance with violence would only have meant more conflict, suffering, and even death. These imperial ideologies forced the marginal peoples into a life of suffering, conflict and unlimited competition among themselves.

To the margins of this world in this situation, the Johannine Jesus delivers a message of forgiveness. He teaches his people that forgiveness is the key to overcome the world (20:19). To a world, which killed Jesus, which persecuted his followers, he teaches forgiveness. Under persecution by the

---

119. As God the Father loves the world (3:16), as Jesus loves the world (15:12–13), the followers of Jesus should love the world, even unto death, through the demonstration of this ideology to bring about the Johannine new world.

Jewish leaders and also Rome, the Gospel brings its readers/hearers a clear message of forgiveness from king Jesus.

3. Love, service, peace, and forgiveness are therefore the important features of the Johannine new world. This message begins in the Prologue, where it presents a breaking down of barriers in the world. Jesus' journey motif[120] can be read as going beyond the boundaries. His mission to the world means the beginning of the establishment of a new world of liberation and peace. Through boundaries being destroyed at the center and at the margins, the world could enter into the new relationship of love, freedom, service, peace, and forgiveness. In addition, the collapse of territory in the Gospel shows that the new world is an open world, which does not restrict access to others. Anyone who wants to enter may do so without any geographical, ethnic, national, religious, status, or gender restriction. It declares that the new world that the Johannine community pursues is not exclusive and unsociable. The only key to open and enter into the new world is Jesus himself. People are invited into the new world of love, freedom, service, peace, and forgiveness in both the earthly and the spiritual realms.

The Gospel of John speaks not in terms of earthly power, but instead with love, freedom, peace, service, and forgiveness to reverse the order of this world into that of the new world. The Johannine new world is the world united against exploitation and oppression.

Summary of the Chapter

The Johannine Gospel leads the readers to see beyond this world/Rome by presenting Jesus as the universal king of the new world. In addition, the Gospel shows the ruling ideology of the new world through the teaching of the Johannine Jesus. This ideology (love, freedom, forgiveness, service, and peace) is different from that of the contemporary world of the Johannine community, the ideology of the darkness (oppression, exploitation, slavery, and so on). The Johannine Gospel also presents Jesus as the decolonizer who comes to his own to liberate his people from darkness. Therefore, to know this Johannine Jesus, to believe in him, is the way of freedom. The only way of liberation from material oppression, tyranny and power, bondage of religions, and the limitation of a social position, is to believe in Jesus and to be his disciple. It is true that the conditions of the world in which the darkness reigned at the time of the Johannine Gospel is similar to that of today. To this world, the Johannine Gospel proclaims

---

120. See the section, "The Coming of the King Into the World," of this chapter.

that the margins will be liberated from its reality, which is full of political, religious, and economic conflict.

In short, the Fourth Gospel shows that in the Johannine new world where Jesus reigns as king, the new ruling ideology applies, and invites the readers to enter this new world in order to apply this new ideology themselves. Therefore, this message is appropriate for this world, which has passed through the colonial era.

7. Conclusion

I BEGAN THIS BOOK with an emphasis on the Gospel of John as a postcolonial text, namely as a product of a multiple, complex and hybridized society under Roman imperial rule. At the same time, by reading this Gospel from a postcolonial perspective I sought to answer the following questions: Why does John employ a variety of royal christological titles? Does John's Gospel portray Jesus as the universal king? What is the Johannine Jesus' function in the (post)colonial world? To answer these questions, in the first part of the book, I examined a variety of christological titles in the Fourth Gospel in terms of the kingship, and in the second part, as a Korean reader, I attempted a postcolonial reading of the Gospel in terms of the function of the Johannine Jesus as king.

At the same time, I pointed out that the Gospel of John represents a melting pot of the knowledge of various backgrounds, particularly Jewish and Graeco-Roman (hybridentity). In other words, as a literary strategy, the combination of a variety of cultural elements into one category is found in the Gospel. This Gospel uses many ambiguous and complex terms, concepts, and motifs originating in the multicultural world of its author and readers, and among them is the kingship motif applied to the Johannine Jesus. In particular, in the revelation of the complex identity of the Johannine Jesus, the royal christological titles play a particularly important role. I have demonstrated numerous examples and usage of the royal christological titles which John applies to portray Jesus as the universal king, decolonizer, and liberator. These titles include Christ (Messiah), Son of God, Son of Man, Prophet, Savior of the World, Lord (Lord and God), and the King of Israel/the Jews. I have also demonstrated their interchangeability and employment of series in the immediate passage to identify the Johannine Jesus as king.

At the same time, I also argued that John might employ both christological titles and many literary devices to deepen the kingship of the Johannine Jesus in the narrative. In particular, the christological titles employed to describe Jesus as a king in the Johannine Gospel were used in contrast with similar ones of other marginal groups (Jewish, Samaritan, Qumran) and those of the center (Graeco-Roman) as well. Although their meanings are indirect and suggestive, among many interpretations concerning them and the common meaning of those titles, the kingship of Jesus could be easily recognized by people of diverse origins, because the terms and concepts connoting kingship were adapted from their diverse backgrounds and used in the Gospel.

Accordingly, it is my argument that, with the presupposition that John envisages a reading community with a wide spectrum of origins, the author adapts and employs many christological titles in order to identify, without any possibility of misunderstanding, the Johannine Jesus as a universal king. The Johannine Gospel not only pursues a new world, in which the various groups live together in unity and harmony, but also seeks to open larger and more extensive solidarities in the name of Jesus, the universal king. In other words, the Johannine Jesus is designated as the king who sets out to liberate his people from the darkness, which ruled the world, and to lead them into his new world. Particularly relevant for an exploration of the kingship of Jesus and his function are the Johannine christological titles.

Thus, I argued that the disclosure of the complex and ambivalent relationships between the center and the margins in the narrative is necessary to explain the function of the Johannine Jesus. That is, the Gospel presents a means of decolonization, but it never justifies violence as a way of decolonization. The Johannine Jesus does not attempt to overturn the colonial power; rather, he puts his life at the mercy of the violence of the colonizer in order to liberate the world from this violence. For example, whereas the Jewish leaders as well as the Roman Empire attempt to bring together regions, religious and ethnic groups in a united opposition, which leads to competition, struggle and oppression, to maintain their ruling positions, the Johannine Jesus attempts neither to overturn the colonial world, nor to bring together regions, religious and ethnic groups in a united opposition. On the contrary, the Johannine Jesus collapses the barriers among the opposing groups to bring them to a new world where all the people live in harmony without competition, struggle, and oppression. He teaches how to live a liberated life with forgiveness, service, peace, and love instead of competition, struggle, and oppression. He combines the center and the margin into one with his life and teaching. The Johannine Jesus is the Universal King in this sense.

Furthermore, I submitted at this point that the Johannine Jesus as the universal king, the decolonizer, as well as the liberator, could be recognized by the readers of every generation, just as the first century readers in the hybridized colonial world could recognize him as such. I also emphasized that the Gospel presents the postcolonial ideology of the Johannine new world, which is quite different from that of the Imperial world; that its postcolonial ideology has validated the purposes of the Gospel for its readers from generation to generation, just as it did for the first century readers, that is, to consolidate the Johannine community in faith and accomplish their mission to the world.

In these respects, therefore, my investigation was an examination of postcolonial theory in the Gospel of John. The postcolonial attempt is to make a new utopian society through mutual transactions of the two, the center and the margin, overcoming institutionalized violence and sufferings. That is, the message of the Johannine new world pursued in the Gospel is like this: entering into the new ordered society and overcoming institutionalized violence and sufferings through the universal king, that is, entering into the new world of forgiveness, service, peace, freedom, and love through the Johannine Jesus. In this sense, the postcolonial attempt is linked to the Johannine utopia where Jesus as the universal king reigns for all the people regardless of their origins at the center or the margin.

This Johannine ruling ideology, therefore, gives a positive alternative for the oppressed, exploited, and struggling world. In this book, I, as a postcolonial reader, also pointed out that just as it presented the Johannine Jesus as king to first century readers, the Gospel proposes to various readerships through all generations that Jesus is the way to reach a new world where every one lives in harmony without conflict, oppression, and exploitation.

Therefore, as I have argued, the better future can be found in the message of the Gospel of John. In this respect, the Johannine christological titles are relevant for an exploration of the kingship of Jesus and his function. This Gospel demonstrates that the Johannine Jesus lived a non-violent life offering postcolonial hope in a violent world. It shows that a new society, more, a new world could be constructed by imitating the life of Jesus who lived a non-violent life pursuing a utopian vision. The Fourth Gospel also delivers a message that all groups could enter into the new ideal world in spite of the barriers, which exist by collaborating with one another and putting Jesus in the center. The Gospel proposes the cross-cultural benefits of a non-violent society displayed in love, forgiveness, freedom, service, and peace.

The Johannine Gospel suggests solutions to the marginal groups in society, whose aim should be trying to resolve the problems to which the Roman or the Jewish leaders had not been able to find answers. This Gospel presents the only way to be free of oppression and conflict, which exist both in the center and the margins; moving the center from this world to Jesus. The Johannine Jesus is the only way to the Father (14:6) whose kingdom is for all his followers (14:1). Jesus will receive them to himself (14:3). That is, the followers of Jesus will be there where Jesus is and they know the way where he is going (14:4). Just like the Johannine Jesus, the Johannine community are invited to play a role in setting others free from oppression through faithfulness to the new ruling ideology of Jesus, the postcolonial message of this Gospel: loving one another (13:34–5; 14:15); forgiveness (20:23); service (13:5–17); freedom (8:31–32); and peace which is given by Jesus, which the world cannot give (14:27; 15:33; 20:19, 26).

Bibliography

Aalen, Sverre. "'Reign' and 'House' in the Kingdom of God in the Gospels." *NTS* 8 (1961–62) 215–40.
Alcoff, Linda M. "Cultural Feminism vs. Post-Structuralism: The Identity Crisis in Feminist Theory." *Signs* (1988) 405–36.
Alexander, Loveday. "The Acts of the Apostles as an Apologetic Text." In *Apologetics in the Roman Empire: Pagans, Jews, and Christians*, edited by Martin Goodman, Mark Edwards, and Simon Price, 15–44. Oxford: Oxford University Press, 1999.
———. "Ancient Book Production and the Circulation of the Gospels." In *The Gospels for All Christians: Rethinking the Gospel Audiences*, edited by Richard Bauckham, 71–105. Grand Rapids, MI: William B. Eerdmans, 1998.
———. "Introduction." In *Images of Empire*, edited by Loveday Alexander, 11–18. JSOTSup 122. Sheffield: Sheffield Academic, 1991.
———. "The Relevance of Greco-Roman Literature and Culture to New Testament Study." In *Hearing the New Testament: Strategies for Interpretation*, edited by Joel B. Green, 109–26. Grand Rapids, MI: William B. Eerdmans, 1995.
———. "Rome, Early Christian Attitudes to." In *ABD* 5:835–39.
———, ed. *Images of Empire*. JSOTSup 122. Sheffield: Sheffield Academic, 1991.
Alexander, Philip S. "The Family of Caesar and the Family of God: The Image of the Emperor in the Heikhalot Literature." In *Images of Empire*, edited by Loveday Alexander, 276–97. JSOTSup 122. Sheffield: Sheffield Academic, 1991.
Allegro, J. M. "Further Messianic References in Qumran Literature." *JBL* 75 (1956) 174–87.
Allison, Dale C. *The New Moses: A Matthean Typology*. Edinburgh: T&T Clark, 1993.
Althusser, Louis. "Ideology and Ideological State Apparatuses." In *Literary Theory: An Anthology*, edited by Julie Rivkin and Michael Ryan, 294–304. Oxford: Blackwell, 1998.
Anderson, Robert T. "Samartians." *ABD* 5:946.
Applebaum, S. "Judaea as a Roman Province: The Countryside as a Political and Economic Factor." *ANRW* II/8 (1989) 355–96.
Ashcroft, Bill, Gareth Griffiths, and Helen Tiffin. *The Empire Writes Back*. 2nd ed. London: Routledge, 2002.
———. *Postcolonial Studies: The Key Concepts*. London: Routledge, 2000.
———, ed. *The Post-Colonial Studies Reader*. 2nd ed. London: Routledge, 2006.

Ashton, John. "The Identity and Function of the ΙΟΥΔΑΙΟΙ in the Fourth Gospel." *NovT* 27 (1985) 40–73.
———. *Understanding the Fourth Gospel*. New ed. Oxford: Clarendon, 1991.
———, ed. *The Interpretation of John*. Issues in Religion and Theology 9. London: SPCK, 1986.
Atkinson, Kenneth. "On the Herodian Origin of Militant Davidic Messianism at Qumran: New Light from Psalm of Solomon 17." *JBL* 118 (1999) 435–60.
Attridge, H. "Genre Bending in the Fourth Gospel?" *JBL* 121 (2002) 3–21.
Aune, D. E. "Biography." In *The Westminster Dictionary of New Testament and Early Christian Rhetoric*, by D. E. Aune, 78–81. Louisville, KY: Westminster John Knox, 2003.
———. *The Cultic Setting of Realized Eschatology in Early Christianity*. NovTSup 28. Leiden: E. J. Brill, 1972.
———. "Gospels, Literary Genre of." In *The Westminster Dictionary of New Testament and Early Christian Literature and Rhetoric*, by D. E. Aune, 204–6. Louisville, KY: Westminster John Knox, 2003.
———. *The New Testament in Its Literary Environment*. Philadelphia: Westminster, 1987.
———. "Roman Emperors." In *DPL*, 233–35.
———. *The Westminster Dictionary of New Testament and Early Christian Literature and Rhetoric*. Louisville, KY: Westminster John Knox, 2003.
Bacon, B. W. *The Gospel of the Hellenists*. New York: Holt, 1993.
Barclay, John M. G. *Jews in the Mediterranean Diaspora: From Alexander to Trajan (323 BCE—117 CE)*. Edinburgh: T&T Clark, 1996.
Barnard, L. W. "Clement of Rome and the Persecution of Domitian." *NTS* 10 (1964) 251–60.
Barrett, C. K. *The Gospel according to St. John*. 2nd ed. Philadelphia: Westminster, 1978.
———. *The New Testament Background*. Rev. ed. San Francisco: HarperCollins, 1989.
Barthes, Roland. "The Death of the Author." In *Modern Criticism and Theory: A Reader*, edited by David Lodge, 167–72. London: Longman, 1988.
Barton, John. "Historical Criticism and Literary Interpretation: Is There Any Common Ground?" In *Crossing the Boundaries*, edited by Paul Joyce, Stanley E. Porter, and David E. Orton, 3–15. Leiden: Brill, 1994.
———. "The Messiah in Old Testament Theology." In *King and Messiah in Israel and the Ancient Near East*, edited by John Day, 365–79. JSOTSup 270. Sheffield: Sheffield Academic, 1998.
Barton, Stephen C. "Can We Identify the Gospel Audiences?" In *The Gospels for All Christians: Rethinking the Gospel Audiences*, edited by Richard Bauckham, 173–94. Grand Rapids, MI: William B. Eerdmans, 1998.
———. "Christian Community in the Light of the Gospel of John." In *Christology, Controversy, and Community: New Testament Essays in Honour of David R. Catchpole*, edited by David G. Horell and Christopher M. Tuckett, 279–301. NovTSup 99. Leiden: Brill, 2000.
———. "The Relativisation of Family Ties in the Jewish and Graeco-Roman Traditions." In *Constructing Early Christian Families*, edited by Halvor Moxnes, 81–102. London: Routledge, 1997.
Bassler, J. M. "The Galileans: A Neglected Factor in Johannine Community Research." *CBQ* 43 (1981) 245–57.

———. "Mixed Signals: Nicodemus in the Fourth Gospel." *JBL* 108 (1989) 635–46.
Bauckham, Richard. "The Economic Critique of Rome in Revelation 18." In *Images of Empire*, edited by Loveday Alexander, 47–90. JSOTSup 122. Sheffield: Sheffield Academic, 1991.
———. "For Whom Were the Gospels Written?" In *The Gospels for All Christians: Rethinking the Gospel Audience*, edited by Richard Bauckham, 9–48. Grand Rapids, MI: Williams. B. Eerdmans, 1998.
———. "Introduction." In *The Gospels for All Christians: Rethinking the Gospel Audience*, edited by Richard Bauckham, 1–8. Grand Rapids, MI: William B. Eerdmans, 1998.
———. "John for Readers of Mark." In *The Gospels for All Christians: Rethinking the Gospel Audiences*, edited by Richard Bauckham, 147–71. Grand Rapids, MI: William B. Eerdmans, 1998.
———. "Messianism According to the Gospel of John." In *Challenging Perspectives on the Gospel of John*, edited by John Lierman, 34–68. Tübingen: Mohr Siebeck, 2006.
———, ed. *The Gospels for All Christians: Rethinking the Gospel Audiences*. Grand Rapids, MI: Williams. B. Eerdmans, 1998.
Beasley-Murray, G. R. *Jesus and the Kingdom of God*. Grand Rapids: Eerdmans, 1986.
———. *John*. 2nd ed. WBC 36. Nashville: Thomas Nelson, 1999.
Bernard, J. H. *A Critical and Exegetical Commentary on the Gospel according to John*. 2 vols. ICC. Edinburgh: T&T Clark, 1928.
Beutler, J. "Faith and Confession: The Purpose of John." In *Word, Theology, and Community in John*, edited by R. Alan Culpepper, John Painter, and Fernando F. Segovia, 19–32. St. Louis, MO: Chalice, 2002.
———. "The Use of 'Scripture' in the Gospel of John." In *Exploring the Gospel of John: In Honor of D. Moody Smith*, edited by R. A. Culpepper and C. C. Black, 147–62. Louisville, KY: Westminster John Knox, 1996.
Beutler, Johannes, and Robert T. Fortna, eds. *The Shepherd Discourse of John 10 and Its Context*. Cambridge: Cambridge University Press, 1991.
Bhabha, Homi. *The Location of Culture*. London: Routledge, 1994.
———. "Of Mimicry and Man: The Ambivalence of Colonial Discourse." *October* 28 (1984) 125–33.
Bieringer, R., D. Pollefeyt, and F. Vandecasteele-Vanneuville, eds. *Anti-Judaism and the Fourth Gospel*. Louisville, KY: Westminster John Knox, 2001.
———. "Wrestling with Johannine Anti-Judaism: A Hermeneutical Framework for the Analysis of the Current Debate." In *Anti-Judaism and the Fourth Gospel*, edited by R. Bieringer, D. Pollefeyt, and F. Vandecasteele-Vanneuville, 3–40. Louisville, KY: Westminster John Knox, 2001.
Black, Matthew. "Jesus and the Son of Man." *JSNT* 1 (1978) 4–18.
Black, David Alan, and David S. Dockery, eds. *Interpreting the New Testament: Essays on Methods and Issues*. Nashville: Broadman & Holman, 2001.
Blomberg, Craig L. "The Diversity of Literary Genres in the New Testament." In *Interpreting the New Testament: Essays on Methods and Issues*, edited by David Alan Black and David S. Dockery, 272–95. Nashville: Broadman & Holman, 2001.
———. *The Historical Reliability of John's Gospel: Issues & Commentary*. Leicester: InterVarsity, 1987.
Böcher, O. "Πλάναω." In *EDNT* 3:98–100.
Boer, M. C. de. "The Depiction of 'the Jews' in John's Gospel: Matters of Behavior and Identity." In *Anti-Judaism and the Fourth Gospel*, edited by D. Pollefeyt, R.

Bieringer, and F. Vandecasteele-Vanneuville, 141–57. Louisville, KY: Westminster John Knox, 2001.

———. "Narrative Criticism, Historical Criticism, and the Gospel of John." *JSNT* 47 (1992) 35–48.

Boismard, M. É. *Moses or Jesus: An Essay in Johannine Christology*. Translated by B. T. Viviano. Leuven: Leuven University Press, 1993.

Bond, Helen K. *Caiaphas: Friend of Rome and Judge of Jesus?* Louisville, KY: Westminster John Knox, 2004.

Borgen, Peder. "John 6: Tradition, Interpretation and Composition." In *From Jesus to John: Essays on Jesus and New Testament Christology in Honour of Marinus de Jonge*, edited by Martinus C. de Boer, 268–91. JSNTSup 84. Sheffield: Sheffield Academic, 1993.

———. *Logos was the True Light*. Trondheim: Tarip, 1983.

———. "Moses, Jesus, and the Roman Emperor: Observations in Philo's Writings and in the Revelation of John." *NovT* 38, 2 (1996) 145–59.

———. "'There Shall Come Forth a Man': Reflections on Messianic Idea in Philo." In *The Messiah: Developments in Earliest Judaism and Christianity*, edited by J. H. Charlesworth, 341–61. Minneapolis, MN: Fortress, 1992.

Boring, M. Eugene. *Revelation*. IC. Louisville, KY: John Knox, 1989.

Bousset, Willelm. *Kyrios Christos: A History of the Belief in Christ from the Beginnings of Christianity to Irenaeus*. Translated by John E. Steely. Nashville: Abingdon, 1970.

Bowman, John. "Samaritan Studies." *BJRL* 40 (1958) 298–327.

Boyd, W. J. P. "The Ascension according to St. John." *SE* VI (1973) 20–27.

Brent, Allen. *The Imperial Cult and the Development of Church Order: Concepts and Images of Authority in Paganism and Early Christianity before the Age of Cyprian*. VCSup 45. Leiden: Brill, 1999.

Brooke, George J. "Kingship and Messianism in the Dead Sea Scrolls." In *King and Messiah in Israel and the Ancient Near East*, edited by John Day, 434–55. JSOTSup 270. Sheffield: Sheffield Academic, 1998.

———. "The Kittim in the Qumran Pesharim." In *Images of Empire*, edited by Loveday Alexander, 135–59. JSOTSup 122. Sheffield: Sheffield Academic, 1991.

Brown, Raymond E. *The Community of the Beloved Disciple*. London: Geoffrey Chapman, 1979.

———. *The Gospel according to John (I–XII)*. AB 29. New York: Doubleday, 1966.

———. *The Gospel according to John (X–XXI)*. AB 29A. New York: Doubleday, 1970.

———. *An Introduction to the Gospel of John*. Edited by Francis. J. Moloney. New York: Doubleday, 2003.

———. "Other Sheep Not of This Fold: The Johannine Perspective on Christian Diversity in the Late First Century." *JBL* 97 (1978) 5–22.

Bruce, F. F. *The Gospel of John*. Rep. ed. Grand Rapids, MI: William B. Eerdmans, 2004.

———. *New Testament History*. New York: Doubleday, 1980.

Bruggen, Jacob van. *Jesus the Son of God: The Gospel Narratives as Message*. Translated by Nancy Forest-Flier. Grand Rapids, MI: Baker, 1999.

Buchanan, G. W. *Jesus: The King and His Kingdom*. Macon, GA: Mercer, 1984.

———. "The Samaritan Origin." In *Religions in Antiquity: Essays in Memory of E. R. Goodenough*, edited by J. Newsner, 148–75. Leiden: E. J. Brill, 1968.

Bultmann, Rudolph K. *The Gospel of John: A Commentary*. Translated by G. R. Beasley-Murray. Oxford: Basil Blackwell, 1971.

———. *Theology of the New Testament*. Translated by Kendrick Grobel. 2 vols. London: SCM, 1952, 1955.
Burge, Gary M. *The Anointed Community: The Holy Spirit in the Johannine Tradition*. Grand Rapids, MI: William B. Eerdmans, 1986.
———. "Territorial Religion, Johannine Christology, and the Vineyard of John 15." In *Jesus of Nazareth: Lord and Christ (Essays on the Historical Jesus and New Testament Christology)*, edited by Joel B. Green and Max Turner, 384–96. Grand Rapids, MI: William B. Eerdmans, 1994.
Burkett, Delbert. *The Son of the Man in the Gospel of John*. JSNTSup 56. Sheffield: Sheffield Academic, 1991.
Burnett, Andrew, Michael Amandry, and Pere Pau Repolles, eds. *Roman Provincial Coinage*. Vol. 1. London: British Museum, 2007.
Burridge, Richard A. "About People, by People, for People: Gospel Genre and Audience." In *The Gospels for All Christians: Rethinking the Gospel Audiences*, edited by Richard Bauckham, 113–45. Grand Rapids, MI: William B. Eerdmans, 1998.
———. *What Are the Gospels? A Comparison With Graeco-Roman Biography*. SBLMS 70. Cambridge: Cambridge University Press, 1992.
Byrne, Brendan. "The Faith of the Beloved Disciple and the Community in John 20." *JSNT* 23 (1985) 83–97.
Caird, G. B. *A Commentary on the Revelation of St. John the Divine*. 2nd ed. BNTC. London: Black, 1984.
Caragounis, Chrys C. "The Kingdom of God: Common and Distinct Elements Between John and the Synoptics." In *Jesus in Johannine Tradition*, edited by Robert T. Fortna and Tom Thatcher, 125–34. Louisville, KY: Westminster John Knox, 2001.
———. "The Kingdom of God in John and the Synoptics: Realized or Potential Eschatology?" In *John and the Synoptics*, edited by Adelbert Denaux, 473–80. BELT 101. Leuven: Peeters, 1992.
———. "Kingdom of God/Kingdom of Heaven." In *DJG*, 417–30.
Carson, D. A. *The Gospel according to John*. PNTC. Grand Rapids, MI: William B. Eerdmans, 1991.
———. "The Purpose of the Fourth Gospel: John 20:30–31 Reconsidered." *JBL* 108 (1987) 639–51.
Carter, Warren. *John and Empire: Initial Explorations*. New York: T&T Clark, 2008.
———. *John: Storyteller, Interpreter, Evangelist*. Peabody, MA: Hendrickson, 2006.
———. *Matthew and Empire: Initial Explorations*. Harrisburg, PA: Trinity Press International, 2001.
———. *Matthew and the Margins: A Socio-Political and Religious Reading*. JSNTSup 204. Sheffield: Sheffield Academic, 2000.
———. *The Roman Empire and the New Testament*. Nashville: Abingdon, 2006.
Casey, P. M. "Aramaic Idiom and the Son of Man Problem: A Response to Owen and Shepherd." *JSNT* 25.1 (2002) 2–32.
———. *From Jewish Prophet to Gentile God: The Origins and Development of New Testament Christology*. Cambridge: James Clarke, 1991.
———. "General, Generic and Indefinite: The Use of the Term 'Son of Man' in Aramaic Sources and in the Teaching of Jesus." *JSNT* 29 (1987) 21–56.
———. *Is John's Gospel True?* London: Routledge, 1996.
———. "Method in Our Madness, and Madness in Their Methods: Some Approaches to the Son of Man Problem in Recent Scholarship." *JSNT* 42 (1991) 17–43.

Cassidy, R. J. *Christians and Roman Rule in the New Testament: New Perspectives*. New York: Crossroad, 2001.

———. *John's Gospel in the New Perspective: Christology and the Realities of Roman Power*. Maryknoll, NY: Orbis, 1992.

Catchpole, David R. "The 'Triumphal' Entry." In *Jesus and the Politics of His Day*, edited by Ernst Bammel and C. F. D. Moule, 319–34. Cambridge: Cambridge University Press, 1984.

Césairé, A. *Discourse on Colonialism*. Translated by Joan Pinkham. New York: Monthly Review Press, 1972.

Chang, Paul Yunsik. "Carrying the Torch in the Darkest Hours: The Sociopolitical Origins of Minjung Protestant Movements." In *Christianity in Korea*, edited by Robert E. Buswell Jr. and Timothy S. Lee, 195–220. Honolulu: University of Hawaii Press, 2006.

Charles, R. H., ed. *The Apocrypha and Pseudepigrapha of the Old Testament*. 2 vols. Oxford: Oxford University Press, 1913.

Charlesworth, James H., ed. *The Messiah: Developments in Earliest Judaism and Christianity*. Minneapolis, MN: Fortress, 1992.

———, ed. *The Old Testament Pseudepigrapha*. Vol. 1, *Apocalyptic Literature and Testaments*. London: Darton, Longman & Todd, 1983.

———, ed. *The Old Testament Pseudepigrapha*. Vol. 2, *Expansions of the "Old Testament" and Legends, Wisdom and Philosophical Literature, Prayers, Psalms, and Odes, Fragments of Lost Judeo-Hellenistic Works*. London: Darton, Longman & Todd, 1985.

Charlesworth, M. P. *Documents Illustrating the Reigns of Claudius and Nero*. Cambridge: Cambridge University Press, 1939.

———. "Some Observations on Ruler-Cult Especially in Rome." *HTR* 28 (1935) 26–42.

Chennattu, Rekha M. *Johannine Discipleship as a Covenant Relationship*. Peabody, MA: Hendrickson, 2006.

Childs, Peter, and Patrick Williams. *An Introduction to Post-Colonial Theory*. Harlow, Essex: Pearson Education, 1997.

Chilton, B. D. *God in Strength: Jesus' Announcement of the Kingdom*. Sheffield: JSOT, 1987.

Cho, Sukmin. "Jesus as Prophet in John's Gospel: The Meaning, the Role in Characterization and the Christological Significance." PhD diss., University of Bristol, 2004.

Chung, Hee Chae. "From Development Dictatorship to Civilian Democracy: The South Korea Case." In *Korea and the World: Strategies for Globalization*, edited by Eui Hong Shin and Yun Kim, 151–68. Columbia, SC: Center for Asian Studies at the University of South Carolina, 1995.

Clark, Allen D. *History of the Korean Church*. Seoul: Christian Literature Society of Korea, 1961.

Collins, Adela Yarbro. *Crisis and Catharsis: The Power of the Apocalypse*. Philadelphia: Westminster, 1984.

Collins, J. J. *The Scepter and the Star: The Messiahs of the Dead Sea Scrolls and Other Ancient Literature*. New York: Doubleday, 1995.

———. "The Son of God Text from Qumran." In *From John to Jesus: Essays on Jesus and New Testament Christology in Honour of Marinus de Jonge*, edited by Martinus C. de Boer, 65–82. JSNTSup 83. Sheffield: Sheffield Academic, 1993.

Collins, Raymond F. *John and His Witnesses.* Collegeville, MN: Liturgical, 1991.
———. *These Things Have Been Written.* Grand Rapids, MI: William B. Eerdmans, 1990.
Coloe, M. L. *God Dwells with Us: Temple Symbolism in the Fourth Gospel.* Collegeville, MN: Liturgical, 2001.
———. "Households of Faith (Jn 4:46–54; 11:1–44): A Metaphor for the Johannine Community." *Pacifica* 13 (2000) 326–35.
———. "Raising the Johannine Temple (Jn 19:19–37)." *ABR* 48 (2000) 47–58.
Conway, Colleen M. "The Production of the Johannine Community: A New Historicist Perspective." *JBL* 121 (2002) 479–95.
Cook, S. A., F. E. Adcock, and M. P. Charlesworth, eds. *The Cambridge Ancient History: The Augustan Empire, 44 B.C.–A.D. 70.* Vol. 10. Cambridge: Cambridge University Press, 1966.
Cribbs, F. Lamar. "A Reassessment of the Date of Origin and the Destination of the Gospel of John." *JBL* 89 (1970) 38–55.
Croix, G. E. M. de Ste. "Why Were the Early Christians Persecuted?" In *Studies in Ancient Society*, edited by M. I. Finley, 210–49. London: Routledge and Kegan Paul, 1974.
Crossan, J. D. "Roman Imperial Theology." In *In Shadow of Empire*, edited by R. A. Horsley, 59–73. Louisville, KY: Westminster John Knox, 2008.
Cullmann, Oscar. *The Christology of the New Testament.* Translated by Shirley C. Guthrie and Charles A. M. Hall. Rev. ed. Philadelphia: Westminster, 1963.
———. *The Johannine Circle: Its Place in Judaism, among the Disciples of Jesus and in Early Christianity.* Translated by John Bowden. London: SCM, 1976.
———. "Samaria and the Origin of the Christian Mission." In *The Early Church: Five Essays*, edited by A. J. B. Higgins, 185–92. London: SCM, 1966.
Culpepper, Alan R. *Anatomy of the Fourth Gospel: A Study in Literary Design.* Philadelphia: Fortress, 1983.
———. "Anti-Judaism in the Fourth Gospel as a Theological Problem for Christian Interpreters." In *Anti-Judaism and the Fourth Gospel*, edited by D. Pollefeyt R. Bieringer, and F. Vandecasteele-Vanneuville, 61–82. Louisville, KY: Westminster John Knox, 2001.
———. "The Christology of the Johannine Writings." In *Who Do You Say That I Am?*, edited by Mark Allan Powell and David R. Bauer, 66–87. Louisville, KY: Westminster John Knox, 1999.
———. "The Gospel of John as a Document of Faith in a Pluralistic Culture." In *What is John?: Readers and Readings of the Fourth Gospel*, edited by F. F. Segovia, 107–28. Atlanta: Scholars, 1996.
———. *The Johannine School: An Evaluation of the Johannine-School Hypothesis Based on an Investigation of the Nature of Ancient Schools.* SBLDS 26. Missoula, MT: Scholars, 1975.
Cuss, Dominique. *Imperial Cult and Honorary Terms in the New Testament.* Paradosis: Fribourg University Press, 1974.
Dahl, Nils Alstrup. "The Johannine Church and History." In *The Interpretation of John*, edited by John Ashton, 122–40. London: SPCK, 1986.
Danker, Frederick W. "Benefactor." In *DJG*, 58–60.
———. *Benefactor: Epigraphic Study of a Graeco-Roman and New Testament Semantic Field.* St. Louis, MO: Calyton, 1982.

Davies, Margaret. *Rhetoric and Reference in the Fourth Gospel*. JSNTSup 69. Sheffield: JSOT, 1992.

Davies, P. J. E. *Death and the Emperor: Roman Imperial Funerary Monuments from Augustus to Marcus Aurelius*. Cambridge: Cambridge University Press, 2000.

Davies, W. D. *The Gospel and the Land: Early Christianity and Jewish Territorial Doctrine*. Sheffield: JSOT, 1994.

Day, John. "The Canaanite Inheritance of the Israelite Monarchy." In *King and Messiah in Israel and the Ancient Near East*, edited by John Day, 72–90. JSOTSup 270. Sheffield: Sheffield Academic, 1998.

———, ed. *King and Messiah in Israel and the Ancient Near East*. JSOTSup 270. Sheffield: Sheffield Academic, 1998.

De Jonge, Henk Jan. "'The Jews' in the Gospel of John." In *Anti-Judaism and the Fourth Gospel*, edited by D. Pollefeyt, R. Bieringer, and F. Vandecasteele-Vanneuville, 121–40. Louisville, KY: Westminster John Knox, 2001.

De Jonge, M. "Christology, Controversy and Community in the Gospel of John." In *Christology, Controversy and Community*, edited by David G. Horrell and Christopher M. Tuckett, 209–30. NovTSup 99. Leiden: Brill, 2000.

———. *God's Final Envoy: Early Christology and Jesus' Own View of His Mission*. Grand Rapids, MI: William B. Eerdmans, 1998.

———. *Jesus: Stranger from Heaven and Son of God: Jesus Christ and the Christians in Johannine Perspective*. Translated by John E. Steely. Sources for Biblical Study 11. Missoula, MT: Scholars, 1977.

———. *Jewish Eschatology, Early Christian Christology and the Testaments of the Twelve Patriarchs*. NovTSup 63. Leiden: Brill, 1991.

———. "Jewish Expectations about the 'Messiah' according to the Fourth Gospel." *NTS* 19 (1975) 246–70.

———. "The Main Issues in the Study of the Testaments of the Twelve Patriarchs." *NTS* 26 (1980) 508–24.

———. "The Radical Eschatology of the Fourth Gospel and the Eschatology of the Synoptics." In *John and the Synoptics*, edited by Adelbert Denaux, 481–87. BETL. Leuven: Peeters, 1992.

———. "The Use of the Word *Kristos* in the Johannine Epistles." In *Studies in John*, edited by J. N. Severnster, 65–74. NovTSup 24. Leiden: E. J. Brill, 1970.

Deissmann, Adolf. *Light from the Ancient East*. Translated by Lionel R. M. Strachan. London: Hodder and Stoughton, 1910.

Dodd, C. H. "Behind a Johannine Dialogue." In *More New Testament Studies*, edited by C. H. Dodd, 41–57. Manchester: Manchester University Press, 1968.

———. *The Founder of Christianity*. London: Collins, 1971.

———. *Historical Tradition in the Fourth Gospel*. Cambridge: Cambridge University Press, 1963.

———. *The Interpretation of the Fourth Gospel*. Cambridge: Cambridge University Press, 1953.

Donaldson, Laura E., and R. S. Sugirtharajah. *Postcolonialism and Scriptural Readings*. Semeia 75. Atlanta: Scholars, 1996.

Droge, A. J. "Apologetics, NT." In *ABD* 1:302–7.

Dube, Musa W. "Reading for Decolonization (John 4.1–42)." In *John and Postcolonialsim: Travel, Space and Power*, edited by Musa W. Dube and Jeffrey L. Staley, 51–75. London: Sheffield Academic, 2002.

———. "Savior of the World But Not of This World: A Post-Colonial Reading of Spatial Construction in John." In *The Postcolonial Bible*, edited by R. S. Sugirtharajah, 118–35. Sheffield: Sheffield Academic, 1998.

Dube, Musa W., and Jeffrey L. Staley, eds. *John and Postcolonialism: Travel, Space and Power*. London: Sheffield Academic, 2002.

Duke, Paul D. *Irony in the Fourth Gospel*. Atlanta: John Knox, 1985.

Dunn, James D. G. "The Embarrassment of History: Reflections on the Problem of 'Anti-Judaism' in the Fourth Gospel." In *Anti-Judaism and the Fourth Gospel*, edited by D. Phllefeyt, R. Bieringer, and F. Vandecasteele-Vanneuville, 41–60. Louisville, KY: Westminster John Knox, 2001.

Eagleton, Terry. *Literary Theory*. 2nd ed. Oxford: Blackwell, 1996.

Eco, Umberto. *The Role of the Reader: Explorations in the Semiotics of Texts*. London: Hutchinson, 1981.

Edwards, D. "Tyre." In *ABD* 6:686–92.

Edwards, R. B. "Hellenism." In *DJG*, 317–17.

———. "Rome." In *DJG*, 710–15.

Ehrenberg, Victor, and A. H. M. Jones. *Documents Illustrating the Reigns of Augustus and Tiberius*. 2nd ed. Oxford: Clarendon, 1955.

Elliott, J. H. "Jesus the Israelite was Neither a 'Jew' nor a 'Christian': On Correcting Misleading Nomenclature." *Journal for the Study of the Historical Jesus* 5.2 (2007) 119–54.

Engberg-Pedersen, Troels. "Introduction: Paul Beyond the Judaism/ Hellenism Divide." In *Paul Beyond the Judaism/Hellenism Divide*, edited by Troels Engberg-Pedersen, 1–16. Louisville, KY: Westminster John Knox, 2001.

Esler, Philip F. *Community and Gospel in Luke-Acts: The Social and Political Motivations of Lucan Theology*. Cambridge: Cambridge University Press, 1987.

———. "Jesus and the Reduction of Intergroup Conflict." In *The Social Setting of Jesus and the Gospels*, edited by Bruce J. Malina, Wolfgang Stegemann, and Gerd Theissen, 185–205. Minneapolis, MN: Fortress, 2002.

Evans, C. A. *Mark 8:27—16:20*. WBC. Nashville: Thomas Nelson, 2001.

———. "Messianism." In *DNTB*, 698–707.

Evans, Craig A., and William Richard Stegner. *The Gospels and the Scriptures of Israel*. JSNTSup 104. Sheffield: Sheffield Academic, 1994.

Faierstein, Morris M. "Why Do the Scribes Say That Elijah Must Come First?" *JBL* 100 (1981) 75–86.

Fanon, Frantz. *The Wretched of the Earth*. Translated by Constance Farrington. London: Penguin, 1967.

Fantin, Joseph D. "The Lord of the Entire World: *Lord Jesus*, a Challenge to *Lord Caesar*?" PhD diss., University of Sheffield, 2007.

Fee, G. N. "On the Text and Meaning of John 20:30–31." In *The Four Gospels*, edited by F. van Segbroeck, C. M. Tuckett, Belle G. Van, and J. Verheyden, 193–206. BETL 100. Leuven: Leuven University Press, 1992.

Ferguson, Everett. *Backgrounds of Early Christianity*. 3rd ed. Grand Rapids, MI: William B. Eerdmans, 2003.

Fiensy, David A. *The Social History of Palestine in the Herodian Period: The Land Is Mine*. Studies in the Bible and Early Christianity 20. Lewiston: Edwin Mellen, 1991.

Fiorenza, E. S. *Jesus and the Politics of Interpretation*. London: Continuum, 2000.

———. "Miracles, Mission and Apologetics: An Introduction." In *Aspects of Religious Propaganda in Judaism and Early Christianity*, edited by E. S. Fiorenza, 1–25. Notre Dame: Notre Dame University Press, 1976.

Fitzmyer, Joseph A. "The Contribution of Qumran Aramaic to the Study of the New Testament." *NTS* 20 (1974) 382–407.

———. *The One Who Is to Come*. Grand Rapids, MI: William B. Eerdmans, 2007.

Ford, Josephine Massyngberde. "Jesus as Sovereign in the Passion according to John." *BIB* 25 (1995) 110–17.

Fortna, Robert T. *The Fourth Gospel and Its Predecessor: From Narrative Source to Present Gospel*. Edinburgh: T&T Clark, 1989.

———. *The Gospel of Signs: A Reconstruction of the Narrative Source Underlying the Fourth Gospel*. SNTSMS 11. London: Cambridge University Press, 1970.

———. "Theological Use of Locale in the Fourth Gospel." In *Gospel Studies in Honor of Sherman Elbridge Johnson*, edited by Massey H. Shepherd Jr. and Edward C. Hobbs, 58–95. AThRSup 3. London: Anglican Theological Review, 1974.

Fox, Robin Lane. *Pagans and Christians*. New York: Knopf, 1987.

Fredriksen, Paula. *Jesus of Nazareth, the King of the Jews: A Jewish Life and the Emergence of Christianity*. London: McMillan, 2000.

Freed, Edwin D. "Did John Write His Gospel Partly to Win Samaritan Converts?" *NovT* 12 (1970) 241–56.

———. "The Entry Into Jerusalem in the Gospel of John." *JBL* 80 (1961) 329–38.

———. *Old Testament Quotations in the Gospel of John*. Leiden: Brill, 1965.

———. "Samaritan Influence in the Gospel of John." *CBQ* 30 (1968) 580–87.

———. "The Son of Man in the Fourth Gospel." *JBL* 86 (1967) 402–6.

Frend, W. H. C. *Martyrdom and Persecution in the Early Church*. Grand Rapids, MI: Baker, 1981.

———. *The Rise of Christianity*. London: Darton, Longman and Todd, 1984.

Friesen, Steven J. *Imperial Cults and the Apocalypse of John: Reading Revelation in the Ruins*. Oxford: Oxford University Press, 2001.

Fuglseth, Kare Sigvald. *Johannine Sectarianism in Perspective: A Sociological, Historical, and Comparative Analysis of Temple and Social Relationships in the Gospel of John, Philo, and Qumran*. NovTSup 119. Leiden: Brill, 2005.

Gandhi, Leela. *Postcolonial Theory: A Critical Introduction*. Edinburgh: Edinburgh University Press, 1998.

Geisler, N. L. "Johannine Apologetics." *BSac* 136 (1979) 333–43.

Georgi, Dieter. "Who Is the True Prophet?" In *Paul and Empire*, edited by Richard A. Horsley, 36–46. Harrisburg, PA: Trinity Press International, 1997.

Glasson, T. Francis. *Moses in the Fourth Gospel*. London: SCM, 1963.

Goodenough, Erwin Ramsdell, and Jacob Neusner. *Religions in Antiquity: Essays in Memory of Erwin Ramsdell Goodenough*. SHR 14. Leiden: E. J. Brill, 1968.

Goodman, Martin. "The First Jewish Revolt: Social Conflict and the Problem of Debt." *JJS* 22 (1982) 417–27.

———. *The Roman World 44 BC to AD 180*. London: Routledge, 1997.

———. *The Ruling Class of Judea: The Origins of the Jewish Revolt against Rome A.D. 66–70*. Cambridge: Cambridge University Press, 1987.

Goulder, Michael D. "Nicodemus." *SJT* 44 (1991) 153–68.

———. "Psalm 8 and the Son of Man." *NTS* 48 (2002) 18–29.

Grabbe, Lester. "The Terminology of Government in the Septuagint—in Comparison with Hebrew, Aramaic, and Other Languages." In *Jewish Perspectives on Hellenistic Rulers*, edited by Tessa Rajack et al., 225-37. Los Angeles: University of California Press, 2008.
Grant, F. C. *The Economic Background of the Gospel*. Oxford: Oxford University Press, 1926.
Green, W. S., J. Neusner, and E. S. Frerichs, eds. *Judaism and Their Messiahs at the Turn of the Christian Era*. Cambridge: Cambridge University Press, 1987.
Griffin, Miriam. "*Urbs Roma, Plebs* and *Princeps*." In *Images of Empire*, edited by Loveday Alexander, 19-48. JSOTSup 122. Sheffield: Sheffield Academic, 1991.
Grundmann, W. "The Decision of the Supreme Court to put Jesus to Death (John 11:47-57) in Its Context: Tradition and Redaction in the Gospel of John." In *Jesus and the Politics of His Day*, edited by C. F. D. Moule and E. Bammel, 295-318. Cambridge: Cambridge University Press, 1988.
Gundry, Robert H. "'In My Father's House Are Many Monai (John 14,2)." *ZNW* 58 (1967) 68-72.
Gunther, J. J. "The Alexandrian Gospel and the Letters of John." *CBQ* 41 (1979) 581-603.
Halliday, Michael A. K. "Anti-languages." *American Anthropologist* 78 (1976) 570-84.
———. *Language as Social Semiotic: The Social Interpretation of Language and Meaning*. Baltimore, MD: University Park, 1978.
Hamel, G. *Poverty and Charity in Roman Palestine, First Three Centuries C.E.* Berkeley: University of California Press, 1990.
Hanson, A. T. *Prophetic Gospel: A Study in John and the Old Testament*. Edinburgh: T&T Clark, 1991.
Harris, W. *Ancient Literacy*. Cambridge: Harvard University Press, 1989.
Haynes, Stephen R., and Steven L. McKenzie, eds. *To Each Its Own Meaning*. Rev. and exp. ed. Louisville, KY: Westminster John Knox, 1999.
Hengel, Martin. *The Johannine Question*. London: SCM, 1989.
———. *Judaism and Hellenism: Studies in Their Encounter in Palestine During the Early Hellenistic Period*. Translated by John Bowden. London: SCM, 1974.
———. *The Son of God: The Origin of Christology and the History of Jewish-Hellenistic Religion*. Translated by John Bowden. London: SCM, 1976.
Hengel, Martin, and John Riches. *The Charismatic Leader and His Followers*. Edinburgh: T&T Clark, 1981.
Higgins, A. J. B. *Jesus and the Son of Man*. London: Lutterworth, 1964.
Hill, David. *New Testament Prophecy*. Atlanta: John Knox, 1975.
Holladay, Carl R. *Theios Aner in Hellenistic Judaism: A Critique of the Use of This Category in New Testament Christology*. Missoula, MT: Scholars, 1977.
Horbury, William. *Jewish Messianism and the Cult of Christ*. London: SCM, 1998.
———. "Messianism in the Old Testament Apocrypha and Pseudepigrapha." In *King and Messiah in Israel and the Ancient Near East*, edited by John Day, 402-33. JSOTSup 270. Sheffield: Sheffield Academic, 1998.
Horsley, Richard. *Bandits, Prophets, and Messiahs: Popular Movements at the Time of Jesus*. San Francisco: Harper & Row, 1985.
———. "Introduction." In *Paul and Empire: Religion and Power in Roman Imperial Society*, edited by Richard A. Horsley, 10-24. Harrisburg, PA: Trinity Press International, 1997.

———. "Jesus and Empire." In *In the Shadow of the Empire*, edited by R. A. Horsley, 75–96. Louisville, KY: Westminster and John Knox, 2008.

———. *Jesus and Empire: The Kingdom of God and the New World Disorder*. Minneapolis, MN: Fortress, 2003.

———. *Jesus and the Spiral of Violence: Popular Jewish Resistance in Roman Palestine*. San Francisco: Harper & Row, 1987.

———. "Popular Messianic Movements around the Time of Jesus." *CBQ* 46 (1984) 471–95.

———, ed. *Paul and Empire: Religion and Power in Roman Imperial Society*. Harrisburg, PA: Trinity Press International, 1997.

Hoskins, Paul M. *Jesus as the Fulfilment of the Temple in the Gospel of John*. Eugene, OR: Wipf & Stock, 2007.

Hoskyns, Edwyn. *The Fourth Gospel*. 2nd rev. ed. London: Faber & Faber, 1947.

Hurtado, L. W. "Christ." In *DJG*, 106–17.

———. "Gospel (Genre)." In *DJG*, 276–82.

Jeremias, J. *Jerusalem in the Time of Jesus*. Translated by F. Cave and C. Cave. London: SCM, 1969.

Johnson, D. H. "Shepherd, Sheep." In *DJG*, 751–54.

Johnson, Sherman E. "The Davidic-Royal Motif in the Gospels." *JBL* 87 (1968) 136–50.

———. "Early Christianity in Asia Minor." *JBL* 77 (1958) 1–17.

Jones, Donald L. "Christianity and the Roman Imperial Cult." In *ANRW II. 23, 2*, edited by H. Temporini-W. Haase, 1023–54. Berlin: W. de Gruyter, 1980.

Kang, Wi Jo. "Church and State Relations in the Japanese Colonial Period." In *Christianity in Korea*, edited by Robert E. Buswell Jr. and Timothy S. Lee, 97–115. Honolulu: University of Hawaii Press, 2006.

Karris, Robert J. *Jesus and the Marginalized in John's Gospel*. Collegeville, MN: Liturgical, 1990.

Kaylor, David R. *Jesus the Prophet: His Vision of the Kingdom on Earth*. Louisville, KY: Westminster John Knox, 1994.

Keener, Craig S. *The Gospel of John*. 2 vols. Peabody, MA: Hendrickson, 2003.

———. "Shepperd, Flock." In *DNLT*, 1090–93.

Kerr, Alan. *The Temple of Jesus' Body: The Temple Theme in the Gospel of John*. JSNTSup 220. Sheffield: Sheffield Academic, 2002.

Kim, Yun, and Eui Hang Shin, eds. *Korea and the World: Strategies for Globalization*. Columbia: Center for Asian Studies at the University of South Carolina, 1995.

Kim, Gye-Dong. *Foreign Intervention in Korea*. Aldershot: Dartmouth, 1993.

Kim, Hyung-Kook. *The Division of Korea and the Alliance Making Process*. New York: University Press of America, 1995.

Kim, Sehyun. "Jesus as 'Good Man' in the Gospel of John." *Scripture and Interpretation* 3 (2009) 79–94.

Kim, Se Yoon. *The "Son of Man" as the Son of God*. WUNT 30. Tübingen: J. C. B. Mohr, 1983.

Kim, Tae Hun. "The Anarthrous υἱός θεοῦ in Mark 15.39." *Biblica* 79 (1998) 221–41.

Kim, Wonil. "Minjung Theology's Biblical Hermeneutics: An Examination of Minjung Theology's Appropriation of the Exodus Account." In *Christianity in Korea*, edited by Robert E. Buswell Jr. and Timothy S. Lee, 221–37. Honolulu: University of Hawaii Press, 2006.

Kimelman, Reuven. "Birkat Ha-Minim and the Lack of Evidence for an Anti-Christian Jewish Prayer in Late Antiquity." In *Jewish and Christian Self-Definition: Aspects of Judaism in the Graeco-Roman Period*. Vol. 2. Edited by A. I. Baumgarten, E. P. Sanders, and Alan Mendelson, 232–44. London: SCM, 1981.

Kinman, Brent. *Jesus' Entry Into Jerusalem*. Leiden: Brill, 1995.

Klappert, B. "King, Kingdom." In *NITDNT* 2:372–90.

Klausner, Joseph. *The Messianic Idea in Israel: From Its Beginning to the Completion of the Mishnah*. Translated by W. F. Stinespring. London: Allen & Unwin, 1956.

Kleinknecht. "βασιλεύς." In *TDNT* 1:564–65.

Klink, E. W., III. *The Sheep of the Fold: The Audience and Origin of the Gospel of John*. Cambridge: Cambridge University Press, 2007.

Koenig, J. *Jews and Christians in Dialogue: New Testament Foundations*. Philadelphia: Fortress, 1979.

Koester, Craig R. "Messianic Exegesis and the Call of Nathanael (John 1.45–51)." *JSNT* 39 (1990) 23–34.

———. "The Savior of the World (John 4:42)." *JBL* 109/4 (1990) 665–80.

———. "The Spectrum of Johannine Readers." In *What Is John?: Readers and Readings of the Fourth Gospel*, edited by Fernando F. Segovia, 5–20. Atlanta: Scholars, 1996.

———. *Symbolism in the Gospel of John: Meaning, Mystery, Community*. 2nd ed. Minneapolis, MN: Fortress, 2003.

Koester, Helmut. *History, Culture, and Religion of the Hellenistic Age*. 2 vols. Philadelphia: Fortress, 1982.

Köstenberger, Andreas J. "Jesus the Good Shepherd Who Will Also Bring Other Sheep (John 10:16): The Old Testament Background of a Familiar Metaphor." *BBR* 12.1 (2002) 67–96.

Kovacs, Judith L. "'Now Shall the Ruler of This World Be Driven Out': Jesus' Death as Cosmic Battle in John 12:20–36." *JBL* 114.2 (1995) 227–47.

Kümmel, Werner G. *Introduction to the New Testament*. Translated by Howard Clark Kee. Rev. ed. London: SCM, 1975.

Kuhn, K. G. "βασιλεύς." In *TDNT* 1:571–74.

———. "Ἰσραήλ." In *TDNT* 3:359–69.

Kvalbein, Hans. "The Kingdom of God and the Kingship of Christ in the Fourth Gospel." In *Neotestamentica et Philonica*, edited by David Edward Aune, Torrey Seland, and Jarl Henning Ulrichsen, 215–32. Leiden: E. J. Brill, 2002.

Kysar, Robert. "Community and Gospel: Vectors in the Fourth Gospel Criticism." *Int* 31 (1977) 355–66.

———. *The Fourth Evangelist and His Gospel: An Examination of Contemporary Scholarship*. Minneapolis, MN: Augsburg, 1975.

———. "Johannine Metaphor-Meaning and Function: A Literary Case Study of John 10:1–18." In *The Fourth Gospel from a Literary Perspective*, edited by R. Alan Culpepper and Fernando F. Segovia, 81–111. Semeia 53. Atlanta: Scholars, 1991.

———. *John, the Maverick Gospel*. Atlanta: John Knox, 1976.

Ladd, G. E. *A Theology of the New Testament*. Grand Rapids, MI: Williams B. Eerdmans, 1974.

Lagrange, M. J. *Evangile selon Saint Jean*. 2nd ed. Paris: Gabalda, 1984.

Lambert, W. G. "Kingship in Ancient Mesopotamia." In *King and Messiah in Israel and the Ancient Near East*, edited by John Day, 54–71. JSOTSup 270. Sheffield: Sheffield Academic, 1999.

Leaney, A. R. C. "John and Qumran." *Studia Evangelica* VI (1973) 296–310.
Lee, Manyeol, ed. *An English Sourcebook of Shinto Shrine Problem II: A Volume of Board of Foreign Mission of the Presbyterian Church in the U. S. A.* Seoul: Institute of Korean Christianity History, 2004.
Levin, Yigal. "Jesus, 'Son of God' and 'Son of David': The 'Adoption' of Jesus into the Davidic Line." *JSNT* 28.4 (2006) 415–42.
Lierman, John. "The Mosaic Pattern of John's Christology." In *Challenging Perspectives on the Gospel of John*, edited by John Lierman, 210–34. Tübingen: Mohr Siebeck, 2006.
Lincoln, Andrew T. *The Gospel According to Saint John*. BNTC 4. London: Continuum, 2005.
———. *Truth on Trial: The Lawsuit Motif in the Fourth Gospel*. Peabody, MA: Hendrickson, 2000.
Lindars, Barnabas. *The Gospel of John*. Rep. ed. NCBC. Grand Rapids, MI: Williams B. Eerdmans, 1995.
———. *Jesus Son of Man: A Fresh Examination of the Son of Man Sayings in the Gospels in the Light of Recent Research*. London: SPCK, 1983.
———. *New Testament Apologetic: The Doctrinal Significance of the Old Testament Quotations*. London: SCM, 1961.
———. "Son of Man." In *A Dictionary of Biblical Interpretation*, edited by R. J. Coggins and J. L. Houlden, 639–42. London: SCM, 1990.
———. "The Son of Man in the Johannine Christology." In *Christ and Spirit in the New Testament*, edited by B. Lindars and S. S. Smalley, 43–60. Cambridge: Cambridge University Press, 1973.
Ling, Timothy J. M. *The Judaean Poor and the Fourth Gospel*. Edited by John Court. SNTSMS 136. Cambridge: Cambridge University Press, 2006.
Longman, Tremper, III. "Fictional Akkadian Royal Autobiography: A Generic and Comparative Approach." PhD diss., Yale University, 1983.
Loomba, Ania. *Colonialism/Postcolonialism*. London: Routledge, 1998.
Louw, Johannes P., and Eugene A. Nida, eds. *Greek-English Lexicon of the New Testament Based on Semantic Domains*. 2 vols. New York: United Bible Societies, 1988.
Lowe, Malcolm. "Who Were the ΙΟΥΔΑΙΟΙ?" *NovT* 18 (1976) 101–30.
MacDonald, Donald Stone. *The Koreans: Contemporary Politics and Society*. Boulder, CO: Westview, 1988.
MacDonald, John. *The Theology of the Samaritans*. New Testament Library. London: SCM, 1964.
MacRae, G. W. "The Fourth Gospel and *Religionsgeschichte*." *CBQ* 32 (1970) 13–24.
Maddox, R. "The Function of the Son of Man in the Gospel of John." In *Reconciliation and Hope: New Testament Essays on Atonement and Eschatology presented to L. L. Morris on His 60th Birthday*, edited by R. J. Banks, 186–204. Exeter: Paternoster, 1974.
Malina, Bruce J. *Christian Origins and Cultural Anthropology: Practical Models for Biblical Interpretation*. Atlanta: John Knox, 1986.
Malina, Bruce J., and Richard L. Rohrbaugh. *Social-Science Commentary on the Gospel of John*. Minneapolis, MN: Fortress, 1998.
Manning, Gary T., Jr. *Echoes of a Prophet: The Use of Ezekiel in the Gospel of John in Literature of the Second Temple Period*. JSNTSup 270. London: T&T Clark International, 2004.

Marcus, Joel. "Entering Into the Kingly Power of God." *JBL* (1988) 663–75.
Martyn, J. L. *The Gospel of John in Christian History*. New York: Paulist, 1978.
———. *History and Theology in the Fourth Gospel*. 3rd ed. Louisville, KY: Westminster John Knox, 2003.
Mason, Rex. "The Messiah in the Postexilic Old Testament Literature." In *King and Messiah in Israel and the Ancient Near East*, edited by John Day, 338–64. JSOTSup 270. Sheffield: Sheffield Academic, 1998.
Mattingly, D. J., ed. *Dialogues in Roman Imperialism: Power, Discourse, and Discrepant Experience in the Roman Empire*. Portsmouth: JRA, 1997.
Mbembe, Achille. "The Intimacy of Tyranny." In *The Post-Colonial Studies Reader*, edited by Gareth Griffiths, Bill Ashcroft, and Helen Tiffin, 66–69. London: Routledge, 2006.
McCaffrey, James. *The House with Many Rooms: The Temple Theme of Jn. 14,2–3*. Roma: Editrice Pontificio Instituto Biblico, 1988.
McCrum, M., and A. G. Woodhead, eds. *Select Documents of the Principates of the Flavian Emperors Including the Year of Revolution A.D. 68–96*. Cambridge: Cambridge University Press, 1966.
McCune, George M. *Korea Today*. Westport, CT: Greenwood, 1950.
McDonald, John. *The Theology of the Samaritans*. London: SCM, 1964.
McGrath, James F. *John's Apologetic Christology: Legitimation and Development in Johannine Christology*. SNTSMS 111. Cambridge: Cambridge University Press, 2001.
Mckenzie, F. A. *Korea's Fight for Freedom*. 2nd ed. Seoul: Yonsei University Press, 1969.
McKnight, Edgar V. "Reader-Response Criticism." In *To Each Its Own Meaning*, edited by Steven L. Mckenzie and Stephen R. Haynes, 230–52. Louisville, KY: Westminster John Knox, 1999.
Mead, A. H. "The *Basilikos* in John 4:46–53." *JSNT* 23 (1985) 67–72.
Meeks, Wayne A. "'Am I a Jew?' Johannine Christianity and Judaism." In *Studies in Judaism in Late Antiquity 12: Christianity, Judaism and Other Greco-Roman Cults, Part I. Studies for Morton Smith at Sixty*, edited by Jacob Neusner, 163–86. Leiden: Brill, 1975.
———. "The Divine Agent and His Counterfeit in Philo and the Fourth Gospel." In *Aspects of Religious Propaganda in Judaism and Early Christianity*, edited by E. S. Fiorenza, 43–67. Notre Dame: University of Notre Dame Press, 1976.
———. "Galilee and Judea in the Fourth Gospel." *JBL* 85, 2 (1966) 159–69.
———. "The Man from Heaven in the Johannine Sectarianism." *JBL* 91 (1972) 44–72.
———. *The Prophet-King: Moses Traditions and the Johannine Christology*. NovTSup 14. Leiden: E. J. Brill, 1967.
Memmi, Albert. *The Colonizer and the Colonized*. Translated by Howard Greenfield. London: Souvenir, 1965.
Metzger, Bruce M. "Recently Published Greek Papyri of the NT." *BA* 10 (1947) 25–44.
———. *A Textual Commentary on the Greek New Testament*. Corrected ed. Stuttgart: United Bible Societies, 1975.
Millar, Fergus. *The Roman Near East, 31 BC–AD 337*. Cambridge: Harvard University Press, 1993.
Millar, Fergus, and Erich Segal, eds. *Caesar Augustus: Seven Aspects*. Oxford: Clarendon, 1984.

Moloney, F. J. *Belief in the Word: Reading the Fourth Gospel, John 1–4*. Minneapolis, MN: Fortress, 1993.

———. *Glory not Dishonor: Reading John 13–21*. Minneapolis, MN: Fortress, 1998.

———. *The Johannine Son of Man*. 2nd ed. Rome: Las-Roma, 1978.

Moore, G. F. *Judaism in the First Centuries of the Christian Era: The Age of the Tannaism*. 3 vols. Cambridge: Harvard University Press, 1927–30.

Moore, Stephen. *Empire and Apocalypse: Postcolonialism and the New Testament*. Sheffield: Sheffield Phoenix, 2006.

Moore-Gilbert, Bart. *Postcolonial Theory: Contexts, Practices, Politics*. London: Verso, 1997.

Moore, Hamilton, and Philip McCormick. "Domitian (Part i)." *IBS* 25 (2003) 74–101.

———. "Domitian (Part ii)." *IBS* 25 (2003) 121–45.

Morris, Leon. *The Gospel according to John*. Rev. ed. NICNT. Grand Rapids, MI: William B. Eerdmans, 1995.

Motyer, Steve. "Method in Fourth Gospel Studies: A Way Out of the Impasse?" *JSNT* 66 (1997) 27–44.

———. *Your Father the Devil?: A New Approach to John and "the Jews"*. Carlisle: Paternoster, 1997.

Moule, C. F. D. *The Birth of the New Testament*. 3rd rev. ed. BNTC. London: Adam and Charles Black, 1981.

Mowery, Robert L. "Son of God in Roman Imperial Titles and Matthew." *Bib* 83 (2002) 100–110.

Murray, G. R. B. *John*. 2nd ed. WBC. Nashville: Thomas Nelson, 1999.

Na, Young-Wha. *A Criticism of Radical Theology*. Seoul: Christian Literature Crusade, 1984.

Na'aman, N. "Death Formulae and the Burial Place of the Kings of the House of David." *Biblica* 85 (2004) 245–54.

Neusner, Jacob, William S. Green, and Ernest Frerichs, eds. *Judaisms and Their Messiahs at the Turn of the Christian Era*. Cambridge: Cambridge University Press, 1987.

Neyrey, Jerome H. "God, Benefactor and Patron: The Major Cultural Model for Interpreting the Deity in Greco-Roman Antiquity." *JSNT* 27 (2005) 465–92.

———. *An Ideology of Revolt: John's Christology in Social-Science Perspective*. Philadelphia: Fortress, 1988.

———. "The Jacob Allusions in John 1:51." *CBQ* 44 (1982) 586–605.

———. "Spaces and Places, Whence and Whither, Homes and Rooms: 'Territoriality' in the Fourth Gospel." *BTB* (2002) 60–74.

Nicholson, Godfrey C. *Death as Departure: The Johannine Descent-Ascent Schema*. SBLDS 63. Chico, CA: Scholars, 1983.

Nickelsburg, G. W. E. *Ancient Judaism and Christian Origins: Diversity, Continuity, and Transformation*. Minneapolis, MN: Fortress, 2003.

———. "Salvation Without and With a Messiah: Developing Beliefs in Writings Ascribed to Enoch." In *Judaisms and Their Messiahs at the Turn of the Christian Era*, edited by William S. Green, Jacob Neusner, and Ernest Frerichs, 58–64. Cambridge: Cambridge University Press, 1987.

Nicol, W. *The Semeia in the Fourth Gospel: Tradition and Redaction*. NovTSup 32. Leiden: Brill, 1972.

Nielsen, K. *There Is Hope for a Tree: The Tree as Metaphor in Isaiah*. Translated by C. Crowley and F. Crowley. Sheffield: Continuum International, 1989.

Nissen, Johannes. "Community and Ethics in the Gospel of John." In *New Readings in John: Literary and Theological Perspectives*, edited by Johannes Nissen and Sigfred Pedersen, 194–212. JSNTSup 182. Sheffield: Sheffield Academic, 1999.

———. "Mission in the Fourth Gospel: Historical and Hermeneutical Perspectives." In *New Readings in John: Literary and Theological Perspectives*, edited by Johannes Nissen and Sigfred Pedersen, 213–31. JSNTSup 182. Sheffield: Sheffield Academic, 1999.

Nissen, Johannes, and Sigfred Pedersen, eds. *New Readings in John: Literary and Theological Perspectives*. JSNTSup 182. Sheffield: Sheffield Academic, 1999.

North, Wendy E. Sproston. *The Lazarus Story within the Johannine Tradition*. JSNTSup 212. Sheffield: Sheffield Academic, 2001.

Novak, Ralph Martin, Jr. *Christianity and the Roman Empire: Background Texts*. Harrisburg, PA: Trinity Press International, 2001.

Odeberg, Hugo. *The Fourth Gospel: Interpreted in Its Relation to Contemporaneous Religious Currents in Palestine and the Hellenistic-Oriental World*. Amsterdam: Grüner, 1974.

Ohler, Markus. "The Expectation of Elijah and the Presence of the Kingdom of God." *JBL* 118 (1999) 461–76.

Okure, Teresa. *The Johannine Approach to Mission: A Contextual Study of John 4:1–42*. WUNT 2. Reihe 31. Tübingen: Mohr, 1988.

Olsson, Birger. *Structure and Meaning in the Fourth Gospel: A Textual-Linguistic Analysis of John 2:1–11 and 4:1–42*. Translated by Jean Gray. Lund, Sweden: CWK Gleerup, 1974.

O'Neill, J. C. "The Kingdom of God." *NovT* 34 (1993) 130–41.

Orchard, Helen Claire. *Courting Betrayal: Jesus as Victim in the Gospel of John*. JSNTSup 161. Sheffield: Sheffield Academic, 1998.

Osborne, Grant R. *The Hermeneutical Spiral: A Comprehensive Introduction to Biblical Interpretation*. Downers Grove, IL: InterVarsity, 1991.

Painter, John. "The Farewell Discourses and the History of the Johannine Christianity." *NTS* 27 (1981) 525–43.

———. "The Point of John's Christology: Christology, Conflict and Community." In *Christology, Controversy and Community: New Testament Essays in Honour of David R. Catchpole*, edited by David G. Horrell and Christopher M. Tuckett, 231–52. NovTSup 99. Leiden: Brill, 2000.

———. *The Quest for the Messiah: The History, Literature, and Theology of the Johannine Community*. 2nd ed. Edinburgh: T&T Clark, 1993.

Pak, Ung Kyu. *Millenialism in the Korean Protestant Church*. New York: PeterLang, 2005.

Pancaro, Severino. "'People of God' in St. John's Gospel." *NTS* 16 (1969–70) 114–29.

Park, Chung-Shin. *Protestantism and Politics in Korea*. Seattle: University of Washington Press, 2003.

Perkins, P. *The Love Commands in the New Testament*. New York: Paulist, 1982.

Perrin, N. *The Kingdom of God in the Teaching of Jesus*. Philadelphia: Westminster, 1963.

Peterson, N. R. *The Gospel of John and Sociology of Light*. Valley Forge, PA: Trinity Press International, 1993.

Pomykala, K. E. *The Davidic Dynasty Tradition in Early Judaism: Hits History and Significance for Messianism*. Atlanta: Scholars, 1995.

Pratt, M. L. *Imperial Eyes: Travel Writing and Transculturation*. London: Routledge, 1992.
Price, S. R. F. "Rituals and Power." In *Paul and Empire: Religion and Power in Roman Imperial Society*, edited by Richard R. Horsley, 47–71. Harrisburg, PA: Trinity Press International, 1997.
———. *Rituals and Power: The Roman Imperial Cult in Asia Minor*. Cambridge: Cambridge University Press, 1984.
Pryor, John W. "Jesus and Israel in the Fourth Gospel: John 1:11." *NovT* 32 (1990) 201–18.
———. *John: Evangelist of the Covenant People*. Downers Grove, IL: InterVarsity, 1992.
Purvis, James D. "The Fourth Gospel and the Samaritans." *NovT* 17 (1975) 161–98.
Rajak, Tessa. "Introduction." In *Jewish Perspectives on Hellenistic Rulers*, edited by Sarah Pearce, Tessa Rajak, James Aitken, and Jennifer Dines, 1–9. Berkeley: University of California Press, 2007.
———. *Josephus: The Historian and His Society*. London: Duckworth, 1983.
Rajak, Tessa, et al., eds. *Jewish Perspectives on Hellenistic Rulers*. Berkeley: University of California Press, 2007.
Reasonor, M. "Emperor, Emperor Cult." In *DLNT*, 321–26.
Reim, Gunter. "Jesus as God in the Fourth Gospel: The Old Testament Background." *NTS* 30 (1984) 158–60.
Reimund Bieringer, D. Pollefeyt, and F. Vandecasteele-Vaneuville. "Wrestling with Johannine Anti-Judaism: A Hermeneutical Framework for the Analysis of the Current Debate." In *Anti-Judaism and the Fourth Gospel*, edited by D. Pollefeyt R. Bieringer, and F. Vandecasteele-Vaneuville, 3–40. Louisville, KY: Westminster John Knox, 2001.
Reinhartz, Adele. "The Colonizer as Colonized." In *John and Postcolonialism: Travel, Space and Power*, edited by Musa M. Dube and Jeffrey L. Staley, 170–92. London: Sheffield Academic, 2002.
———. "'Jews' and Jews in the Fourth Gospel." In *Anti-Judaism and the Fourth Gospel*, edited by D. Pollefeyt R. Bieringer, and F. Vandecasteele-Vaneuville, 213–30. Louisville, KY: Westminster John Knox, 2001.
———. "The Johannine Community and Its Jewish Neighbors: A Reappraisal." In *What Is John? Literary and Social Readings in the Fourth Gospel*, edited by F. F. Segovia, 111–38. SBLSymS 7. Atlanta: Scholars, 1998.
———. *The Word in the World: The Cosmological Tale in the Fourth Gospel*. Atlanta: Scholars, 1992.
Rensberger, David. *Johannine Faith and Liberating Community*. Philadelphia: Westminster, 1988.
Ricoeur, Paul. *Interpretation Theory: Discourse and the Surplus of Meaning*. Fort Worth: Texas Christian University Press, 1976.
Ridderbos, Herman N. *The Gospel according to John*. Translated by John Vriend. Grand Rapids, MI: William B. Eerdmans, 1997.
Roberts, J. J. M. "The Old Testament's Contribution to Messianic Expectations." In *The Messiah: Developments in Earliest Judaism and Christianity*, edited by J. H. Charlesworth, 39–51. Minneapolis, MN: Fortress, 1993.
Robey, David, and Ann Jefferson, eds. *Modern Literary Theory: A Comparative Introduction*. London: Batsford, 1986.

Robinson, J. A. T. "The Destination and Purpose of St. John's Gospel." *NTS* 6 (1959–60) 117–31.
———. "Elijah, John and Jesus: An Essay in Detection." *NTS* 4 (1957–58) 263–81.
———. *The Priority of John*. London: SCM, 1985.
———. *Redating the New Testament*. London: SCM, 1976.
Roloff, Jürgen. *The Revelation of John*. CC. Minneapolis, MN: Fortress, 1993.
Rowland, Christopher. "Christ in the New Testament." In *King and Messiah in Israel and the Ancient Near East*, edited by John Day, 474–96. JSOTSup 270. Sheffield: Sheffield University Press, 1998.
———. "John 1:51, Jewish Apocalyptic and Targumic Tradition." *NTS* 30 (1984) 498–507.
Said, E. W. *Culture and Imperialism*. London: Chatto & Windus, 1993.
———. *Orientalism: Western Conceptions of the Orient*. London: Penguin, 1991.
Salier, Bill. "Jesus, the Emperor, and the Gospel According to John." In *Challenging Perspectives on the Gospel of John*, edited by John Lierman, 284–301. Tübingen: Mohr Siebeck, 2006.
Sanders, E. P. *The Historical Figure of Jesus*. London: Penguin, 1993.
Samkutty, V. J. "Samaritan Mission in Acts." PhD diss., University of Sheffield, 2004.
Samuel, Simon. "A Postcolonial Reading of Mark's story of Jesus." PhD diss., University of Sheffield, 2002.
Sanders, E. P. *Judaism: Practice and Belief, 63 B.C.E–66 C.E.* London: SCM, 1992.
Sandmel, Samuel. *Anti-Semitism in the New Testament?* Philadelphia: Fortress, 1978.
Sartre, Jean-Paul. "Preface to The Wretched of the Earth by Frantz Fanon." In *The Wretched of the Earth*, by Frantz Fanon, 7–26. London: Penguin, 1967.
Scherrer, Stephen J. "Signs and Wonders in the Imperial Cult: A New Look at a Roman Religious Institution in the Light of Rev 13:13–15." *JBL* 103 (1984) 599–610.
Schnackenburg, R. *The Gospel according to St. John*. Translated by David Smith and G. A. Kon. 3 vols. Kent: Burns & Oates, 1982.
Schoeps, H. J. *Jewish Christianity*. Philadelphia: Fortress, 1969.
Schmidt, Karl Ludwig. "βασιλεύς, βασιλεία." In *TDNT* 1:564–93.
Schmiz, P. "Sidon." In *ABD* 6:17–18.
Schneider, J. and C. Brown. "σωτήρ." In *NITNTT* 3:216–21.
Schürer, E. *The History of the Jewish people in the Age of Jesus Christ (175 B.C.–A.D. 135)*. Edited by F. Miller, G. Vermes, M. Black, and M. Goodman. Rev. ed. 3 vols. Edinburgh: T&T Clark, 1973–87.
Schweizer, Eduard. "The Son of Man." *JBL* 79 (1960) 119–29.
Scobie, Charles H. H. "The Origins and Development of Samaritan Christianity." *NTS* 19 (1973) 390–414.
Scobie, C. S. "The Use of Source Material in the Speeches of Acts III and VII." *NTS* 25 (1978–79) 339–421.
Scott, K. *The Imperial Cult Under the Flavians*. New York: Arno, 1975.
Segal, Alan F. "Universalism in Judaism and Christianity." In *Paul in His Hellenistic Context*, edited by Troels Engberg-Pedersen, 1–29. Edinburgh: T&T Clark, 1995.
Segovia, F. Fernando. "Biblical Criticism and Postcolonial Studies: Toward a Postcolonial Optic." In *The Postcolonial Bible*, edited by R. S. Sugirtharajah, 49–65. Sheffield: Sheffield Academic, 1998.
———. *Decolonizing Bible Studies: A View from the Margins*. Maryknoll, NY: Orbis, 2000.

---. "The Final Farewell of Jesus: A Reading of John 20:30–21:25." *Semeia* 53 (1991) 167–90.

---. "Interpreting Beyond Borders: Postcolonial Studies and Diasporic Studies in Biblical Criticism." In *Interpreting Beyond Borders*, edited by Fernando F. Segovia, 11–34. Sheffield: Sheffield Academic, 2000.

---. "John 1:1–18 as Entrée into Johannine Reality." In *Word, Theology, and Community in John*, edited by R. Alan Culpepper, John Painter, and F. F. Segovia, 33–64. St. Louis, MO: Chalice, 2002.

---. "The Journey(s) of the Word of God: A Reading of the Plot of the Fourth Gospel." *Semeia* 53 (1991) 23–54.

---. "The Love and Hatred of Jesus and Johannine Sectarianism." *CBQ* 43 (1981) 258–72.

Seldon, Raman, Peter Widdowson, and Peter Brooker, eds. *A Reader's Guide to Contemporary Literary Theory*. 4th ed. London: Prentice Hall, 1997.

Senior, Donald, and Carroll Stuhlmueller. *The Biblical Foundations for Mission*. Maryknoll, NY: Orbis, 1983.

Shepherd, David, and Paul Owen. "Speaking Up for Qumran, Dalman and the Son of Man: Was Bar Enasha a Common Term for 'Man' in the Time of Jesus?" *JSNT* 81 (2001) 81–122.

Sheppard, Beth M. "The Gospel of John: A Roman Legal and Rhetorical Perspective." PhD diss., University of Sheffield, 1999.

Sherk, Robert K. *Roman Documents from the Greek East*. Baltimore, MD: Johns Hopkins University Press, 1969.

Sidebottom, E. M. *The Christ of the Fourth Gospel in the Light of First Century Thought*. London: SPCK, 1961.

Sim, David C. "The Gospels for All Christians? A Response to Richard Bauckham." *JSNT* 84 (2001) 3–27.

Smalley, S. S. "The Johannine Son of Man Saying." *NTS* 15 (1968–9) 278–301.

---. *John: Evangelist and Interpreter*. Exeter: Paternoster, 1978.

Smallwood, E. Mary. *Documents Illustrating the Principates of Gaius Claudius and Nero*. Cambridge: Cambridge University Press, 1967.

---. "Domitian's Attitude toward the Jews and Judaism." *CP* 51 (1959) 1–14.

---. *The Jews Under Roman Rule: From Pompey to Diocletian*. Edited by Jacob Neusner. SJLA 20. Leiden: E. J. Brill, 1976.

Smith, D. Moody. "Johannine Christianity: Some Reflections on Its Character and Delineation." *NTS* 21 (1974–75) 222–48.

---. "The Presentation of Jesus in the Fourth Gospel." *Int* 31 (1977) 367–78.

Smith, D. Moody, R. Alan Culpepper, and C. Clifton Black. *Exploring the Gospel of John: Essays in Honour of D. Moody Smith*. Louisville, KY: Westminster John Knox, 1996.

Smith, Jonathan. *Drudgery Divine: On the Comparison of Early Christianities and the Religions of Late Antiquity*. Chicago: University of Chicago Press, 1990.

---. *Map Is Not Territory: Studies in the History of Religions*. Leiden: E. J. Brill, 1978.

Smith, T. C. *Jesus in the Gospel of John*. Nashville: Broadman, 1959.

Song, Gil Sop. *History of Theological Thought in Korea*. Seoul: Christian Literature Society, 1987.

Sordi, Marta. *The Christians and the Roman Empire*. Translated by Annabel Bedini. London: Croom Helm, 1986.

Spivak, Gayatri. *A Critique of Postcolonial Reason: Toward a History of the Vanishing Present*. Cambridge: Harvard University Press, 1999.
Staley, J. L. "'Dis Place, Man': A Postcolonial Critique of the Vine (the Mountain and the Temple) in the Gospel of John." In *John and Postcolonialism*, edited by Musa W. Dube and Jeffrey L. Staley, 32–50. London: Sheffield Academic, 2002.
Stauffer, Ethebert. *Jesus and His Story*. Translated by Dorothea M. Barton. London: SCM, 1960.
Stegemann, Wolfgang, and Ekkehard W. Stegemann. *The Jesus Movement: A Social History of Its First Century*. Translated by O. C. Dean Jr. Minneapolis, MN: Fortress, 1999.
Strauss, M. L. *The Davidic Messiah in Luke-Acts: The Promise and Its Fulfillment in Lukan Christology*. JSNTSup 110. Sheffield: Sheffield Academic, 1995.
Sugirtharajah, R. S. *Asian Biblical Hermeneutics and Postcolonialism: Contesting the Interpretations*. Sheffield: Sheffield Academic, 1998.
———. *Bible and the Third Word: Precolonial, Colonial and Postcolonial Encounters*. Cambridge: Cambridge University Press, 2001.
———, ed. *The Postcolonial Bible*. Sheffield: Sheffield Academic, 1998.
———. "Postcolonial Biblical Interpretation." In *Voices from the Margins: Interpreting the Bible in the Third World*, edited by R. S. Sugirtharajah, 64–84. Maryknoll, NY: Orbis, 2006.
———. "A Postcolonial Exploration of Collusion and Construction in Biblical Interpretation." In *The Postcolonial Bible*, edited by R. S. Sugirtharajah, 91–116. Sheffield: Sheffield Academic, 1998.
Suh, Changwon. *Minjung and Christian Faith: Theology and Christian Ethics of the Third World*. Seoul: Nadan, 1989.
Sullivan, Richard D. "The Dynasty of Judaea in the First Century." In *ANRW Part II principat 8*, edited by W. Haase and H. Temporini, 296–354. Berlin: Walter de Gruyter, 1978.
Swanson, Tod D. "To Prepare a Place: Johannine Christology and the Collapse of Ethnic Territory." In *John and Postcolonialism: Travel, Space and Power*, edited by and Jeffrey L. Staley and Musa W. Dube, 11–31. London: Sheffield Academic, 2002.
Tanzer, Sarah J. "Salvation Is for the Jews: Secret Christian Jews in the Gospel of John." In *The Future of Early Christianity: Essays in Honor of Helmut Koester*, edited by A. Thomas Kraabel, Birger A. Pearson, George W. E. Nickelsburg, and Norman R. Petersen, 285–300. Minneapolis, MN: Fortress, 1991.
Teeple, Howard M. *The Mosaic Eschatological Prophet*. Philadelphia: Society of Biblical Literature, 1957.
Thatcher, Tom. *Greater than Caesar: Christology and Empire in the Fourth Gospel*. Minneapolis, MN: Fortress, 2009.
Thiong'o, Ngugi wa. *Decolonialising the Mind: The Politics of Language in African Literature*. London: James Currey, 1986.
———. *Moving the Center: The Struggle for Cultural Freedoms*. London: James Currey, 1993.
Thomas, John Christopher. *Footwashing in John 13 and the Johannine Community*. JSNTSup 61. Sheffield: Sheffield Academic, 1991.
Thompson, Leonard L. *The Book of Revelation: Apocalypse and Empire*. Oxford: Oxford University Press, 1990.

Thompson, Michael B. "The Holy Internet: Communication Between Churches in the First Christian Generation." In *The Gospels for All Christians: Rethinking the Gospel Audiences*, edited by Richard Bauckham, 49–70. Grand Rapids, MI: William B. Eerdmans, 1998.

Tiede, David L. *Charismatic Figure as Miracle Worker*. SBLDS 1. Missoula, MT: Scholars, 1972.

Tilborg, Sjef van. *Reading John in Ephesus*. NovTSup 83. Leiden: Brill, 1996.

Tomson, P. J. "'Jews' in the Gospel of John as Compared with the Palestinian Talmud, the Synoptics, and Some New Testament Apocrypha." In *Anti-Judaism and the Fourth Gospel*, edited by D. Pollefeyt, R. Bieringer, and F. Vandecasteele-Vanneuville, 176–212. Louisville, KY: Westminster and John Knox, 2001.

———. "The Names 'Israel' and 'Jew' in Ancient Judaism and the New Testament." *Bijdr* 47 (1986) 120–40, 266–89.

Toy, C. H. "The King in Jewish Post-Exilian Writings." *JBL* 18, 1/2 (1899) 156–66.

Tyson, Joseph B. *A Study of Early Christianity*. London: Collier-Macmillan, 1973.

Unnik, W. C. van. "The Purpose of the Fourth Gospel." *SE* (1959) 382–411.

Vermes, Geza. *Jesus the Jew: A Historian's Reading of the Gospels*. 2nd ed. London: SCM, 1983.

———. *Jesus and the World of Judaism*. Philadelphia: Fortress, 1984.

———. "The 'Son of Man' Debate." *JSNT* 1 (1978) 19–32.

———, ed. *The Complete Dead Sea Scrolls in English*. London: Penguin, 1998.

Veyne, Paul. *"Bread and Circuses": Euergetism and Municipal Patronage in Roman Italy*. Translated by Kathryn Lomas and Tim Cornell. London: Routledge, 2003.

———. *Bread and Circuses: Historical Sociology and Political Pluralism*. Translated by Brian Pearce. London: Penguin, 1992.

Vod Rad, G. "βασιλεύς." In *TDNT* 1:565–71.

Wahlde, Urban C. von. "The Johannine 'Jews': A Critical Survey." *NTS* 28 (1982) 33–60.

———. "The Terms for Religious Authorities in the Fourth Gospel: A Key to Literary-Strata?" *JBL* 98 (1979) 231–53.

Wallace, Daniel B. "John 5,2 and the Date of the Fourth Gospel." *Biblica* 71 (1990) 237–56.

Webster, J., and N. Cooper, eds. *Roman Imperialism: Post-Colonial Perspective*. Leicester: University of Leicester Press, 1996.

Weinstock, S. *Divus Julius*. Oxford: Oxford University Press, 1971.

Williamson, H. G. M. "The Messianic Texts in Isaiah 1–39." In *King and Messiah in Israel and the Ancient Near East*, edited by John Day, 238–70. JSOTSup 270. Sheffield: Sheffield Academic Press, 1998.

Wind, A. "Destination and Purpose of the Gospel of John." *NovT* 14 (1972) 26–69.

Witherington, Ben, III. *The Christology of Jesus*. Minneapolis, MN: Fortress, 1990.

———. *Jesus, Paul and the End of the World: A Comparative Study of New Testament Eschatology*. Downers Grove, IL: InterVarsity, 1992.

Wright, N. T. *The New Testament and the People of God*. London: SPCK, 1992.

Young, Franklin W. "Jesus the Prophet: A Re-examination." *JBL* 68 (1949) 285–99.

Young, Robert J. C. *Postcolonialism: A Very Short Introduction*. Oxford: Oxford University Press, 2003.

Younger, Lawson K. *Ancient Conquest Account: A Study in Ancient Near East and Biblical History Writing*. JSOTSup 98. Sheffield: JSOT, 1990.

www.ingramcontent.com/pod-product-compliance
Lightning Source LLC
Chambersburg PA
CBHW070240230426
43664CB00014B/2366